ANZACS, EMPIRES

AND

ISRAEL'S RESTORATION

1798 - 1948

KELVIN CROMBIE

 Vocational Education & Training Publications

First published 1998
Second Printing 1998
Third Printing 2000

Vocational Education & Training Publications
PO Box 1305
Osborne Park WA 6916

Ph: 08 9445 8308
Fax: 08 9446 8573

National Library of Australia
Cataloguing in publication data

Crombie, Kelvin
Anzacs, Empires and Israel's Restoration 1798-1948

Includes index

ISBN 0-646-35298-9

Printed in Western Australia

What Some Of The Reviewers Say:

"This fascinating book tells the story of the 150 years from Napoleon's invasion of the Eastern Mediterranean (as part of his plan to destroy Britain in 1798) to David Ben Gurion's declaration of the State of Israel in 1948.
Of special interest is the way in which the ultimate victory of Britain in the Middle East in World War II - the burden of which was borne largely by the Anzacs, as Churchill acknowledged - had its issue in the emergence of a Jewish State........
........Altogether a good read, which I warmly recommend......"
  Rt. Rev. Donald Robinson, former Archbishop of Sydney, in the Southern Cross newspaper of the Diocese of Sydney.

".......Kelvin Crombie has bought all the politics, all of the fighting, and the ANZAC enquiry together and produced a special title which emphasises the ANZAC contribution to a modern nations history.....
The title.......deserves the widest circulation among military historians and those who follow the ANZAC spirit."
  Dr. Frank Glen. Editor. NZ Journal of Military History.

"The text is a celebratory tale that sits comfortably in the traditions of Christian Zionism.......
Crombie's fundamental thesis is that the declaration of Jewish Statehood in 1948 was the culmination in modern times of a long and circuitous journey which began with Napoleon's call to the Jews to return to Eretz Israel and revive their ancient homeland. The background surveyed is the clash of empires over the region from ancient times to the present.
.....the writer achieves this in a prose which is simple, straight forward, and disarming, broken into short digestible themes for easy consumption"
  Dr. Rodney Gouttman, University of South Australia, in the Australian Jewish News.

"This book is truly global in it's scope. It is not light reading, but it is a must for all those interested in the background to Israel's restoration."
  Margot Hodson, Editor, Shalom, the magazine of the Church's Ministry among Jewish People, UK.

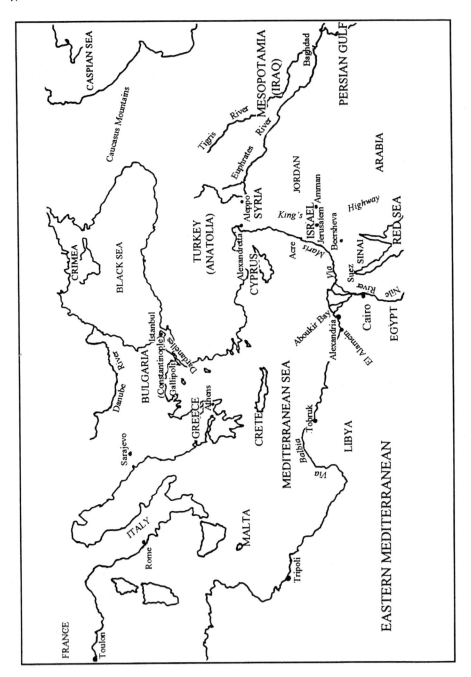

Dedication

This book is dedicated to some of those who helped make this subject relevant to me.

John Crombie
VX 17303 2/7th Battalion, 6th Division, Australian Imperial Force.
Died on active service 20 January 1941 near Tobruk
and buried on Libya-Egypt border.

James Crombie
WX 13435 2/28th Battalion 9th Division, Australian Imperial Force.
Repatriated to Australia sick while on active service
at Gaza, British *Palestine*, 1942.

Colonel John Patterson
Commander *Zion Mule Corps* and *Jewish Legion.*
A firm believer in Israel's destiny.

Zev Jabotinsky (z.l)
Initiator of Jewish fighting forces during World War One.

Lieut.-General Edward Chaytor
Commander of New Zealand Mounted Rifles Brigade
and Anzac Mounted Division.
An admirer of the Jewish people.

Yitzak Rabin (z.l)
Former Israeli general and Prime Minister,
and Uzi Narkiss (z.l), former Israeli general.
Listening to their admiration of the Anzacs further inspired me.

Winston Churchill, to me a profound thinker,
with at times almost 'prophetic' insight.

And to

Betty Monger
Youngest of four daughters of
Trooper Reg Walters, 10th Light Horse Regiment.

Acknowledgments

There are many who I would like to thank for their involvement in this project. First and foremost to my wife Lexie and daughters Orit, Nirel and Talia. Others include Reuven Achimeir, Lindsay and Martha Bear, The Crombie Clan, especially Grant and Jill, Peter Darg, Ivor Davies, Murray and Rosemary Dixon, (and *Prayer for Israel NZ)* Owen Eatwell, the late David Forbes, Dr Chaim Goren, John Haldane, Wes and Gwen Hill, Owen Hoskin, Bev Huch, Carol Jeffrey, Ray and Jill Lockhart, Alison Marchant, Jan Marriot (*Celebrate Shalom Magazine)*, Bill and Rachel Millward (*ICEJ, NZ*),Wendy Monger, Rod Monger, Sybil Parry, David Pileggi, Pat Ramsay (*Shalom Israel*), Bruce and Heather Reekie, Jackie Reinhalda, Marie Shaw, Len and Bev Sherwood, Ruth Stark, Kim Sutton, Vic and Peg Wolters (and prayer group in Newcastle), and many others.

To the many who have loaned or presented materials, especially photographs, for use, including: General Uzi Narkiss (z.l), Ed Plenty and family, Duncan Brocket, the Jeffrey family, Margaret Robbins, Christ Church Jerusalem, the Zionist Archives Jerusalem, and in particular Mr. Reuven Koffler, the Jabotinsky Archives in Tel Aviv, Rishon le Zion Museum and Archive, and Jewish Legions Museum, Avihayil.

Also to the family of Moses Mosenson for permitting me to use his letters from the desert. Mrs. Beryl Sincock, for allowing me to use diary entries of her late husband Thomas Derrick. Wendy Monger for allowing me to use the diary and photographs of her late grandfather Reg Walters. Mrs. Marie Holt for permission to use extracts of her late husband's book *From Ingleburn to Aitape.* ETT Imprint (Sydney) for permission to use Ion Idriess book *The Desert Column.* Mr. Tony Harkins (Auckland) for permission to use excerpts from the book *New Zealanders in the Sinai and Palestine* by Lieut-Col C. Guy Powles. John Burridge (Perth) for permission to use *Westralian Cavalry* by Major Olden. The Australian War Memorial for permission to use the *AIF IN Sinai and Palestine* by H.S. Gullett. And the other publishers and authors who permitted me to quote from their works. Full credits are given in the Footnotes and Bibliography.

The writings of Sir Winston Churchill: Reproduced with permission of Curtis Brown Ltd, London, on behalf of C & T Productions Limited and the Estate of Sir Winston Churchill. Martin Gilbert WINSTON S. CHURCHILL Vol IV copyright C &T Productions 1975. Winston S. Churchill THE SECOND WORLD WAR Volumes I, II, III, IV, VI copyright Winston S. Churchill. Winston S. Churchill, THE WORLD CRISIS.

Also to the Auckland War Memorial Library; Australian War Memorial, Canberra; the Queen Elizabeth II New Zealand Army Museum, Waiouru; the *Jerusalem Post* Archives, Jerusalem; the Jabotinsky Institute Archives, Tel Aviv; the Imperial War Museum, London; the Public Records Office, London; Yad Ben Zvi Archive, Jerusalem; the National Library, Jerusalem; the British Library, London.

Contents

page

List of Maps

Illustrations

Introduction

While reflecting upon the world situation at the beginning of 1915, (when plans were being formulated for an attack upon Turkey at Gallipoli near the Dardanelles Straits), Winston Churchill wrote in his classic book *The World Crisis*:

> From the uttermost ends of the earth ships and soldiers are approaching or gathering in the Eastern Mediterranean in *fulfilment of a destiny as yet not understood by mortal man* ... the arrival of the Anzacs[1] in Egypt created the nucleus of the Army, needed to attack the heart of the Turkish Empire.[2]

Churchill's statement presents us with some thought-provoking questions, such as: 'What were ships and soldiers from the uttermost ends of the earth actually doing in the Eastern Mediterranean? 'Why were they attacking the heart of the Turkish Empire?' And: 'What could all this have to do with the fulfilment of a destiny as yet not understood by mortal man?'

Another thought provoking statement, referring to the same general period of time, was made by an Israeli citizen in 1992. This representative of Kibbutz Be'eri[3] was speaking at an anniversary event at the Anzac Memorial overlooking Gaza. The event recalled the tragic battles at Gaza in 1917 when thousands of British, Australian and New Zealand soldiers died. Speaking to many Israeli, Australian, British and New Zealand officials, and veterans from the 50th anniversary event at El Alamein in Egypt, this Israeli said:

> We sense the importance of living so close to this historic site of battle that took place so long ago, and yet paved the way for our own kibbutz to grow and flourish here in the Northwest Negev. We honour the memory of those who gave their lives here. We salute those of you, who, in your youth, took part in either World War One or World

---

1   Anzac is an acronym for Australian and New Zealand Army Corps, first coined in 1915 while troops from these two countries were training in Egypt.

2   Churchill, W. *The World Crisis*. Charles Scribner's Sons, (New York, 1949), p. 289. Italics mine. Reproduced With permission of Curtis Brown Ltd, London, on behalf of C & T Productions Limited and the Estate of Sir Winston Churchill.

3   Kibbutz - a collective farm in Israel, which alongside the moshav (where the farm members have more autonomy) served as the agricultural, ideological and defence backbone of the pioneer Jewish settlement in the Land of Israel - Eretz Israel.

War Two. Could you, while looking over the fields of destruction, have pictured fields of life built upon the havoc of war? Was it at all possible to envision the laughter of children, the roses in the gardens? We at Be'eri thank and honour you. As Israelis, we understand the sacrifice you made here. *Your fight here helped change the destiny not only of this region, but of the world.* [4]

This time we must ask the questions: 'What connection did two bloody defeats at Gaza, again involving Anzacs from the uttermost ends of the earth, have with paving the way for an Israeli agricultural settlement to flourish in the Negev region?' And: 'What connection does this have with changing the destiny of the region, and indeed the world?'

My contention, and the subject of this book is that the answers to these questions, and those associated with Churchill's statement, are closely connected with the restoration and rebirth of modern Israel. Such a theory becomes plausible when considering a comment made by another Israeli, a local historian, at Beersheva, also on 1 November 1992, during an event celebrating the seventy-fifth anniversary since that town's capture by British infantry and Anzac horsemen. After outlining how the Australian horsemen galloped in and effected the final capture of Beersheva on 31 October 1917, this Israeli said, 'Had Beersheva not been captured that day then we Israelis may not be here today.' [5]

Beersheva, the town associated with the Jewish patriarch Abraham (to whom God promised the Land of Israel) thereafter became a strong connecting point for Israel, the British and the Anzacs. For on the day that Beersheva was captured, the British War Cabinet agreed to what became historically known as the *Balfour Declaration* - the promise of a Jewish homeland in the Land of Israel, then known as Turkish *Palestine.* [6]

These statements, when considered together, seem to present some interesting themes: the Eastern Mediterranean region; Empires; soldiers, primarily Anzacs, from the uttermost ends of the earth; and the rebirth of modern Israel.

The presence of soldiers from Australia and New Zealand in the region of the Eastern Mediterranean, some 16-20,000 kilometres from their homelands, between 1914-1919 (and again between 1940-1943), was due to their attachment to the British Empire. And the presence of soldiers of the British Empire brought with it the inevitability of a clash with the other rival empires of the time.

---

4   From speech of Kibbutz representative, copy in author's possession. Italics mine.

5   Similar sentiments were expressed by *Jerusalem Post* columnist Meir Ronnen in an article which appeared on 4 December 1992, which commemorated the seventy-fifth anniversary since General Allenby's entrance into Jerusalem on 11 December 1917.

6   The term Palestine only came into common usage for the Land of Israel following the Roman defeat of the second Jewish Revolt, 132-135 AD, known as the Bar Kockba Revolt. To erase any Jewish connection to the land, the Romans changed its name to *Syria Palestina*. I prefer to use the ancient and Biblical term 'Eretz Israel' or 'the Land of Israel.'

This modern day clash of the empires in the Eastern Mediterranean region actually stretched from Napoleon's invasion of Egypt and the Land of Israel in 1798-99 till the battle of El Alamein in 1942, and then the establishment of the State of Israel in 1948. A period of 150 years.

During that fascinating period far-off places such as Aboukir Bay, the Pyramids, El Arish, Jaffa, Acre, Navarino, Crimea, Sebastopol, Jerusalem, Bethlehem, Suez, Cyprus, Alexandria, Rishon le Zion, Gallipoli (Gelibolu), the Dardanelles, Romani, Maghdaba, Gaza, Beersheva, Ayun Kara, Jericho, Es Salt, Megiddo, Semakh, Damascus, Amman, Aleppo, Tobruk, Benghazi, Mersa Matruh, Larisa, Thermopylae, Kalamata, Maleme, Suda Bay, Sfakia, Marjayoun, Beirut, Minqar Qaim, El Alamein and many others, became household names throughout the world.

Attached to these far-off places were such familiar names as Napoleon, Nelson, Mehmet Ali, Shaftesbury, Palmerston, Czar Nicholas, Emperor Napoleon III, Disraeli, Herzl, Kaiser Wilhelm (William) II, Churchill, Chauvel, Chaytor, Trumpeldor, Jabotinsky, Lloyd George, Allenby, Lawrence, Balfour, Weizmann, Wavell, Freyberg, Blamey, Rommel, Montgomery, Ben Gurion, and many others.

Many of these places and names are associated with the Jewish hope of a restoration to their homeland after centuries of dispersion throughout the earth. And here lies the heart of the story, the silver lining running from beginning to end.

Napoleon's invasion stirred the jealousy, ambitions and opposition of rival European powers, especially Britain. Thereafter they, and especially Britain, eyed closely the activities of the French and indeed any rival European power in that region. Why? For Napoleon's goal was to use that very region as a halfway house for his ultimate purpose of ousting the British from India. The Eastern Mediterranean, and especially the area either side of where the Suez Canal would ultimately be cut, was the region between the European powers and their imperial domains in the east. It was the *land between empires.*

But Napoleon's invasion did more. It aroused the interest of some Jewish people concerning a future restoration. This interest began with news of the direction of the invasion fleet, and escalated following Napoleon's bold declaration in April 1799, while in the Galilee, calling upon the exiled Israelites to return to their ancestral homeland.

Ironically though it was Bible-believing Christians in Britain, primarily the Evangelicals,[7] who showed the greatest interest in this future restoration. Believing that a return of the Jewish people to the Land of Israel would precede the return of Jesus Christ to reign in Jerusalem, they saw Napoleon's invasion, his interest in the

---

7   Evangelical is the name given to a popular movement which began within the British church during the eighteenth and nineteenth centuries. Evangelicals were found within all denominations. Their basic beliefs were: the centrality of the death and resurrection of Jesus Christ; that a changed life came only through personal belief in Jesus; and, that the Bible was the Word of God.

Jewish people, and proclamation, as signs of the impending restoration of Israel. One prominent Evangelical was James Bicheno. His prolific writings on the subject influenced countless Britons of the time. He wrote in the aftermath of Napoleon's venture:

> Whatever ... the result of the expedition of the French in the East may be, yet as the consequence of it ... their extraordinary expedition may not lead, directly to the casting out of the Turks from Egypt and Syria, and to the restoration of the Jewish people to their own land; *but these events* [the casting out of Turkey and restoration of Israel] *may be brought about in a more circuitous way, and by means and instruments not thought of* ... For as it is not from one particular event that our hope of a speedy restoration of the Jews is drawn, but from the combined direction of many, so it is not this or that particular circumstance, favourable or unfavourable, that can materially affect it.[8]

The events of this one hundred and fifty year period seem to clearly substantiate those amazing words and predictions of James Bicheno. For the return of the Jewish people to the Land of Israel was brought about in a circuitous way, by various ways and means, and by the combined direction of many, both favourable and unfavourable circumstances.

Besides Jewish involvement in their restoration, countless British Evangelicals prayed for and were actively involved in this vision. The height of their activity was during the period of the 1830's and 1840's, the time of the 'Eastern Question', when people such as Lord Shaftesbury petitioned the British Government to support Israel's restoration. Their efforts succeeded only in part. But their vision persisted and was taken up by later generations of Britons.

One of the more fascinating and even circuitous ways associated with Israel's restoration was the special role played by Anzac soldiers in this process, and indeed the special relationship formed between the Jewish people and the Anzacs. This began in the environs of Egypt prior to the Gallipoli venture. There the wild colonial boys from 'down under' interacted with the Jewish refugees who had just been mercilessly thrown out of the Land of Israel by the Turks. And later, as the men of Anzac prepared for their first military campaign as sovereign nations, the Jewish men of Zion agitated to be involved in the war against the Turks, and in particular in the conquest of their homeland. And so was born the *Zion Mule Corps* through the inspiration of Vladimir (Zev) Jabotinsky and Victor Trumpeldor. Even though Gallipoli was far from the Land of Israel, yet Trumpeldor believed that all roads ultimately led to Jerusalem. And so it was that political events before and during the Gallipoli campaign slowly but surely introduced the subject of the future of Jerusalem and the Land of Israel onto the political agenda.

---

8   Bicheno, J. *The Restoration of the Jews, And the Crisis of all Nations,* (London, 1800), p. 111.

The *Zion Mule Corps* was the first Jewish fighting unit to embellish the Star of David, for some 1800 years. And the unit was brilliantly led by an Anglo-Irish Evangelical named John Patterson. This very same Gentile Zionist[9] later led the *Jewish Legion* as it served alongside the British and Anzac forces during their campaign to wrest the Land of Israel from the Turks. It was during that campaign that the Anzac horsemen became a legend to the Jewish people

The victory at Beersheva laid the foundations for legend status. That status was built upon during the following weeks as the Jewish colonists in Judea were liberated from the Turks, on many occasions by the Anzac horsemen. The Jewish people marvelled at the warm-hearted men riding on their large horses. Such an attitude was held also by the townsfolk of Jaffa and Jerusalem.

Perhaps the most significant act of this sphere of the campaign against Turkey occurred in Jerusalem on 11 December 1917. There, during the Jewish festival of *Hanukah,* (purification and liberation) Anzac soldiers stood alongside Britons at the base of the Tower or Citadel of David, as 400 years of Turkish rule over the Land of Israel ended. For the Jewish people this event, and the associated *Balfour Declaration* increased their hopes for an ultimate restoration.

Memories of the Anzacs remained when some twenty-five years later their sons returned to the region to battle the Fascist and Nazi threat. The English-language newspaper, the *Palestine Post* wrote under the bold front page headlines, **'ANZACS BACK AGAIN'** on 13 February 1940:

> The arrival of Australian and New Zealand forces in this part of the world is an event of prime importance ... and ... it recalls one of the most stirring chapters of the last War. The forces which landed in Egypt on Sunday are the successors of those who almost twenty-five years ago made the battlefields of Gallipoli immortal.[10]

Several days later the same newspaper wrote of the arrival of the Australians at their bases 'somewhere in Palestine.'

> The chief topic of conversation in Palestine is the arrival of the Australians ... To quite a number they recall the part played by the Anzacs in Palestine in the last War ... For some years after they left this country their fame was celebrated in story and anecdote.'[11]

One of those thousands of Jewish people who affectionately recalled the popularity of the Anzacs was a young Uzi Narkiss.[12] Narkiss is well known historically as one of that famous trio alongside Yitzak Rabin and Moshe Dayan striding purposely into

---

9   The name given to non-Jewish people who support the return of the Jewish people to Eretz Israel.
10 *Palestine Post,* 13 February 1940, p. 6.
11 Ibid., 16 February 1940, p. 8.
12 General Narkiss died following my interview with him and before the release of this book and the associated documentary.

Jerusalem's Old City in June 1967. Narkiss in fact commanded the *Jerusalem Brigade* which captured Jerusalem during the Six Day War. One of his treasured possessions was an Aussie slouch hat, which he 'borrowed from an Australian soldier.'

During the Second World War, while the anti-Allied, anti-Zionist Arab nationalist movement awaited a German victory, tens of thousands of Jewish people from the Land of Israel joined British units and served in other capacities against the Nazi threat. Their very existence as a community was seriously threatened. The Nazi machine made no secret of its sympathy to the nationalist Arab ambitions of completely eradicating the Jewish presence in British *Palestine*. At one stage the Jewish community prepared for a modern day Masada - resolved to fight the Germans to the bitter end as their illustrious forefathers had done against the Romans almost 1900 years before. It was then that the Jewish people were forcibly expelled from their homeland and endured some 1800 years of wandering and persecution in the Gentile nations of the world. They began returning in sizable numbers from the 1880's onwards.

And now, in the 1940's, Jewish survival in the Land of Israel was reliant upon an Allied victory in the region. Initial defeats in North Africa, Greece and Crete were compensated by the liquidation, especially in Crete, of large numbers of the impending German invasion force. Fears of an invasion of British *Palestine* from the north were largely overcome with the capture of Syria in June-July 1941 by a predominantly Australian force - in which both Moshe Dayan and Yitzak Rabin played minor supporting roles. Yet while Rommel's forces remained in North Africa, the Nazi threat to the Land of Israel remained. The final victory at El Alamein in November 1942 caused most of these anxieties to dissipate. Relief at that final victory is expressed in the words of gratitude which accompanied a beautiful Hebrew Bible which the Jewish leaders presented to Montgomery. It is inscribed:

> Field Marshal Viscount Montgomery the gallant leader of the victorious British forces
> in whose hands God has placed salvation in Zion in the days of El Alamein.

Unfortunately the role of the British in aiding the survival of the Jewish people during that period was later forgotten as the British attempted to thwart the establishment of a Jewish State in the Land of Israel. A bitter conflict between these two parties ended on a sour note; the mighty British Empire being forced to withdraw in humiliation in May 1948. Yet on that very day, some one hundred and fifty years after Napoleon's invasion fleet left France en-route to the Eastern Mediterranean, the Jewish leadership proclaimed the establishment of the State of Israel.

The year of 1998 commemorates the anniversary of these two important historical events. It will be two hundred years since Napoleon's invasion, and fifty years since Israel's establishment. The year 1998 also heralds several other important historical anniversaries. It will be one hundred years since the grandiose visit of the German Kaiser, Wilhelm or William II to Jerusalem in 1898, and eighty years since the end of the First World War in 1918.

All these four events are part of what some may see as Divine intervention in the affairs of mankind, bringing forth the fulfilment of Biblical prophecy with the restoration of Israel. Some Jewish people would advocate that this restoration would predate the *coming* of the Jewish Messiah. Countless Evangelicals and Bible-believers would advocate that this event would predate the *return* of the Jewish Messiah, namely Jesus of Nazareth, to Jerusalem. Yet many others, both Jewish and non-Jewish would see this as the combination of many unrelated events, or of man inspired nationalism, leading to the creation of a political entity named the State of Israel.

I have my particular viewpoint concerning the importance and relevance of the period from May 1798 till May 1948. Yet, despite my bias, I have attempted to present as much of the bigger picture as possible. I emphasize *attempted* because with such a broad subject and such a length of time as one hundred and fifty years, there is so much more that could be written. This book is not and does not presume to be a military history, nor a political history, nor even a history of the Jewish people. It is a combination of these factors, although none of them is covered in-depth. Countless other books have been written providing more detailed information. It looks at this period of history from a particular angle.

The writing of this book is partly due to my personal residence in Israel for over fifteen years, and to my childhood impressions gained while growing up on an Australian wheat and sheep farm. The presence of an Israeli family in the farming community for several years, the Six Day War of 1967, and knowledge that two uncles had served in *Palestine* during the Second World War, augmented greatly this boyhood fascination in the region. I was also familiar with the stories of the Anzacs at Gallipoli, of the Light Horse in *Palestine*, and of the heroic *Rats of Tobruk* and the importance of El Alamein.

My father and three of his brothers fought in the Second World War, two serving in the Eastern Mediterranean. Uncle John, a soldier in the 6th Australian Division, lost his life near Tobruk and is buried in Egypt. Uncle Jim came out with the 9th Australian Division, but fell sick while stationed near Gaza and was repatriated. While stationed in British *Palestine* uncle John sent a letter to uncle Jim in Australia in 1940, and wrote:

> Whilst away we visited a War Cemetery and were struck by the beautiful way it is being kept. The land itself is a free gift from the people of Palestine and there seem to be troops buried there from all over the world. There are quite a number of Anzac graves there.[13]

Soon after writing this letter, he too was buried in an Anzac grave. One of those many Anzac graves from the First World War which he may have seen was that of a

---

13 Copy of uncle's letter in author's possession.

great uncle, George Ridley, who died as a Gallipoli reinforcement in July 1915, and was buried at Suez.

Some years ago, after attending the Anzac Service at the Commonwealth War Cemetery on Mount Scopus, adjacent to the Mount of Olives overlooking Jerusalem, my Dutch wife Lexie asked, 'What on earth are all these young men from Australia and New Zealand doing buried here, on a hillside overlooking Jerusalem?' It was a good question and one which begged an answer.

I write this book therefore with the knowledge that I'm not alone in holding an interest in the affairs of the Eastern Mediterranean. A very high proportion of New Zealanders and Australians, had family members who served and fell there. There are up to 20,000 Anzac graves in the Eastern Mediterranean region, and many thousands more British, Indian and South African, as well as French, German and Austrian. Countless more Evangelical Christians and Jewish people throughout the world likewise pay particular interest in the affairs of the region in question.

It seems to me that despite their far-flung situations on the earth's surface, the geographical locations of Britain, India, Australia and New Zealand, (and to a lesser extent South Africa), indicates that they were key instruments in restoring Israel to her land. Yet it also seems that many are unaware of the deeper significance of those battles in which young men from those nations fought and died.

Such a sentiment is more-or-less borne out by a letter which appeared in the *Jerusalem Post* on Armistice Sunday 1994:

> I think the time has come to make up with the British and to restore the friendship of the Balfour Days, without which there would have been no State of Israel. Moreover, without the British victory at El-Alamein (which occurred on about the same day as the Balfour Declaration, but about 25 years later), the Yishuv[14] would have perished and Israel could not have been born.
>
> These facts are hardly known to the younger generation and it is high time to bring them to the fore.[15]

This then is my *attempt* to present these facts to the younger (as well as to the older) generation. And perhaps at the end you may agree with me that the service and sacrifice of soldiers of the British Empire-Commonwealth within the Eastern Mediterranean, and particularly as it related to the Jewish people and the Land of Israel, could actually have helped *change the destiny of that region, and the world.* And more-so, that they may even have played a part in the *fulfilment of a destiny as yet not understood by mortal man.*

---

14 Yishuv is the term used to describe the Jewish settlement in the Land of Israel. Prior to the Zionist movement, the Jewish settlement was known as the *old* Yishuv, and thereafter that associated with the Zionist movement, known as the *new* Yishuv.

15 Letter to the Editor, *Jerusalem Post*, 13 November, 1994.

*C*hapter 1

The Land Between Empires

By Geographical Chance

From antiquity past the region stretching from Egypt through to Mesopotamia and Anatolia (encompassing the modern day nations of Egypt, Israel, Jordan, Lebanon, Syria, Iraq and Turkey) has been called the 'fertile crescent', the 'centre of civilization', the 'centre of the world' and more. It was a political, cultural and economic crossroads. Anything or anyone travelling north-south, or east-west, of necessity passed through this region.

Major trade routes crisscrossed this region. From Egypt the *Via Maris (Way of the Sea)*, for the most part hugged the coastal plain through the Sinai Peninsular into the Land of Israel. At the Carmel Range it diverged. One branch headed due north into the Lebanon and then into Anatolia. A second branch swept north east past the Sea of Galilee over the Jordan River, into the Bashan or Golan and onto Damascus. And a third branch continued eastwards along the Jezreel Valley over the Jordan River, up the hills of Edom to the plateau above. Here it met the route from Arabia, the *King's Highway*, which had steered its course from Jedda through Mecca, Medina, Rabbat Ammon (Amman), Deraa and then onto Damascus. From Damascus routes spread eastward to the Mesopotamian region, and northward through Homs, Hama and Aleppo into Anatolia - Turkey proper.

Anatolia itself was a major centre for routes coming from Asia overland, or via the Black Sea. Produce also traversed by sea from the Black Sea through the Bosphorus and Dardanelles Straits to the Mediterranean and vice versa. Produce coming from India and the islands even further east again, were often shipped to the Persian Gulf or Red Sea and Gulf of Suez, and then transported overland to Levantine ports and then onto their European destinations.

Such routes assisted not only trade, but relayed information, ideas and foreign armies seeking after self aggrandizement, glory and power. And by geographical accident the most central land within this overall region was the Land of Israel. 'The emphasis ... upon this land' wrote James Monson, 'must always be understood against the larger geographical and historical context of the Eastern Mediterranean, Egypt and Mesopotamia. In light of these larger forces the country ... is rather insignificant, *except as a land bridge between great powers.'* [1] It was a *land between empires.*

Enter the Israelites

The great empires of antiquity, be they Assyrian, Egyptian, Babylonian or Persian coveted this *land between.* Their covetousness however was not guided by any material need. The fertility or beauty of the land endeared them not. It was the area's location as a buffer zone between the other superpower of the day which guided their interests and appetites.

Such imperial rivalry did not auger well for the independence of any smaller power in this strategic buffer zone. If such a nation did exist, it did so at the bequest of one empire or another, and for that particular empire's strategic interest, or it existed due to a temporary power vacuum in the region.

Sometime during the period of the second or third millennium before the common era Abraham the Aramean wandered into the land and soon afterwards received a promise from El Shaddai, the God Almighty, that from his loins would spring forth a people who would inherit the Land of Israel (then Canaan) as an eternal possession. More than likely an imperial power vacuum existed midway through the second millennium BCE, when Moses and Joshua, descendants of Abraham led the Hebrew or Israelite people out of Egypt, through the Sinai and into the Land of Israel.

Throughout the next thousand or so years the people of Israel rarely held sovereign control over their destiny within the Land of Israel, a notable exception being during the reigns of David and Solomon. The imperial powers were always involved in some way, or waiting on the boundary lines.

Although the God of Abraham gave the people of Israel this land as an eternal possession, blessing and prosperity within the land depended upon their obedience to the teachings of Abraham's God - His law or Torah. Whenever these laws were obeyed, blessing, prosperity and security followed. Disobedience however resulted in pestilence, plague, drought and the sword. And in times of great apostasy, the land was first divided, and then invaded and ravaged by the imperial powers.

In 722 BCE the mighty Assyrian Empire captured the northern kingdom of Israel and led her people away to captivity. The southern kingdom of Judah followed suit, when in 586 BCE the Babylonian Empire completed a humiliating defeat upon the people of Judah, destroyed Jerusalem and led the people away. Their captivity however was only temporary.

Several generations later Cyrus, king of the Persian Empire subdued Babylon. Endeavouring to endear himself to the subjugated peoples, and desiring, most probably,

---

1   Monson, J. *The Land Between - A Regional Study Guide to the Land of the Bible.* (Jerusalem, 1983), p.13. Italics mine.

to strengthen his southern defences, Cyrus permitted a remnant of Israelites to return to their homeland. It was much in Persia's interest to have a strong and friendly people holding this strategic buffer zone. Besides, it would assist him by not having to support a garrison force there. The priest state of Judea was founded.

Greeks and Hasmoneans

Yet Israel's geographical location soon came to haunt her again. Alexander the Great, king of the Greek Empire, crossed the Dardanelles Straits near Gelibolu (Gallipoli), in 332 BCE and conquered the Eastern Mediterranean as part of his quest for establishing an empire stretching from Greece to India.

Within ten years Alexander himself was dead, and his vast empire was divided among his leading generals. Egypt was ceded to Ptolemy, who claimed the Land of Israel, while Syria fell to Seleucus. Conflict soon broke out between these ambitious generals. Syria battled for control of Eretz Israel, and gained it following victory over Egypt in 198 BCE.

The spirit of imperial rivalry was never satisfied. Syria, under Antiochus Epiphanes IV later attempted the subjugation of Egypt itself. He also desired to centralize his empire, and attempted to enforce a uniform religious system. He desecrated the Jewish Temple and attempted to stop them worshipping their God. His policy brought him into conflict with the Jewish people, stimulating at first a local and later a national revolt led by the Hasmoneans or Maccabees against Greek-Syrian control.

The Maccabees ultimately defeated the Greek-Syrians, rededicated their Temple, and established an independent Jewish reign over the Land of Israel. This deliverance and rededication was thereafter celebrated by the festival of *Hanukah* in the month of December.

The Jewish people enjoyed the benefits of little or no foreign interference. It seemed that a return to the glory days of David and Solomon were at hand. Such however was not to be. The Maccabees soon lost their patriotic zeal and endeavoured even to establish a hereditary monarchy. Many devout Jewish people, anticipating the coming of a Messiah, deliverer, from the family of King David, refused to accept this non-Davidic monarchy. Rival claimants then staked claims to the throne and civil war raked the land.

The Roman Eagle Appears

During the very same period the Roman Empire was hovering on the boundaries of the Land of Israel, and responding to the request from one of the rival Hasmonean claimants, General Pompey entered Jerusalem in 63 BCE. Roman rule in Eretz Israel varied over the following decades between direct and indirect rule, depending upon the internal conditions. All the while most Jewish people resented the presence of a pagan power over the land, and in particular in their holy city, Jerusalem.

It was into this tense and complicated environment that Jesus of Nazareth emerged and spoke of another Kingdom, a kingdom of righteousness and peace and everlasting life. Many Jewish people responded to his message, while most did not. He ultimately fell foul of both the Jewish religious and Roman political authorities and was executed outside Jerusalem as a common criminal. Above His head, written in three languages, was the sign *King of the Jews.* To vindicate his message God raised Jesus from the grave after three days. He soon after commanded His followers to take this message of the Kingdom of God from Jerusalem to Judea, Samaria and *to the uttermost ends of the earth.*

While Jesus' followers were setting out to achieve this enormous task, other movements were occurring within the boundaries of Eretz Israel. Dissatisfaction with Roman rule overflowed and in 66 CE Jewish zealots provoked a revolt against Rome. Concerned lest the revolt spread to other distant parts of its scattered empire, Rome rushed large forces and senior generals to the region.

Raked by internal divisions, and militarily overwhelmed, the Jewish Revolt was doomed to failure. In 70 CE Roman forces besieged Jerusalem, destroying both the Temple and much of the city. Only one outstanding building was left standing, the fortress at the western entrance, later affectionately named David's Citadel, (although it was built by King Herod) - left as a testimony of Roman victory and Jewish defeat.

Most of the Jewish survivors of the Revolt were dispatched as slaves to various parts of the Roman Empire. A similar fate befell the survivors of a second unsuccessful uprising, the Bar Kockba Revolt between 132-135 CE. Following this unsuccessful Revolt, Jewish people were forbidden entrance into Jerusalem, which was henceforth known as *Aeolia Capitolina*, a Roman pagan city. The province of Judea was renamed *Syria Palestina*, an attempt to erase the Jewish connection to the land.

Jewish national hopes seemed vanquished for good. Only tradition and the writings of the prophets kept awake any thought of a future national restoration to the Land of Israel. For all practical purposes, the possibility seemed remote indeed. Rome was determined to erase the possibility of a Jewish national presence in Eretz Israel.

Byzantium and Roman Christianity

Despite often violent opposition the small band of Jewish and later Gentile followers of Jesus spread His message throughout the Roman Empire. By the fourth century it was a force to be reckoned with. Emperor Constantine did just that and provided the now Gentile dominated movement with official recognition following the year 312 CE. The movement, now known as Christianity, soon became the official Roman religion. What began as a movement of people placing personal faith in Jesus as King, now began to be transformed into an institutional religious system.

A new Roman religion and character called for a new Roman capital. Emperor

Constantine moved his capital in 330 CE to the ruins of a former city known as Byzantium on the shores of the strategic Bosphorus Straits bridging Europe and Asia and there built a new Rome, named Constantinople.

The huge Roman Empire then divided into two administrative halves at the end of the fourth century. Old Rome remained as capital of the Western Roman Empire, while Constantinople remained capital of the Eastern Roman Empire, henceforth known as the Byzantine Empire or Byzantium. Over the next few hundred years both these halves diverged and became two separate empires.

Initially the religion of these two administrative halves was synonymous - Roman Christianity. But as the political characters of the two halves diverged with time, so too did the religious character of each. The western church evolved into the Roman Catholic Church centred upon Rome, while the eastern church became the Greek Orthodox Church centred upon Constantinople.

The religious character of the land of Israel was thereafter characteristically Byzantine Christianity. The two physical representatives of this religious system were the Church of the Holy Sepulchre in Jerusalem, and the Church of the Nativity in Bethlehem, the building of which began after 326 CE.

The Jewish people in the Land of Israel throughout this period were tolerated, but had little political clout, except during the period of Emperor Justinian in the fifth century, who at one point offered them the opportunity of rebuilding their Temple. The effort was fruitless. Thoughts of a national Jewish resurrection however remained constant.

Byzantium was never a unified system. It expended much energy upon the rebellious minority groups within its borders, many of which resented the imperial designs of the rulers from Constantinople. And there was that continual menace of Persia on the extreme eastern border. Such exertions sapped Byzantium's strength, and reduced her ability to successfully retain control. Into this ready made environment another force, Islam, entered into the *land between* as would-be rulers.

The Islamic Invasion

Mohammed the Arabian made his famous pilgrimage from Mecca to Medina in 622 CE, signalling the beginning of the Muslim movement - or Islam, which means 'submission.' Once fully established in Arabia this movement sent forth its tentacles throughout the region, engulfing nation after nation.

Entrance into the Land of Israel was sealed following defeat of the Byzantine forces around 636 at the Yarmuk River, which runs into the Jordan River just south of the Sea of Galilee. Subjugation of Jerusalem followed soon after. In time Muslim Arabs moved in and settled the Land of Israel, changing the character of the Jewish homeland once again, this time in a more drastic way.

The indigenous inhabitants of the Land of Israel either converted, fled, or remained, and became respected minority groups, *dhimmi's,* under Islamic control. And this new imperial power lived up to the meaning of its name, *submission.* It commanded the respect and submission of these *dhimmi* peoples. It proclaimed that Mohammed the prophet was the final revelation of Allah, fulfilling all that had been previously established by Moses and Jesus. Islam therefore could not accept any Divine connection between the Jewish people and the Land of Israel, or for that matter any Divine connection between the followers of Jesus and the Land of Israel. The Land of Israel was now a part of *dar al Islam,* the land of Islam.

This was the status quo in the Land of Israel until the middle of the eleventh century, when a new type of Muslim, the Seljuk Turk, swept into the region from the central Asian highlands and subdued the region. These conquerors respected still less the traditions of the local non-Muslim peoples and began to harass what were in their eyes, the 'infidels'.

The Crusades

This Turkish invasion coincided with a religious revival within the boundaries of the Roman Catholic Church. News of 'infidel' Muslims harassing local Christians in the 'Holy Land' and even harassing pilgrims coming from the West, stirred such religious passions into action. Following a speech from Pope Urban in 1096, devout Catholics, primarily French and German and to lesser extent from other nations like England, enlisted for service to expel the Muslim 'infidel' from the Land of Israel. The Crusades had begun.

All the way from the Rhine to Jerusalem these zealous warriors spilled innocent blood in the quest for seeking higher 'spiritual' glories. And it was the Jewish people as much as the Muslims who felt the brunt of this ill-conceived zeal. In Jerusalem, apart from killing many Muslims, they also massacred almost the entire Jewish population, after which the blood-stained zealots attended the Church of the Holy Sepulchre for evening mass. The Crusaders also ousted the reigning Greek Orthodox Patriarch of Jerusalem, replacing him with their own Catholic Patriarch.

Motives other than assisting the Eastern Orthodox Christians were paramount in this ill-conceived venture, be they political, economic and seeking after self aggrandizement. And most definently these ill-directed zealots did not represent Jesus, whose life and teachings were the complete opposite to those associated with the Crusaders. Yet whatever the motives, the Crusades marked the first incursion into the Eastern Mediterranean of Western or Roman Christianity. Its presence thereafter played a significant role in determining the character and destiny of the Land of Israel.

The Crusaders ultimately failed in their goals and by the thirteenth century the Land of Israel had reverted to Muslim rule. Yet its legacy remained. Thereafter the two Roman Churches, Western and Eastern claimed the place of rightful authority over the so-called Holy Places of Eretz Israel, while France, the foremost Crusader nation, even regarded herself as a guardian of Christian interests in the region. Also the trading centres set up by the Italian city states, mostly from Venice and Genoa, remained and became the commercial middleman between Europe and the spices and riches of the East.

Return to Islamic Control - the Mamelukes

Control over the Land of Israel and Syria did not revert to the previous Muslim rulers, be they Arab or Seljuk, but fell instead into the hands of the Mameluke regime from Egypt. In their efforts to thwart any further European invasion of the region, the Mamelukes destroyed many of the coastal cities and ports in the Land of Israel. The Mamelukes however were not only concerned with the European menace, but also with the southward movements of northern hordes, especially the Mongols and Othami Turks, whose eyes looked covetously towards *the land between* in order to extend their own imperial boundaries.

*C*hapter 2

To the Uttermost Ends of the Earth

India and trade to the East

Finally in the fifteenth century the Othami Turks swept eastwards and engulfed the Roman Byzantine Empire. Constantinople, the symbol of *Christian* Rome, was subdued in 1453. Jerusalem was spared this new invading horde until 1517, when it too came under the dominion of the Turkish crescent, and remained so for the next four hundred years.

The Turkish Empire inherited the ancient trade routes from the east to the west, the trade of porcelain, silks and spices from China, India and the Spice Islands, challenging the Italian monopoly. The Italian monopoly was by this stage drawing conflict from the other Europeans who had to purchase the produce at exorbitant rates. New and more economic means to trade with the East were sought.

This period saw the beginnings of European expansionism as the sea faring countries, Portugal, Spain, Holland, England (Britain) and later France sent expeditions farther and farther from their territorial waters. Their goal - the discovery of the sea route to India and the Spice Islands. This goal was like a magnet drawing them forward to more and more reckless ventures. Once the Portuguese discovered the route around the Cape of Good Hope in the late fifteenth century, competition intensified between the European powers.

The discovery of these sea routes diminished the importance of the Levantine or Eastern Mediterranean ports, and of the power of the Italian city states. The French capitalized upon this vacuum and entered into an agreement, or *Capitulation*[1] with the Turks in 1535. Besides numerous political privileges, there were economic and other benefits from this *Capitulation* as well. France, the traditional protector of the Roman Catholic Church in Europe, now became the official protector of all Christians, especially Catholics within the Turkish Empire.

---

1   The word *Capitulation* comes from the chapters of the trade agreements previously made between the Turks and the Italian city states.

Initially Portugal commanded the newly found sea routes and European trade with the East. By the close of the sixteenth century however Holland began to challenge this monopoly. By 1602 the Dutch had set up their own Dutch East India Company, with emphasis being given to trade with the Spice Islands, later named the Dutch East Indies, and present-day Indonesia. While seeking further areas of trade, or while being blown off course by the trade winds, many a Dutch ship floundered upon the coast of a large land mass to the south of the Spice Islands. They named this mass Nieuw Holland, while two large islands to the east of this land mass they named Nieuw Zeeland. The Dutch, eager for trade and not for colonization, recorded their existence but showed little active interest in them.

With Britain's defeat of the Spanish Armada in 1588, she too began rising as a sea power to be reckoned with. England had already challenged the French monopoly of Levantine trade by entering into a trade agreement, or *Capitulation* with Turkey in 1579. English merchants then set up the Levantine Company in 1581 and trade with the Levant thereafter increased. Such a Company however was still disadvantaged by the monopoly which Portugal and Holland held upon the Indies trade. English merchants had to pay high duties for the produce which they purchased coming overland to the Levantine and Turkish ports. A more expedient means of trade was needed and found in the formation of the English East India Company in 1600. Now they directly challenged the Portuguese and Dutch monopoly.

The Dutch won the first round, by ousting the English from the East Indies. The English then were forced to focus upon India where they encountered the hostility of the Portuguese. An armed conflict ended in an English victory in 1614, and thereafter the East India Company entered into an agreeable relationship with the local Mogul emperor, and began expanding its activities and setting up trading stations at strategic points of the sub-continent.

By the late seventeenth century, with the demise of Spain as a sea power, competition began in earnest between the French and the English. No longer content with the 'Turkey trade' France began sending covetous eyes eastwards to where the Dutch, Portuguese and English were battling it out. Collision with these other powers became inevitable especially after the French East India Company was founded in 1664. Over the following years Portuguese and Dutch interests in India slowly decreased, being replaced by British and French.

The search for the quickest and most convenient route to the east continued, and as competition stiffened, this quest intensified. It was the French who first proposed the suitability of establishing a link between the Red Sea, where the squalid port of Suez was positioned, and the Eastern Mediterranean. As the other European powers had by now more-or-less vacated the Mediterranean, the French envisaged opening trading warehouses at Suez, and transporting produce over the Isthmus of Suez to the Mediterranean, either via the Nile or directly overland. Such a proposal was made to the Turkish authorities in 1665, but was turned down.

The German philosopher Gottfried Leibniz then advised Louis XIV of France in 1671 that to truly establish French authority in the Eastern Mediterranean, he should reconstruct the ancient canal connecting the Mediterranean and the Red Sea. He predicted that the true commercial route to India would be found via Egypt.[2] His proposal, again unsuccessful, nevertheless revealed how the region of Egypt and the Land of Israel could very easily become of great importance in this quest for the riches of the East.

By geographical 'chance' the Eastern Mediterranean was sandwiched between Europe and the East. Yet for the present, while Turkey was strong and in control of its destiny, the region would not be contested by the ambitious and greedy European nations-cum-Empires. But once they smelled the weakening of Turkey, conflict between them there would surely be.

Turkey and Russia

Turkey began to weaken following its failure to capture Vienna in 1683. Soon afterwards Russia inflicted defeat upon her and at the subsequent Peace of Carlowitz, Turkey was forced for the first time to relinquish territory. Endeavouring to exert some control over the Turkish Empire, Russia attempted, unsuccessfully, to insert religious factors into the settlement, especially the return of the Church of the Holy Sepulchre to Greek Orthodox authority.

This matter of the status of the Orthodox Church concerned Russia. In the tenth century she had accepted Byzantine Christianity as the state religion, and since the fall of Constantinople, many Russians viewed Russia as having adopted the mantle of the Byzantine Empire and Orthodox Church. They even viewed Moscow as the new Constantinople. The Russian king adopted the title Tsar, the Byzantine title for Emperor. Many Russians therefore believed they had certain titular rights to Constantinople, and parts of the former Byzantine Empire, including the Land of Israel and in particular the 'Holy Places' there.

Clashes between Turkey and Russia increased, especially when Russia, in the eighteenth century under Catherine the Great, began a process of creeping expansion southward. Catherine fomented rebellion in the Turkish areas of Crimea, Morea and Georgia, forcing Turkey to war in 1769, and winning convincingly. The resulting *Treaty of Kucuk Kaynarca* (which in effect became a *Capitulation*) of 1774 forced considerable concessions upon Turkey. Amongst them was the right for Russia to henceforth protect Orthodox Christians living in certain parts of the Turkish or Ottoman Empire. Russia unofficially however expanded this right to all regions of the Turkish Empire, including the 'Holy Places' of Eretz Israel.

Russia then annexed the Crimea in 1783. It was another stage in that long and

---

2   Tuchman, B. *Bible and Sword,* Minerva Press, (New York, 1956), p. 164.

fervent quest of gaining access from the Black Sea to the Mediterranean through the Bosphorus and Dardanelles Straits and to the wide world beyond. Such access was vital for Russia if she was ever to compete with the other European Empires.

Britain and Israel

Britain during the sixteenth and seventeenth centuries was also a nation undergoing far reaching-changes. The birth of her seafaring Empire was being set in motion. Simultaneously she was completing her break with the Roman Catholic Church, a process already set in motion by the movements of Luther and Calvin on the Continent.

One group of reformers, the Puritans, desired to completely purify the church in Britain of all taints of Roman Catholicism. The Puritans, known for producing the Pilgrim Fathers who sailed to America, also developed a keen interest in the Jewish people. This came about due to the Puritan desire to refute all Roman Catholic doctrines and positions. The standard Roman position concerning Israel was basically, that as the Jewish nation (represented by the leadership) had rejected Jesus as their King and Messiah, therefore Israel had forfeited all privileges as pertaining to God's chosen nation. All such unfulfilled promises and privileges recorded in the Bible henceforth were entrusted to the Gentile (Roman) Church, which became, in effect, the new or the spiritual Israel.

According to this theology there was to be no further restoration of Israel to her land, and no pre-eminent position for the Jewish 'church'. Israel according to the flesh, so this line of thinking ran, was under an eternal Divine curse.

This doctrine concerning Israel was challenged by certain Puritan scholars. They surmised, that if the Roman Church was erroneous in key doctrines, then such doctrines concerning Israel too were erroneous. Andrew Willett wrote a treatise in 1590 entirely devoted to this question of the *Calling of the Jews*. The term Israel, he argues, must be taken literally, as referring to the nation and people of Israel. He also wrote that before the return of Jesus Christ, the Jewish people would again be established in the Land of Israel.[3]

Perhaps it was Thomas Brightman though who laid the firmest foundation of a belief in Israel's future restoration. In his book *Apoclypsis Apocalypseos*, published in 1609, he predicted the future overthrow of the Antichrist, whom he and many others acquainted with Rome, to be followed by the overthrow of Turkey, then the 'Calling of the Jews' and their restoration to the Land of Israel. Brightman was quickly followed by other writers, all adding their slightly different shades to this fascinating topic.

3   Verete, Meir. *The Restoration of the Jews in English Protestant Thought 1790-1840.* Middle East Studies, Frank Cass Publishers, (London, January 1972), p.15. I am extremely grateful to the research and writings of the late Professor Verete, which provided me with a platform from which I could further explore this fascinating period and subject.

Of all Brightman's followers, probably Sir Henry Finch was the most prominent. Finch was a member of Parliament, a man acquainted with law and jurisprudence, and of high social and political standing. In his *The World's Great Restauration, or the Calling of the Jews, and (with them) of all the Nations and Kingdoms of the earth, to the faith of Christ*, published in 1621, Finch painted a picture of a restored Israel living in millennial glory, with the nations of the world paying homage to this restored Jewish nation.

Such a testimony produced interesting reactions, including King James I, who detested the idea of bowing down before the ruler of a Jewish kingdom. Finch and his publisher were summarily thrown into prison, and only released when they recanted of their 'treasonable' opinions.

It was Finch who laid down some clear guidelines for interpreting Scripture and in particular the prophecies in the Old Testament. He again emphasized that wherever the name Israel was mentioned, it did not mean anyone else but the people of Israel. The same he said concerning Jerusalem, Judah and Zion. These terms do not apply to the 'spiritual Israel', Jewish and Gentile believers in Jesus, but they apply to the original people or places so named. He too, wrote conclusively of a future return of Israel to her land, as prophesied by Ezekiel, Hosea, Zephaniah, Isaiah, Daniel, and John.[4]

The return of Israel to her land, according to these writings, was to be closely associated with the personal return of Jesus to Jerusalem, although there were discrepancies as to the relationship between the two events. Most however saw a direct connection between these two events and the decline of the Roman Catholic Church. Much of their exegesis came from the books of Daniel and Revelations. Daniel chapter 7 reveals the presence of four successive beasts, depicting four successive kingdoms - Babylonian, Persian, Greek and Roman. The final kingdom would ultimately fall, and then would come an everlasting Kingdom. This, they believed, would be the ultimate Kingdom of Christ.

These Puritan writers viewed the Roman kingdom or Empire as being preserved in their day by the existence of the Roman Catholic Church and the Holy Roman Empire (primarily Germany) and France, the protector nation of the Catholic Church. The Pope, as the leader of the Roman Catholic Church, they viewed as the Anti-Christ. They predicted therefore, that in the latter days the fourth beast or kingdom would receive a strong blow, and that this event would signal the beginning of the end, culminating in the return of the Messiah Jesus and the return of Israel to her land.

The writings of Willet, Brightman and Finch influenced many other thinkers and writings in both England and Scotland. Two in particular, Joseph Mede and Samuel Lee, then further consolidated the viewpoint that the dispersed nation of Israel would

---

4   Verete, Meir. ibid., p. 16.

one day be restored to their homeland.[5]

During periods of Catholic dominance in Britain, many Protestants and Puritans fled, a number settling in Holland. Here they spread their teachings concerning the restoration of Israel. Even the Jewish people, many of whom being descendants of refugees from the Spanish Inquisition, were influenced by the Puritan viewpoint. One renowned rabbi, Menasseh ben Israel later journeyed to England to meet with Oliver Cromwell, the leader of the Puritan Commonwealth. He pleaded for the re-entry of Jewish people into England who had been expelled from England in 1290, during a period of strong anti-Semitism engendered by the Roman Catholic Church. Cromwell however was not fully convinced by Ben Israel's plea, and re-admission only occurred some years later under James II.

Holland was host to other refugees from Catholic persecution. One was Frenchman Pierre Jurieu. Jurieu, like the Puritan restorationists, believed in a future return of Israel to her ancient homeland. In 1687, while in Holland, he wrote *The Accomplishment of the Scripture Prophecies,* in which he predicted, amongst other matters, that a revolution would engulf France in the later 1700's which would have long-term ramifications. Jurieu also wrote an address *To the Nation of the Jews,* and stated : 'I confess the hopes they conceive of a *Kingdom of the Messiah,* which shall be chiefly for them, is built upon express and unquestionable *Prophecies*: that even their *Ierusalem* [Jerusalem] should be *rebuilt,* and that *they* shall be again gathered together in their own Land.' [6]

Britain, France and the Eastern Empires

While the theological belief concerning Israel's restoration to her land was taking hold in various parts of Europe, and especially in Britain, the battle of the European Empires for world wide dominance was intensifying. The Russian and Turkish Empires were continuing to battle it out around the Black Sea region, while the emerging French and British Empires were now entering into a long period of serious confrontation.

Trade in the East, especially in India, was now gradually being caught up into this new political reality. From 1707 the once powerful Mogul Empire began a process of quick disintegration. Several rival Indian dynasties and the British and French trading companies vied to fill this vacuum. The French companies had steadily increased their activities in the first half of the 1700's, and at one stage stood to oust Britain from certain areas.

The first serious conflict occurred between 1756-1763, the Seven Years War,

---

5   Ibid., p. 18.
6   Jurieu, Peter. *The Accomplishment of the Scripture Prophecies,* (London, 1687), p. 2-3. Copy in British Library, London.

during which the French attempted to make strong military alliances with local Indian princes and thence to eradicate the British presence. At one point the French again raised the idea of cutting a canal from the Mediterranean through to the Red Sea and thereby establishing a quick route to India. It proceeded no further due to a British victory and most former French holdings were taken over by the English East India Company.

Victory forced Britain to consolidate her holdings in India. The power of the East Indies Company became more far reaching and India became essential for Britain's imperial designs. But the French had not completely given up. They merely embarked on other ventures. Probably the most ambitious of these was the proposal to actually gain control over Egypt - the halfway house between India and Europe. The Duc de Choiseul set the venture in motion in 1769, hoping to gain control over the Mameluke (Mamluk) Bey (local ruler ostensibly under Turkish control) Ali Bey. But within a few years the venture faded out, as both De Choiseul and Ali became politically obsolete.[7] Nevertheless the French did maintain a small trading station at Suez, which was however being joined by the British towards the close of the eighteenth century.

During the American Revolution France endeavoured to oppose Britain, not only in America, but again in India, where they encouraged uprisings by the princes of Mysore, Hyderabad and Mahratta. Warren Hastings, the British Governor-General ultimately prevailed against the opposing forces. Britain may have lost America, but she gained India.

Even before the American Revolution and subsequent problems throughout the world, Britain was wary of the presence of rival European, especially French activities in the East. With this in mind Captain James Cook set out in 1769 on a voyage of discovery and possession on behalf of the Britain Government. Part of his task was to determine if in fact there was a large southern land mass, the legendary *Terra Australis*, and if in fact this was the same as Nieuw Holland. Cook in the process of his journey rediscovered first Nieuw Zeeland, and then the eastern coast of Nieuw Holland in 1770.

Great interest was aroused by Cook's discoveries. They were quickly overshadowed however by the American Revolution. Britain was also beset at this time by the Industrial Revolution. Although providing positive benefits to her economy, the Industrial Revolution greatly affected her social structure. Britain's urban population had grown steeply during this period. Industrialization meant the displacement of much of the traditional rural lifestyle of the country. In the cities housing was poor, wages low and conditions harsh.

Many people, unable to survive economically in such harsh conditions, resorted

---

7   Kinross, Lord, *Between Two Seas*. William Morrow & Company, Inc, (New York, 1969), p. 10.

to petty crime so as to eke out a basic existence. Most were not criminals in the real sense, but desperate ordinary people, desirous to survive with a degree of dignity. Yet according to the very stringent British law system, if caught for such minor offenses as stealing a chicken, a loaf of bread or the likes, they were classified as criminals and received a heavy punishment. In most cases the punishment was much severer than the 'crime' warranted. They were packed into the few prisons then in the nation.

The prisons were degrading and disgraceful. Men and women were often thrown in together. Worse still, petty criminals and children were placed in the same cells as hard core murderers, rapists and the likes. It seemed that society and the legal system made little distinction between minor and major crimes. All had broken the law, and therefore all deserved to rot in the same prison cell. With the loss of America as a dumping ground for such criminals, and the overcrowding of the already crowded prisons, the policy makers pondered on how best to deal with this problem while the aristocracy wanted society cleaned up of this 'scum'.

Prime Minister William Pitt was confronted by two problems; the French and the overcrowded prisons in Britain. Pitt needed to keep France away from Britain's vital interests in the East. This concern was amplified by France's agreement with the Bey or ruler of Cairo in 1785. For the French this was 'a distant gambit to a possible invasion of India.'[8] A bigger problem then arose with the signing of an agreement between the French and Dutch in the same year. Pitt worried lest the Dutch avail their eastern ports to access by the French, as actually happened at the Cape Colony.

The other problem, that of the overcrowded prisons was, by 1786, becoming a major and desperate issue. Several proposals had been made over the previous years, incorporating to various degrees strategic matters with the need to open a new base for dispatching the 'scum' of British society. It does not appear that Pitt took too much notice of such proposals.[9] A Memo on the matter was submitted to the Cabinet in August 1786. At this juncture Joseph Banks, who had accompanied Cook, submitted testimony on the advantages of settling at Botany Bay on the east coast of Nieuw Holland. Nieuw Zeeland was ruled out as a possible location due to the more warrior like character of their inhabitants.

Colony New South Wales

Finally a decision was reached in 1787 to establish a convict settlement on the east coast of Nieuw Holland, (now New South Wales), which Cook had be claimed for Britain. Captain Arthur Phillip would lead the first convoy of convicts to *the uttermost ends of the earth.* His convoy, which finally departed Britain on 13 May 1787, consisted

---

8   Hughes, Robert. *The Fatal Shore.* Pan Books/Collins, (London, 1987), p. 59.
9   Ibid., pp. 61-64.

of some eleven ships, carrying 1,030 passengers, including 548 male and 188 female prisoners, on what would become the longest journey ever attempted with such a number of people. In fact these 736 outcasts of British society would be the harbinger of some 160,000 who would be sent out to Australia over the following years. There was no historical precedent for the birth of a country in such a manner.

Phillip's First Fleet reached Botany Bay on the east coast of Nieuw Holland on 20 January 1788. Finding conditions there unsuitable, he set sail for Sydney Cove several kilometres north on 26 January. Upon leaving Botany Bay two French warships were spotted in the vicinity, prompting Phillip to hasten to Port Jackson and quickly proclaim British sovereignty over what now became New South Wales.

Phillip had supplies for two years But it became apparent very quickly that rationing was required. No relief ships arrived from the 'Mother Country' until June 1790. And this convoy brought not just relief, but also hundreds of real outcasts including the sick, disabled and helpless. A third convoy in 1791 brought another 1,500 convicts.

Indeed British society was being cleansed of the so-called scum of society. But such a policy brought undue hardship upon those being transported, and upon their families who remained behind. Very seldom were those separated families reunited. And conditions were indeed rough in the new convict colony. Mercy was in small quantity, while the cat-o-tails lash was in much use. The soldiers, being at the lower rung of the British military scale, were often worse than the convicts themselves, and indeed terribly abused them. This was the beginnings of the new British society in the south seas, an extension of the British Empire to *the uttermost ends of the earth*.

C hapter 3

French Revolution and Israel's Return

While the foundations for an extension of the British Empire were being laid in the Far East, foundations for Israel's restoration were being laid in France and Britain. The stimulant was the beginning of the French Revolution in 1789. 'Several months after its outbreak,' wrote the late Professor Meir Verete of Jerusalem's Hebrew University, 'Englishmen began to hear and to read that it was this great event that heralded the end of the generations and the impending advent of the kingdom of Christ.'[1]

Evangelicals to the Fore

A number of Evangelical Christians in Britain at this time had become acquainted with the writings of the Puritan theologians, Pierre Jurieu and others, on the issue of the restoration of Israel. One of them, Edward May had read Jurieu's *The Accomplishment of the Scripture Prophecies,* and his prediction of a future revolution in France. May wrote an initial treatise entitled *The Accomplishment of the Scripture Prophecies* which was printed in London in 1790. In it he drew a number of far-reaching conclusions, among them that the fall of the French Monarchy, to be quickly followed by the fall of the Pope, would usher in the countdown to the fulfilment of the prophecies.

Subsequent events, both in France and elsewhere in the region seemed to substantiate what Jurieu, May and others had predicted. And by 1792 the number of other writers on the subject began to increase. Perhaps the most significant of these writers was James Bicheno, a Baptist minister in England. Bicheno, who had read Jurieu's work, and others besides, wrote *The Signs of the Times,* in 1792. Bicheno provided much more of a systematic outline for interpreting the events in France. He combined the writings of the books of Daniel and Revelation, with other prophecies of the Old Testament, and looking at the events happening in his own day, saw that

---

1   Verete, Meir. *The Restoration of the Jews,* p. 5.

the fourth beast or kingdom as referred to by Daniel, was now entering its final stages of life. If this was so, he predicted, then the last days had begun, the Antichrist would be finally overthrown, the Jewish nation would be reborn and the nations of the world would accept Christ.[2]

Until Bicheno's book the standard viewpoint was, that the Jewish people would firstly acknowledge Jesus as Messiah and then be restored to the Land of Israel. Yet, Bicheno predicted that the Jewish people would initially return to Eretz Israel in unbelief and thereupon turn to Jesus. This viewpoint had a tremendous bearing upon subsequent writings and attitudes. Others followed him and either adopted his viewpoint, modified it, or even ridiculed it. Both positive and negative reactions all helped increase the interest level in Israel's restoration.

It seemed that even some members of the Establishment were seeing the events in neighbouring France as of eternal significance. In 1793 the *Evangelical Magazine*, a joint magazine of both Evangelical Anglicans and non-Anglicans (Dissenters) wrote an article entitled *Remarks on the Prophecies and Promises Relating to The Glory of the Latter Day*. Having described at length the hope and glory of the future, the article then referred to the 'present period' or the grand jubilee as they called it, as 'a crisis replete with great events.' It then adjudged that this was the time when 'The power of Antichrist is falling ...' Referring to the Roman Church as Antichrist, vessel of 'bigotry and superstition,' the article then referred to the gradual decay of the *papal power*, meaning the Roman Church, and that it, 'has received a surprising and unexpected blow, by those late events, which have taken place in a neighbouring nation, and still alarm the world.'[3]

At this point the article detracts from the opinions of Bicheno and company. It makes no specific mention of Israel's restoration, but emphasizes the preaching of the Gospel to the nations as the necessary next step and of Christ Jesus' ultimate victory over the spirit of Antichrist. Nevertheless, such sentiments alluding to the events in a neighbouring country as harbingers of the beginning of these latter days in such an influential magazine revealed the extent to which this opinion, that the French Revolution and its consequences was precursor of the latter days, was spreading.

During the following years subsequent editions of Bicheno's *Signs of the Times* were printed, and during the period 1794-95 more than ten separate works on the subject of Israel's restoration, were published.[4] Included was a work by the eminent scientist and theologian, Dr. Joseph Priestley, entitled *The Present State of Europe compared with ancient Prophecies.*

---

2   Bicheno, James. *The Signs of the Times.* (London, 1792), p. 72.
3   *Evangelical Magazine*, October 1793, London, p. 162.
4   Verete, Meir. *The Restoration of the Jews.* p. 44.

As could be expected with such millenarian[5] excitement, there were a number of interlopers. One, Richard Brothers, a retired naval officer, actually took matters into his own hands and predicted that he was the saviour of England and the world, and that as a descendant of David, he would lead the Jewish people back to their homeland. He immediately attracted widespread attraction. Numerous editions of his writings were printed and thousands distributed. People from all over Britain believed he was the Messiah. He caused such havoc in London that he was arrested, and even appeared before the Privy Council, where in the presence Prime Minister Pitt and some other ministers he was extensively examined by the Lord Chancellor.[6]

The activities of Brothers reveal again the depth of feeling amongst the populace of the country at the time concerning the events then occurring 'in a neighbouring land,' and their association to the approach of the last days, the imminent return of Israel to her homeland, and the return of Jesus. Yet the manner in which Brothers propagated his viewpoint caused many to issue cautions against wild predictions, calculating of dates and the likes. The distinguished *Evangelical Magazine* wrote such a caution in its 1796 edition.[7]

Indeed many within the Establishment in Britain were becoming unsettled by this increasing interest in the millennium and Jewish restoration. It could easily undermine the solidity of British society. This especially so as a good number of Dissenters favoured the views coming from France, seeing in them an opportunity for deliverance from their inferior status in their own establishment ruled society.[8] Some of such opinion even refused to assist in the construction of anti-invasion defences on the south coast.[9] The ideas, both of the French Revolution and the millenarians, found ready prepared ground with many members of the non-establishment.

Members of the Established Church did however, in time, begin showing an interest in the millenarian concept. One of the first was Edward King, a fellow of the Royal Society. In his *Remarks on the Signs of the Times*, published in 1798, he actually predicted that France was to be the restorer of the Jewish people. Such views from a member of the Establishment were certainly to be frowned upon at this time, when concern of the French invasion was tantamount. Henry Kett, another Anglican, and scholar from Cambridge, held similar views. A leading bishop of the day, Samuel Horsley, was led to refute these sentiments, and wrote a book in 1799 entitled *Critical disquisition's on the Eighteenth chapter of Isaiah.*

---

5   Millennium - thousand years. In this context referring to the thousand year reign of Christ from Jerusalem prior to the final downfall of Satan. Evangelical Christians looking for the return of Israel anticipated Christ's thousand year reign.
6   Verete, Meir. *The Restoration of the Jews.* p. 9.
7   *Evangelical Magazine*, London, 1796. p. 303.
8   Verete, Meir. *The Restoration of the Jews.* p. 10.
9   Ibid. p. 10.

The reviewer from the *Gentleman's Magazine* however picked up a strong millenarian hint in Horsley's book and wrote that perhaps Horsley held 'his own latent sentiment that the deliverance of the Jews ... may possibly be effected by means of England.' [10] This hint of Horsley was taken seriously by some, due to his high standing as a leading bishop. Yet for most of the millenarian thinkers and writers, thoughts of England being the restorer of Israel were, at this point, rather vague.

Meanwhile the excited populace waited expectantly for the future fulfilment of the remaining predictions of the millenarian writers. Many of their expectations were met when the French forces overthrew the temporal power of the Pope when they invaded Italy and established the Roman Republic in 1797-1798, forcing Pope Pius into exile.

With the extinguishing of the temporal power of the Roman Church, the Turks, another of the forces of Antichrist, were next in line to be vanquished, a necessary requirement before the actual Jewish restoration and return of Jesus could take place. Indeed Jesus had warned his disciples that as part of the birth pangs of the last days 'Nation would rise against nation and kingdom against kingdom.' But there was another essential requirement, which many of these Evangelicals saw, before Jesus would return.

Jesus spoke to His disciples and instructed them that, 'this gospel of the kingdom will be preached in the whole world as a testimony to all nations, and then the end will come.'[11] In obedience to this commandment many Evangelical Christians garnered their resources in the last decade of the century and formed numerous missionary societies. These included the Baptist Missionary Society in 1792; the non-denominational London Missionary Society in 1795; the Anglican Church Missionary Society in 1799; and the non-denominational Bible Society followed in 1804. The Evangelical movement was dedicated in one form or another to taking the gospel of the kingdom to the uttermost ends of the earth.

What of the Jewish People?

If numerous Evangelical Christians in Britain were preparing for the return of the Jewish people to their homeland, what of the Jewish people themselves? Were they ready for such a return? Were they in any position to effect it even if they so desired? Basically no. There were already a few thousand Jewish people living in Turkish *Palestine*, but the majority of these were aged, primarily there to study the Torah and die in the 'Holy Land'. They looked to the coming of their Messiah, *after which* the exiled Israelites would return.

Yet the French Revolution promoted a process of emancipation for the Jewish

---

10 *Gentleman's Magazine,* London, July 1799. p. 549.
11 Matthew 24: 6-8,14. New International Version.

people which paved the way for their ultimate return to Eretz Israel. In 1791 the French National Assembly proclaimed liberty for all Frenchmen, regardless of their religious affiliation. Thereafter the Jewish people of France, and later other nations as well, enjoyed, for the first time, civil rights and equality. Not only were Jewish people emancipated from the squalid ghettos but also from the control of their own religious leaders.

Amongst the first to experience the reality of this new chapter in Jewish history were the Jewish people of Italy after part of their land was occupied in 1796 by the army of Republican France. One French commander was a young Napoleon Bonaparte. At that time the Jewish people lived separately in squalid ghettos, and were forced to wear demeaning yellow badges. Napoleon was stirred by the sight of this persecuted minority. 'In every Italian city which the French army entered,' wrote Kobler, 'the ghetto gates were removed, hacked to pieces and burned, the shameful badges thrown away, and the symbols of freedom -Trees of Liberty - planted by the delivered Jews.'[12]

These were positive signs for the liberation and emancipation of the Jewish people in Europe. But they seemed to contribute very little to the actual return of the Jewish people to the Land of Israel itself. Amazingly though this process was also soon set in motion, and it was again the French who were to the fore, and the prime mover was the very same French general, Napoleon Bonaparte.

---

12   Kobler, F. *Napoleon and the Jews*. Massada Press, (Jerusalem, 1975), p. 18.

*C*hapter 4

Napoleon and the Road to India

Invasion Plans

While the French were implanting their message of liberty, fraternity and equality throughout Europe, they began making plans to invade Britain. An invasion army, named the *Army of England* was formed under the command of General Bonaparte. Preparations in Britain for a French invasion had been in progress since 1797, and the nation was being prepared as best it could. To prevent the French Mediterranean Fleet at Toulon slipping past Gibraltar into the Atlantic and joining the rest of the French invasion fleet at Brest, the Admiralty dispatched Admiral Sir Horatio Nelson to the Mediterranean on 2 May 1798.

While Pitt and the Government awaited the movements of the French Fleet, Napoleon, as early as January 1798 had changed the battle plan. The *Annual Register*, an official British publication wrote of Napoleon in 1798:

> He had often expressed in conversation even for several years before, his opinion, that there could not be a nobler enterprize, or one more conducive to the interests of the human race, than to relieve India from the domination of the English, and to open the richest commerce to the whole world ... he conceived the design of shutting it [India] out from England, by the possession of Egypt.[1]

Napoleon duly informed the French Government, the Directory, that in order to ultimately destroy Britain it would be necessary to take Egypt.[2] The strategic reasons being to cut Britain's link to India, and to preserve French trade in the Levant, the Eastern Mediterranean.

There were other minor motives for wanting the expedition to Egypt. Napoleon's secretary, Fauvelet de Bourrienne wrote many years later that prior to the expedition to Egypt, Napoleon desired to emulate the exploits of Alexander the Great.[3] There was still another factor. A restless general needed action, and if it wasn't Britain, then why not Egypt?

---

1   *The Annual Register*, (London, 1798), pp. 134-135. Copy in Public Records Office, Kew.
2   *Correspondence de l'armee francaise en Egypte*. Paris, Year VII, Vol. III., p. 235. Quoted in Herold, J. Christopher. *Bonaparte in Egypt*. Hamish Hamilton, (London, 1963), p. 14.

Destination - Egypt

Napoleon's fleet of some one hundred and eighty vessels and over 50,000 men left Toulon on 19 May 1798, the largest force France had dispatched overseas. The course of the history of the Eastern Mediterranean and indeed the world was about to change. 'The path to Constantinople and India' wrote Trevelyan, 'seemed open to the most ambitious spirit since Alexander the Great.'[4] Napoleon's movement from France, quickly alerted the British. Even before news of the French Fleet's true whereabouts became public, *The St. James Chronicle (or British Evening Post)* wrote:

> Curiosity and conjecture have been equally exercised with respect to the object of the expedition of Buonaparte up the Mediterranean, but nothing satisfactory or conclusive has yet been presented to the Publick (sic.) Even the overthrow of the Torkish (sic.) Government, and the plunder of its capital, are considered as objects too trivial for an armament so formidable ... and it has been assumed by many, that the conquest of India can alone bound the views, and satisfy the ambitions of the French Chief.[5]

Nelson arrived at Toulon eight days after the French Fleet had set sail, and then set off in hot pursuit. From Italy he discovered the true destination of the French Fleet. 'I shall believe,' he wrote to the First Lord of the Admiralty, 'that they are going on their scheme of possessing Alexandria, and getting troops to India ...' Nelson then assured his superior that he would discover and destroy the French Fleet, and subsequently set course for Egypt. [6]

The French Fleet meanwhile captured the tiny strategic island of Malta on 11 June. Then several days later they set sail for Egypt, but after having received intelligence of the presence of a pursuing British fleet, Napoleon altered his course, and the two fleets unknowingly passed each other.

Calls for Israel's Restoration

Napoleon's departure to the East stirred the hearts of a number of Jewish people in Europe. One Italian Jew, wrote an anonymous letter which appeared in the leading French literary magazine *La decade philosophique; litteraire et politique,* which Napoleon may possibly have read prior to his departure. Then it appeared in full in the *Courier* newspaper in London on 19 June 1798. The *Letter* called for Israel's restoration as a nation among the other nations of the world, a realization to be assisted by 'the invincible nation which now fills the world with her glory', meaning of course France. Speaking to his Jewish brethren, the writer concludes:

---

3   Herold, J. Christopher. ibid. p. 3.
4   Trevelyan, G.M. *The History of England.* Longmans, Green and Co, (London, 1948), p. 576.
5   *The St. James Chronicle (or British Evening-Post),* From Thursday, July 12 to Saturday July 14, 1798. No 6329. No page number. Under heading: *The British Review.* Copy at British Library.
6   Nelson, Horatio, Viscount Nelson. *Dispatches and Letters.* Ed by Sir Nicholas Harris Nicolas. Vol. III. (London, 1895), p. 31. Quoted in Herold, J. Christopher. *Napoleon in Egypt.* p. 50.

O my Brethren, what sacrifices ought we not make to attain this object? We shall return to our country, we shall live under our own laws - we shall behold those places where our ancestors demonstrated their courage and their virtues. Already I see you all animated with a holy zeal. Israelites! the end of our misfortunes is at hand. The opportunity is favourable - take care that you do not allow it to escape.[7]

Other British magazines, *The Gospel Magazine* and *St. James Chronicle* followed suit and reproduced excerpts. Many of the millenarian writers and advocates were excited when they read this article, and then heard of Napoleon's subsequent invasion of Egypt.

Bicheno in the postscript to his *A Glance at the History of Christianity and of English Non Conformity*, published in late 1798, wrote:

Now we are to be looking for the restoration of the scattered Jews ... To pretend to determine, positively, *how* this is to be brought about, would be arrogance; the probability is that the Turkish power being overturned in Palestine, by some invading enemy, that enemy will think it politic and necessary, for the promotion of its own schemes, to invite the Jews to take possession of their ancient patrimony, and to make one cause with themselves. For without the support of some powerful nation, how are the dispersed, disorganized Jews, to collect their numbers and unite their energies, so as to produce the effects predicted? We know God can work miracles; but we know also that he usually works by second causes.

I shall now only add that Egypt, it is probable, will be an easy conquest, (Isa xi) and a thoroughfare for the returning sons of Abraham, to the country of their ancestors.[8]

Even the pro-Establishment *The Gentleman's Magazine*, wrote in September 1799 '... it is surely no rash conjecture to suppose that they [the Jews] may be restored to their own land under the power and protection of another mighty empire.'[9] Other writers earlier in the 1700's had also predicted that an empire, even Britain, would be the restorer of Israel.[10] The signs of the times in 1798 seemed to point to France as being the restorer of Israel, or at least the possessor of the Land of Israel. Henry Kett seemed to adhere to this belief. In his *History the Interpreter of Prophecy* published in 1799, he wrote in explaining some aspects of the book of Daniel:

It certainly is not *impossible* that the French may offer them [the Jewish people] their ancient land ... in order to render them subservient to their vast designs of universal conquest ... I do not think this likely to happen. It seems to me *more* probable, that the

---

7   *The Courier*, 19 June 1798. See also Kobler, Franz. *The Vision Was There: A History of the British Movement for the Restoration of the Jews to Palestine*. World Jewish Congress, British Section/Lincolns-Prager Publishers Ltd, (London, 1956), p. 44.

8   Bicheno, James., *A Glance at the History of Christianity and of English NonConformity*, (London, 1798), p. 28.

9   *The Gentleman's Magazine*, September 1799, p. 738. Quoted in Verete, M. *The Restoration of the Jews*. p. 45.

10   Whiston, W. *The Full and Final Restoration*. London, 1753., pp. 14-15. Quoted in Verete, M. *The Restoration of the Jews*. p. 50.

French should choose to retain possession of a country so well adapted to their acknowledged views; and that thus this people may be the means of recovering the land from its present desolation ...[11]

Subsequent events seemed to further the expectation that Britain would not be the nation to restore Israel to her land. This thought was quite repugnant to some British millenarian writers, including Bicheno, who wrote:

> What the designs of Providence are none can say; or how things may be over-ruled in favor of this nation or that, it is impossible to conjecture; but, if the Jews are to be soon restored, I freely acknowledge, that, from the awful events which we have lately witnessed in Europe; from the footing which the French have got in the Turkish empire, near to the promised land, if not in it; from the general disaffection of the Turkish provinces, and from the deep policy of our enemy, and the principles which they disseminate - whether they succeed in this or that particular object or not - I cannot help fearing that we are not the favoured nation. I wish our prospects were more promising.[12]

Battles at Alexandria, the Pyramids and the Nile (Aboukir Bay)

Napoleon's Fleet arrived off the coast of Egypt on 1 July and the following day the French attacked and captured Alexandria. Murad Bey the Mameluke bey or ruler of Cairo quickly summoned together a force to battle Napoleon, whose troops had immediately begun moving southwards towards Cairo. Napoleon met and quickly defeated a smaller Mameluke army on 13 July. He then moved towards Cairo where, with the Pyramids as a backdrop, he defeated, on 21 July a much larger force. The Battle of the Pyramids was a turning point in the affairs of Egypt, and indeed of the entire region. A modern European army had entered the heartland of Islam, and defeated an Islamic army.

These victories further alarmed the British in India. In a letter to the Governor of the small British colony at the Cape, the Government of Bombay wrote an appeal for assistance. Referring to the French as an enemy 'so notoriously and malignantly jealous of our Eastern Empire' it read:

> The object of this expedition appears ... to be decidedly directed in its ultimate end against the British possessions in India & probably by way of the Red Sea ... The different ports in the Red Sea, will afford more than ample tonnage for the accommodation of this Army ... it seems very probable, that part of this Force would be left to annoy us this side of India ...[13]

---

11 Kett, Henry. *History the Interpreter of Prophecy.* (London, 1799), p. 227. Copy in the British Library.
12 Bicheno, James. *The Restoration of the Jews: The Crisis of All Nations.* (London, 1800), p. 65. Copy in the British Library.
13 Government of Bombay to Earl Macartney, 28 September 1798. WO 1/893. Public Records Office [PRO] Kew, London.

It was imperative that Nelson seek out and destroy the French Fleet, if it still remained in Egyptian waters, before it moved to obtain those strategic objectives. On 1 August, while Napoleon and his army were celebrating victory in Cairo, Nelson discovered and attacked the bulk of the French Fleet nestling in the Bay of Aboukir, at the mouth of the Nile. Only four French ships managed to escape, what became known as the Battle of the Nile. The first clash between the European Empires over the destiny of the Eastern Mediterranean had claimed its first casualties. It also resulted in the forging of better diplomatic relations between Britain and Turkey.

Turkish-British-Russian Alliance

The Turks knew of the intended destination of the French Fleet as early as May 1798. When the French explained that it amounted to no more than settling a score with the Mamelukes, the Turks, who also were upset with the semi-autonomy of the Mamelukes, were almost convinced. But, the Turks contended, if the French meant no harm towards them, why had they not sent a fully fledged ambassador to Turkey to explain their intentions?

Relations between France and Turkey thereafter deteriorated. Despite this, Charles Talleyrand, representing the Directory, sent Ruffin, the French charge d'affaires in Constantinople, a secret communiqué on 4 August stating France's real intentions:

> All trade in the Mediterranean must ... pass into French hands ... and ... Egypt, a country France always has desired, belongs of necessity to the Republic ... The Directory is determined to maintain itself in Egypt by all possible means.[14]

Throughout this period the British and Russian ambassadors at Constantinople had been pressuring the Turkish Government to declare war against France. Yet it was not until 9 September, after news of the defeat at Aboukir Bay had reached Turkey, did they take such drastic action. Shortly afterwards the Russian Fleet left the Black Sea, passed through the Bosphorus, to cheers from the Turkish populace, through the Dardanelles Straits and into the Mediterranean. In December 1798 Britain, Russia and Turkey signed treaties of alliance, each pledging not to make separate peace treaties with the French.

The French in Egypt

The credibility of the French in Egypt waned following the destruction of their Fleet. It further decreased following the Turkish declaration of war against France, which even provoked a serious uprising against the French in Cairo. Napoleon nevertheless endeavoured to ingratiate himself before the leaders of the region, and sent letters of

---

14 La Jonquiere, C. de. *L'Expedition en Egypt, 1798-1801*. Paris, 1899-1907. Vol II, page 607-608. Quoted in Herold, J. Christopher. *Bonaparte in Egypt*. pp. 132-133.

introduction as far afield as Acre, Damascus, Mecca and Tripoli. The response was usually one of silence or opposition. Ahmed or Djezzar (the Butcher) Pasha, governor of Acre was indignant, refusing to receive Napoleon's messenger. The international scene looked ominous for France.

Napoleon meanwhile invested time in one of his favoured projects, indeed the centre of his strategic objective, the construction of a canal connecting the Mediterranean and Red Sea. From the Isthmus of Suez he wrote on 29 December 1798 of his intentions to complete a survey of the Suez Canal.[15] Of course there was no Suez Canal but there had been in antiquity various canals which connected the Isthmus of Suez to the Mediterranean. At his departure in early January he left behind a small band of engineers and surveyors to survey the Isthmus of Suez. Due however to a miscalculation these surveyors wrongly deduced that the level of the Red Sea was higher than that of the Mediterranean.

Part of his plan to conquer India, required establishing bases along the Red Sea and then cutting Britain's sea link. To aid him he wrote to Tippoo Sahib, a local Indian prince and opponent of British rule, on 25 January: 'You have already learned of my arrival on the shores of the Red Sea with an innumerable and invincible army, anxious to free you from the yoke of England ... I take the first opportunity of letting you know that I am anxious that you should send me information through Moca and Muscat as to your political situation. I hope you can send to Suez or Cairo, some able and trustworthy person with whom I can discuss matters.'[16]

His invasion of Egypt had captivated the imagination of Tippoo Sahib and indeed all who opposed British rule in India. Yet by May 1799 his would-be ally in India was dead, defeated in battle against the British.

The Invasion of the Land of Israel, Sinai, El Arish and Gaza

The Anglo-Russo-Turk Alliance bode ill for Napoleon. The French Consuls throughout the Turkish Empire had been arrested, and Djezzar Pasha was commissioned to form an army to oust him from Egypt. Aware of the intentions of Djezzar Pasha to invade Egypt and rout him, Napoleon decided to take the offensive. He wrote to the Directory on 10 January 1799 boasting that by the time they read his letter, he might be in Jerusalem standing upon the ruins of Solomon's Temple.[17] His strategic reasons for the campaign, as explained to the Directory, were, to consolidate the French presence in Egypt by conquering the Sinai Peninsular and forming a buffer zone between himself and the Turkish forces, to force the Turks to explain their

---

15   Johnston, R.M. *The Corsican: A Diary of Napoleon's Life in His Own Words.* Macmillan and Co, (London, 1910), p. 89.

16   Napoleon I. *Correspondence de Napoleon I publiee par ordre de 'lEmperor Napoleon III.* (Paris, 1858-70) Vol, V. p. 278. Quoted in: Johnston, R.M., ibid., p. 90.

17   Johnston, R.M. ibid. p. 92

intransigence towards him, and, to deprive the British Fleet of using the province of Syria to draw their supplies.[18]

His ultimate objective within the province of Syria was the conquest of Acre, the most strategic coastal port. After this, he could subdue the cities of Damascus and Aleppo, and with the help of the local Mamelukes and Arabs, march onto Constantinople. From there he would follow the footsteps of Alexander the Great and march onto the Indus and subdue India.[19]

Although unprepared for a campaign into Syria, Napoleon's 13,000 strong force left Cairo on 10 February 1799. His first move was to fortify Katia, an oasis on the ancient *Via Maris*, and from there move across the harsh Sinai Peninsular and rout the remnants of the Mameluke army which had fled to El Arish.

El Arish was finally captured on 19 February. General Kleber's division then led the vanguard towards Gaza, which fell without any fighting five days later. The ancient city, the gateway into the Land of Israel, was then looted and all available provisions commandeered. From here the French Army headed towards Ramle, which was reached and taken on 1 March. The French forces left here on 3 March and headed for Jaffa which they reached that same day. Jaffa, reputed to be one of the oldest ports in the world, was to be a more formidable opponent.

Massacre at Jaffa

Having refused Napoleon's offer to surrender, the Turkish and Mameluke force was subjected to a concentrated bombardment on 7 March. Several hours later the city walls were breached, and the French tricolour was flying in triumph. Then, unfortunately, the soldiers of France totally sacked the town, killing, raping and maiming all who came in their sight, Moslem, Christian or Jew, man, female or child, young or old.

Worse was to come. Between 2,500 to 3,000 Turkish soldiers were barricaded in the citadel, and sued for surrender. The French emissaries promised them freedom of passage, a matter which infuriated Napoleon who stated his inability to feed, guard or escort so many prisoners. Under the pretext that a number of these prisoners in fact were some that he had set free following the capture of El Arish, Napoleon ordered their execution.

The French name had now been tainted. And as if a curse befell them, the following day French troops fell victim to the plague, and daily thereafter soldiers were brought dead and dying to the hospitals. Despite these setbacks Napoleon left a garrison behind to care also for the sick and wounded, and marched north on 14 March, to confront the other butcher, Ahmad Pasha.

---

18   Quoted in Kobler, Franz. *Napoleon and the Jews.* Massada Press, (Jerusalem, 1975), p. 41.
19   Herold, J. Christopher. *Bonaparte in Egypt.* p. 265.

Siege of Acre

Napoleon's forces occupied Haifa on 17 March. Two days later the French Army was approaching Acre, which was defended on the land by Djezzar Pasha and at sea by Admiral Sir Sidney Smith of the British Navy. Distasteful of sieges, and short of siege guns, which were en-route by boat, the impatient Napoleon began his assault against Acre on 28 March.

The battle was lost on the first day. Sidney Smith landed 800 British Marines to assist in the defence of the city which greatly assisted in stemming the flow of French troops into the city after the walls had been breached. Many Turks, fully aware of the fate of their brethren at Jaffa, began to panic and flee. Djezzar stopped the panic, sent the soldiers back and the incursion was halted.

Two days after this assault Djezzar Pasha, the Butcher, massacred two hundred innocent Christian citizens of the town. More death followed when the French attempted another frivolous assault on 1 April. This failure pacified Napoleon's impatience, and he opted to await the arrival of the siege guns. But man of action that he was Napoleon chose to take the initiative elsewhere.

Declaration to the Jewish People

Djezzar Pasha had summoned help from as far afield as Damascus and Aleppo. Napoleon needed to rout these forces before they arrived at Acre. He initially secured victories over smaller Turkish and Arab forces. But in mid April the bulk of the army of Damascus crossed the Jordan River to the north of the Sea of Galilee. This army, comprised of some 35,000 men of whom about 25,000 were horsemen, assembled in the Jezreel Valley below the majestic Mount Tabor. General Kleber met them with a force of only 2,000.

The battle began early in the morning of 16 April and raged throughout the day. The French were in a precarious position. Then at about 4 o'clock in the afternoon, when matters seemed desperate, and with ammunition running low, Napoleon appeared to the south and sent a cannon volley towards the Turkish lines. The Turks fled, quickly pursued by the tired, but now revived French troops. The Battle of Mount Tabor had been won by Napoleon's timely intervention.

This was now an opportune time for Napoleon to ingratiate himself with the discontented peoples of the region, those who disdained Turkish rule. At this juncture he issued another of his by now famous proclamations, **this time to the Jewish people.** The Paris based *Moniteur Universal* wrote on 22 May 1799 that 'Napoleon has published a proclamation in which he invites all the Jews of Asia and Africa to gather under his flag in order to re-establish the ancient Jerusalem. He has already given arms to a great number, and these battalions threaten Aleppo.'[20] The alleged

---

20 *Moniteur Universal*. Paris, May 22, 1799. Quoted by Schwarzfuchs, Simon. *Napoleon the Jews and the*

manifesto proclaimed 'Israelites, arise!':

> Ye exiled, arise! Hasten! Now is the moment which may not return for thousands of
> years, to claim the restoration of civic rights among the population of the universe
> which have shamefully been withheld from you for thousands of years, to claim your
> political existence as a nation among nations, and the unlimited natural right to worship
> Jehovah according to your faith, publicly and most probably forever ...[21]

Napoleon addressed his proclamation to the Jewish people as 'the rightful heirs of
Palestine.' He also promised them the support of the French nation, who would help
the Jewish people to not only regain their inheritance, but to 'remain master of it and
maintain it against all comers.'[22]

Defeat at Acre and Retreat to Egypt

All of Napoleon's victories and this profound proclamation to the Jewish people
were worthless however if he could not subdue Acre. To this purpose he returned
there and invested all his energies. The assaults resumed on 24 April and continued
thereafter for several weeks. On several occasions large breaches were made in the
city walls and Frenchmen managed to penetrate beyond. Inside however they were
cut down by the combined forces of Djezzar Pasha and Sidney Smith.

Sir Sidney made several desperate attempts to persuade Napoleon and the French
forces to accept defeat. None proved successful. Summoning reinforcements from
the garrison forces located elsewhere, Napoleon decided upon one last attempt for 10
May 1799. He had not given up hope of winning, then gathering a large army,
marching on Damascus and Aleppo and then subduing Constantinople, where he
would establish a new and great Empire. Yet throughout that May day of 1799 the
army of France rushed the walls of Acre, but could not capture the ancient city.
Napoleon conceded defeat and embarked upon a speedy and honourable retreat.

To conceal his withdrawal Napoleon shelled Acre continuously for several days.
Withdrawal began on 20 May and to slow down the Turkish pursuit, the French
embarked upon a scorched earth policy. It was a painful, daunting withdrawal in
which the injured, wounded and sick were often jettisoned and left to the mercies of
the local populace and pursuing Turkish forces. At Tantura, when it was evident that

---

Sanhedrin. (London , 1979), p. 24.

21 Quoted in: Sacher, Harry. *A History of Israel.* Alfred A. Knopf, Inc., (New York, 1976), p. 22.

22 Tuchman, Barbara. W. *Bible and Sword.* p. 163. Tuchman continues: 'The original of this Proclamation
has never been found. Its wording remained unknown until a manuscript copy in German translation came
to light in 1940 in the archives of a Viennese family with rabbinical connections tracing back to Napoleon's
entourage in the East. Until then only the fact of the Proclamation was known through two dispatches
concerning it that appeared in May of 1799 in *Le Moniteur,* the official organ of the French Directory.'
Simon Schwarzfuchs doubts the authenticity of this discovery. See Schwarzfuchs, Simon. *Napoleon the
Jews and the Sanhedrin.* p. 24.

no French ships would arrive to assist the withdrawal, due to the intervention of the British Fleet, Napoleon jettisoned his heavy guns, and the march continued.

The retreating French force rested up in Jaffa, from where many of the sick and wounded were sent ahead, most by land back across the Sinai sands, and some by sea. These were picked up by Smith, who treated them kindly and even transported them to Egypt. Smith had actually offered to carry Napoleon's sick and wounded on his ships to save them the fate of falling into the hands of Djezzar's soldiers. Napoleon refused the offer. He even ordered the remaining few invalid wounded in the hospitals in Jaffa to be poisoned. Thankfully the attempt failed.

The French rearguard left Jaffa on 28 May, and travelled back the same route on which they came several months before. One soldier wrote:

> May 30: the army reaches Gaza. May 31: the march through the Sinai Desert begins. June 1: having marched from sunrise to sunset for two consecutive days across the desert, the army reaches, or rather falls down in exhaustion, at El Arish, in Egyptian territory. June 3: the march through the desert is resumed.[23]

The dejected and exhausted French soldiers and Christians, fleeing in dread of Djezzar's retributions, marched for nine solid hours before reaching Katia. At the sight of Egypt proper they were overwhelmed with excitement - compared to what they had just endured, it was heaven on earth.

Back in Egypt

Aware of France's perilous position in Europe, Napoleon had decided even while at Acre, the expediency of returning to France at the first opportunity. His initial concern however was the imminent landing of the pursuing Turkish Army. The expected Turkish Fleet arrived off Aboukir Bay in mid-June, prompting Napoleon to quickly attack. His impetuosity this time succeeded, and the Turkish force was defeated. One of the survivors of the battle was a young Albanian officer named Mehmet Ali, who managed to swim to one of Sidney Smith's ships.

Shortly later, on 22 August Napoleon managed to slip away from Egypt and returned to France. As he left he was still haunted by his failure at Acre, and rued the name of Admiral Sir Sidney Smith. His successor, General Kleber, was ordered to make peace with Turkey, but also not to evacuate the country. 'The Turkish Empire ...' Napoleon wrote, 'is crumbling, and the evacuation of Egypt would be all the more disastrous for France since we would see that fertile country fall into the hands of some other European power in our lifetime.'[24]

---

23 Richardot, Charles. *Nouveaux Memoires sur l'armee francaise en Egypte et en Syrie.* Paris, 1848. page 178. Quoted in Herold, J. Christopher. *Bonaparte in Egypt.* p. 309.
24 *Correspondence,* Vol. V., ibid., p. 577. Quoted in Herold, J. Christopher. *Bonaparte in Egypt.* p. 343.

General Kleber made a solid start in upholding these instructions. At Heliopolis, en-route to Cairo the large Turkish Army was soundly defeated by a far inferior French force on 20 March 1800. He then proceeded to drive the remnant of this vast army out of Egypt.

Peace at Last

Following his return to France Napoleon initially gave little consideration to the diabolical situation in Egypt. Yet after becoming the First Consul and consolidating his power in France, he finally took this situation in hand. Russia had withdrawn from the triple alliance with Britain and Turkey, so now France was at war only with Britain and Turkey. Both Britain and France however wanted a peace treaty upon their own terms, from a position of strength in the remaining major theatre of war in the Eastern Mediterranean.

In late 1800 a British expeditionary force, commanded by General Sir Ralph Abercromby, and comprised of troops from Britain, India and the Cape Colony began assembling on the coast of Asia Minor. Almost simultaneously Napoleon and Tsar Paul of Russia became aligned and agreed to contest British possessions in Asia. Russia prepared to march against British India. Napoleon wrote to Tsar Paul on 27 February:

> The pride and arrogance of the English are unparalleled ... The English have attempted to land in Egypt. The interest of all the Mediterranean and Black Sea Powers is that Egypt should remain in the possession of France. The Suez Canal, which would join the Indian Ocean to the Mediterranean is already surveyed; the work is easy and will not take long, it will confer incalculable benefits on Russian commerce.[25]

Yet despite his political manoeuverings, Napoleon's ambitions in the East were again thwarted. Abercromby's troops landed at Aboukir Bay in March 1801, and defeated the French forces. The routed French hastened back to Alexandria and Cairo where they were besieged by the British. Finally, by September 1801, peace treaties were agreed upon and all the besieged French forces surrendered, and were then transported back to France. Egypt and Turkish *Palestine* were finally freed from French troops and Britain could now enter into negotiations with the French for a formal peace treaty, which was completed in London on 1 October 1801.

Consequences of the Campaign

Napoleon's campaign in Egypt and the Land of Israel marked the beginning of a new era in the history of that region. It revealed to the Islamic world how easily a western

25 *Correspondence*, Vol. VII. p.40. Quoted in: Johnston, R.M. *The Corsican.* p. 150.

'infidel' power could penetrate into the heart of *dar al Islam*. And, more importantly at this point, it revealed to Britain how easily a rival European power could interfere with her coveted link to India.[26] A battle between the European empires had been triggered, and after 1798 there was no turning back.

Britain henceforth would carefully observe every movement in that region and would challenge any she thought were contrary to her national interests. And France could not relinquish her ambitions in the region, and time and again over the next one hundred and more years she agitated to regain a pre-eminent position there.

Despite the political motives of Napoleon's proclamation to the Jewish people, the very fact that such an offer was made, indicated an awareness of the special connection between the Jewish people and the Land of Israel. This campaign was another important step forward in the restoration of Israel, as prophetically understood by the Italian Jewish man and James Bicheno. Bicheno's prophetic statements, especially those in his *The Restoration of the Jews* from 1800,[27] will be seen to be very accurate over the succeeding decades.

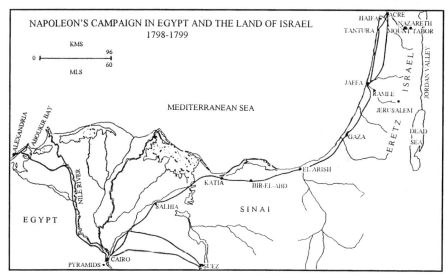

▲ *Napoleon's Campaign in Egypt and the Land of Israel, 1798-1799*

---

26 Lewis, Bernard. *The Middle East and the West.* Harper Torchbooks, (New York, 1964), p. 34
27 Found on page 4 of the Introduction.

Chapter 5

Empire and Evangelicals: 1800-1842

Consolidation in India, Australia and New Zealand

Napoleon's invasion of Egypt stirred opposition to British rule in India. But after the defeat of Sultan Tippoo Sahib, British influence increased. She took control over much of the centre and south of the sub-continent by entering into alliances with the Indian princes. These regions, now under direct British rule, accepted British garrisons. The northern regions however troubled Britain, for they provided an opportunity for rival European powers, namely Russia, to move south. During the following decades these areas too were subdued. By the 1840's the British controlled, either directly or indirectly through treaties with local rulers, the entire Indian subcontinent. [1]

The emphasis at the colony of New South Wales until 1800 had been upon survival. Having attained this goal the colony thereafter grew and expanded. Governor Phillip began offering land to convicts who had served out their sentences. Then some of the officers of the New South Wales [Army] Corps, those entrusted with the security of the colony, began to establish various agricultural initiatives, with the help of convict labour.

Only twenty-three free settlers came out to New South Wales before 1800. Thereafter, when news of growth and expansion reached the shores of 'Mother' Britain, that number steadily increased. Colonies were established in other areas, some for strategic reasons, to ensure the French never claimed these regions. Two colonies were set up at Hobart and Launceston in Van Diemen's Land (later Tasmania) in 1804. Newcastle to the north of Sydney was settled in 1804 and Port Macquarie further north still in 1821. Moreton Bay, (near where Brisbane was built), which became the centre of the colony of Queensland, was settled in 1824. Then, to ensure the stability of the entire continent, the western region (later Western Australia) was colonized, King George's Sound (Albany) in 1826 and the Swan River (Perth-Fremantle) in 1829. The southern coast of the land mass was then settled, firstly Melbourne (later the capital of Victoria) in 1835, and Adelaide (capital of South Australia) in 1836. Simultaneous with the establishment of these settlements, pioneers

---

1 Wallbank, Walter T., *A Short History of India and Pakistan.* (New York, 1958), p. 64.

moved further inland from the coast and discovered the large agricultural and desert regions of the hinterland. Colony New South Wales had now expanded into the colonies of Australia.

The adventurers, traders and pioneers also moved east. Traders, especially whalers and sealers plied the seas around the two large islands, now known as New Zealand, traded with the local inhabitants, the Maoris, and returned to Sydney with their wares. By the early 1800's trading posts were established in various locations, especially in the Bay of Islands region in the north. New Zealand was slowly becoming an established satellite of New South Wales.

William Marsden an Anglican missionary from the Church Missionary Society landed in the Bay of Islands in December 1814 and began proclaiming the Gospel of Jesus Christ *in the uttermost ends of the earth.* New Zealand was the furthermost point of the earth from Jerusalem from whence that command was given by Jesus many centuries before.

For the most part however it was the face of the often covetous trader and the outcasts of New South Wales which characterized the European presence in New Zealand. J.D Lang, the senior Presbyterian minister in New South Wales wrote of New Zealand society in 1839 that it consisted primarily of escaped convicts, convicts who had completed their sentences, adventurers and others trying to escape the more established regime in Sydney and Hobart.[2]

By the 1830's, as the colonies of Australia changed character from penal settlements to established society, a more serious interest began in New Zealand, especially by business entrepreneurs, who sensed that Britain at some point might add it to her possessions. Ships crossing the Tasman Sea from New South Wales carried men eager for land.[3]

Such an influx of new settlers dramatically changed the character of the society. There was a desperate need for more law and order. Many of the more stable residents, especially the missionaries, constantly petitioned the British Crown to intervene. The situation was more than the Governor of New South Wales was able to effectively administer. The British Crown took all these matters very seriously and in 1839 sent out an official representative, William Hobson, to govern New Zealand on behalf of Britain.

Hobson congregated many of the leading Maori and British leaders on 6 February 1840 at Waitangi in the Bay of Islands, and had them sign a treaty of understanding. This *Treaty of Waitangi* effectively marks the beginning of an 'independent' New Zealand. The colony remained, technically, part of New South Wales until May 1841, when it finally became a separate colony. Britain's eastern Empire, although continually being added to, henceforth was primarily linked to these three areas;

---

2   Sinclair, K. *A History of New Zealand.* Penguin Books, (Auckland, 1988), p. 47.
3   Sinclair, K. ibid.. p. 53.

India, Australia and New Zealand. For this reason the maintenance and security of the link between Britain and her eastern Empire, was at the top of Britain's foreign policy agenda.

Napoleon and Jewish Emancipation

While his efforts to restore Israel to her land may have failed, Napoleon never forgot his interest in the Jewish people. Recognizing their distinctiveness, and desiring to garner their energies for the benefit of the French Empire, Napoleon convened an *Assembly* in Paris on 25 April 1806, comprised of one hundred and eleven, mostly French and Italian Jewish leaders. Of this historic *Assembly* Kobler wrote: 'Now Napoleon identifying the new French Empire with imperial Rome, tried to bring about a partnership of the Jewish people with the French nation.'[4]

The assembled Jewish delegates affirmed their allegiance to France, and to the French people as their brethren. The *Assembly* was a further, significant development in the emancipation of the Jewish people, not only in France, but in time, throughout Europe. The Jewish people could maintain dual citizenship, recognized as part of a distinct religion-nation, yet also as citizens of a host nation.

Napoleon confirmed this direction by calling for the formation of a *Great Sanhedrin*, a Jewish Parliament, designed for the Jewish people to determine how they were to best combine their national distinctiveness with full and active involvement in the national life of France and the host nations. The Great *Sanhedrin* finally met on 4 February 1807, and caused a general sensation as a result.[5]

Letters of support arrived from all over Europe. James Bicheno, in a new edition of the *Restoration of the* Jews claimed that the *Sanhedrin* 'constituted a link in the chain of events which was to bring about the restoration of the Jewish commonwealth in Palestine.'[6] But there was also serious opposition, mostly from orthodox Jewish leaders throughout Europe, and from the French Catholic Church. Napoleon ended the session of the *Sanhedrin* prematurely. Despite this the *Assembly* and *Sanhedrin,* although short in duration, allowed Jewish people to savour for the first time, the delights of civil and religious liberty.

British Evangelicals and Israel

Almost simultaneous to the developments in France the writings of Bicheno, Kett, Priestley, Horsely and others became widely disseminated in Britain. Interest grew to such an extent that by 1809 a non-denominational missionary society, named 'The London Society for Promoting Christianity among the Jews' was formed. This society,

---

4   Kobler, F. *Napoleon and the Jews.* p. 143.
5   Kobler, F. ibid. p. 155.
6   Kobler, F. ibid. p. 167.

known as the London Jews Society or LJS, became the main channel of expression for that Evangelical hope in Israel's restoration over the following decades. After 1815 it became an Anglican society.

Leading Evangelicals such as Charles Simeon and William Wilberforce were actively involved, while among the early vice-presidents were the Duke of Devonshire, as well as seven earls, five viscounts and several members of Parliament. The Duke of Kent, Queen Victoria's father became the patron in 1813. The Society then constructed a large complex, known as *Palestine Place* in London's East End, an ambitious project in the midst of the Napoleonic Wars.

Following the conclusion of the Napoleonic Wars in 1815 the LJS desired to branch out into Europe. The initial venture was undertaken by the enthusiastic Lewis Way.[7] Way left London in 1817 and passing through Holland and Prussia, arrived in Russia. There he met the Czar Alexander I on three occasions, during which he addressed the issue of the civil welfare and future restoration of the three million or so Jewish people within the Czar's realm, most of whom lived within an area named the *Pale of Settlement*.

The Czar was so impressed by Way and his message that he invited him to attend the Peace Conference of Aix-la-Chapelle (today Aachen in Germany) to be held in October 1818. Way accepted the invitation and spoke passionately in front of the leaders of the European nations on behalf of the Jewish people. A clause pertaining to the Jewish people was then included in the protocol of the Conference. Although little of a tangible nature came of this clause, it nevertheless highlighted how the issue of Israel's restoration was beginning to gain more official interest.

From the early 1820's the LJS also began in earnest to establish itself in Jerusalem. Yet all efforts failed due to the opposition from the Muslim-Turkish authorities and other ecclesiastical bodies, especially the Roman Catholic and Greek Orthodox. Concerning the climate then prevailing in Jerusalem, one missionary, Rev W.B. Lewis wrote:

> Here the Jews find no ease, though they love the land, for it is the land of their forefathers, and the land of promise ... With respect to the foreign Jews, those who are not subjects of the Ottoman Empire, the difficulties ... might certainly be a great deal diminished ... by the residence of a Consular Agent or protector among the oppressed.[8]

Lewis was the first proponent of the establishment of a British Consulate in

---

7   Way had inherited some 300,000 pounds sterling, which he determined to use for the glory of God. One day while travelling in the south of England, he noticed a rather odd shaped building, and upon inquiry was told that it was build by two sisters, Jane and Mary Parminter, descendants of Huguenot refugees from France. Way was informed that these ladies planted some trees, and in their will dictated that these were not to be cut down until the Jewish people had been restored to their land. It was later discovered that no such clause existed, yet the sentiment was there. Way then knew to which cause his fortune would be directed, and soon afterwards came into contact with the LJS.

8   *Jewish Expositor.* London, 1825. pp. 16-17.

Jerusalem, to be closely associated with the status of the Jewish people. Other workers of the Society who followed, especially Dr. George Dalton, Jerusalem's first doctor, and John Nicolayson from Denmark, maintained the same position.[9] These pioneer British missionaries, looking to forward the object of missions, and ever ready to forward the return of the people of Israel to their land, were realistic of the abysmal conditions of the land under Turkish rule, and continually prayed for a change of government in Turkish *Palestine*. Such expectation was fulfilled in the early 1830's.

Egypt on the Move

Following the defeat of the French and the departure of the British occupying forces in 1801 Mehmet (or Mohammed) Ali, the survivor of the battle of Aboukir Bay, became pasha, or ruler, with the aid of the Mameluke leaders, whom he later massacred. Although it was the British who saved his life, Mehmet Ali was more favourably inclined towards the French. So when in 1807, after the resumption of hostilities between France and Britain, the British attempted a landing in Egypt, ostensibly to keep the French out, Mehmet Ali repelled them.

Mehmet Ali, a keen and close observer of Napoleon's invasion of Egypt, saw modernization as the key to success. He turned to the French for assistance. His reform and modernization of the army paid dividends. When the Greeks rose in revolt against their Turkish overlords in 1821, the Sultan, hard pressed, invited help from Mehmet Ali, who sent his son Ibrahim in command of the Egyptian forces. Egypt was promised, in return, (at least according to Mehmet), certain areas, including Syria.

Russia, the traditional protector of Orthodox Christians in the Ottoman Empire, did not want to see a Christian, Orthodox state emerge, unless Russia was in control. She aligned herself with the Greeks. Despite reservations about opposing Turkey, the British and French could not allow Russia to battle this one out by herself. If Greece and Russia were victorious, then Russia stood to gain a pre-eminent position in the Eastern Mediterranean.

The conflict climaxed in 1827 when the combined Turkish and Egyptian Fleets were blown out of the water by the British, French and Russian Fleets at the Battle of Navarino in Greece. The British then laid siege to Alexandria, forcing Mehmet Ali to withdraw his armies from Greece, which seriously imperiled the Turkish cause. Greek independence was formally recognized in 1832.

Mehmet Ali's demand for the promised provinces, especially Syria, were withheld by the Sultan, who stated that the Egyptian effort had been unsuccessful. Incensed at this betrayal, Mehmet Ali embarked upon other campaigns of expansion, including the Sudan and Arabian Peninsular. In 1831 he demanded the area of Syria for his son

---

9   *Jewish Intelligence*, London, 1826. p. 76.

Ibrahim to govern. The Sultan refused, and using an argument with the Pasha of Acre as a pretext, Mehmet Ali's forces, under the command of Ibrahim, invaded the *land between*. Crossing the Sinai, as Napoleon had done some years before, the armies of Egypt entered the province of Syria on 1 November 1831. They first captured Gaza. The army then met the Egyptian Fleet at Jaffa which quickly fell, followed by Jerusalem, on 7 December, again with little opposition. Turkish rule by this time was not popular. Tougher opposition was found in the north. Acre, capital of the pashalic,[10] was finally captured on 26 May 1832. Where Napoleon had failed, Ibrahim succeeded. And he kept advancing. John Nicolayson recorded in his diary on 19 June 1832: 'This morning the surrender of Damascus to Ibrahim Pasha was announced ... Thus he is advancing rapidly and everywhere the spell of Islamism is broken.'[11]   Hama, Homs and Aleppo fell thereafter one by one. The armies of Egypt kept advancing, destroying the large Turkish Army which had been sent to defeat him at Konya in Anatolia. By the middle of 1833 Ibrahim had reached Bursa in Anatolia and nothing stood between the Egyptian Army and Constantinople.

The Turkish Sultan, Mahmoud, appealed to Britain to send the Royal Navy to Alexandria and the Dardanelles. Britain was pre-occupied with internal reform, its Navy was occupied in Holland, and the Cabinet, with the exception of Foreign Secretary Lord Palmerston, was unprepared to become embroiled in a conflict in the Eastern Mediterranean. Besides this, she was also attempting to establish better relations with France, and with France aligned with Egypt, Britain feared involvement could be detrimental to her foreign policy. In fact, with each Egyptian success French support of Egypt increased.

The Turks had no choice but to seek the help of their arch enemy, Russia. In no time at all Russian troops were in Constantinople, and the Russian Fleet was in the Bosphorus and Dardanelles, both of which were fortified.[12]

The Egyptians quickly halted their advance. The European powers were alarmed at the presence of the Russians at the entrance to the Mediterranean, and in the streets of Constantinople, and demanded their withdrawal. The Russians in turn demanded firstly the withdrawal of Ibrahim from Syria. Ibrahim refused, so too did the Russians. The Russians then forced upon the Turks the *Treaty of Unkiar Skelessi*, signed on 8 July 1833. The *Treaty* provided for the presence of Russian troops in Turkey, the presence of the Russian Fleet in the Bosphorus and Dardanelles, and an agreement that neither Russia nor Turkey would take any step in foreign affairs without consulting each other. There was also a secret clause (which British ambassador Ponsonby discovered through a spy) that in the event of a future war between Russia and non-

---

10   Pashalic - administrative region within the Turkish Empire, governed by a pasha.
11   LJS Report. London, 1833. p. 155
12   Parkes, James. *Whose Land?* Penguin Books. (London, 1949), p. 180.

Turkish belligerents, the Bosphorus would be open to Russian vessels but closed to non-Turkish vessels.

Both Foreign Secretary Palmerston and Ambassador Ponsonby immediately realized their enormous blunder once news of the *Treaty* became known. 'There is nothing that has happened since I have been in this office which I regret so much,' Palmerston later wrote to a friend, 'as that tremendous blunder of the English government. But it was not my fault; I tried hard to persuade the Cabinet to let me take that step.'[13]   This blunder determined all his future dealings concerning the Eastern Mediterranean.

Ibrahim abolished the pashalics of Acre and Damascus, and created the province of Syria, with Damascus as capital, from where he ruled as pasha. He ruled the non-Muslim minority groups leniently, especially the Catholics and Orthodox, protected as they were by France and Russia. He realized too the importance of maintaining good relations with Britain, the only major power with no protected minority group. Mehmet Ali then met with the British Consul-General in Egypt, Colonel Campbell on 22 July 1833. 'His Highness assured me with great earnestness,' wrote Campbell to Palmerston following the meeting, 'that his anxious desire was to give to British subjects every support in order to cultivate his relations with us, and to show his respect for His Majesty's government, and that every necessary order had been given by him in Syria to that effect.'[14]   In October 1833 John Nicolayson became the first permanent Evangelical resident in Jerusalem.

Palmerston, Shaftesbury and the Evangelicals

Like the period of Napoleon's invasion, these events in the east also stirred the Evangelical interest in the 'signs of the times'. The LJS wrote in their Annual Report of 1833:

> We beg to draw attention to the countries of the East, now almost every day exhibiting changes of an important and interesting nature, and in them striking signs indicative of the near approach of those glorious events to which the Christian is directed to look forward with confidence and joy.
>
> Political changes are permitted, by a wise and over-ruling Providence, to introduce a milder and more tolerating order of things ...[15]

Many believed these events furthered the cause of Israel's restoration and strongly advocated further active British involvement in the region. Following a visit to Jerusalem in 1834, John Farren, the British Consul-General of Syria wrote to the Foreign Office suggesting the establishment in Jerusalem of a Consulate. His stated

---

13   Lord Palmerston to Frederick Lamb, 22 May 1838. Quoted in Ridley, Jasper. *Lord Palmerston.* Constable, (London, 1970), p. 160.
14   PRO:F.O. 78/227 .
15   LJS Report, 1833. p. 161.

reasons being; to protect the British subjects, of which Nicolayson was one and the Gibraltar Jew Haim Amzalag the other; offering protection and assistance to British travellers; and of offsetting the French and Russian presence there through their protected communities the Catholics and Orthodox.

Foreign Secretary Palmerston finally consented in 1836, stating, 'I think it would be expedient to have an English Consular Agent at Jerusalem.'[16] This decision was based upon pressure exerted by the Evangelicals, led by Palmerston's relative Anthony Ashley Cooper (later Lord Shaftesbury), and due to Palmerston's desire to offset any French and Russian pretensions in the region. *The Treaty of Unkiar Skelessi* still haunted him, while France's relationship with Egypt concerned him.

These overtures for the establishment of a British Consulate in Jerusalem were virtually synonymous with the appeal by the LJS to build a Protestant Church in Jerusalem. Such a proposal however ran contrary to existing Islamic law, which clearly forbade the building of new churches anywhere in the area of *dar al Islam,* the region of Islam.

Shaftesbury and the LJS President, Sir Thomas Baring, (former Chancellor of the Exchequer) approached Palmerston, who accordingly contacted both Consul-General Campbell in Egypt, and Ambassador Ponsonby in Constantinople to acquire the necessary permission. Campbell fully supportive of the idea, replied that the only way he foresaw of receiving such permission would be to firstly have a Consulate in Jerusalem. Having previously agreed in principle to the sending out of a consul, Palmerston now made the formal move, and William Tanner Young was appointed in 1838.

Shaftesbury and the Evangelicals were ecstatic, seeing this as a further sign of Israel's impending restoration, and that Britain would be her restorer. 'What a wonderful event it is,' Shaftesbury recorded in his diary, 'The ancient city of the people of God is about to resume a place among the nations, and England is the first of Gentile Kingdoms that ceases to tread her down.'[17] Anything Shaftesbury accredited was sure to have widespread influence, such his high standing in British society at the time as one of the leading social reformers and Evangelicals. Hence the impact of an article he wrote in the December 1838 edition of *Quarterly Review.* The article was actually a review of Lord Lindsay's recently published book *Travels in Egypt and the Holy Land.*

'The main object of Lord Ashley in this article,' wrote his biographer Edwin Hodder, 'was to give publicity to movements in which he took an intense personal interest, and which were to become, chiefly through his instrumentality, subjects of the same absorbing interest in the religious and political world.' Referring then to

---

16 PRO:FO 78/295.
17 Hodder, Edwin. *The Life and Works of the Seventh Earl of Shaftesbury.* Cassell, (London, 1886), p. 233, entry 29 September 1838.

Napoleon's failed efforts on behalf of the Jewish people, Ashley remarked in the context of seeking the maintenance of the British Empire, that, 'the affairs of the East are lowering on Great Britain.'[18] These comments bear witness to the increasing sentiment, that Israel's future restoration would be synonymous with Britain's task of spreading her enlightened empire throughout the world, including the Eastern Mediterranean.

Such sentiments came closer to fulfillment following Consul Young's arrival in Jerusalem in early 1839. This was an event, Young believed, that Jewish people, even in the remotest villages in Europe, would hear about.[19] And the Jewish people had every reason to be thankful, for among Young's official instructions, he was told 'to afford protection to the Jews generally.'[20]

Young, a member of the LJS, made every effort to protect the Jewish people and uphold the interests of Britain. 'There are two parties here' he wrote to Palmerston on 14 March 1839, 'who will doubtless have some voice in the future disposition of affairs - "The one is the Jew - unto whom God originally gave this land for a possession, and the other, the Protestant Christian, his legitimate offspring." Of both these,' he concluded, 'Great Britain seems the natural guardian.'[21]

By mid 1839 Britain was slowly being drawn into an active involvement in the affairs of Jerusalem and the Land of Israel. This involvement, especially politically, was as much a reaction against possible French and Russian involvement there as it was concerning Israel's restoration. Yet in the context of the politics of the region, these two issues were becoming inseparably connected.

Egypt Again on the Move

Despite two local uprisings against Egyptian rule, Ibrahim Pasha established a sound regime in the province of Syria. Yet all the while his regime threatened the Turkish Sultan. This was contrary to Britain's policy, preferring a weak yet stable Turkish Empire, rather than a strong Egypt supported by France. But Britain also needed a Turkey separate from dependence upon Russia. Turkey, as far as Britain was concerned needed to be a bulwark against Russian aggression in the region, especially against India. Yet Palmerston was reluctant to back Mehmet Ali in any confrontation with Turkey, as he feared a direct confrontation with Russia.

When, therefore in 1838, Mehmet Ali announced his intention of forming Egypt and Syria into a hereditary kingdom, an Egyptian confrontation with Turkey seemed inevitable. Tensions escalated between the rival powers. Finally, in mid 1839, a

---

18   Quoted in *Jewish Intelligence*, 1839. p. 38.

19   PRO:F.O. 78/368. Young to Campbell, 19 April 1839. Quoted in Hyamson, Albert. *The British Consulate in Jerusalem in Relation to the Jews in Jerusalem*. (London, 1934), Volume 1, p. 8

20   PRO:F.O. 78/368 (NO 2) Bidwell to Young, 31 January 1839. Quoted in Hyamson, Albert, *The British Consulate*, Vol. 1, p. 2.

21   PRO:F.0. 78/368, no 8. Quoted in Hyamson, Albert. *The British Consulate*, Vol. 1, p. 6.

Turkish Army crossed the Euphrates and entered Syria, where it was met and soundly defeated by Ibrahim. Shortly afterwards the entire Turkish Fleet surrendered to the Egyptians at Alexandria. And then on 30 June, the Sultan died. The signs were ominous for Turkey as Ibrahim's army was again poised to move towards Constantinople. Mehmet Ali wisely restrained Ibrahim, lest the European powers be provoked.

But all was too late. The ingredients were now there for a major European confrontation. If Ibrahim continued his march onto Constantinople, then Russia would intervene on behalf of Turkey. The French, not eager to see an increase in the Russian position within the Turkish Empire, proposed to the British Government that they should give warning to Russia by sending their fleets to the Dardanelles. Palmerston, keen to thwart Russian as well as French ambitions, agreed, and the British and French Fleets were dispatched to the strategic Dardanelles waterway.[22]

News of the Egyptian victory provoked an interesting reaction in Constantinople. A number of Turkish ministers (viziers) agreed in July 1839 to recognize Mehmet Ali as Viceroy of Syria. Yet numerous European statesmen, including Count Metternich of Austria, preferred to allow the future status of the Levant to be decided by the European Powers.

Palmerston, supported by the Russians, Austrians and Prussians wanted to expel Ibrahim from Syria. France stalled. There was a ground swell of support for Mehmet in France, and besides, memories of Napoleon's vision of a veiled French empire in Egypt and Syria were still present.

At this critical time, when he was totally dependent upon the European powers, the new Sultan Mahmud II issued a decree, the *Hatti Sherif of Gulhane*, or the *Decree of the Rose Chamber*. This *Decree*, enacted to appease the European powers, guaranteed equal rights for the non-Muslim citizens of the Ottoman Empire, granting them the same civil rights as the Muslims. They were also guaranteed complete freedom of their religion.

During August and September 1839 the French began to backtrack from their previous position, and declared their reluctance to use force to cause Mehmet Ali to withdraw from Syria. Palmerston informed them that the other powers would force Egypt out. The French in turn voiced their objection to the presence of the Russian Army fighting against the Egyptians.[23] The Russians on the other hand wanted Egypt ousted, as it would increase their power base in the region as Turkey's main protector.

In mid 1840 Palmerston and the European statesmen submitted a proposal to France which was then handed to Mehmet Ali: that Mehmet Ali retain southern Syria, up to Acre, and Turkey regain the remainder of Syria. The French Prime Minister Thiers rejected the plan outright, while at the same time a French agent at

22   Ridley, Jasper. *Lord Palmerston*, p. 220.
23   Ibid. p. 226.

Constantinople had attempted to persuade the Turks to compromise with Egypt and exclude the European powers altogether. Such a deal would have placed France in a very favourable position in the region.[24]

At this point the British Cabinet, cautious of offending France, procrastinated. Palmerston offered his resignation, unwilling to suffer another embarrassment like that of 1833. If, he maintained, his advice was not accepted, it would lead to 'the practical division of the Turkish Empire into two separate and independent states, whereof one will be the dependency of France, and the other a satellite of Russia.' Britain's political and economic influence, in the region, he further stated, would be seriously curtailed. And, he added, such a division of the Turkish Empire would also give rise to both local insurrection, and in time the involvement of the European Powers.[25]

Prime Minister Melbourne reluctantly agreed to accept Palmerston's anti-French stance. On 15 July 1840 the ambassadors of Austria, Prussia and Russia met in London with Palmerston and signed the *Treaty of London*. The ultimatum consisted of two parts. One, called for Mehmet Ali to accept the European demand to withdraw from Syria and Crete within ten days. If this was done, he would receive southern Syria, including Acre, but excluding Jerusalem (and Mecca and Medina) as an hereditary Pashalic. If however he did not accept these demands within ten days, then according to the second option he would lose Syria, and receive only Egypt. If after twenty days neither of these demands were accepted, then the Sultan, if he felt fit, could even dismiss him from his position as Viceroy of Egypt.

When informed, the French reacted angrily, announcing the end of the Anglo-French Alliance. The situation deteriorated to such a degree that there was talk of another European war. Palmerston maintained however that the French were only bluffing and would not go to war. The ultimatum was presented to Mehmet Ali by the consuls of the Four Powers later in July.

This same period of time witnessed a turning point in the development of Jewish nationalism, due to events in Damascus and Rhodes. In Damascus a Catholic Capuchin priest went missing in the ancient city. As he was last seen leaving the Jewish area, the Jewish community was accused of murdering him, and using his blood for the *Passover*. An anti-Jewish pogrom erupted. The western world especially was shocked, as the *Blood Libel* accusation had not been heard since the days of the Crusades.

Condemnation of the event arose from throughout the world, and Sir Moses Montefiore, scion of the British Jewish community, travelled to the East to show the indignation of the enlightened West of this barbarous accusation. Montefiore received a *Firman* (imperial edict) from the Sultan, condemning the act, and passed it on to Colonel Charles Churchill, stationed in Damascus. Churchill was one of the few

---

24 Ridley, Jasper. *Lord Palmerston*, p. 233.
25 Lord Palmerston to Lord Melbourne, 5 July 1840. Quoted in Ridley, Jasper. ibid., p. 233.

Britons and indeed Europeans to witness this event from close quarters. Matters were later apprehended, but not before many innocent Jewish people were victimized.

Calls for Israel's Restoration

Again these stirring times aroused the Evangelicals. Shaftesbury, as the representative of the restorationist movement, had been awaiting the arrival of the modern day Cyrus who would permit the Jewish people to return to their homeland. He finally was convinced that his step father in-law, Lord Palmerston, was the man chosen by Providence. He wrote on 24 July 1840:

> Anxious about the hopes and prospects of the Jewish people. Everything seems ripe for their return to Palestine ... Could the five Powers of the West be induced to guarantee the security of life and possessions to the Hebrew race, they would now flow back in rapidly augmenting numbers. Then by the blessing of God I will prepare a document, fortify it by all the evidence I can accumulate, and, confiding to the wisdom and mercy of the Almighty, lay it before the Secretary of State for Foreign Affairs.[26]

Ashley propounded his proposal of the Jewish restoration to Palmerston. His desire was for a clause to be inserted into whatever final Treaty resulted from the conflict in the East, guaranteeing the right of the Jewish people to return to the Land of Israel under the protection of the European (and especially British) powers.[27] Shaftesbury wrote on August 1:

> Dined with Palmerston. After dinner left alone with him. Propounded my scheme, which seemed to strike his fancy; he asked some questions, and readily promised to consider it. How singular is the order of Providence! Singular, that is if estimated by man's ways! Palmerston has already been chosen by God to be an instrument of good to His ancient people; to do homage, as it were, to their inheritance, and to recognize their rights without believing their destiny. And it seems he will yet do more. But though the motive be kind, it is not sound. I am forced to argue politically, financially, commercially; these considerations strike him home; he weeps not like his master over Jerusalem....[28]

Palmerston was impressed by Shaftesbury's plea. Several days later, on 11 August, Palmerston wrote to Ambassador Ponsonby in Constantinople:

> There exists at present among the Jews dispersed over Europe a strong notion that the time is approaching when their nation is to return to Palestine; and consequently their wish to go thither has become more keen, and their thoughts have been bent more intently than before upon the means of realizing that wish. It is well known that the Jews of Europe possess great wealth; and it is manifest that any country in which a considerable number of them might choose to settle, would derive great benefit from

---

26 Hodder, Edwin. *Shaftesbury.* p. 166.
27 Ashley to Palmerston, 25 September 1840. Quoted in Hodder, Edwin. *Shaftesbury.* pp. 168-169.
28 Hodder, Edwin. *Shaftesbury.* p. 167.

the riches which they would bring into it.[29]

Palmerston exaggerated, probably for political expediency, the readiness for return and the wealth of the Jewish people. His purpose was to arouse the interest of the Sultan in a possible solution to the future of the Land of Israel. In view of the Turkish need for British support, this was the most opportune time to propose such a policy. Palmerston continued:

> Whether Mehmet Ali accepts the first or the second offer which is to be made to him, in either case, it would be of manifest importance to the Sultan to encourage the Jews to return to, and to settle in, Palestine; because the wealth which they would bring with them would increase the resources of the Sultan's dominions; and the Jewish people, if returning under the sanction and protection and at the invitation of the Sultan, would be a check upon any future evil designs of Mehmet Ali or his successor. [30]

It seems that Palmerston is proposing a Jewish presence in the *land between* as a buffer between Turkey and Egypt. Shaftesbury, and numerous other influential Evangelicals saw the importance of the proposal. Shaftesbury wrote in his diary on 24 August: 'Palmerston tells me that he has already written to Lord Ponsonby, to direct him to open an intercourse with Reschid Pasha at Constantinople respecting protection and encouragement to the Jews. This is a prelude to the Antitype of the decree of Cyrus ...' He added further on 29 August: 'The newspapers teem with documents about the Jews. Many assail, and many defend them.'[31]

War and Turkish Control again over the Land of Israel

By October 1840 French opposition to the ultimatum had seriously increased, even to the point where they began to reinforce their Mediterranean fleet. The French King informed Queen Victoria of the French mood. Palmerston reassured the Queen, in a letter written on 11 November 1840 that it would amount to nothing. He confessed that there was a very strong party within France which favoured the establishment of a united region comprising Egypt and Syria (including the Land of Israel) under French control and influence. However he reassured the Queen that the French would not go to war supporting such a view against the Four Powers aligned against her.[32]

As Mehmet Ali had refused to accept the European and Turkish ultimatums, he needed to be flushed out of Syria. A primarily British Fleet was assembled and the Levantine coastal ports of Beirut and Sidon were bombarded and captured. Many Egyptians were taken captive, and much of the Egyptian army deserted Ibrahim at this critical moment. At Acre the British Fleet under Admiral Sir Charles Napier

---

29   PRO:F.O. 78/390 (No 134) Quoted in Hyamson, Albert. *British Consulate*, p. 33.
30   PRO:F.O. 78/390 (No 134) ibid. p. 34.
31   Hodder, Edwin. *Shaftesbury.*, p. 168.
32   Lord Palmerston to Queen Victoria, 11 November 1840. (Connell, *Regina v. Palmerston*, pp. 25-27). Quoted in Ridley, Jasper. *Lord Palmerston.* p. 239.

heavily bombed the fortress. At about twenty-five past four in the afternoon of 3 November 1840 a bomb hit three main magazines causing a terrific explosion which destroyed a good part of the town and killed many of the garrison soldiers. Acre, which with British support had withstood Napoleon, now fell to a combined Turkish and British-led force. One of those present was Colonel Charles Henry Churchill.

Napier then sailed to Alexandria and met Mehmet. Napier demanded that the Turkish Fleet be returned and that Egypt accept the terms of the *Treaty of London*. If they complied Mehmet's Ali's regime would retain Egypt. Although acting without complete authorization, Napier's promise to Mehmet Ali was ultimately endorsed.

The Egyptian withdrawal went into effect soon afterwards. Nicolayson, who as a British subject remained behind in Jerusalem, wrote on 7 November: 'Last night a firman arrived from the Turkish authority ... to the Kadi here, which invests him with all authority, for the time, to require the surrender of the city, and to organize a provisional Government in the name of the Sultan.'[33]

From November 1840 until July 1841 when the *Treaty for the Pacification of the Levant* was signed in London, the European powers made every effort to alleviate the problems caused by the Egyptian occupation of the province of Syria and to formulate a plan which would provide peace in the region.

Reactions to the Conflict

The War again stirred the interest of the British public, both religious and secular. The editor of the London Jews Society periodical *Jewish Intelligence* wrote :

> The course of events, of late, in Syria, has been attentively watched by all those who are anxiously looking for the restoration of Israel, and awaiting the fulfillment of the sure word of prophecy ... It is true, that the Jewish nation were in no degree involved in the cause of contention, and formed no part of the elements in collision; but who shall say what is the hidden meaning and intention of the array of emphatic events which has lately passed before our eyes in the East?....
>
> The Sultan's authority is now re-established in Syria; but those who have watched the continual and rapid decay of the Turkish empire, will be satisfied that unless there is a sudden and extensive change for the better in its strength and resources, which there is no ground whatever to expect, his authority over Syria must be only nominal; while among the various tribes now inhabiting the land, there is none which, from its numbers or power, is able to exercise any paramount authority over the thinly-populated country.
>
> The way, therefore, seems to be opening remarkably for the restoration of the Jews....[34]

The Scottish Evangelicals too were excited by the signs of the times. The 'Acting Committee of the General Assembly of the Church of Scotland for Promoting

---

33 *Jewish Intelligence*, 1841, p. 44.
34 *Jewish Intelligence*, 1841, p. 34.

Christianity among the Jews' sent a Memorandum to Lord Palmerston on 23 October 1840 - even before the final outcome of the War. They wrote:

Your memorialists take the liberty of laying the following statement before your Lordship ... in consequence of their deep interest in the welfare of the Jewish nation, and the important events now going forward in Syria.

Your memorialists beg to state, that within these late years there has been manifested within the Church and among the people of Scotland, a strong feeling in behalf of the people of Israel ...

Your memorialists look with deep interest on the transactions now going on in Syria, which they trust will result in the more firm and more extensive establishment of British influence in that interesting land; and, deeply impressed with the conviction, that it is a revealed truth of the Word of God, that the blessing of God is promised to those who succour his ancient but now afflicted people, whether nations or individuals, but they are most anxious that, in any future settlement of that country under the auspices of Britain, your Lordship and Her Majesty's Government should take measures, as far as possible, for protecting the Jews against oppression and injustice ...[35]

The secular press too was calling for a solution favourable to the Jewish cause. The *Times* newspaper wrote:

Let the four Allied Powers now publish to the four quarters of the world their determination to restore the Jews from all nations to the Holy Land, and to assist them in rebuilding the walls and Temple of Jerusalem ...[36]

But neither the Turks nor the other European countries, especially Russia, Austria and France were enthusiastic about this British proposal for the restoration of Israel. The matter was taken seriously though by Palmerston, who hereafter made every effort to forward the Jewish cause. On 24 November 1840 he sent a copy of the Church of Scotland Memorial to Ambassador Ponsonby in Constantinople, and added: 'With reference to this Memorial, I have to state to Your Excellency that *the matters to which it relates excite a very deep interest in the minds of a large number of Persons in the United Kingdom, and the Sultan would enlist in his favour the good opinion of numerous and powerful classes in this country,* if he were immediately to issue some formal edict or declaration granting and assuring to such Jews as may choose to fix themselves in any part of the Turkish Dominions, but more especially in Syria, full security for their Persons and Property, and free liberty to go and come: and it would probably contribute much to give confidence to such Jews as might determine to settle in Palestine, in consequence of such an Edict ...[37]

---

35 'Acting Committee of the General Assembly of the Church of Scotland for Promoting Christianity among the Jews' to Viscount Palmerston, 23 October 1840. Quoted in *Jewish Intelligence*, 1840., pp. 370-371.

36 Quoted in *Jewish Intelligence*, 1841., p. 35.

37 PRO:F.O. 78/391 (No 248). Viscount Palmerston to Viscount Ponsonby, 24 November 1840. Quoted in Hyamson, Albert. *The British Consulate*, Vol. I. p. 35. Italics mine.

Palmerston did not exaggerate concerning the number of powerful people espousing this viewpoint. There were many. One of them, George Rose, Member of Parliament and former British Ambassador in Berlin, said at the annual meeting of the LJS in 1841:

> ... there are circumstances which in these days, when the great purposes of God in the restoration of Israel are evidently approaching to their accomplishment, appear to mark out England, or Englishmen, at least, as destined to act a peculiar part in that accomplishment. Twice has the torrent of war rolled over Syria from Egypt, within the last forty-three years; and each time has the invader been sent back whither he went, frustrated mainly by British naval means ... Let one read Sir Sydney Smith's despatches describing the discomfiture of Bounaparte, till then irresistible and unconquered, before the miserable land defences which Acre opposed to him, and he will learn with wonder a success inexplicable and unparalleled. Acre was saved, and the whole of Syria, by that event; ... And now, again, we see consequences as astonishing produced by means whose results in extent and rapidity exceed the most daring calculations; and, again, the deeds were wrought by the hands of a British seaman ... [38]

Rose's sentiments were held by many a Briton. The province of Syria, and in particular the Land of Israel had twice been saved from conquest by British arms. The underlying sentiment was that Turkey was our debtor. However Britain gained no great political advantage in the Land of Israel, although the *Treaty of Unkiar Skelessi* was revoked and a convention signed concerning navigation in the Dardanelles, whereby no European warships were permitted access through the Dardanelles while Turkey was in a state of peace.

Another factor which emerged from this episode was the unpreparedness of the Jewish people for a return to their ancestral homeland. One Briton, Colonel Charles Churchill, was aware of this Jewish apathy, and expressed his feelings in a letter to Sir Moses Montefiore, unofficial spokesman for the Jewish community in Britain, on 14 June 1841:

> I cannot conceal from you my anxious desire to see your countrymen endeavour once more to resume their existence as a people. I consider the object to be perfectly obtainable. But two things are indispensably necessary: Firstly that the Jews themselves will take up the matter universally and unanimously. Secondly that the European powers will aid them in their views. It is for the Jews to make a commencement.[39]

The crisis of 1840, similar to that of 1798-99 again highlighted the significance of the Land of Israel and Syria, to the European Empires. It now remained to be seen which Power, in the aftermath of the crisis of 1840, was most likely to take the pre-eminent position in the Land of Israel, and to what extent the Jewish people would take a more active role in determining their own destiny there.

---

38 *Jewish Intelligence,* 1841. page 165.
39 Churchill to Sir Moses Montefiore. 14 June 1841. Quoted in Wolf, Lucien., *Notes on the Diplomatic History of the Jewish Question* (London, 1919), pp 119-20.

Chapter 6

Jerusalem, Crimea and the Suez Canal

Enter Prussia-Germany

The active involvement of the European powers in the affairs of the Land of Israel until 1840 had been minimal. After 1841 this situation changed dramatically, and yearly the Land of Israel became the focal point of the conflict between the European Empires, who were now joined by a small, yet potentially significant Prussia. King Frederick William IV of Prussia, had in 1840 envisioned the establishment of a world wide Protestant church, with Jerusalem as its centre and starting point. His involvement, albeit rather minimal, in the war of 1840 provided him with the opportunity to introduce Prussian-German interests into Eretz Israel. Prussia however, was a small European power. The support of a larger power was needed if the King's dream was to be fulfilled.

Frederick William was acquainted with Shaftesbury, and knew of the presence in Jerusalem of the various British institutions. In June 1841 he dispatched his private envoy, Chevalier de Bunsen, to London to meet with Shaftesbury as well as delegates of the British Government and English Church, to ascertain the possibility of entering into an alliance with Britain and thereby gaining political advantage out of the war of 1840.

De Bunsen was enthusiastically welcomed. Ultimately though only one of his three proposals, to establish a Protestant Bishopric in Jerusalem, met with success. In no time at all, a *(Jerusalem) Bishopric Act* passed through both Houses of Parliament and received the Royal Assent. A Protestant bishop, a former rabbi named Michael Solomon Alexander, was consecrated at Lambeth Palace in November 1841. One of those officiating at the consecration was George Selwyn, the newly appointed Anglican Bishop of the new colony of New Zealand (now officially separate from New South Wales). So while Selwyn was preparing to sail to the uttermost ends of the earth, Alexander, his family and entourage soon afterwards set out for Jerusalem, aboard a British warship.

The establishment of the Bishopric greatly increased British and Prussian interest in the affairs of Jerusalem and the Land of Israel, while at the same time provoking negative reactions from the other, especially non-Protestant, European powers. They saw the move as an act of aggrandizement by the Protestant empires and sought to either hinder or to counter the progress of the Protestant Bishopric. Within a short time both the Roman Catholic and Greek Orthodox Churches restored their patriarchates to Jerusalem.

The Protestant presence was further enhanced with the completion in 1849 of an Evangelical Anglican church named Christ Church. This church, whose construction violated the principles of Islam, was built by the LJS opposite the Citadel or Tower of David, and resplendent with Jewish symbols and Hebrew inscriptions, resembled in part a synagogue.

The Prussians also dispatched a Consul to Jerusalem in 1842, quickly followed by France and then the other European powers. What was in 1838 a small insignificant walled town in the Turkish Empire with only one European consulate, the British, had by 1845 become a focal point of interest throughout the European capitals.

Clash of Imperial Ambitions - the Crimean War

While British and Prussian concerns and interests in the Land of Israel steadily increased after 1842, those of Russia and France grew substantially. Both sought every opportunity to increase their position and prestige in the region through their protected minorities, the French through the Catholic Church, and the Russians through the Orthodox Church.

By the early 1850's two ambitious personalities were ruling these nations, Napoleon III in France, and Nicholas I in Russia. Nicholas actually proposed to Palmerston in 1844 that the Turkish Empire be partitioned, Russia taking European Turkey, Britain taking Egypt and Crete, while Constantinople would temporarily remain a Turkish province.[1] Nicholas also agitated for Constantinople to further endorse and confirm Russia as the protector of Orthodox Christians in the Turkish Empire. Turkey refused to grant Russia the opportunity of any further encroachment upon her territory, fearing the loss of her independence.

The Russian demand was exacerbated by an incident in 1847 in far-away Turkish *Palestine*. A silver star in the Catholic section of the Church of the Nativity in Bethlehem had been stolen. The Catholics blamed the Greeks, whom they accused of attempting to usurp their rights in the Holy Places in both Jerusalem and Bethlehem. A Catholic accusation against the Greek Orthodox was construed by the Czar as an accusation against him, as Russia *claimed* the right of protector of Orthodox rights (although the *Treaty of Kucuk Kaynarca* only provided a limited jurisdiction to exercise such rights). Nicholas appealed to the Sultan to intervene.

Louis Napoleon, like his most illustrious forebear, Bonaparte, hankered after international fame, and likewise looked to the East. He was anxious to uphold the

---

1   Tuchman, B., *Bible and Sword.*, p. 254

role as protector of the Roman Catholics within the Turkish Empire. There was no doubt that such demands, more-or-less forgotten by France since the Napoleonic Wars, would antagonize Russia, complicate Turkey, and embarrass Britain. He likewise demanded Turkish intervention in the scandal at Bethlehem, in favour of the French of course! The Sultan, caught between these two major Powers, conciliated by replacing the silver star at his own cost. This move upset the Orthodox and Russians, who felt slighted by the Catholic-French accusations and in February 1853 the Russian envoy, Prince Menshikov, demanded that the Turkish Government intervene on their behalf.

Russia simultaneously assembled troops along the borders of some of Turkey's European dominions and in her Black Sea ports. The British and French ambassadors immediately summoned their respective governments, as in 1839, to send their fleets to the Dardanelles, again as a warning to Russian aspirations. Britain remained ambivalent over the issue, and the French Fleet sailed alone. Palmerston was indignant that Britain should oppose Russia, seeing Russia's stance as a dangerous threat to the stability of the Eastern Mediterranean. He wasn't alone. Sir Austen Layard said in the House of Commons, 'We should not forget that, although Egypt is *a* high road to India, Syria and the valleys of the Tigris and Euphrates form *the* high road, and any power holding those countries would command India.'[2]

Despite the presence of the French Fleet at the Dardanelles, Russia still threatened to invade the Turkish regions of Wallachia and Moldavia if her demands were not met. Pamerston and Lord John Russell increased their pressure upon the Cabinet, which finally agreed to the dispatch of the British Fleet to the Dardanelles. But when the weather fell foul, the ships anchored within the Straits, causing Russia to claim that this was a violation of the *Straits Convention* of 1841, and she thereupon invaded the Turkish provinces.

A peace conference was convened in Vienna, and all parties agreed to a compromise agreement; except Turkey, who believed that any concessions granting Russia protection rights over Orthodox Christians, would gravely affect her independence. Turkey replied by declaring war upon Russia. Popular support in Britain was for supporting Turkey against Russia. The thought of Russia controlling Constantinople was repugnant to most Britons. This feeling increased following the destruction of a Turkish Fleet at Sinope on 30 November 1853. Shortly afterwards the British and French Fleets sailed into the Black Sea and towards the harbour of Sebastopol in the Crimea.

Nicholas, looking for a pretext for war against Turkey in order to accumulate more Turkish territory and to attain the goal of controlling the Black Sea region and

---

2   *The Turkish Question, Speeches delivered in the House of Commons,* on 16 August 1853, and 17 February 1854, by Austin Henry Layard (London 1854) p. 10, cited in Sokolow, N. *History of Zionism* . London 1919. Vol 1, p. 157.

the exits into the Mediterranean, now increased his demands. Despite efforts to effect a peaceful solution, Britain and France were forced to declare war upon Russia on 28 March 1854. In 1798-99 it had been Britain, Russia and Turkey against France. In 1827 it had been Britain, France and Russia against Turkey. Now it was Britain, France and Turkey against Russia.

The British and French objective was the capture of the Russian stronghold of Sebastopol by a combined force of some 60,000 men. As these British and French troops steamed up the Dardanelles, past a little village named Gelibolu, into the Sea of Marmara, under the guns of Constantinople, through the Bosphorus and into the Black Sea, Palmerston, the proposer of the scheme, and the generals saw the matter as a *fait accompli*. The first landings occurred on 14 September 1854, but within two months half the British force was dead, wounded or sick with cholera. Despite some heroic victories, the expected quick victory over Sebastopol evaded the British-French command.

Jewish Concerns and Initatives

Once war was declared no further *haluka*[3] distributions could be transferred from the Jewish people of Russia to the Jewish subjects in the Land of Israel. This caused tremendous distress for the Jewish population who relied heavily upon these contributions. Many in desperation turned to the British consul, James Finn and his energetic wife Elizabeth, and the LJS Mission for support.

Once the plight of the Jewish community in Jerusalem and the Land of Israel became known in western Europe, support was quickly forthcoming. The Paris based Rothschild family immediately dispatched an envoy, Dr. Albert Cohen, with instructions to open a Jewish Hospital, and establish other Jewish institutions so that Jewish people would not have to resort to the services of the 'Jewish Mission'.

James and Elizabeth Finn also purchased land outside the Old City upon which they established an 'industrial plantation', known as Abraham's Vineyard, to employ Jewish men who could then earn their own bread. It was the first such venture in Jerusalem. Finn, seeing the benefit of British support of Turkey at this time, also sent a dispatch to Ambassador de Redcliffe in Constantinople, with a petition from the Ashkenazi Jews of Jerusalem, seeking permission for the establishment of a synagogue.[4]

Shaftesbury too was active. He wrote to the British Foreign Secretary, Lord Clarendon, stating that 'the Sultan should be moved to issue a Firman[5] granting to

---

3   *Haluka* - the Hebrew word for distribution, refers to the system whereby Jewish people in Europe sent alms to their brethren in Eretz Israel, which was distributed there by the rabbis.

4   Finn to de Redcliffe., 13 July 1854. F.O. 195/445 (No 23). Quoted in Hyamson, Albert., *The British Consulate*. Vol I., p. 225

5   *Firman* - Imperial edict.

the Jewish people power to hold land in Syria or any part of the Turkish domains.'[6] Clarendon in turn passed this information to the British Ambassador in Constantinople. The following year Moses Montefiore stopped in Constantinople en-route to Jerusalem, and beyond all expectations, received official permission to purchase small plots of land at Jaffa and at Jerusalem. When in Jerusalem in July 1855, he purchased land outside the Old City, upon which the first Jewish 'suburb', Mishkenot Shaananim, was ultimately built.

Although seemingly insignificant within the broader political picture, these operations of Montefiore, Finn and Rothschild in the Land of Israel were important as they marked the beginning of practical Jewish activities there. Jewish people were now being encouraged to move outside the walls of the Old City of Jerusalem and become involved in agricultural projects.

Ferdinand de Lesseps Vision

Also in 1854 Napoleon's vision to construct a canal across the Isthmus of Suez was resurrected. The proponent was a French diplomat, Ferdinand de Lesseps. De Lesseps had grown up in Egypt, and was acquainted with the family of Mehmet Ali, especially one of his son's, Mohommad Said. While in France in 1854 De Lesseps heard that Said had become Viceroy of Egypt, and after gaining the support of some French businessmen concerning the building of a canal across the Isthmus of Suez, he departed for Egypt.

There De Lesseps broached his plans to Said Pasha, who agreed in full. Said Pasha in turn granted De Lesseps a Concession on 30 November 1854, instructing him to form a Company, subsequently named the *Compagnie Universelle du Canal Maritime de Suez*, comprised of leading European shareholders. The French Consul-General was closely involved in the deliberations. This French involvement and interest attracted British suspicion, especially by Palmerston, who wrote to Ambassador de Redcliffe:

> If ... the Canal is meant to be one for seagoing ships, the expense would be enormous and the undertaking would never pay. But it would be injurious to England because, in any quarrel between England and France, France, being so much nearer to the Canal, would have much the start of us in sending ships and troops to the Indian seas.[7]

Problems arose when Turkey began to threaten Said Pasha to drop the scheme. The Egyptian Viceroy duly informed Turkey in no uncertain terms of his determination to see the project through. He reiterated that the project would not benefit France

---

6   Shaftesbury's dairy, 17 May 1854. Quoted in Hodder, Edwin., *The Life and Work of the Seventh Earl of Shaftesbury*, p. 493.

7   F.O. 78/1156 (1854-1855) Quoted in Lord Kinross, *Between Two Seas.*, William Morrow & Company, Inc. (New York, 1969), p. 79.

alone, but Britain, Turkey, Egypt and the world. Said Pasha's counter-offensive succeeded in swinging the mood in Constantinople in favour of the Canal. De Lesseps then returned to France in June 1855 to begin agitating for shareholders to join the Suez Canal Company.

Such moves increased Palmerston's concerns and he again wrote to de Redcliffe:

> It is quite clear that this scheme is founded on ulterior motives hostile to British views and interests and the secret intention no doubt is to lay a foundation for a future severance of Egypt from Turkey and for placing it under French protection. A deep and wide canal interposed between Egypt and Syria studded with fortifications could be a military defensive line which, with the desert in front of it, would render the task of a Turkish army very difficult.[8]

This crisis with France was further complicated by the matter in Crimea, where Britain was allied to France. The War was now the more critical issue.

Palmerston Takes the Reins

The ill-fated prosecution of the war effort led to the downfall of the British government, and Palmerston took over as Prime Minister in February 1855. Shortly afterwards Nicholas I died and was replaced by Alexander II. The new Czar was prepared for peace, and talks soon began in Vienna.

Palmerston wanted Russia cut down to size, so that she would never again threaten Turkey's stability, and therefore the stability of the Eastern Mediterranean and Britain's link to India and her eastern Empire. Russia would not consent to Palmerston's harsh demands, the talks were terminated and the war prolonged. In September 1855 Sebastopol fell to the French forces, and following other set backs Russia finally, in January 1856 agreed to the British-French peace terms.

The Peace Congress began in Paris in February 1856. Two of the British aims were, the demilitarization of the Black Sea, and the stripping away of any protection rights Russia exercised over the Orthodox Christians. Russian interests in the Turkish Empire had to be minimized. Both these points were ultimately agreed upon. In addition, the Sultan issued a new reform, the *Hatti Humayan*, granting further reforms for the non-Muslim inhabitants of the Turkish Empire. The *Treaty of Paris* was signed on 30 March 1856. Again, at least for the time being, Palmerston and Britain had managed to preserve Britain's link to India, and had kept Russia at bay.

Russia's New Tactic

Stripped of its mostly self given status as protector of the Orthodox Church, the Russians now adopted a new tactic in their efforts to undermine the stability of Turkey.

---

8   F.O. 78/1156 (1854-1855). Quoted in Lord Kinross, ibid., p. 79.

She would establish a purely Russian presence in the Land of Israel. Immediately after the signing of the peace treaty Boris Mansurov was sent to Jerusalem to study the possibility of establishing a Russian presence there, and of introducing a Russian shipping line to bring Russian pilgrims to the 'Holy Land'. He reported back that:

> ... Western institutions were making a greater impression upon the indigenous population than both the local Ottoman authorities and the administration of the Greek Orthodox Church together, and he perceived correctly that Russia's part in the rivalry was negligible. The local population saw no Russian monasteries, schools, hospitals or hospices, institutions which the other powers had been busy setting up throughout the country.[9]

Mansurov recommended to his superiors that Russia set up a shipping line for the transport of pilgrims, establish a consulate in Jerusalem, and hostels in various parts of the country to assist the pilgrims. His plan was accepted by the Czar, and the 'Palestine Committee' was formed, with the Czar himself as Patron. Then negotiations began in 1857 for the purchase of a large plot of land outside the walls of Jerusalem's Old City, known as the Maidan.

The Grand Duke Constantine visited Jerusalem in 1859, to complete the purchase, as well as to purchase plots of land on the Mount of Olives and also near the Church of the Holy Sepulchre to fulfill Russia's imperialist goals. Building upon the huge complex at the Maidan, thereafter known as the Russian Compound, began soon after, and was the most impressive building programme in Jerusalem. Antonin Kapustin, the Russian representative overseeing the project wrote of his motives for being in Jerusalem:

> I have abandoned all ambition in life and followed with all my being one end - that of confirming and strengthening Russia's name in the Holy Land so that we should not be merely guests there, but to a certain extent rightful owners.[10]

The Russian Compound was so enormous, that many, especially the Catholic-French representatives believed it was being built to be a Russian army barracks in the event of a Russian invasion. But this was not the only large Russian enterprise. Through Kapustin's involvement, large plots of land were purchased and buildings constructed throughout the land, one of the biggest being at Abu Kabir, near Jaffa, where the Russian pilgrims would stay after landing, prior to the ascent to Jerusalem. By the mid 1860's, it seemed for all intents and purposes that Russia was a major candidate for taking control over the Land of Israel if and when the Turkish Empire fell. And Russia lost the war!

---

9   Carmel, Alex. *Activities of the European Powers in Palestine 1799-1914.*, Asia and Africa Studies 19 (1985), Institute of Middle Eastern Studies, University of Haifa, p. 67.

10   Hopwood, D. *The Russian Presence in Syria and Palestine, 1843-1914: Church and Politics in the Near East.*(Oxford, 1969), p. 95.

French Initiatives

The French too were not idle. Apart from the efforts of the Rothschild family on behalf of the Jewish community, French initiatives increased tremendously in the years following the Crimean War. Baron de Cauchy established the *Oevre des ecoles d'Orient* the purpose of which was to further a Catholic education system throughout the Turkish Empire, and more specifically in the Land of Israel. This effort was assisted by using the already established Catholic institutions. Thus, wrote Tibawai 'apart from the usual opening of schools for boys and girls of their own sect, the French missions, often in alliance with the Propaganda Fide[11], formed seminaries for the Melkites, Maronites, Armenian Catholics and Syrian Catholics.'[12]

The most prestigious French/Catholic building was the Latin Patriarchate, completed in 1864. Yet, wrote Carmel, 'The crown of French activity in Palestine ... was the reconstruction of the Crusader Church of St. Anna [13] ... The ruined church ... had been a gift from the Sultan to Napoleon III for the services he rendered to Turkey in the Crimean War.'[14] Numerous other French-Catholic institutions were established in Jerusalem and throughout the region of the Land of Israel and Syria. By the mid 1860's it seemed that France was joining Russia as the main contenders for inheriting the Land of Israel when the Turkish Empire finally fell apart.

British Interests

British interests in the Land of Israel remained quite unobtrusive, and revolved around the operations of the Consulate, Bishopric and the LJS. But a growing number of British strategists were dedicated, like Pitt before them, to eradicating any possibility of either a French or Russian takeover in the Eastern Mediterranean, and of confirming and strengthening Britain's presence there. Colonel George Gawler, a veteran of Waterloo and former Governor of the colony of South Australia, was one. Gawler, who actually accompanied Montefiore on a visit to Jerusalem in 1849, wrote in the context of Empire, that Britain:

> ... urgently needs the shortest and safest lines of communication ... Egypt and Syria stand in intimate connection. A foreign hostile power in either would soon endanger British trade ... and it is now for England to set her hand hard to the renovation of Syria through the only people whose energies will be extensively and permanently in the work - the real children of the soil - the sons of Israel.[15]

---

11 Roman Catholic educational institution.
12 Tibawi, A.L. *British Interests in Palestine*, (Oxford, 1961), p. 171.
13 Located inside the Old City of Jerusalem, adjacent to the traditional site of the Pool of Bethesda, and close to the *Via Dolorosa* and Temple Mount.
14 Carmel, A. *European Activities*, pp. 49-50.
15 Gawler, Colonel George. Found in *British Projects for the Restoration of the Jews*, British Palestine Commission, (London, 1917), p. 17.

Gawler's concern for Israel's return and the security of Britain's link to the East was similar to that proclaimed by a long line of distinguished Britons, including Bicheno, Shaftesbury and Churchill.

In the early 1860's another form of British activity in Eretz Israel was set in motion. Captain Charles Wilson had been sent to Jerusalem by the Army Ordnance Survey Department to assist in a project funded by the wealthy Angela Boudett-Coutts to establish a proper water supply in the revered city. Simultaneously he was to draw up maps of Jerusalem and its environs. News of his work helped prompt A. P. Stanley and George Groves, two prominent English churchman, to form a society to help promote such projects, as well as archaeological and scientific studies of the Land of Israel.

This society, named the *Palestine Exploration Fund* (PEF) was officially formed on 12 May 1865 in the Jerusalem Chamber of Westminster Cathedral. Shaftesbury was one of the founding members. Its operations, on both sides of the Jordan River, proved of tremendous value over the following decades in deepening that already strong British interest in the land of the Bible.

The Suez Canal

Thanks to the vision and initiative of De Lesseps, France also took a quantative step forward in the imperial stakes following the ending of the Crimean War. Despite lack of official Turkish permission, as well as opposition from Palmerston and De Redcliffe, he managed to foster support throughout Europe, and even in Britain itself for his ambitious scheme.

Ironically it was the Indian Mutiny in 1857 which revealed the viability, for Britain, of at least the overland route between Alexandria and Suez. What began as a disagreement between Indian sepoy troops and their officers, quickly spread, especially in the north of India into a widespread revolt against British rule. After suppressing the revolt drastic changes were made to the British administration in India. Thereafter the government of India became a direct responsibility of the British Government and the operations of the East India Company were greatly curtailed.

Despite now seeing the viability of the quicker Suez route, the British Government, led by the strongly imperialist spokesman Benjamin Disraeli continued to oppose the cutting of a canal, seeing it as nothing other than a French effort to control the Eastern Mediterranean. The French official line however was somewhat ambivalent.

Finally in November 1858 the subscription list for the Suez Canal Company was opened to the public. More than half the 400,000 shares were purchased by French investors. Said Pasha was reluctantly persuaded by De Lesseps to buy up the remainder thereby allowing De Lesseps to finally register his Company. Despite the lack of official Turkish recognition De Lesseps enlisted Egyptian workers, and on 25 April

1859, struck the first blow at the point where the Red Sea would later enter the Mediterranean. These were the first blows in what would soon provide a rival to the Dardanelles as the most strategic waterway in the world.

This move by De Lesseps was a calculated gamble - it would either move Said Pasha, the Sultan and the British to openly oppose, or support the venture. British opposition mounted. France, pressured more and more by the 21,000 French investors, decided it was time to make an official policy. French prestige, De Lesseps claimed, would be damaged in the East, if British pressure succeeded and the venture failed. Turkey continued its official opposition, in part due to British pressure, lest 'the Isthmus might make Egypt the theatre of conflict in any future European War.'[16]

In October 1859 the Porte (Turkish Government) stated their final word - work on the Canal must stop. All seemed lost. But not to De Lesseps. He met Emperor Napoleon in France in October 1859, and convinced him that the enterprise was sound, and for the benefit of France. Napoleon was won over and announced his support of the project. While Britain and Turkey remained unmoved, the rest of Europe slowly came to support the scheme.

Crisis in Lebanon and Syria

During this same period the first widespread outbreak of opposition to the liberal policies of the *Hatti Humayan* broke out in 1860. Muslims and Druze, a Muslim sect, incensed with the increase of freedom granted to the Christians, attacked the Maronite Christian community in the Lebanon region of Syria for three days. France, the traditional protector of Catholic concerns in the Turkish Empire, called for an international Convention. Despite British resistance to a French monopoly, warships from Britain, France, Russia and Prussia moved to Beirut, where an almost exclusively French international force landed. Napoleon received a six month mandate to restore peace and order.

When Napoleon secured an extension of a further four months in Syria, Britain became suspicious of French ambitions. Britain wanted France out. 'We do not want to create a new Papal state in the East, and to give France a pretext for indefinite occupation', wrote Lord John Russell the Foreign Secretary.[17] Britain was so determined to get France out that the Turkish Government was forced to set up a semi autonomous Christian region in Syria, henceforth known as Lebanon, to be governed by a Christian. When Napoleon's forces finally left Lebanon in 1861, they left behind a more stable environment for the Christians of the region, as well as an enhanced respect for France.

---

16 Lord Kinross, *Between Two Seas*, p. 131.
17 Quoted in Tuchman, B. *Bible and Sword*, p. 257.

The Canal Takes Shape

Despite the troubles in Syria, the Suez Canal took shape. A new port, Port Said, emerged at the Mediterranean end, and along the projected route the towns of Kantara and Ismailia quickly grew. All had a distinct French character, much to the distaste of Ambassador Bulwer, who visited the project in 1862. His visit caused him to surmise that construction of the Canal was indeed a *fait accompli*, although opposition against too much French connection must continue. All the while the Turks withheld official permission.

Said Pasha died in 1863 and was replaced by Ismail Pasha. He was immediately confronted with the large debt he inherited due to Said's purchase of Company shares. He needed to determine the best course to follow. If, he surmised, Egypt managed to finance the completion of the Canal, without seeking foreign financial assistance, she would gain more independence from Turkey, and greatly increase her political and commercial value.

Ismail (after whom Ismailia was named) decided to proceed, with or without Turkish and British permission. He also then made efforts to pay, from the Treasury, most of the outstanding money from Said's shares in the Company. The Egyptian Government was now financially as well as politically committed to the project.

The Porte then finally agreed, conditionally, to the construction of the Canal, in April 1863. Those conditions were: the Egyptians could no longer use forced labour; the Suez Canal Company had to surrender some lands conceded to her; and there needed to be international guarantees of the Canal's neutrality, similar to those granted to the Dardanelles and Bosphorus.[18] These conditions provoked many difficulties for De Lesseps and Ismail, who turned to France, and the Emperor for guidance. Napoleon in 1864 again endorsed the project.

British opposition was maintained by Palmerston's successor, Lord Russell, whose government wished to ensure that, even with the completion of the Canal, there would be no opportunity for French colonists to settle on the lands owned by the Canal Company. Ultimately by 1866 most of the Turkish and British apprehensions were sufficiently satisfied, at least so as not to offend France which was now a committed supporter of the Canal Company. On 19 March 1866 the Sultan finally signed a *firman* authorizing the construction of the Suez Canal - a matter which had by now become a *fait accompli.*

As De Lesseps and his engineers pushed ahead, the status of France increased, while that of Britain decreased. Month by month the Canal began to take shape. Port Said, Kantara, Ismailia, and Suez on the Red Sea, were all transformed from sleepy Arab villages, into thriving ports and stations. Yet the unnecessary delays over the

---

18   Lord Kinross, *Between Two Seas*, pp. 169-170.

years had caused innumerable financial burdens for De Lesseps and the Canal Company, debts which would later seriously compromise Egypt. In March 1869 the Prince and Princess of Wales visited the almost completed Suez Canal, and lamented that due to Palmerston's lack of foresight, this great work, vital for Britain's link to India, had been achieved by the French. The Prince's true sentiments were repeated some years later, while passing through the Canal en-route to India. 'The Suez Canal,' the Prince said to Lord Granville, 'is certainly an outstanding work, and it is an everlasting pity that it was not made by an English company and kept in our hands, because, as it is the highway to India, we should be obliged to take it - and by force of arms if necessary.'[19] The Suez Canal was finally officially opened on 17 November 1870, the most distinguished guest present being Napoleon's wife the Empress Eugenie.

The Rise of Germany

No sooner had the Empress returned to France, when war broke out with neighbouring Prussia. Prussia had united many of the Germanic provinces, and embarked upon a war against her traditional antagonist France in 1869. Inspired by Otto von Bismark, German troops quickly subdued imperial France, forcing the Emperor and his wife into exile, and bringing down the Second Empire. As one empire fell, another emerged. At the Palace of Versailles near Paris, the German Empire was proclaimed.

Defeat at the hands of Germany in the Franco-Prussian War ruined French prestige throughout the East. She now again had the daunting task of stabilizing her nation after the humiliation of defeat, and then of slowly restoring her international credibility. And, as Germany ruled the nest in continental Europe, France's ambitions in the Eastern Mediterranean were again checked.

Problems for Egypt

The Turkish Government heavily reprimanded Ismail for his apparent move towards independence, and for taking large loans at high interest rates from overseas. Such matters would seriously jeopardize the financial stability of Egypt, making it increasingly reliant upon overseas investment.

The vacuum created by France's loss in the Franco-Prussian War, allowed Britain to regain the lead in the Imperial stakes. After 1869 it was she, more than any other country, which monopolized the usage of the Canal, linch-pin as it now was to her expanding eastern Empire, primarily in India, Australia and New Zealand. This factor, coupled with Egypt's financial problems were paving the way for further British involvement in the region.

---

19 Lee, Sidney. *King Edward VII.* Ch 7. London, 1925. Quoted in Lord Kinross, ibid., pp. 233-234.

Despite heavy usage of the Canal, the delays in construction and lower than expected profits steered De Lesseps and the Canal Company into considerable debt. The shareholders were losing patience. De Lesseps, the staunch Frenchman took the only option open to him - he sought further British investment. The British Government in turn were interested in securing controlling interests on the Board, although the idea of a non-French dominated Board was repugnant to De Lesseps. But before such drastic moves occurred, usage increased and the Canal Company's financial predicament improved.

The same could not be said for the financial problems of the Egyptian Government (the Khedive). The annual interest on the loans the Egyptian Government had taken out over the previous years amounted to almost the same amount as the gross national income of Egypt, apart from her Canal returns. The situation by November 1875 was critical for Ismail. He seriously contemplated the sale or mortgaging of the Khedive's 177,642 shares in the Suez Canal Company.

News of the Egyptian dilemma filtered through to Government circles in Britain. Benjamin Disraeli the new imperialistic Prime Minister, was intrigued by the situation, having previously discussed with Baron Lionel de Rothschild the possibility of Britain gaining a lion's share of the Canal. Disraeli gained the support of his Cabinet, and sent word to Ismail via the Consul-General in Alexandria, to forestall selling the shares to the other consortiums, primarily French.

De Lesseps strongly encouraged the French Government to assist in purchasing the shares. France was reluctant, as Germany was threatening a renewal of war. With Britain restraining Germany, France was unwilling to overtly oppose any strong British initiatives. Although the French Government opted out, French interests were maintained by the interest of two French banking consortiums. But Disraeli was not going to lose this opportunity. He quickly raised a loan of 4 million pounds from Rothschild, and outbid the French consortiums.

Yet another opportunity for France to complete the vision of Napoleon Bonaparte had slipped from its grasp. Its victory of 1869 was counteracted by Britain's in 1875. And Britain's move was one more knot in that rope which would ultimately compel her to make every conceivable move to ensure her retention of that strategic waterway. Until 1875 she had basically endeavoured to prop up the Turkish Empire so as to keep the vultures, France and Russia, away from the Isthmus of Suez and the Dardanelles. Now her policy was being forced to change primarily due to French initiatives.

One interesting aspect of this saga was the role of the Jewish born Benjamin Disraeli. Disraeli had previously written two novels dealing with the issue of Israel's return to Eretz Israel. The second, *Tancred*, published in 1847, was the better known of the two. And now as Prime Minister of Britain, he had enacted a policy which was to ultimately play a significant role in bringing about that ultimate restoration.

The Noose Tightens

The establishment of the Suez Canal and increasing interests of Britain and France in the affairs of Egypt, and the apparent independence of Egypt, were all signs to the non-Turkish peoples of the Turkish Empire, that now was the time to throw off the yoke of Turkish control. In 1875 a revolt broke out in the Bulgarian region of the Turkish Empire. It was put down brutally by the Turks.

Russia again saw the opportunity of fighting Turkey, by supporting the Bulgarian cause, and gaining land in the process. The Russo-Turkish War began in 1877. Britain was left in a quandry. Half the populace were anti-Russia, decrying the fact that if Russia won, her forces may occupy Constantinople.

Fear of Russian expansion was counterbalanced by disgust at Turkish brutality and numerous Britons, including William Gladstone, called for the ousting of barbaric Turkey from European soil. Yet Britain's stance was determined, once it became known that the Russian Fleet was approaching Constantinople. Disraeli overcame Cabinet opposition and sent a British Fleet through the Dardanelles and into the Bosphorus. He also brought up reinforcements from India - via the Suez Canal - to Malta. The Russian advance was halted, but not before she gained heavy concessions from Turkey in the *Treaty of San Stefano.*

A peace conference was summarily convened in Berlin to review and revise the *Treaty of San Stefano,* primarily to curtail Russian influence in the region. Prior to this Conference Disraeli and Gladstone met the Turks. Foreign Secretary Salisbury had instructed Ambassador Layard in Constantinople, that it was vital for Britain to ensure that Turkey did not come under Russia's control, and that it was essential for the Sultan to obtain an alliance with Britain. For Britain, it was vital, if she was to keep Russia away from her link to India, to seek an alliance with Turkey. 'We shall have to choose' Salisbury continued, 'between allowing Russia to dominate over Syria and Mesopotamia *or taking the country for ourselves,* and either alternative is formidable.'[20]

Britain was very aware of the vulnerability of the region, and the potential of Russia gaining a pre-eminent position there. A Russian conquest of Constantinople was a distinct possibility. With control of Constantinople and the Bosphorus, the Russian Fleet could easily move through the Dardanelles, into the Eastern Mediterranean - and towards the Suez Canal. The so-called *Cyprus Convention* was signed on 4 June 1878, with Britain pledging to support Turkey if Russia again attempted to usurp her territory. In return Britain gained security rights over Cyprus.

At the following Treaty of Berlin in 1878, Turkey was treated leniently, while some of Russia's gains were stripped from her. When the Treaty was signed and

---

20 Salisbury letter to Laynard, 10 May 1878. Temperley, H.W.V., *Near East: Disraeli and Cyprus. English Historical Review,* XLVI, (April, 1931), Quoted in Tuchman, B. *Bible and Sword,* p. 263.

sealed, Disraeli informed the delegates of Britain's defensive alliance with Turkey. The other countries, when hearing of this arrangement, demanded their share in the spoils - France demanding Tunisia while Italy demanded Albania and Tripoli (Libya). These dramatic events again stirred an interest in Israel's restoration, both amongst the Evangelicals and the secular. A female novelist, writing under the name of George Eliot wrote *Daniel Deronda* which spoke of Jewish emancipation. Others like Edward Cazalet and Laurence Oliphant took a more active interest in Israel's return to her land. Oliphant, a Member of Parliament and friend of the Prince of Wales, wrote and spoke in the strongest terms on behalf of Israel - and then actually went to live in the Land itself. His move was synonymous to a larger scale immigration to Eretz Israel.

Jewish Nationalism Awakens

Like every other major conflict in the region since Napoleon's invasion this one too influenced the Jewish people. Many Jewish observers in eastern Europe were impressed by the passion of the people of the Balkan region to be liberated from Turkish control and establish their own national identity. Although national movements had previously propelled Greece, Italy and Germany into nationhood, these recent events coincided with an awakening Jewish nationalist movement.

During the previous decades men such as Rabbi Judah Alkalai, Rabbi Zev Kalischer, Rabbi Elijah Guttmacher and others had espoused various forms of Jewish nationalism. Moses Hess formulated a type of Jewish nationalism based upon developments then occurring in Western Europe, and wrote *Rome and Jerusalem* in 1860. There was a steady movement towards a clearer form of Jewish nationalism, steering away from the traditional belief that first the Messiah would come, then the Israelites would return to Eretz Israel.

One Russian Jewish nationalist and observer was Eliezer Perlman (later Eliezer Ben Yehuda), a writer for the Hebrew newspaper *Ha-Shahar (The Dawn).* Perlman believed that the Jewish people had all the attributes for nationhood, a common history, language (Hebrew) and culture, but they lacked the essential attribute - a national home.[21]

Other Jewish nationalists then formed small groups and clubs during the late 1870's. Unfortunately their activities helped spark off anti-Jewish riots, called pogroms, as the host nations, especially Russia, were by now becoming wary of national sentiment among the ethnic peoples within her domains. The pogroms caused a further consolidation of this Jewish nationalist movement, A covering body was formed named the *Hibbat Zion (Love of Zion)* and its members the *Chovevei Zion (Lovers of Zion).* This movement began agitating towards the establishment of a Jewish national home in the Land of Israel.

---

21   Sacher, H. *A History of Israel*, p. 263.

The Egyptian Crisis

Egypt's financial crisis, precipitated by the extravagances of Said and Ismail, forced her to seek international advice. Britain and France complied by sending economic advisors. When their sound advice was not completely followed, the French and British appealed to Turkey to intervene. The Turks deposed Ismail in 1879. Ismail's successor Tewfik, adopted various policies aimed at stemming the tide of bankruptcy. One policy was the reduction of the Egyptian army. This move was resented by numerous officers, and resulted in a riot by nationalist agitators. The insurrection, led by Colonel Arabi, intensified, culminating in a *coup d'etat* in September 1881. The nationalists adopted the slogan, 'Egypt for the Egyptians.'

Britain and France were concerned lest this military dictatorship lead to further problems. They called for the Khedive, Pasha Tewfik, to stave the power of Arabi. Such a move further incensed the Egyptians. Britain and France further feared for the safety and security of the Suez Canal and for the foreign nationals living in Egypt. They dispatched warships to Alexandria. This move provoked Arabi and his supporters, who subsequently massacred fifty foreign nationals. Arabi then proceeded to fortify Alexandria.

The British Fleet fired on these fortifications, and landed troops, purportedly 'in the name of the Khedive.' British ships and troops then obtained permission to occupy Port Said, Suez and other points along the Canal, again in the name of the Khedive. At this juncture, a weak vacillating French Government, mainly under George Clemenceau's influence, refused to permit further French intervention. As the French Fleet left Egypt's waters, France's last opportunity of achieving what Napoleon had set out to do some 83 years before - the conquest of Egypt - was lost.

Despite protestations concerning the neutrality of the Canal, British troops landed at Port Said and Ismailia on 19 August 1882. Reinforcements quickly arrived at Suez from India. Arabi rallied his troops and several days later fought a pitched battle against the British forces at Tel-el-Kebir, and lost. The following day the British troops occupied Cairo. Egypt was now under British control. Although there ostensibly to protect the legitimate ruler, the Khedive Tewfik, Britain was in fact there to protect her strategic interests - the link to India and the eastern Empire.

C hapter 7

Zionism and Imperial Alliances

The Russian Jews are Coming

While a bout of Arab nationalism provoked the intervention of Britain in the affairs of Egypt, so too did a bout of Russian nationalism in 1881 and 1882 provoke the movement of several thousand Jewish refugees to live in Turkish *Palestine*. This immigration, known as the first *aliyah*, or immigration, marked the beginning point of a Jewish national home in the Land of Israel.

Czar Alexander II was assassinated in 1881. The period was one of uncertainty. Ethnic and national groups throughout the region were fighting for their historic national rights. Russia needed to stem the tide, and some quick decisive action was necessary. A scapegoat was needed by which to set an example. They chose the Jewish people as that scapegoat, implicating them because a Jewish lady was involved in the plot to assassinate the Czar.

A number of government inspired pogroms, erupted throughout the *Pale* region in the summer of 1881. The situation continued to worsen, culminating with the publication, in 1882, of harsh anti-Jewish laws. The hardships and restrictions these laws placed upon the Jewish people were for many unbearable, and tens of thousands uprooted and left. The majority of these Jewish refugees sailed to the west, to Britain, Canada and the United States. Some ventured further afield, to South America, South Africa, Australia and even New Zealand. But a few thousand chose the Land of Israel. Their movement coincided with the strongly nationalist book *Auto Emancipation* written by Leon Pinsker.

The vanguard of this movement was a small group of *Chovevei Zion,* naming themselves the *Bilu*, an acronym for 'House of Jacob let us go'. This small group was nationalist, while the majority of the refugees merely sought a refuge in the land of their forefathers. But whatever the motive, the arrival of the Russian refugees marked the beginning point of a new chapter in the history of the Land of Israel. For the first time large numbers of non-religious Jewish people had come to settle in the Land of Israel. The character and destiny of the Jewish community was about to change dramatically.

Life was very difficult for these newcomers. There was no economic infrastructure for them. The religious Jewish community didn't particularly want them, and even if they did, could not financially support them. And the Turkish authorities were unwilling to assist their absorption. Although several Jewish agricultural colonies had been established in the country, notably at Motza in 1869 and at Petach Tikva (Muleubis) in 1878, the Jewish presence was by no means synonymous with such ventures. From 1882 that changed.

The *Bilu* and then other refugees endeavoured to set up Jewish agricultural colonies. They were doomed to failure from the outset, as the Turkish bureaucracy, lack of finances and experience, and local Arab opposition combined to make the ventures unsuccessful. Previous approaches to wealthy European philanthropists like Barons Rothschild and Hirsch had failed. If help was not soon forthcoming, the would be colonists would fail in their efforts to establish a new Jewish life in the land of their forefathers.

The situation of these Jewish refugees became so bad that many chose to resort to the services of the British based London Jews Society. The LJS missionaries provided much tangible assistance, causing even the correspondent of the *Jewish Chronicle* to conclude: 'The treatment of these poor Jews is kind in the extreme, and whatever our views as Jews on this subject may be, certain it is that the missionaries have saved many Jewish lives.'[1]

When he became aware of the role the missionaries played Rothschild's obstinate stance ultimately gave way. He wrote to Samuel Hirsch the director of the French sponsored Mikve Israel colony that 'This movement has been established in my opinion, with the encouragement of the English, who knew very well, that when these people would come to Eretz Israel, starving to death and destitute, they would be easy game for the missionaries.'[2]

With Rothschild's benevolent assistance soon forthcoming, these Jewish refugees established several colonies, namely Rishon le Zion (First in Zion), Khirbet Dieran (later Rehovoth), Rosh Pina, Gedera and Hadera. One other colony for the Russian refugees not associated with Rothschild was Artuf, which was established in 1883 by the British missionaries. It was sold in 1892 to Romanian Jewish colonists.

In the same year a young Eliezer Margolin came from Russia with his family and settled at Khirbet Dieran (Rehovoth). Young Eliezer adapted very quickly to the agricultural lifestyle. In time he also helped with the defence of the new Jewish *Yishuv* (settlement), earning the accolades of the local Arabs: 'He sits on his horse like a Bedouin and shoots like an Englishman.'[3]

Although this Jewish colonist movement had little political clout, it did gradually establish facts upon the ground. More colonies were founded and more Jewish workers came, buying up for the most part unwanted and unused lands from Arab landowners.

---

1   *Jewish Chronicle*, London, 15 September 1882, p. 13.
2   Rothschild to Hirsch, 6 April 1883, quoted in S. Yavniely, *Sefer Ha Zionist* (Tel Aviv, 1944) p. 81.
3   Jabotinsky, V., *The Story of the Jewish Legion.*, Bernard Ackerman, (New York, 1945), p. 102.

Although seeking the establishment of a Jewish national home, they were content for the most part to eke out an existence, and overcome the often harsh Turkish opposition. But their aspirations gained support in Europe, as more Jewish people, mainly in eastern Europe, but also in the west, became aware of the venture, and endeavoured to support it.

The Zionist Movement and Germany

Political support would ultimately be necessary if there was to be a viable Jewish national home in Eretz Israel. Piecemeal colonialisation would not force the Turkish authorities to grant a Jewish autonomy in the region. The support of one or the other European governments would be imperative. That realization began the road to reality in 1896. A secular Austrian Jew, Theodor Herzl, startled by the extent of anti-Semitism even in western Europe, wrote a book entitled *Der Judenstaat* - the Jewish State, declaring that the only tangible solution to the plight of the dispersed and despised Jewish people, was for the establishment of a Jewish State.

The concept was quickly taken up by those of like mind, including a visionary English priest, William Hechler, the chaplain of the British Embassy in Vienna. Hechler supported Herzl's vision, and encouraged him to make contact with the leaders of Germany, and to call for a Congress to discuss the vision. In 1897 several hundred Jewish delegates, mostly from eastern Europe, assembled in Basle, Switzerland, and at the First Zionist Congress, laid the political foundations for what would become the future State of Israel.

It became obvious to the leaders of this newly formed Zionist movement that their vision could be fulfilled only with the support of a leading European power. Hechler wrote: 'I cannot help thinking, that if Germany and England were to take this movement and such a new state under their protection, and Palestine were declared to be a neutral country, something like Belgium, the Return of the Jews would become a great blessing to Europe, and put an end to the anti-semitic spirit of hatred, which is detrimental to the welfare of all nations.'[4]

Germany at the time seemed the most accessible, primarily because Herzl had made, with Hechler's assistance, contact with members of the German ruling aristocracy. A meeting with the Kaiser himself would be the next and most important step. The Kaiser and his German Empire had, since 1871, been slowly establishing a power base in central Europe. Sandwiched between France and Russia, it was a force soon to be reckoned with by the major powers. And by the art of deduction, it became progressively clear to the Sultan, that of all the major European Empires, only Germany had no ages long desire to usurp her territory. From 1878 and the Congress of Berlin, and then since 1882 and Britain's occupation of Egypt, the Sultan

---

4   Hechler to the Grand Duke of Baden, 26 March 1896. Quoted in Ellern, H and B., *Herzl, Hechler, the Grand Duke of Baden and the German Emperor, 1896-1904,* (Tel Aviv, 1961), p.6.

had been making gradual moves towards Germany. And these moves had been reciprocated.

In 1898 the new and imposing German Church of the Redeemer was completed in the middle of Jerusalem's Old City. The Kaiser was to travel to Jerusalem to officially open the church and en-route was to meet the Sultan in Constantinople. It was the ideal opportunity for Herzl, the leader of the political wing of the Jewish nationalist movement, to meet the Emperor of Germany, who could, it was anticipated, act on behalf of Zionism before the Sultan. Herzl first met the Kaiser in Constantinople, where little of any significance resulted, and then followed him to the Land of Israel.

In October 1898, 100 years since Napoleon's expedition, the German Emperor entered the Land of Israel. The Turks ingratiated themselves before the Kaiser and his entourage, even permitting the walls of the Old City of Jerusalem to be breached so as to allow the Kaiser, riding his huge white horse, and his entourage to proceed into the city (an issue which did not go unnoticed by the British press, who ridiculed this ostentatious show) on 31 October 1898. Jerusalem, despite its presence of large Russian and French-Catholic institutions, its growing Jewish population, and large Moslem presence, was, in October 1898, the Kaiser's city. The German connection had well and truly been forged - and would become more-so in the following years as she built huge edifices upon the lands bestowed to them by the Turks. The most imposing became the Augusta Victoria Hospice, named after the Kaiser's wife, on the Mount of Olives, with the most imposing view in all four directions. Many later claimed it was no more than a German fortress built for an invading army!

No wonder then that Herzl and his entourage, including Hechler, envisioned Germany as the would be protector of the Jewish nationalist movement.[5] Herzl met briefly with the Kaiser first at Mikveh Israel. Several days later, on 2 November Herzl met with the Kaiser in Jerusalem. This meeting it was hoped would determine if Germany would support a Jewish future in Jerusalem and Eretz Israel. Although showing some interest in the scheme during the meeting, disappointment followed. Kaiser Wilhelm II was aware of the need to foster good relations with Turkey. And as Turkey viewed any nationalist movement, especially one with European connections, with suspicion and disdain, Germany, and the Kaiser were unwilling to forge relations with a Jewish nationalist movement.

This was just one of many disappointments for Herzl and his newly founded movement. Dedicated to something more grandiose than mere gradual colonization, the Zionists needed some form of political backing. Turkey, being a Muslim state, most definitely would not permit the establishment of a Jewish national home in her domain. France, despite Napoleon's declaration of April 1799, had no sympathy towards such a concept, espousing the Land of Israel for her own cause. Russia, the

---

5   *The Diaries of Theodor Herzl.* Translated and Edited by Marvin Lowenthal. The Universal Library, Grosset & Dunlap. (New York, 1962), p. 276.

most virulently anti-Semitic of the Empires, was most definitely not sympathetic to such a concept. If (and when) she gained control over the region, Eretz Israel would have a Russian-Orthodox-Byzantine character. That left Britain as the only Empire which could support the Zionist cause and encourage the return of the Jewish people to the Land of Israel.

Egypt and the Zionists

Following the failure of Herzl's attempt to interest the Kaiser to support their goals, the Zionist movement began looking towards Britain. The Fourth Zionist Congress therefore was held in London in 1900. It was here that the Jewish Colonial Fund was finally established, to raise funds for the purchase of land in Eretz Israel.

During the same period further pogroms erupted in the east, primarily in Romania, forcing thousands more Jewish refugees westwards. Some endeavoured to enter Britain, causing fears of cheap labour competition. The British Government set up a royal commission to determine the best solution to this dilemma. Lord Rothschild was a member. Although he, like many influential British Jews, was opposed to the wild Zionist scheme, Rothschild nevertheless saw the potential for the Zionist move-ment at this juncture. Perhaps the Zionists could assist by drawing off these refugees to Turkish *Palestine*, and thus saving Rothschild and the British Jews an embarrass-ing situation. He met with Herzl.

Herzl explained to Rothschild that he wanted to establish a Jewish colony on British territory. Eretz Israel was still Turkish territory, so Herzl had conceived the idea of having a half-way station. On a piece of paper he wrote to Rothschild 'Sinai Peninsular, Egyptian Palestine, Cyprus.'[6]

Rothschild then discussed the suggestion with the British Colonial Minister, Joseph Chamberlain. Chamberlain liked the proposal, not because he was pro-Zionist, but because he saw another opportunity to expand the interests of mankind - and the British Empire. Chamberlain, like many Britons of the time, saw the two concepts as virtually synonymous. And here was an excellent opportunity to settle and hold that delicate piece of real-estate, the east bank of the Suez, by colonialists under British protection. The Suez Canal region was by now the jugular vein of the British Empire. It was an idea straight from the history books - perhaps he knew of the strategies of Cyrus the Persian and more recently of Napoleon in using the Jewish people as their imperial agents.

These events occurred during 1902. After his initial meetings with Chamberlain, Herzl returned to Constantinople to bargain and negotiate again with the Turks about a charter for the Land of Israel. His chances were slim. He returned to London, and discussed again the Sinai-Cyprus proposal with Chamberlain. Chamberlain explained

---

6   Tuchman, B. *Bible and Sword.*, p. 293.

that Cyprus was out of the question, as both the Greek and Moslem inhabitants would oppose such a proposal. But, after Herzl showed Chamberlain the location of El Arish on a map, the most probable location in Sinai for a colony, the Colonial Secretary showed interest in the scheme. For Herzl, any place on the borders of Turkish *Palestine* would suffice.

Herzl later met with the Foreign Secretary, Lord Landsdowne and discussed the scheme. At this point however some of the difficulties involved in the proposal began to surface, like, what form would this colonization project take? Would it be a British colony? Or a colony with statehood as the objective? And, what of the legal difficulties. Egypt was still, legally, a part of the Turkish Empire. Therefore the settlers would need to become Turkish citizens, living under Egyptian law. Then there were the disputes between the Turkish and Egyptian administrations concerning the exact boundary line separating the two regions. Nevertheless delegations were dispatched to determine the feasibility of the venture, especially concerning the possibility of irrigating the region for a large number of people.

Britain's Imperial Concerns - The Boer War

During the latter decades of the nineteenth century Britain and the European powers increased their penetration into Africa. During this period Sir Cecil Rhodes, the British Premier of the Cape Colony alienated the Dutch residents of South Africa, also known as Boers, who rallied to oppose British rule. The burning issue resolved around who would govern South Africa - Britain or the Boers. As a result the South African, or Boer War began, in 1899. Almost immediately the Australian colonies, New Zealand and Canada offered volunteer forces.

The first Australian colony to offer troops was Queensland, where one of the prime movers was an officer named Harry Chauvel. The Australian colonies, on the verge of receiving a degree of independence from Britain, sent several thousand volunteers. These were primarily mounted infantry, men from the bush who knew how to ride a horse and exist in harsh country. The New Zealand volunteers, the New Zealand Mounted Infantry, were of a similar stock, and among their number was Edward Chaytor. In the midst of the War, on 1 January 1901, the Australian colonies federated and became the Commonwealth of Australia.

The British forces serving in South Africa were led by Field Marshall Lord Roberts, whose Chief-of-Staff was Major General Lord Kitchener. Amongst the thousands of British troops were Irishman John Patterson, who commanded a Yeomanry regiment for three years; Edmund Allenby 6th Royal Dragoons (Inniskillings); Philip Chetwode, and others who later played prominent roles in the region of the Middle East. One very interesting combatant was Winston Churchill, who escaped from a Boer prisoner of war camp in 1900 - and who within several months was seated in the House of Commons!

East Africa and Kishinev

Chamberlain toured British possessions in Africa in 1902 with the goal of restoring confidence after the Boer War. While in the region of East Africa he was informed that more settlers were required. He made a small note that this could be ideal for Herzl's Zionist settlers. During the same time it was becoming clear that a Jewish presence in Sinai would not be favoured by the British authorities in Egypt.

Upon returning to Britain he met with Herzl in April 1903, and explained to the Zionist leader of the area in East Africa as a possibility for the Zionist movement. Nevertheless Herzl, although by now aware of governmental opposition, pressed on with his Sinai scheme. But the events of the next three weeks changed all of his plans. During Easter terrible pogroms erupted against the Jewish people in Kishinev, Russia. The desperate plight of the Jewish people again went to the top of the agenda. The Zionist movement needed a quick breakthrough in order to succour their people following this traumatic event. Then in early May reports came through from Egypt that the possibility of irrigating the El Arish region was completely impractical. This report was the last nail in the Sinai colonization coffin, and in mid May 1903 the British Government finally rejected the Sinai scheme.

Chamberlain reaffirmed the East Africa offer to the Zionists. Herzl, dedicated on one hand to the welfare of the Jewish people, and on the other to the colonization of the Land of Israel, was caught in a dilemma. Yet he brought the proposal to the Zionist Congress at Basle in 1903. Although a majority of delegates voted to send a delegation to spy out the land in question, those in opposition, mostly Russian Jews, vehemently opposed. For them the Zionist movement was synonymous to Eretz Israel - Biblical Zion. There could be no other place for a Jewish national home. The Zionist movement was divided.

Soon afterwards the chief architects of this initial official 'agreement' between the Zionists and the British Empire, Chamberlain and Herzl, passed from the scene. Chamberlain resigned at the end of 1903, and Herzl died prematurely in 1904. Thereafter the Zionist movement passed into other hands. In time the two main streams, practical Zionism, epitomized by the more pragmatic Russians, and political Zionism, epitomized by the more idealistic western Europeans, converged. Together they laboured for the accomplishment of their goals. Slowly lands were purchased in Turkish *Palestine* and settlements established. All the while the political leaders pressed on with their goal of bringing the movement to the higher levels of politics.

Several years later a new and more enterprising form of Zionism emerged: Socialist Zionism. Led by men later known as Yitzak Ben Zvi and David Ben Gurion, this movement worked for a synthesis of the socialist ideals then developing in Russia, with the vision of a restored Zion. A fourth stream of Zionism, Cultural Zionism, was also being espoused. Led by Ahad Ha'Am, it was dedicated to forming a Jewish cultural centre, as opposed to a purely political entity, in Zion.

Britain and the Sinai

The Zionist-Sinai scheme confirmed British concern for the east side of the Suez Canal, her imperial jugular vein. Lord Cromer, the British Agent in Cairo, had, in 1892, made an agreement with the Turkish authorities, that the border of Sinai would run from Rafa down to near Aqaba on the Red Sea. While remaining part of Turkey, the Sinai would be administered by the Anglo-Egyptian authorities. It seemed to be a sound scheme.

But the Turks, in 1906, tested the degree to which Britain was willing to defend this agreement. They staged an incident at Taba. The Anglo-Egyptian Government immediately responded. 'This incident,' wrote Friedman, 'combined with the construction of the Hedjaz railway, re-emphasized the strategic importance of the Sinai Peninsular and opened British eyes to the possibility of a serious invasion of Egypt from the east by Turkey.'[7]

Over the following years a number of British military analysts attempted to determine what was the best form of defence of the Suez in the event of a Turkish, or Turkish led, invasion. There was not always a consensus. Some maintained that the present status quo was sufficient and that no sizable army could cross the Sinai. Others however maintained that the 1906 incident disproved this theory, and that the only effective barrier was the Land of Israel itself. Still others maintained that the most effective barrier was the maintenance and integrity of Turkey. Despite such concerns and opinions, British policy since 1882 had concentrated upon Egypt and neglected any serious interest in the Land of Israel.

Imperial Activities and Agreements

While the British presence in Egypt was consolidated, France, Germany and to a lesser extent Russia were now the main contenders for taking large slices of the Turkish Empire in the event of its fall. The Turks had granted Germany a major concession in 1899 to build a railway to the Persian Gulf - the ultimate goal being to link Berlin with Baghdad. A branch of this line spread to Alexandretta, near the Antioch of old, a strategic port at the Bay of Alexandretta where Anatolia and Syria meet. The main line south east passed through Aleppo, and by 1912 it was about to cross the Euphrates near the ancient city of Carchemish then being excavated by British archaeologists, one of whom was a young Oxford graduate named Thomas Edward Lawrence.

Meanwhile France invested heavily in Turkey by supporting various projects, including the construction of a railway from Damascus to Haifa at the base of Mount Carmel south of Acre. The concession also called for the construction there of a large port.

---

7   Friedman, I. *The Question of Palestine*. Transaction Publishers, (New Jersey, 1992), p. 2.

The early part of the twentieth century witnessed a continuation of the traditional rivalry between the British, French and Russians. But the growing strength of Germany, and the pending relationship between Germany, Austria and even Turkey, stimulated a drastic change of strategy between these three historical protagonists.

Britain and France made an initial yet important *Treaty of Agreement* in 1904 which removed a number of key confrontational situations between them. Russia and Britain finally realized the stakes were too high in their confrontations along the northern approaches to India, especially through Afghanistan, and signed the *Anglo-Russian Agreement* in 1907. There was, by now, the makings of a *Triple Entente* between the three former protagonists.

The Breakup of Turkey Begins

The growth of European investment in the Eastern Mediterranean was synonymous with the stagnation of Turkey. The Turkish Empire was crumbling. Many Turks could see the writing on the wall. One keen observer of this situation was a young Russian Jewish journalist named Vladimir (Zev) Jabotinsky who was then living in Constantinople. Jabotinsky was the editor of four Zionist newspapers, and was convinced by 1909 'that where the Turk rules neither sun may shine nor grass may grow, and that the only hope for the restoration of Palestine lay in the dismemberment of the Ottoman Empire.'[8]

The surrounding countries agitated to assist this dismemberment for their own nationalist and imperialist ambitions. Bulgaria declared its independence in October 1908. Then almost immediately, the Austro-Hungarian Empire annexed Bosnia and Herzegovina, a move which grieved Serbia, who coveted these two states as forming in the future part of a large Slav state. The move also upset Russia, Serbia's protector nation.

Also in 1908 a group of young Turkish army officers in Salonika rose in revolt and ultimately prompted a change in the Government of Turkey. Led by Enver Bey (Pasha) this movement, known as the Young Turks set up a *Committee of Union and Progress* (C.U.P.) and was committed to the reformation of Turkey.

The Young Turks, shocked by the events around them endeavoured to shore up the foundations of their tottering Empire. But the rot just continued. Italy, under a flimsy pretext, declared war against Turkey in 1911 and amongst her war gains, claimed Tripolitania/Cyrenaica (modern day Libya) and Rhodes Island (part of the Dodecanese). The Balkan League, comprising Bulgaria, Greece and Serbia followed suit and declared War against Turkey in 1912. After winning convincingly they helped themselves to portions of the former Turkish Empire. The following year saw the beginning of the Second Balkan War, after which Turkey managed to salvage

---

8   Jabotinsky, V. *The Story of the Jewish Legion.*, p. 30.

some of her lost possessions.

The writing was on the wall. The Turkish Empire was tottering and its collapse seemed inevitable. Self-preservation was now deemed impossible. Her only option was for the establishment of a strong alliance with an European power. Only Germany was acceptable. General Otto Liman von Sanders arrived in Turkey in 1913 as the spearhead of a large German effort to reform and reorganize the Turkish Army.

British, French and German Agreements

Since her occupation of Egypt, Britain had virtually relinquished the region of Syria and the Land of Israel to French, German and even Russian involvement. By 1912 however rumours were filtering into Syria that British agents from Egypt were stirring up Arab nationalists against France. Indeed there was a large group within Egypt (including perhaps Cromer's replacement Lord Kitchener) who were apprehensive about the prospect of having France facing them on the east side of the Suez. This group saw value in a union of sorts between Egypt and Syria.

To dispel French fears Foreign Minister Grey informed the French in December 1912, that Britain had no strategic interests in the region. The French Prime Minister Poincare told his Parliament on 21 December 1912, that concerning Lebanon and Syria 'the British Government has in a very friendly manner declared to us that in these regions it has no intention of taking any action nor has it any designs or political aspirations of any kind.' [9] The British Ambassador to Paris, Francis Bertie wrote to Grey on 26 December 1912, that 'Your assurances which Poincare quoted in the Senate that we have no designs in Syria have excited the appetite of the French newspapers. They appear to conclude that our disinteressement is equivalent to a free hand for France.' [10]

Despite Poincare's statement there were some ambiguities. Did he give the same meaning to Syria as did the British? And was Britain in fact surrendering Turkish *Palestine* - on the opposite side of the Suez, to France? Subsequent agreements between the French and Germans over the railway concessions however made the matter clear as far as the French were concerned.

France, sensing the dangerous proximity of the new German initiatives, initiated negotiations with the new European superpower aimed at lessening any potential conflict. An agreement was reached by February 1914 whereby Germany recognized

---

9   Stein, L. *The Balfour Declaration.* Vallentine Mitchell & Co,(London, 1961)., p. 48. Stein concluded : 'This account of what Poincare said is taken from his own extracts from his speech as set out in *Au Service de la France*, VI, 411-412. An editorial in *The Times* of 23 December 1912, notes with satisfaction that Poincare had been able to say that there was no difference between France and Britain concerning Syria. The passage in question is not, however, to be found in the official report of the Senate debate on 21 December 1912, and it may be that, though Poincare describes his statement as having been made to the Senate, it was made to the Foreign Affairs Commission of that body.'

10 PRO:F.O. 800/53.

the French zone of interest in the southern regions of the Turkish Empire, primarily in Syria, which for the French meant Turkish *Palestine*. In return France recognized the German zone as being to the north and east of the Turkish Empire.

It was over the issue of railroads however that Grey was forced to oppose French aspirations. The French and the Turks proposed extending the Ramle-Jaffa railroad in Turkish *Palestine* southward to El-Arish - and perhaps further westward still - towards the Suez. This possibility was repugnant to Grey and many other British imperialists. One member of Parliament, Mark Sykes highlighted his concern in a speech before Parliament on 18 March 1914, cautioning that French activities in Syria could result in Britain being faced with a 'European frontier in the Sinai Peninsular.'[11]

Despite the misgivings of Sykes, and others, France seemed the most likely inheritor of the Land of Israel in 1914, come the eventual dismemberment of the Turkish Empire. Only where the Holy Places were concerned was she likely to share ownership, with Russia or some international body. France, wrote Stein, 'was not slow to make it clear to her Allies that in any partition of the Turkish Empire her claims would extend to a Greater Syria, including *Palestine*.'[12]

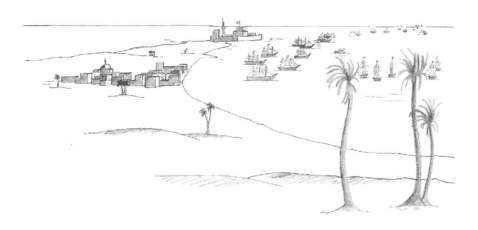

▲ *Battle of the Nile at Aboukir Bay, 1798*

---

11 Stein, L. *The Balfour Declaration*, p. 49.
12 Ibid., p. 44.

▲ *Battle of Mount Tabor, 1799. Napoleon's forces defeating Turkish Army.*

▲ *British forces landing at Aboukir Bay, 1801.*

▲ *The Evangelical Anglican Christ Church opposite the Tower of David, Jerusalem c.1850*

▲ *The Suez Canal*

▲ *The German Kaiser's entourage enters Jerusalem's Old City between Christ Church and Tower of David, 31 October 1898*

▲ *Jewish agricultural pioneers in Eretz Israel, c.1890*

▸ *Theodor Herzl meets Kaiser Wilhelm II, Eretz Israel, October 1898*

*C*hapter 8

The Anzacs are Coming

Europe at War

By the middle of 1914 it appeared that many of the international problems of previous years were dissipating. Yet, recalled an energetic Winston Churchill, the First Lord of the Admiralty, 'National passions, unduly exalted in the decline of religion, burned beneath the surface of nearly every land with fierce if shrouded fires.'[1] The fire finally burst onto the surface when on 28 June 1914 Archduke Franz Ferdinand of Austria was assassinated by Serbian radicals in Sarajevo, Serbia. The assassination set off an immediate ripple effect. Austria demanded a Serbian apology. Russia sided with her client nation Serbia. Germany backed Austria's demands - and when no side was willing to back down, the fuse blew, and the fire was no longer shrouded. In no time at all Europe went to war. 'The 4th August is one of the world's fateful dates.' Wrote David Lloyd George, the Chancellor of the Exchequer. 'The decision taken on that day in the name and on behalf of the British Empire altered the destiny of Europe.'[2] The respected evangelical Bible teacher Oswald Chambers wrote in the September 1914 edition of the evangelical magazine *Tongues of Fire,* 'This question is on the lips of people today "Is war of the devil or of God?" It is neither. It is of man, though God and the devil are both behind it. War is a conflict of wills either in individuals or in nations, and just now there is a terrific conflict of wills in nations.'[3]

Such a war was inevitable as the gluttonous appetites of the European Empires would ultimately need to be fully satisfied - at the expense of each other. Yet ironically Britain, France and Russia, the main protagonists during the previous one hundred years, were now lined up on the same side, members of the Triple Entente, the *Entente Cordial.* Opposing them were the armies of the Central Powers - Germany and the Austro-Hungarian Empire.

---

1   Churchill, W. *The World Crisis.*, p. 97.
2   Lloyd George, D. *War Memoirs.* Odhams, (London, 1939), p. 42.
3   McClasland, David. *Oswald Chambers: Abandoned to God.* Discovery House Publishers, (Nashville, Tennessee, 1993), p. 194.

Australia and New Zealand Enter

Feelings of commitment towards the 'Mother Country' and the Empire, ran high on both sides of the Tasman Sea. Even before war was declared the Australian Government offered the British Admiralty control of Australian vessels and offered

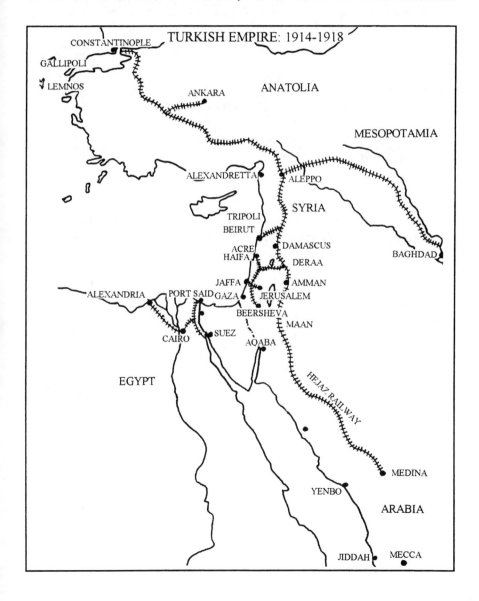

to raise an Australian Expeditionary Force of 20,000 men, the cost of which would be covered by Australia. 'There is indescribable enthusiasm and entire unanimity throughout Australia in support of all that tends to provide for the security of the Empire in war' wrote the Governor-General in a telegram to London on 5 August. [4] Recruitment for the Australian Imperial Force (AIF) to be commanded by Major-General William Bridges began on 19 August - the recruitment centres including show grounds and race tracks. The recruits came from all walks of life, and a variety of ages. The AIF would consist of infantry, mounted (the Light Horse), and auxiliary forces.

Albert Facey was part of a boxing troupe which travelled Australia and was in New South Wales when news of the outbreak of war was heard. Finally, when the rumours of sending an expeditionary force became fact, Facey, like thousands of other young men felt he should go. He wrote: 'we were fit, and another thing that appealed to us was that we would be travelling overseas and would be able to see what the other part of the world was like.' [5]

Amongst the twenty thousand and more other recruits were Leslie Morshead, Iven Mackay, Thomas Blamey and three interesting Jewish men, John Monash, [6] who was to command the 4th Australian Infantry Brigade; Eliezer Margolin who had left Turkish *Palestine* at the turn of the century and held the rank of lieutenant at the outbreak of war due to his involvement in the Territorials; [7] and Louis Salek.

Salek heralded from Wanganui in New Zealand where his father owned a farm. 'A stoker on a ship making regular runs between New Zealand and Australia, Louis was on the Australian side of the Tasmanian Sea when war was declared.' Wrote Stephen Levin. [8] There he 'heard that the Australian Army wanted accomplished horsemen ... He fitted the bill because before going to sea he had spent all his spare time on horses with the Maori people up the Wanganui river.' [9] Salek joined the Australian Imperial Force.

The mood for recruitment was just the same in New Zealand. The New Zealand House of Representatives agreed on 5 August to form an expeditionary force of some 8,000 men, to be commanded by Major-General Alexander Godley. Enlistment, primarily from the existing Territorial Army began almost immediately.

Like the Australian force, the New Zealand Expeditionary Force consisted of infantry brigades, a mounted brigade - the Mounted Rifles which consisted of the Auckland, Wellington, Canterbury and Otago regiments - and auxiliary forces. One contender for command of the infantry force was Colonel Edward Walter Chaytor,

4   Adam Smith, Patsy. *Anzacs*, Penguin Books, (Australia, 1991), p. 21
5   Facey, A.B. *A Fortunate Life*, Penguin Books, (Melbourne, 1981), p. 234.
6   By the end of the War in 1918 Monash had risen to command the Australian Corps in France.
7   Jabotinsky, V. *The Story of the Jewish Legion*, p. 102.
8   Levine, Stephen, 'The Flag Waved Free', *Jerusalem Post*, 23 May 1990.
9   *New Zealand Jewish Chronicle*. October 1992, p. 1.

from Motueka, but he was deemed a necessary asset in the Staff Corps. Another soldier, who became an officer in the Mounted Rifles, was Charles Guy Powles.

In New Zealand, as in Australia, there were mixed motives for enlistment. For some it was to defend the Empire. For others a sense of adventure. For yet others a chance to get away from home - and perhaps even from the authorities. Hartley Palmer was a farmer from Nelson, the only son of a family of nine. He wrote of his motives for enlisting: 'The British Empire wasn't in my thoughts: I didn't know a great deal about it. I wanted to have the trip around the world, and I thought it was a chance to have it. And I wanted to have adventure ... Sailing off to war with all the other Nelson boys made it even more of an adventure.'[10]

'I was schoolteaching in Northland,' recalled Tony Fagan, '... When I heard about the war, I went down to Auckland and joined up. I suppose you could say I was looking for adventure.'[11] Whatever the motive for enlistment, polling stations on both sides of the Tasman Sea had little difficulty finding the numbers to fill the Government's quota, and by late September both forces were ready for moving. Departure from the ports was delayed however while several German warships in the Pacific were neutralized.

First Convoy (not Fleet) Leaves for Britain

The New Zealand ships carrying 8,574 men and some 3,818 horses left Wellington Harbour on 16 October en-route to join their 20,000 Australian brothers, and their horses, who were moving towards Albany in Western Australia. 'There are over two thousand of us on board' wrote Victorian Thomas Gardner of this journey 'so it is rather cramped as we have a number of transport horses on board, and they take up a lot of room on the deck, so we can't get much exercise ... I believe there will be about thirty ships at Albany.'[12]

With the battlefields of France and Belgium before them, these wild colonial boys departed from Albany on 1 November 1914, the convoy of some thirty nine ships being one of the largest in modern times. It was in effect a reversal in history - the sons of the outcasts and adventurers were returning to Britain, to train and then fight for the 'Mother' Country. The convoy remained under the watchful eye of British, Australian and Japanese warships, as the German cruiser *Emden* was lurking somewhere in the Indian Ocean.

The month long journey was hot, boring and tiring, punctuated by a few incidents. A stop at Colombo was greeted with much cheer. There was also some excitement, as *HMAS Sydney* gave chase to the *Emden* which was stalking the convoy. 'When passing Cocos islands' wrote Fred Jones of Taranaki 'one of the convoy intercepted

---

10   Shadbolt, Maurice. *Voices of Gallipoli.* Hodder & Stoughton, (Auckland, 1988), p. 29.
11   Shadbolt, Maurice. *Voices of Gallipoli,* p. 17.
12   Morice, Janet. *Six Bob A Day Tourist* , Penguin Books, (Australia, 1985), p. 11

a message from the *Emden* to another German cruiser, and the *Sydney* was sent in pursuit ... sending the *Emden* ashore on the islands and disabling her.'[13]

Turkey Enters The War

As the convoy cruised through the Indian Ocean, Turkey entered - or was pushed as some claimed - into the War. Churchill, as First Lord of the Admiralty, cancelled a Turkish order for two large battleships in early August, requisitioning them for the British Navy. Although he offered the Turkish Government full compensation, the Turks were incensed as they had been financed by contributions from the general populace. Soon afterwards two German battleships, the *Goeben and Breslau,* being hounded in the Mediterranean by British ships, managed to elude the net and made for Constantinople. There the German crews donned Turkish caps and claimed that the Turks had purchased the two ships.

The presence of German battleships in the Mediterranean was so menacing that many ships took evasive action. Two passengers aboard a Russian steamer plying the waters between Constantinople and Jaffa, were watching with interest these and the associated political developments. David Ben Gurion and Yitzak Ben Zvi, founding members of the *Poale Zion* or Labour Zionist movement, had just completed three years studying law in Constantinople, and were returning to Turkish *Palestine.*[14]

Unbeknown to Churchill or the British at the time, one of the Turkish leaders, Enver Pasha, had concluded a secret agreement with the German Ambassador Wagenheim on 2 August. Turkey at this point was ruled by a triumvirate of envious rulers - Enver Pasha, Minister of War and commander of the Third Turkish Army; Djemal Pasha, Minister of Marine and later Commander of the Fourth Turkish Army, headquartered at Damascus the capital of the province of Syria; and Talaat Bey, Minister of the Interior.

Members of the British Government and in particular Churchill, and David Lloyd George, foresaw that Turkey would ultimately join the Central Powers. They proposed the formation of a Balkan confederation comprising Greece, Bulgaria, Romania and Serbia. The purpose of the confederation being to attack Turkey, and to ensure there would be no overland route between Germany and Turkey. Churchill, on 6 September mentioned to Grey the possibility of Russia joining this alliance and helping to capture the Gallipoli Peninsular.

'The price to be paid in taking Gallipoli' wrote Churchill 'would no doubt be heavy, but there would be no more war with Turkey. A good army of 50,000 men and sea power' and, he predicted ' that is the end of the Turkish menace.' [15] Both

---

13   Jones, Fred. Letter to sister Rita. Auckland War Memorial Library MS 89/105.
14   Teveth, Shabtai. *Ben Gurion: The Burning Ground 1886-1948.* Houghton Mifflin Company, (Boston. 1987), pp. 87-88.
15   Churchill, Winston. *The World Crisis,* p. 284.

Churchill and Lloyd George also saw the danger of one or more of the Balkan countries either joining with, or being defeated and overrun by the Central Powers.

Foreign Minister Grey was not supportive of these suggestions. He feared the issue of Constantinople. When, for instance, the Greeks offered their army to capture the Dardanelles and Constantinople, Grey refused the offer, fearing that if they succeeded and conquered Constantinople, their former imperial capital, they might decide to keep it. Russia, Grey feared, might eveñ contemplate changing sides in the War if it appeared that an Allied country might seize Constantinople.[16]

Any military option, no matter how logical it sounded and appeared on paper, was sure to incur problems when associated with the old jealousies, rivalries and ambitions associated with Constantinople and her environs, which included the Bosphorus and Dardanelles.

Circumstances soon precipitated action. The two German-Turkish ships bombed Russian ports on 27 October. Russia declared war upon Turkey on 2 November. Britain followed suit on 5 November. Turkey then revoked all previous agreements, including the *Capitulations* with the Triple Entente countries. On 9 November Prime Minister Asquith speaking at the Lord Mayor's Banquet in London declared: 'It is the Ottoman Government and not we who have rung the death knell of Ottoman dominion not only in Europe but in Asia.'[17]

One member of the Cabinet, Herbert Samuel took this declaration to heart, and wrote on that day:

> I spoke to Sir Edward Grey to-day about the future of Palestine. In the course of our talk I said that now that Turkey had thrown herself into the European War and that it was probable that her empire would be broken up, the question of the future control of Palestine was likely to arise. The jealousies of the great European Powers would make it difficult to allot the country to any one of them. Perhaps the opportunity might arise for the fulfillment of the ancient aspiration of the Jewish people and the restoration there of a Jewish State.

Samuel impressed upon Grey that, 'British influence ought to play a considerable part in the formation of such a State, because' he concluded, 'the geographical situation of Palestine, and especially the proximity to Egypt, would render its goodwill to England a matter of importance to the British Empire.' He then spoke to Lloyd George at the Cabinet meeting that day about the subject of Israel's restoration. Samuel recorded that Lloyd George '... had referred in the Cabinet to the ultimate destiny of Palestine, and said to me that he was very keen to see a Jewish state established there.' [18]

---

16   Fromkin, David. *A Peace to End All Peace* Avon Books, (New York, 1989), p. 127

17 *The Times.* 10 November, 1914.

18 Viscount Samuel. *Memoirs.* Cresset Press, (London, 1945), pp. 140-142

Meanwhile Britain began the process of dismembering the Turkish Empire by proclaiming Egypt a British Protectorate on 18 December under the authority of a High Commissioner. Lord Kitchener, who had returned to Britain to become the Minister of War, was replaced by Sir Henry McMahon, who arrived in Egypt in January 1915.

The Suez Canal - Britain's Jugular Vein

The Turkish Empire boasted the two most strategic water-ways in the world - the Dardanelles-Bosphorus and the Suez Canal. Both became of high strategic importance at the outset of the war. The Suez Canal was Britain's lifeline to the Empire - to India, New Zealand, Australia, Ceylon, (today's Sri Lanka), Malaya, Singapore and Hong Kong. The German press prior to the war had often spoken of the Canal as Britain's jugular vein - cut it, they predicted and Britain would bleed to death. The Germans wanted either its capture or neutralization, for they knew that through that waterway the young men of the Empire would come to aid 'Mother' Britain.

Planning for such an assault had begun as early as August 1914. Djemal and the German Officer Kress von Kressenstein had jointly planned the operation, intended to simultaneously capture the Canal and to incite a local rebellion within Egypt against British rule. An assault through the Sinai was a logistical nightmare. Accordingly a *Desert Line of Communication Inspectorate* was formed, which set up hospital and supply bases, sunk artesian wells, and developed various methods to capture the winter rainfall.

Turkish *Palestine* became the main supply base, with the general population often suffering confiscation of needed property. It was a bleak period for the Land of Israel. '... the Turkish troops' wrote Meir Dizengoff, the mayor of Tel Aviv '... uprooted trees, destroyed gardens and orchards that we had planted with such effort, and generally impoverished both towns people and villagers.' [19]

General Sir John Maxwell had the task of securing the Suez Canal against the expected Turkish attack. His troops included Indian and British forces. The 42nd Division was sent out from England in September. It was comprised of many young and inexperienced men - inexperienced in fighting and the wiles of Oriental life. By the time they arrived in Alexandria they were thirsting for a good beer. Upon arrival, wrote Private Robert Spencer '...a lot of these Gyppos, Egyptians, were offering these bottles supposed to be whisky, but they were more methylated spirits. Some of the men got hold of them and I think there were one or two killed through drinking this so called whisky.' [20]

---

19 Yaari, Avraham., *The Goodly Heritage*, abridged and translated by Israel Schen, Zionist Organization, Jerusalem, 1958. , p. 355

20 IWM SR 11965 Robert Spencer. Quoted in Steel, Nigel & Hart, Peter., *Defeat at Gallipoli*, Macmillan/ Papermac, (London, 1994), p. 34

Not England but Egypt

While the soldiers from India and Lancashire were acquainting themselves with the Pyramids and Egyptian 'whiskey', concern was raised regarding the final destination of the Australians and New Zealanders. It was apparent that facilities in England for their training were inadequate, and so on 20 November Kitchener notified General Maxwell that for various reasons, one being the expected Turkish attack upon the Suez, these New Zealanders and Australians would disembark and train in Egypt.[21]

Bridges and Godley were informed of the decision following their departure from Aden. They were also informed that following training the troops were destined for the Western Front in France and Belgium, and that the force would henceforth be formed into a Corps - the Australian and New Zealand Army Corps under the command of Lieutenant-General William Birdwood. The Corps later received the code name A.N.Z.A.C.

By late November, as the convoy was steaming up the Red Sea, rumours began spreading amongst the soldiers that they were destined not for England but for Egypt. The Anzac convoy reached the port of Suez on 1 December and then proceeded onto Alexandria. 'We arrived in Alexandria' recalled Jones 'after good but rather monotonous voyage. It took 16 hours to steam through the Canal. The banks were lined with Indian troops guarding it against the Turks.'[22]

While the British and Indian soldiers maintained vigilance at the Suez, the Anzacs moved over the following days to their camps at Mena and Zeitoun closer to Cairo. After the awe of being in the land of the Pyramids had worn off, the reality of Egypt hit these south sea islanders. 'Great Scott! What a place', exclaimed New Zealander Pte P.M. Thompson, 'Foreign service is liable to land a man anywhere. We certainly did expect to find some grass, but not so this time - simply sand, sand, sand, everywhere. We are camped on the Sahara Desert.'[23]

Once the tent cities were established, the soldiers were into the daily routine. The drills thrilled none - but the incentive was there. 'We will be camped here for some time before proceeding to the Front, if we ever do' wrote Gardner to his mother on 14 December. 'We are eight miles out from Cairo in the desert' he continued, 'and do all our drill in the sand making trenches etc. When we are proficient we will go to the front. It all rests with ourselves.' He concluded positively, after looking at the option. 'I would not care to live here very long as there is nothing to see but sand ...'[24]

And so Egypt, which over the millenniums had witnessed countless wars and

21 Powles, Lieut.-Col. C. Guy. *The New Zealanders in Sinai and Palestine,* Whitcombe and Tombs, (Auckland, 1922), p. IX.
22 Letter of Fred Jones to sister Rita. Auckland War Memorial Museum Library MS 89/105.
23 Diary of Pte P.M. Thompson, Queen Elizabeth II Army Museum, Waioru. Quoted in Pugsley, Christopher, *Gallipoli: The New Zealand Story* Hodder & Stoughton/Sceptre, (Auckland, 1990), p. 72.
24 Morice, Janet., *Six Bob A Day Tourist,* p. 23.

foreign soldiers, now listened to the strange accents of soldiers from the uttermost ends of the earth - British, Indian, New Zealand and Australian. They were soon to be joined by another foreign accent, Hebrew, from nearby Eretz Israel.

Jewish People exiled from the Land of Israel

Some 85,000 Jewish people lived in Turkish *Palestine* at the outbreak of the War.[25] The majority of these were European and especially Russian nationals, many of whom enjoyed the privileges of protection from the European consuls, a condition of the *Capitulations*.

Conditions within the Jewish *Yishuv* began deteriorating after the outbreak of War. *Haluka* contributions were disrupted, while the extensive trade between the Jewish colonies and Europe came to a virtual standstill. The very months when most of the cash crops in Eretz Israel were being harvested for export, the countries of destination were locked in armed conflict. Worse still, the revocation of the *Capitulations* was a serious blow for the Zionist movement, which had, under the covering of the various European consuls, extended the Zionist programme throughout the land. Viewed by the Turkish authorities as a subversive foreign movement, it was faced with a major test.

Sensing the seriousness of the situation in Turkish *Palestine*, emergency measures were prepared by various Jewish organizations, primarily in the USA. Through the efforts of the American Jewish ambassador at Constantinople, Henry Morgenthau, support was channeled to the Jewish people in Eretz Israel. In late September 1914 the United States cruiser *North Carolina* anchored off Jaffa and off-loaded of some 10,000 pounds sterling in gold bullion for distribution amongst the Jewish people.

The actual distribution of the gold was carried out by an extraordinary man, Dr. Otis Alan Glazebrook, the American Consul in Jerusalem. Glazebrook, a devout Christian, and admirer of the Jewish people and the *Yishuv's* activities in the Land of Israel, not only admirably handled these finances (a portion of which was also given to the Christian and Muslim communities) but he courageously withstood all terror tactics against him by Djemal Pasha and his minions.

Following Turkey's entrance into the War, Djemal Pasha, commander of the Turkish Fourth Army stationed in Damascus, and ruler of Syria, demanded that all foreigners, especially those belonging to the Triple Entente nations, either relinquish their nationality and become Turkish citizens, or leave the country. Many of the Jewish leaders, including Yosef Chelouche and Meir Dizengoff of Tel Aviv, recommended that such foreign nationals adopt Turkish nationality. Ben Gurion and Ben Zvi went so far as to volunteer to the Turkish governor to help form a Jewish unit for the defence of Jerusalem.

---

25   Yaari, Avraham. *The Goodly Heritage*, p. 348.

Many responded to the call to adopt Turkish nationality. But apprehensions increased when, wrote Chelouche, soon afterwards 'an order was received from Istamboul, that all Ottoman subjects between the ages of 18 and 60 were to be drafted into the army.'[26] Chelouche and Dizengoff, who knew well the avarices of serving in the Turkish Army, remonstrated with the Turkish authorities - but to no avail.

This order was followed soon after by another from Constantinople ordering the immediate deportation of all nationals from the belligerent countries from Turkish *Palestine*. Beha-a-Din, a cousin of Djemal Pasha, and the governor of Jaffa, moved quickly into action. This order was in fact partly prompted by the appearing on 15 December of the United States warship *Tennessee* off the coast of Jaffa. Certain Turkish authorities, supposing it to be a Russian vessel, feared the possibility of a fifth column amongst the Russian nationals living in Jaffa and throughout the land.

In the early afternoon of 17 December, Beha-a-Din, recalls Chelouche 'sent out a large number of soldiers who spread all over the streets of Jaffa and Tel Aviv and indiscriminately rounded up all Jews of foreign nationality, adults and children, and locked them up in the Armenian monastery'.[27] Chelouche and Dizengoff pleaded unsuccessfully with Beha-a-Din for their release, or at least for the reunification of families. All the while the Turkish soldiers heaped indignity upon indignity by fleecing the unsuspecting Jewish people.

They were then taken from the monastery, placed in Arab boats and rowed out to an awaiting Italian steamer with orders to take them to Egypt. The Arab boatmen then brandished knives and extorted money from the panic-stricken passengers, and terrifying mothers by threatening to throw their babies into the water.[28] The correspondent for the English *Evening Standard* wrote of this sad episode:

> Moans, tears, hysterical shouts filled the air. Then without any warning, the steamer weighed anchor and left. It was late in the evening and you could imagine the horror of the situation.
>   The boatmen tried to throw into the water all those who could not be placed aboard the steamer.'[29]

Interestingly, the same correspondent concluded his account of this scene by stating: 'But we are hopeful. The forcing of the Dardanelles means the deliverance of Palestine, which is bound to become a province independent of Turkish rule under the protectorate of a European power.'

The Jewish deportees from Jaffa were off loaded at Alexandria. Others followed. In late December Djemal ordered the deportation of all remaining non-Turkish

---

26 Yaari, Avraham., *The Goodly Heritage*, p. 349.
27 Yaari, Avraham., *The Goodly Heritage*, p. 350.
28 *Jewish Chronicle*, 22 January 1915, p. 10, and *Evening Standard*, quoted in *Jewish Missionary Intelligence*, 1915, p. 46.
29 *Evening Standard*, quoted in *Jewish Intelligence*, 1915, p. 46.

nationals. Many of these were taken aboard the *USS Tennessee*, including Lazar Slutzkin, his wife and seven children. Slutzkin, a prosperous businessman from Melbourne, owned a large house in Rehovot, from where he and his family were expelled by the Turks. Meanwhile, Ben Gurion and Ben Zvi, while protesting the deportations, continued their efforts to promote a pro-Turkish stance by the Jewish community.

By March 1915 there were some 10,000 Jewish refugees in Egypt, causing the British authorities to contemplate under whose jurisdiction they now fell - the Russian Consul, the British authorities, or the local Jewish community?

The refugees were initially placed in various locations, including a hotel and a theatre, and then later in better accommodation offered by the Government. The *Jewish Chronicle* wrote of an eye witness account :

> Everybody who chanced to be in the neighbourhood of the local post office the other day witnessed a most touching sight when several members of the Australian Expeditionary Force went round the small hotels in that district where our poor coreligionists from Palestine were lodged in order to transport them to the "Lazarets", kindly offered by the Government. The degree of kindness with which these fine fellows treated the poor heartbroken refugees and the efforts they made to comfort their poor charges were in marked contrast to the roughness with which they were handled by the Turkish authorities before they left Palestine.[30]

Some of the refugees were able to procure private residences. One such family was that of Lazar Slutzkin. From this house the Slutzkins worked to alleviate the problems of the Jewish community, and kept open house, primarily for Anzac soldiers. One soldier to make the most of this welcome was Louis Salek.[31]

Life became progressively more difficult for those still remaining in Turkish *Palestine*. The Turkish authorities, especially Djemal Pasha and Beha-a-Din, were deeply suspicious of Zionism, and indeed of any Arab nationalist tendencies. They subsequently 'seized men indiscriminately for forced labour,' recalled Chelouche, 'irrespective of their age, health or family responsibilities. The military authorities displayed especial severity towards the Jews. Those who had become Ottoman subjects, including those who had paid for exemption from military service, were taken ... into the Army or made to do forced labour, and were subjected to particularly brutal treatment.'[32] It was imperative for those remaining behind to demonstrate their loyalty to the Turkish Empire.

Plans for a Third Front

Although his September proposal for the opening of a third front aimed at Turkey

---

30 *Jewish Chronicle*, 29 January 1915.
31 Interview with Mrs Ruth Stark, granddaughter of Lazar Slutzkin, in Tel Aviv, 1996.
32 Yaari, Avraham., *The Goodly Heritage*, p. 356.

was thwarted, Churchill persevered in his viewpoint. Of his perspective at the beginning of 1915 he penned:

> The Turks have barred the Dardanelles. It needs but a cry from Russia for help, to make vital what is now void, and to make purposeful what is now meaningless. But as yet no cry has come.[33]

That cry for help was soon to come. Enver Pasha, commanding the Third Turkish Army marched out in mid December 1914 toward the mighty Caucasus mountains separating the Turkish and Russian Empires. He proposed crossing the mountains, crushing the Russians, and then continuing onto British India via Afghanistan. The beleaguered Russian Commander-in-Chief, Grand Duke Nicholas dispatched an urgent request to Kitchener on January 1, 1915, requesting that the Allies stage a diversionary attack against the Turks.[34]

Churchill and Lloyd George had both previously voiced their opinions favouring an attack upon the soft underbelly of the Balkan region. Maurice Hankey, Secretary of the War Council, then proposed, on 28 December 1914 an assault upon the strategic Dardanelles Peninsular, assisted by the Balkan allies.[35] Lloyd George submitted a Memo to the War Council on 1 January 1915 indicating the advantages of attacking Turkey.[36] Churchill wrote immediately to Asquith: 'I wanted Gallipoli attacked on the declaration of war ... Meanwhile the difficulties have increased.' He encouraged immediate action.[37]

The Russian request was discussed at the War Council meeting of 8 January, where Kitchener proposed the Dardanelles as a possible place to attack Turkey. Alexandretta was also proposed.[38] Churchill had meanwhile contacted Vice-Admiral Carden, Commander-in-Chief of the Mediterranean Fleet regarding 'the possibilities of a naval attack on the Dardanelles.' Carden provided an optimistic report of systematically destroying the forts and after several weeks proceeding onto Constantinople and destroying the German battleship *Goeben*. Both Lloyd George and Kitchener thought the idea worth a try.[39]

Churchill continued with his efforts and reported at the next meeting of the War Council on 28 January, as recorded 'that he had communicated to the Grand Duke Nicholas and to the French Admiralty the project for a naval attack on the Dardanelles. The Grand Duke had replied with enthusiasm, and believed that this might assist

---

33 Churchill, W. *The World Crisis*, p. 289.
34 Churchill, W. *The World Crisis*, p. 325.
35 Gilbert, Martin. *Winston S. Churchill, Vol. 3; 1914-1916, The Challenge of War*. Houghton Mifflin, (Boston, 1971), p. 230
36 Lloyd George, *War Memoirs*, p. 224.
37 Churchill W. *The World Crisis*, p. 325.
38 PRO:CAB 21/1 No 21347. 8 January 1915.
39 PRO:CAB 21/1 No 21347. 13 January 1915.

him. The French Admiralty had also sent a favourable reply, and had promised co-operation.' [40]

Lord Balfour provided six advantages for such an attack, concluding 'It would put Constantinople under our control.' The offensive was intended to be a purely naval affair- no ground troops were designated for none would be released from the Western Front.

But while the initial preparations were being made, the very purpose of the assault, the Turkish threat to Russia, ceased being a major factor. The Turkish Third Army was decimated at the battle of Sarikamish in late January 1915 and ceased to exist. Yet despite this reversal, the Dardanelles operation would continue, planning having already begun in earnest. Besides, the advantages of forcing Turkey out of the War were now more apparent.

The Suez Attack

While Enver Pasha licked his wounds, rival Djemal Pasha saw this as an opportune time to stake his claims for supremacy within the triumvirate. It was time to unleash his Fourth Turkish Army against the Suez Canal, the jugular vein of the British Empire. The Turkish 8th Corps Suez Expeditionary Force began assembling at Beersheva and moved out towards the Suez in mid January 1915. The major base in the Sinai was at Jif-Jaffa, location of huge water cisterns along the ancient inland route, from where the surprise attack upon Ismailia was to be staged. British aerial reconnaissance however spotted the Turkish troop movements - and the element of surprise was lost.

The Turkish force emerged from a thick cloud of sand in the early morning of 3 February 1915, and commenced their assault by sliding pontoons and rafts into the Canal. Awaiting them on the opposite bank were the British and Indian soldiers, (with some Anzacs in reserve), who began systematically firing at the oncoming Turks. Only a few Turks made it onto Egyptian soil - and they were quickly dealt with.

Hartley Palmer saw his first action at Ismailia. 'The Turks' he recalled, 'tried to cross the canal right in front of the Motueka platoon of the 12th Nelson Company. No Turk got across. My platoon was 200 yards away and I never fired a shot. But I could hear all the shooting a short distance away. There was only one New Zealander killed, and that was Bill Ham, the first New Zealander to fall in battle.' [41]

The anticipated surprise assault was a complete fiasco, and the Egyptian uprising no more than hot desert air. The defeated and dejected 8th Suez Expeditionary Corps made its return trip to Beersheva. Gone were the hoped for rewards of victory promised

40   PRO: CAB 21/1 No 21347. 28 January 1915.
41   Shadbolt, Maurice. *Voices of Gallipoli*, Hodder & Stoughton, (Auckland, 1988), pp. 29-30. Reproduced with permission of Curtis Brown Ltd, London, on behalf of Maurice Shadbolt. Copyright Maurice Shadbolt.

by Djemal Pasha. Djemal also had the embarrassing task of withdrawing his previous premature announcement of victory.[42]   And the defeat did not bode well for the inhabitants of Eretz Israel.

His search for scapegoats included the Zionists. Beha-a-Din, the newly appointed 'Secretary for Jewish Affairs' outlawed Zionism, forbade all Zionist activities, and closed all Zionist institutions.   Infringements against these standing orders was punishable by death and Arabs were encouraged to ransack Jewish homes.[43]   In Jaffa, Dizengoff wrote that the new Governor Hasan Bek and his minions, 'plundered, confiscated, carried out arrests, and beat up people right and left, making the town and the surrounding area desolate.' Describing the paranoia of the Turks, Dizengoff described how, 'It was forbidden to kindle a light in the houses at night, lest it be used as a signal to the warships which sailed along the coast of Jaffa from time to time. Hasan Bek,' concluded Dizengoff remorsefully, 'plunged the town in darkness by night and in fear by day.'[44]

Djemal Pasha was especially agitated by the presence of Ben Gurion and Ben Zvi, and ordered their expulsion.   They were summarily exiled to Alexandria, en-route to the United States where they were to establish a *Poale* Zion recruiting office - to fight with the Turks against the Triple Entente! Hundreds of other victims of Djemal's suspicions were less fortunate. '... hundreds of young men' wrote Sacher 'were marched off in chains to prisons in Damascus, others exiled to Brusa and Constantinople, yet others sentenced to a living death in the granite pits of Tarsus.'[45] The expulsions and harsh measures against the Jewish community may indeed have been worse had it not been for the active intervention of Consul Glazebrook, and Ambassador Morgenthau.   It was now even more difficult for the Jewish subjects to show their loyalty towards the Turkish Empire.

Djemal's failure to capture the Suez Canal provided a breathing space for the Allied commanders.   It also allowed them to focus their attention upon their other strategic goal within the Turkish Empire, the capture of the Dardanelles, the Bosphorus and Constantinople.

42   Bullock, David. *Allenby's War*. Blandford Press, (London, 1988), p. 19.
43   Yaari, Avraham. *The Goodly Heritage*, p. 357.
44   Yaari, Avraham. *The Goodly Heritage*, p. 358
45   Sacher, H. *A History of Israel*, p. 90.

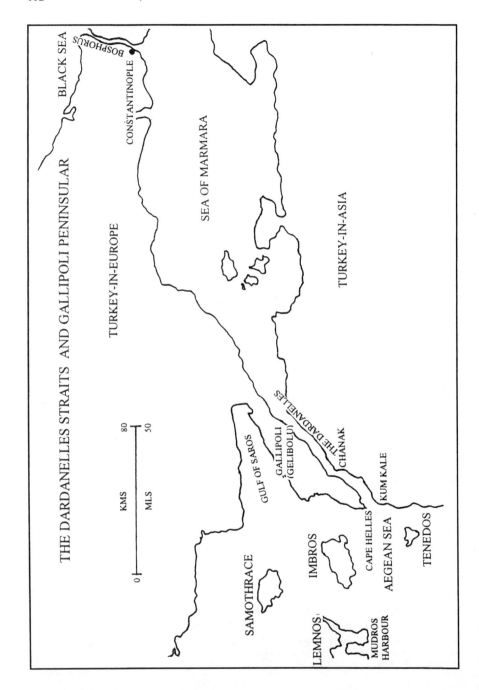

THE DARDANELLES STRAITS AND GALLIPOLI PENINSULAR

Chapter 9

Constantinople - Road to Zion

The months of February and March 1915 were characterized by confusion and muddling over preparations for the Dardanelles campaign. The War Council agreed on 9 February to offer the 29th Division (a French Division was also offered) to the Greeks to encourage them to enter the War on the side of the Allies, and to allay fears of possible repercussions from the Central Powers. The Greeks refused such a minimal offer.

Then Admiral Fisher, the First Sea Lord, informed Churchill that it was imperative to use some land forces. Following the War Council meeting of 16 February Kitchener agreed to release the 29th Division to the Greek island of Lemnos, in readiness for action if required. He also agreed to release the Anzac soldiers if they were required.

Immediately after making this offer Kitchener came under pressure from the generals on the Western Front. On 19 February, the very day when the naval bombardment began on the outer forts of the Dardanelles Peninsular, Kitchener changed his mind concerning the availability of the 29th Division.

Kitchener had meanwhile dispatched General Birdwood to the Dardanelles, to determine the best plan. When it finally became clear that ground forces were required, Kitchener, on 26 February informed Birdwood to prepare the Anzac soldiers for action. Churchill was appalled at the possible involvement of the inexperienced Anzacs - and disclaimed responsibility for the impending operation.

Under mounting pressure Kitchener finally conceded, on 10 March to agree to the release of the 29th Division as well as the Anzacs for the Dardanelles operation. The three week delay in the departure of the 29th Division from Britain would prove disastrous.

Naval Assault on the Dardanelles

The naval attack began on 19 February, causing immediate panic in Turkey. Edwin Morgenthau recalled that the citizens of Constantinople expected the city to fall at any moment. General Liman von Sanders also reported that preparations were being made to transfer the Turkish Government into refuge further inland.[1] 'The success

---

1   Sanders, Liman. von,. *Five Years in Turkey*, The United States Naval Institute, (Annapolis, Md, 1927), p. 72.

of the naval attack upon the outer forts of the Dardanelles and the first penetration of the Straits' wrote Churchill 'produced reactions of high consequence throughout Europe, and their repercussion was apparent all over the world.'[2]

In desperation, the Turks proposed, via Germany, making an alliance with Russia in return for Russia changing sides in the War. In return Turkey would guarantee Russia free passage through the Dardanelles to the Mediterranean. Then Bulgaria, Romania and Greece warmed towards the Allies. On 1 March the Greek Prime Minister Venizelos even offered three army divisions for the impending land assault. The Greeks, quite naturally, were viewing the spoils of victory - their ancient capital Constantinople. Not to be outdone, Bulgaria and Romania too were anticipating some shares in the fall of Constantinople and ultimate dismemberment of the Ottoman Empire.

French and Russian Concerns

France, aware of the imminent dismemberment of the Turkish Empire in the event of a successful campaign at the Dardanelles, dispatched its Foreign Minister Theophile Delcasse to Britain to meet his British counterpart Grey. They 'appear to have agreed' wrote Fromkin 'that if the Ottoman Empire were to be partitioned, Britain would not oppose France's designs on Syria, but that it would be far more preferable for the empire not to be broken up.'[3]

France coveted control of Syria, which included the Land of Israel. Her main opponent would be Britain, and as far as Grey was concerned, Britain was not interested. In the event of dismemberment, France seemed assured of attaining the province of Syria. Russia too had room for concern in the event of victory at the Dardanelles. But her main concern was not Syria, except, naturally, for the Holy Places in Turkish *Palestine*. Russia's main interest was Constantinople, and those strategic waterways, the Bosphorus and Dardanelles, which would determine the character of her future imperial ambitions.

With this in mind the Russian Government informed the British on 3 March, 1915 that they '... could not consent to Greece participating in operations in the Dardanelles, as it would be sure to lead to complications ...'[4] Churchill, like others, was outraged that the Russians could make such a demand.[5] At the War Council meeting on 3 March, Grey declared that now was the time to determine what Britain was willing to concede to Russia, who, Grey understood, clearly wanted access to the Mediterranean.[6]

2   Churchill, Winston. *The World Crisis.*, p. 382.
3   Fromkin, David *A Peace To End All Peace.*, p. 95.
4   Churchill, Winston. *The World Crisis*, p. 385.
5   Ibid., p. 387.
6   PRO:CAB 22/1 No 21347, 3 March 1915., p. 2.

Russia considered itself as the inheritor of the Byzantine Empire, and Constantinople as her rightful possession. But similar ambitions were held by Constantine, the King of Greece and the King of Bulgaria. So in the event of the capture of Constantinople, the question now being asked was: 'Who would inherit ancient Byzantium and enter triumphantly into Constantinople?' Besides all these ancient and sentimental attachments, Russia's concern was that Britain, having attained Constantinople, the Bosphorus and Dardanelles, may keep them for herself, and in the future hinder Russian passage into the Mediterranean and the wide world beyond.

At that 3 March meeting Grey stated that now there was 'a growing feeling in Russia that they ought to control the Straits.' He did not believe the issue of Russian aspirations could await the eventual peace negotiations, but that everything should be done now to ensure Russia would not make a separate peace. 'It would' Grey said 'never do for us to drift into a position of again checking Russian aspirations in the Dardanelles as we had in the past.'[7]

The emphasis that day concerned the future of the Dardanelles, and the position which Britain should adopt towards possible Russian aspirations there. The underlying fear was of Russia making a separate peace with the Central Powers if she felt her 'allies' were not fairly listening to her aspirations.

In conclusion Grey would inform Russia's Foreign Minister Sazanov that Britain would not veto a Russian demand for Constantinople. However, considering France's desire for Syria, Britain would need to 'insist on all sorts of economic questions being settled,' and would 'have to consider our claims in Asia Minor.'[8] Discussions then turned to the character of the proposed occupying force, of the possibility of Greek and Russian troops joining the campaign, and of the conditions to be offered to Turkey.

Russia's Ultimatum

The future of the Turkish Empire took on a new context following the arrival of a telegram to the Foreign Office on 5 March, from Sir. G. Buchanan, the British Ambassador to Russia. Foreign Minister Sazanov had given Buchanan the following *aide memoire*:

> Course of latest events leads His Majesty the Emperor Nicholas to think that the question of Constantinople and the Straits must be definitely solved in accordance with traditional aspirations of Russia.
>
> Any solution would be unsatisfactory and precarious if it did not incorporate henceforward in Russian Empire the city of Constantinople, western shore of the Bosphorus, of the Sea of Marmora, and of the Dardanelles, as well as Southern Thrace up to the Enos-Midia line.
>
> *Ipso facto* and by strategic necessity, part of Asiatic shore included between the

---

7   PRO: CAB 22/1, 3 March 1915., p. 2.

Bosphorus, River Sakharia, and a point to be fixed on the Gulf of Idmid, islands of the Sea of Marmora, islands of Imbros and Tenedos, ought to be incorporated in the empire.

Special interests of France and Great Britain in the region above described will be scrupulously respected.

Imperial Government likes to hope that above considerations will meet with sympathy of the two allied Governments. Said Governments are assured of meeting with, at the hands of Imperial Government, the same sympathy for realisation of desiderata which they may form in other regions of Ottoman Empire and elsewhere.[9]

The prime purpose of the War Council meeting of 10 March was, stated Asquith, to 'consider the political, as well as the strategic, questions likely to arise after the fall of Constantinople.'[10] The discussions and results of this, and the following important Cabinet meetings, played a very important part in determining the future status of the Ottoman Empire, including the Land of Israel, and the ultimate Jewish restoration. Sir Edward Grey placed the matter in its wider context, by reminding the participants, 'In dealing with this question it had to be remembered that Germany was very desirous of concluding a separate peace with France and Russia.'

He also stated that one of Russia's 'principal hopes from this war was to obtain an outlet to the sea.' Also, that Russia had previously vetoed Greek, Bulgarian and Romanian participation in the proposed campaign, for fear that they 'might prejudice her claims for Constantinople.'[11] Russia also feared British opposition due to Britain's historical attitude towards a Russian outlet from the Black Sea to the Mediterranean Sea.

Lord Balfour stated he had no real objections to the Russians receiving her aspirations concerning Constantinople and the Dardanelles, but, he concluded 'We ought to consider what we wanted, for example, in the Persian Gulf and elsewhere.' Lloyd George concurred and stated that the Russians 'were so keen to obtain Constantinople that they would be generous in regard to concessions elsewhere. It was vital for us,' he continued, 'if we made concessions, to say what we wanted in return.'[12] On the matter of concessions, Asquith responded, 'the establishment of Russia at Constantinople, and the granting of all she asks, would make it desirable for us to have an additional naval base in these waters, viz., Alexandretta, the probable terminus on the Mediterranean of the Baghdad Railway.'[13]

The discussion now opened up into discussing Britain's desiderata. Grey reminded everyone that 'France would of course ask for Alsace and Lorraine, and perhaps for

---

8   PRO: CAB 22/1, 3 March 1915., p. 3.
9   Sir. G. Buchanan to Sir. Edward Grey, 4 March 1915. Telegram 249. Produced in Appendix, PRO: CAB 22/1, No 21347, 10 March 1915, p. 8.
10   PRO: CAB 22/1, 10 March 1915., p. 3.
11   PRO: CAB 22/1, 10 March 1915., p. 3.
12   PRO:CAB 22/1, 10 March 1915., p. 3.
13   PRO:CAB 22/1, 10 March 1915., p. 4.

Syria.' Others responded that it was important for Britain to quickly decide what she wanted. Although Alexandretta was a foremost British consideration, Churchill, Grey and Lloyd George all concluded that the French would strongly oppose this request. Lloyd George then steered the discussion towards another area, and 'suggested Palestine as an alternative owing to the prestige it would give us.' Kitchener disagreed stating that 'Palestine would be of no value to us whatsoever'. He favoured Alexandretta. 'With Russia in Constantinople, France in Syria, and Italy in Rhodes,' he stated, 'our position in Egypt would be untenable if any other power held Alexandretta.'

After much lengthy discussion Grey proposed that whatever is suggested to Russia concerning Constantinople be kept secret, otherwise it might upset the other Balkan countries. Also, that there be free passage through the Straits for all nations; that Constantinople be a free port for goods in transit; and that Arabia and the holy places remain in Muslim hands.

In concluding this crucial meeting Asquith suggested, the Minutes record, 'that a hint should be given to Russia that we are abandoning a traditional attitude and that a large section of public opinion in this country would be opposed to it.' It was then agreed to inform the Russian Government that Britain agrees with her proposals presented in the *aide memoire*, provided the War is successfully completed, and provided that Britain receives her *desiderata*. Britain (and France) would soon begin determining exactly what those *desiderata* would be. It was also agreed that the War Office would prepare a Memorandum concerning the strategic significance of Alexandretta.[14]

The key point here was not so much Britain's acceptance of the Russian demands, but her need to determine her own *desiderata* within a dismembered Ottoman Empire. What those *desiderata* actually were was now a matter for her to determine.

As Russia was such an important, yet unreliable ally, her demands were taken very seriously by both the British and the French. Britain relayed her agreement to their demands on 12 March. The French however procrastinated. They first wanted to be sure of Russian consent to her demands to Syria. The French ambassador to Russia informed the Czar concerning France's historic connection and claim to Syria, and of the assets she presently held there. The Russians in turn basically acceded to the French claim upon Syria, yet stipulated that they would not permit a French-Catholic protectorate over the Holy Places of Palestine.[15]

Failure of the Naval Attack

While the British, French and Russian politicians were busy slicing up the Ottoman Empire to suit their imperial ambitions, matters were not progressing according to

14   PRO:CAB 22/1, 10 March 1915, pp. 5-7
15   Stein, L., *The Balfour Declaration.*, p. 63

plan in the Dardanelles. On 18 March a large Allied naval force was about to enter the Narrows near Chanak to destroy the fortifications there and then proceed into the Sea of Marmara and onwards to Constantinople. Unbeknown to them a small Turkish mine-sweeper had re-laid some mines the evening before. A number of Allied ships hit these submerged mines, sinking some and causing the Vice-Commander Admiral de Roebuck to order the withdrawal of the remainder for re-grouping. On that day the Turkish commanders, desperately short of ammunition, had been informed by their superiors to fire their remaining shots and then abandon their positions.

While regrouping De Roebuck confided to Sir Ian Hamilton, the newly appointed commander of the Mediterranean Expeditionary Force, and to Birdwood, that the Navy could proceed no further with the operation without the assistance of the Army. Hamilton in turn insisted that he needed time to prepare, and ordered the 29th Division to sail to Egypt to complete preparations.

French and British Desiderata

On 19 March the day after the abandonment of the naval operations in the Dardanelles, the War Council again met in session. The meeting discussed the military situation - but even more time was spent on the political considerations, under the heading **The Partition of Turkey in Asia**. Asquith explained 'that the French Ambassador in Petrograd had laid claim to a very large part of Turkey in Asia as French desiderata in return for permitting a Russian occupation of Constantinople and the Straits. These desiderata included Cilicia, Syria, and Palestine. The Russians objected most strongly to the Christian Holy Places being in French hands.'[16]

Foreign Secretary Grey suggested the possibility of setting up a Muslim Spiritual entity within Turkey in Asia. This matter, as the following speakers also highlighted, had much to do with the Moslem sentiment in India. Kitchener was apprehensive about leaving the Khalifate[17] in Constantinople, where it could very easily come under Russian dominion - and who could then influence the Moslems in India. He was in favour of transferring the Khalifate to Arabia, where it could be supervised by Britain.

Asquith adequately summed up the sentiments of many by acknowledging that Britain already possessed enough territory, but, he stated, 'we were not free agents.' 'Russia,' he continued, 'intended to take a good slice of Turkey. France, Italy and Greece each demanded a piece. If, for one reason or another, because we didn't want more territory, or because we didn't feel equal to the responsibility, we were to leave the other nations to scramble for Turkey without taking anything ourselves, we should not be doing our duty.'

---

16 PRO:CAB 22/1 No 21347. 19 March 1915, p. 5.
17 Khalifate or Caliphate - centre of Islamic authority.

Concerning the crucial subject of Alexandretta, Mr. Balfour stated 'the French demand to control Cilicia as well as Syria, was excessive.' His remarks echoed a sentiment that henceforth began to grow. With Russia in control of Constantinople, French control over Syria was untenable with Britain's strategic interests. It was inconceivable that Russia be permitted control over Turkey without a counter balance.[18]

France, alarmed by the large Russian demands and distrusting Britain, and realizing that with the continuation of the war her bargaining power may be weakened, wanted the matter dealt with urgently.[19] Thus the French Ambassador, Paleologue again met the Czar on 16 March 1915. Paleologue reminded the Czar of France's historic link to Syria and especially *Palestine*, to which the Czar agreed, apart from reservations concerning the Holy Places.[20]

At later meetings however, Foreign Minister Sazanov made it very clear that the Russians would not acquiesce to all the French demands, especially concerning the Holy Places,[21] and that Russia would never agree to a Roman Catholic protectorate over 'Jerusalem, Galilee, the Jordan, and Lake Tiberius.'[22] In further meetings between representatives of the two great powers the French believed they had received Russian support for *Palestine* except the Holy Places, but the Russian position wasn't quite so clear. What they ended up with was a 'vague assurance that Russia was prepared to let them have what they wanted in Syria and Cilicia.'[23]

France, on 12 April 1915, informed the Russians that they accepted her terms, providing the war was carried through. But already the Russian demand was common knowledge. 'The Russian Premier speaks of Russia's bright, historical future there on the shores of the Black Sea by the walls of Tsargrad,' wrote the *Jewish Chronicle* reporter about the Russian term for Constantinople. He wrote on 'M. Yyves Guyot claims Palestine and Syria for France. The Turkish dominions are already on the dissecting table.'[24]

By mid April 1915 it appeared that soon the Russian flag would fly over Constantinople, the French flag over Damascus and most of the Land of Israel, and the British flag would continue flying over Cairo. But that scenario was soon to be challenged. The secret *Constantinople Agreement* compelled Britain to begin re-

---

18 PRO:CAB 22/1, 19 March 1915, pp. 5-7.

19 Adamov, E. *German Translation of Vol VI of the series of documents from the Archives of the Russian Foreign Office, publ. Moscow,* 1924. No 19. And Grey, E. *Twenty Five Years,* II., p. 230. Quoted in Stein, L. *The Balfour Declaration,* p. 243.

20 Paleologue, M. *An Ambassador's Memoirs,* I, p. 303, & Pingaud, A. *Histoire Diplomatique de la France pendant la Grande Guerre,* Paris, 1940, Vol. I, p. 253. Quoted in Stein, L. ibid., p. 244.

21 Pinquad, A. *Histoire Diplomatique,* I, p. 254, & Adamov, E., ibid., No 29. Quoted in Stein, L. ibid., pp. 244-245.

22 Poincare, R. *Au Service de la France.* Paris, Plon, 1926. VI, p. 118. Quoted in Stein, L. ibid., p. 245.

23 Stein, L. ibid., p. 245, referring to Adamov, E. Nos 29 & 31.

24 *Jewish Chronicle,* 12 March 1915, p. 11.

evaluating her long term policy in the Eastern Mediterranean, primarily to counter French and Russian interests in the region.

The first step towards the re-evaluation of these goals came with the formation by Asquith of an inter-departmental committee named the *De Bunsen Committee* headed by Maurice de Bunsen, on 8 April. Their goal was to determine Britain's *desiderata* within the Eastern Mediterranean. One member of this influential body of men was Mark Sykes, Kitchener's special representative.

Soldiers in Waiting

On 24 March, the very day that Hamilton's forces left Lemnos for Egypt to join the Anzacs, Enver Pasha requested that Liman von Sanders take control and consolidate the fortifications at the Dardanelles. Von Sanders installed a young and energetic officer named Mustapha Kemal to a section of the Dardanelles near the village of Gelibolu - Gallipoli. Von Sanders, Kemal and the Turkish soldiers prepared and waited for the impending Allied assault.

Meanwhile in Egypt the Anzac and other Allied soldiers became increasingly restless. 'Oh, I don't think we will ever get to the front.' A rather pessimistic Claude Pocock of the Canterbury Mounted Rifles bemoaned.[25] 'For the last month we have been merely filling in time' wrote Lieutenant William Johns of Pukekohe to his niece Iris on 20 March, concluding, 'they don't know what to do with us.'[26]

Boredom was a plague. 'Camp life at Mena, for the thirty odd thousand men in training there was very dull indeed,' wrote Anglo-Irishman John Patterson, a non-commissioned British officer then in Egypt. 'There was not much to relieve the monotony,' he continued, 'once the Pyramids had been climbed and the Australian colours had been planted on the summits, save an extra dose of sandstorm.'[27]

Some relieved the boredom by visiting the exotic tourist sites. Others frequented the Haret el Wasser - *Wozzer* to the troops. 'Getting to Egypt, seeing an Eastern city for the first time, was very romantic,' recalled Tony Fagan. 'I saw my first fighting there,' he continued. 'It was the Battle of the Wazzir, the quarter of Cairo where all these brothels and booze dens were.'[28] On 2 April part of the Haret el Wazzir was torched , primarily by New Zealanders (or so the Australians claimed !!) in revenge for certain "injuries" which they and their mates had received.

In June the district received another torching. It seemed that the soldiers who had signed up to fight, seek adventure and see the world, especially Europe, needed some outlet for their frustrations. And the Anzacs weren't alone in their boredom. Private Chadwick of the Lancashire Fusiliers wrote home 'All the boys are looking as well

25 Queen Elizabeth II War Memorial, Waiouru, New Zealand
26 Letter of William Johns, Auckland City Museum, MS 1392. 81/160.
27 Patterson, John. *With the Zionists in Gallipoli*. Hutchinson & Co,(London, 1916)., p. 219
28 Shadbolt, Maurice. *Voices of Gallipoli*, p. 17.

as can be expected, but we are all fed up with this monotonous life.'[29]

Jewish Hopes and Frustrations

The predicament facing the Jewish refugees was much different from that facing the British and Anzac soldiers. Most of the refugees had fled Russia, some due to the virulent anti-Semitism raging there, others due to a compelling Zionist ideology. In their hearts they desired to establish a Jewish society in the Land of Israel based upon the principles of equality and justice. Other Jewish refugees in Egypt were religious, and had made their homes in Turkish *Palestine* for religious rather than nationalist motives. But all now found themselves thrust out of the Land of Israel into British-controlled Egypt. And Britain was allied to the hated Russia.

Due to the position of neutrality espoused by the Zionist leadership, these refugees were unsure as to where their loyalties lay. All they knew was that they now hated Turkey as much as they hated Russia. Their status too was unclear. Under whose jurisdiction did they belong? Their national status was aggravated by the official Russian position. Dr Hirsch Loeb Gordon, who was expelled on December 31st 1914 later wrote:

> The Russian consul who came with us from Jaffa (Razumovsky), the one from Alexandria (Petrov) and the ambassador in Cairo (Smirnov) tried first to persuade and then to force the Russian Jews of military age to return "home" to defend the Czar. Horrifying police raids in the refugees camps were executed in the middle of the night, and able-bodied men registered and re-registered. Alexandria became a trap.[30]

It was into this confusing situation that two brilliant and colourful Russian Jews - Zev Jabotinsky and Joseph Trumpeldor - strode. Together they formulated one of the most controversial Jewish proposals for some years - the formation of a *Jewish Legion* to help liberate the Land of Israel.

Jabotinsky, now a journalist with the Russian newspaper *Russkiya Vyedomosti*, had been travelling through Europe when he heard of Turkey's entry into the War. He felt the time was now right for the formation of a Jewish regiment to help liberate their homeland. He then proceeded onto North Africa to ascertain the Muslim reaction to the Sultan's call of a *Jihad* or Holy War against the Allies. He discovered little response. Many Muslims, he concluded, had lost their faith in the Sultan and Turkey. Jabotinsky could see the death knoll chiming over the Ottoman Empire.

His anti-Turkish prejudices heightened following his arrival in Alexandria in late December 1914. His arrival coincided with the arrival of the first Jewish refugees

---

29 Moorhouse, Geoffrey. *Hell's Foundations: A Town, Its Myths & Gallipoli*. Sceptre. Hodder & Stoughton. (United Kingdom, 1992)., p. 59.
30 Gordon, Dr. H.L. *The Jewish Legions in the British Army During the World War (1914-1918)*, (New York, 1940), p. 2

from Turkish *Palestine*. As a British customs official was fumbling with Jabotinsky's passport, Jabotinsky overheard him commenting to another official: 'A few days ago a boatful of Zionists, almost a thousand of them, arrived from Jaffa - the Turks kicked them out of Palestine.'[31] Jabotinsky immediately volunteered his services to help the refugees and ended up at the Gabbari barracks outside Alexandria.

Being both an observant journalist and a Jewish nationalist, Jabotinsky was intrigued by the situation confronting him in Alexandria. 'Every morning,' he wrote of one impression, 'a huge army wagon used to arrive, driven by an Australian soldier and led by two gigantic Australian horses, for the express purpose of giving the smaller children of the camp a "ride". The Australians' he recalled, 'learned to call out in Hebrew, "Come on, children," and in a moment the wagon would be filled with tiny mites.' One Australian officer he came to know more personally was Lieutenant Eliezer Margolin, who, wrote Jabotinsky, would occasionally visit and 'who stood and watched, and babbled in broken Yiddish ...'[32]

Joseph Trumpeldor had arrived in Egypt under totally different circumstances. Trumpeldor had been a career soldier in the Czar's army, attained the rank of an officer, which was very uncommon for a Jewish soldier, and had distinguished himself during the siege of Port Arthur during the Russo-Japanese War in 1905. Imbued with Zionist beliefs he later moved to Turkish *Palestine* and worked on Kibbutz Degania near the Sea of Galilee, adjacent to the Arab village and railway station of Semakh. It was from here that he voluntarily left in January 1915 following the harsh anti-Zionist policies instituted by Djemal Pasha. Arriving in Alexandria, the one-armed Trumpeldor received special treatment from the Russian consul Petrov, due to his military reputation.

With the exception of individuals like Trumpeldor, the British authorities were in a real predicament as to the future of these Jewish refugees. The most probable solution, especially for those of conscription age, was repatriation to Russia. A delegation of Jewish men, including Jabotinsky, met with the British governor in opposing this scheme, and it was agreed that repatriation was not the best solution. But what was?

At this point Jabotinsky sought out Trumpeldor and propounded his *Jewish Legion* idea. In many ways there could not have been a better qualified Jewish person in Egypt than Trumpeldor to undertake the challenge of forming the first Jewish army for many centuries. He agreed and on 2 March a steering committee, comprising these two plus Chief Rabbi Pergolla and several others, was set up. Then a public meeting was held in the Mafruza barracks outside Alexandria, where a petition was drafted in Hebrew to form a *Jewish Legion* and to propose to Britain to use it for the liberation of the Land of Israel.

31 Jabotinsky, V. *The Story of the Jewish Legion*, p. 29.
32 Jabotinsky, V. ibid., p. 34

'We did not want to be relegated to transport services', wrote Trumpeldor, 'or to be sent anywhere they pleased. We wanted to go into action, to be among the combatants, and only' he continued, 'in the Palestine theatre of war. We wanted to fight for Eretz Israel, upon its soil. Step by step, we would conquer the country from which we had been forcibly exiled; we would liberate our homeland and our comrades who had remained, under terrible conditions, to protect the Yishuv.'[33]

Next Jabotinsky and Trumpeldor traveled to Cairo to meet and submit their proposal to Maxwell. Maxwell however was anything but encouraging, suggesting, instead, the formation of a unit for mule transport to be used on any front against the Turks. To some this offer was disappointing, soliciting debate and disagreement between the members of the delegation. Jabotinsky opposed the offer. 'We civilians' he wrote, 'felt that General Maxwell's offer must be politely declined. The term he used in French, *corps de muletiers*, had a most unflattering sound in our civilian ears: what a shocking combination - Zion, the rebirth of a nation, the first really Jewish troops in the whole history of the Exile, and "mules".'[34]

Jabotinsky, not feeling a part of this offer, left soon afterwards for Europe to agitate for his more grandiose plans of a fully fledged *Jewish Legion*. His travels took him to France, where he received a rebuff from French officials. But the aging Baron Edmund Rothschild encouraged him, saying, 'You must continue at all costs! See that it becomes a real Legion when the time of the Palestine Campaign arrives!'[35]

Zion Mule Corps Formed

Trumpeldor remained in Egypt and accepted Maxwell's offer, believing that any front led to Zion. The acceptance was historic. 'The formation in Alexandria' wrote the *Jewish Chronicle*, 'of the Zion Mule Transport Corps - a Jewish legion comprised almost entirely of Palestine refugees - marks an era in the history of the Jews, as well as that of England. Never has England been known to depart from its policy of admitting none but British subjects of Colonials into its army ...'[36]

Having now secured the formation of the unit, Maxwell needed to find a willing British officer to lead it. Unbeknown to him, he chose the most suitable candidate possible - John Patterson. Patterson was an Irish Protestant with a deep love for the Jewish people and firm believer in their restoration. 'From the days of my youth' Patterson later wrote of the appointment, 'I have always been a keen student of the Jewish people, their history, laws and customs. Even as a boy I spent the greater part of my leisure hours pouring over the Bible ...'

'It was strange, therefore,' he concluded, 'that I, so imbued with Jewish traditions,

---

33 Yaari, Avraham. *The Goodly Heritage*, p. 429.
34 Jabotinsky, V. *The Story of the Jewish Legion*, p. 42.
35 Jabotinsky, V. *The Story of the Jewish Legion*, p. 51.
36 *Jewish Chronicle*, 30 April 1915, p. 11

should have been drawn to the land where the Pharaohs had kept the Children of Israel in bondage for over four hundred years; and it was still more strange that I should have arrived in Egypt just at the psychological moment when General Sir John Maxwell, the Commander-in-Chief, was looking out for a suitable officer to raise and command a Jewish unit.'

'Now, ' he concluded, 'such a thing as a Jewish unit had been unknown in the annals of the world for some two thousand years - since the days of the Maccabees.'[37] Of Patterson the *Jewish Chronicle* concluded 'no man could be better suited to the task of taking a Jewish army to Palestine.'[38] Patterson took up his new command on 19 March and left immediately for Alexandria.

Recruitment for the *Zion Mule Corps* began in earnest after his arrival. By 23 March some 500 men had volunteered, and on that day they paraded at the Gabbari camp and were officially sworn into the British Army. Chief Rabbi Della Pergolla addressed the recruits, explained to them the meaning of an oath, the importance of keeping it, and impressed upon them that 'the honour of Israel rested in their hands.'[39] Soon afterwards, caught up in the euphoria of the moment, these young Jewish exiles, 'dispersed in groups along the streets of Alexandria,' wrote Trumpeldor, 'singing the songs of Eretz Yisrael. They joined company with English soldiers and sang with them the song that was then in vogue, "Tipperary". Within a few days a new camp sprang up in the vicinity of Alexandria, and from it could be heard words of command uttered vigorously and with precision in the Hebrew tongue.'[40]

The new camp at Wardian was soon filled with 500 Jewish recruits, five British and eight Jewish officers, including Trumpeldor, plus twenty horses and some 750 pack mules. The recruits included professionals and lay people, religious and secular, although the majority were secular Zionist nationalists. One of the religious recruits was a lad named Wertheimer, who hailed from the ultra-orthodox section of Jerusalem's Old City. Wertheimer was accompanied to the camp by his equally Orthodox father who insisted that they, the ultra Orthodox and non Zionist Jews too were prepared to lay down their lives for the liberation of Eretz Israel. Yet in such a camp as this, men of the likes of Wertheimer were at a distinct disadvantage - there was no provision for a kosher[41] kitchen. Wertheimer and the other ultra-Orthodox soldiers were forced to adopt a somewhat stringent diet.

The unit finally received standard British uniforms, but embellished with the Star of David insignia. Training then began in earnest on 2 April. 'Drilling and parades were the order of the day;' wrote Patterson, 'horses and mules had to be exercised,

---

37 Patterson, J. *With the Zionists in Gallipoli*, pp. 31-32
38 *Jewish Chronicle*, 30 April 1915, p. 11
39 Patterson, J. *With the Zionists in Gallipoli*, p. 35.
40 Yaari, Avraham. *The Goodly Heritage*, pp. 429-430.
41 Kosher - food prepared according to Jewish dietary laws.

fed and watered three times a day; the men had to be taught how to saddle and unsaddle them, load and unload packs; they had also to be instructed in the use of the rifle and bayonet.'[42]

Following a visit to the camp the *Jewish Chronicle* correspondent wrote of noticing one sergeant 'drilling a squad of raw recruits. His words of command' the correspondent continued, 'borne aloft by the breeze, though quite distinct, sounded strange at the moment. Were they taken from a new list of commands recently published and unknown to the writer? No - a little effort enabled me to recognize the words which proved to be Hebrew. The presence of a few men still wearing the Jewish garb, the Hebrew words of command ringing through the air and the continuous conversations held in Hebrew in the midst of a military camp soon transported me to a Biblical dreamland.'[43]

So while Trumpeldor, Wertheimer and their associates trained for the forthcoming campaign, in the first instance to capture Constantinople, the first step as far as they were concerned to the liberation of Eretz Israel, many Jewish people in Eretz Israel saw things differently. Fearing that the formation of such a unit would only exacerbate the already deep suspicious held by the Turks against them, many feared retributions. It was a valid concern. To help forestall possible retributions, many Jewish-Turkish loyalists marched through the streets of Jerusalem and Jaffa shouting their contempt towards these Jewish 'traitors' in Egypt.[44]

This contempt and concern was shared by two Jewish exiles, David Ben Gurion and Yitzak Ben Zvi in Alexandria itself. They believed the scheme was foolish because they expected Turkey to ultimately win the War. They were diametrically opposed to the other two vibrant Russian Jews then in Egypt, Jabotinsky and Trumpeldor. Jabotinsky and Trumpeldor believed that Britain and the Allies would win, and that it would be beneficial for the Jewish people to have Jewish units serving with the British, especially in the conquest of Eretz Israel.

But the first step in that ultimate conquest would begin at a small part of the Turkish Empire which few had ever heard of, near a little village named Gelibolu - Gallipoli.

42 Patterson, J. *With the Zionists in Gallipoli*, p. 42.
43 *Jewish Chronicle*. 30 April 1915, p. 11.
44 Sacher, H. *A History of Israel*, p. 92.

Chapter 10

Gallipoli

Moving Out

A vanguard of the Mediterranean Expeditionary Force (MEF) left in early April for Lemnos Island, which had been loaned by the Greek Government as the staging post for the offensive. The remainder of the troops began moving from their camps soon afterwards. The embarkation of the *Zion Mule Corps* from Alexandria caused great excitement amongst the Jewish community. 'Embarkation day came,' wrote Yaari, 'and that night, before they set sail, the Jewish soldiers sang the songs and danced the dances of Eretz Yisrael, the girls who had come to see them off adding to the gaiety of the occasion.' Wertheimer however did not join the festivities. When asked why not by Trumpeldor, he replied 'that he was afraid, -lest he should not acquit himself honourably if faced with a serious test, and so disgrace the Zion Corps and the Jewish people.'[1]

One group of disappointed soldiers were the Australian and New Zealand horsemen. The Allied commanders didn't believe the topography of Gallipoli suited the Light Horse and Mounted Rifles. 'I am afraid the Light Horse are rather at a discount in the present war,' wrote a dejected Harry Chauvel, commander of the 1st Light Horse Brigade.[2]

On Lemnos Island the troops of the MEF exercised and contemplated the forthcoming battle. The plan for the offensive called for the French to land on the Asiatic coast near Kum Kale, then after having knocked out the Turkish forts there, to withdraw and join the British force, the 29th Division, at Cape Helles. The main British force there would land at five locations, code named beaches S,V,W,X and Y at the head of the European side of the Peninsula. From there the force was to move up the Peninsula towards Constantinople. This would be the main thrust.

The New Zealanders and Australians would land some twenty kilometres up the west coast, near Gabe Tepe, code named Beach Z or Brighton Beach. Their objective was to capture the strategic Sari Bair mountain ridge, comprising the high points of

---

1   Yaari, Avraham. *The Goodly Heritage*, p. 430.
2   Hill, A.J. *Chauvel of the Light Horse*. Melbourne University Press, (Melbourne, 1978), p. 50.

Chunuk Bair, Hill Q and Koja Chemen Tepe also known as Hill 971. From this ridge the entire region, including the Dardanelles Straits, could be viewed and enemy positions bombed. This force would then move across the Peninsular and join the French and British as they moved northward towards Constantinople. Hamilton planned a diversion by the Royal Naval Division at Bulair well to the north of Gallipoli.

The Anzac Corps was comprised of two divisions, the Australian Division, comprising the 1st, 2nd and 3rd Australian Infantry Brigades; and the New Zealand and Australia Division (Anzac), comprising the New Zealand Infantry Brigade and 4th Australian Infantry Brigade. Although only a secondary movement, the impending attack was important for the Anzacs. Addressing his men General William Birdwood, in an order of the day stated:

> ... Lord Kitchener has told us that he lays special stress on the role the army has to play in this particular operation, the success of which will be a severe blow to the enemy - indeed, as severe as any he could receive in France. It will go down to history to the glory of the soldiers of Australia and New Zealand.[3]

Towards Gallipoli

The Allied convoy, led by the battleship *Queen Elizabeth*, and followed by other battleships, cruisers, destroyers and troops ships, began moving out from Mudros Harbour in the afternoon of 24 April. The Anzac and other troops stood in awe of the spectacle. New Zealander Captain A.B. Morton remarked: 'We felt as we watched it with fascinated interest, that this indeed was the first line of a new page in the history of the Empire.'[4]

As the troopship *Hymettus* carrying the *Zion Mule Corps* was leaving the harbour, it hit a sand bank, and all aboard, men and animals, needed to transfer to another ship. It was a superhuman effort for Patterson and his men in order to be ready for the appointed departure time. At this critical time Patterson was met with a request from Captain Edmunds, the medical officer in charge of the Australian Hospital stores.

Edmunds had been ordered to transfer his supplies to another ship - but had not been allocated any vessels for the transfer. He asked Patterson for the loan of his transport vessels. Under great duress himself, Patterson agreed, realizing that Edmunds' need was a greater one, for Edmunds had explained that so far as he was aware these were the only medical supplies available for the Australian troops. Some time later Patterson received news from Captain Edmunds thanking him for that special favour, which Edmunds said prevented a calamity on the first day of the landing. 'So I think that Australia and New Zealand owe me one' Patterson later

---

3   Morice, Janet. *Six Bob a Day Tourist.*, p. 32
4   Morton, Captain A.B. Diary and Letters (MS 1310) Alexander Turnbull Library, Wellington. Quoted in Pugsley, Christopher. *Gallipoli: The New Zealand Story.*, Sceptre NZ, (Auckland, 1984), p. 103.

wrote of the event, 'for the help I gave them on that strenuous night of 24 April, when I was buried up to my neck in work of my own.' Nevertheless, Patterson concluded, 'I felt very glad that I had risen to the occasion and put the needs of Australia and New Zealand before my own.'[5]

While the *Zion Mule Corps*, the Anzacs, the British and the French began moving towards their destinations, Bernard Freyberg, a young British-born New Zealand member of the Royal Naval Division, slipped into the dark cold water near Bulair and swam the three or so kilometres to shore. There he placed several flares to simulate the bivouac fires of disembarked soldiers, the intended decoy to trick Von Sanders. After achieving his goals, he swam back into the cold dark waters, and was miraculously spotted by the small naval cutter, and picked up.

Baptism of Fire - Cape Helles

The Navy meanwhile had been subjecting the heavily fortified Turkish positions at Cape Helles to a heavy bombardment. Early in the morning of 25 April 1915 the French and British troops began landing at their designated positions. The bombardment at V Beach, the village of Sedd-el-Bahr, was so severe that nothing it was presumed could have survived through it. The men of Dublin, Munster and Hampshire then boarded their boats and began making their way to the beach. 'As the steamers neared the beach' wrote Captain W.L. Weldon aboard one of the transport ships, 'the ships ceased fire, and once within 150 yards of the shore, the boats were cast adrift, when the soldiers got out their oars and raced each other to the beach.' But then in total astonishment Weldon observed how, 'the minute the boats started to row the silence was broken by a terrific rifle and machine-gun fire from the entrenched and concealed Turkish positions.'[6]

A disbelieving Weldon who observed the massacre at short range, recalled, '..the casualties were awful, they grounded and our men leaped out carrying their rifles with bayonets fixed, leaving many dead and wounded behind them.'[7] One ship, the collier *River Clyde,* was moved up to the beach almost simultaneously to these landings, and beached. The soldiers inside then began alighting down the gangplanks. Hundreds of these young men were gunned down by the entrenched Turks. All attempts to consolidate the position at this crucial point failed.

The Lancashire Fusiliers who landed at W Beach near Tekke Burnu, also encountered stiff opposition. Hundreds of young British soldiers were killed and maimed. Yet after suffering terrible casualties Lancashire Landing was secured, and men from the Royal Fusiliers and part of the Royal Naval Division, after securing their position, X Beach to the north, joined the men of Lancashire, Worcestershire

---

5   Patterson, J. *With the Zionists in Gallipoli,* p. 63.

6   Weldon, Captain L.B. *Hard Lying,* (London ,1925), p. 63

7   Weldon, Captain L.B. ibid., p. 63.

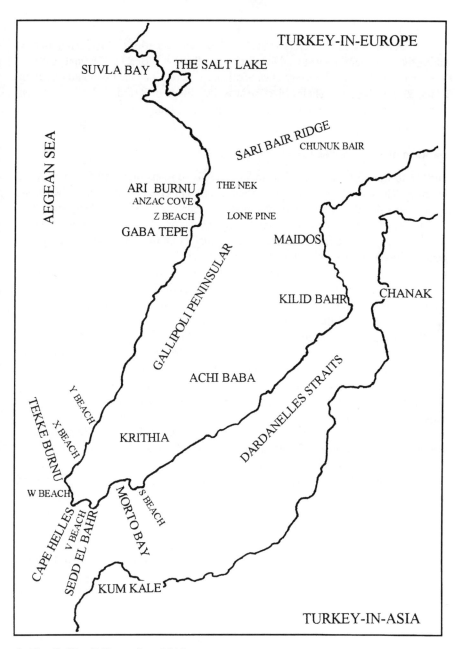

TURKEY-IN-EUROPE

SUVLA BAY   THE SALT LAKE

AEGEAN SEA

SARI BAIR RIDGE   CHUNUK BAIR

ARI BURNU   THE NEK
ANZAC COVE
Z BEACH   LONE PINE
GABA TEPE

MAIDOS

GALLIPOLI PENINSULAR

KILID BAHR   CHANAK

ACHI BABA

DARDANELLES STRAITS

Y BEACH
TEKKE BURNU
X BEACH   KRITHIA

W BEACH
CAPE HELLES
V BEACH   S BEACH
SEDD EL BAHR   MORTO BAY

KUM KALE

TURKEY-IN-ASIA

▲ *The Gallipoli Campaign, 1915*

and Essex.

The South Wales Borderers landed at S Beach near Morto Bay. After finally taking their positions, they moved forward to join those at V Beach. The final position, Y Beach, was taken by the Kings Own Scottish Borderers, and the Plymouth Battalion of the Royal Marines. Their objective was the village of Krithia, which was taken and then lost to a fierce counter attack, forcing them to retire to the beach and then to re-embark.

Baptism of Fire - Anzac Cove

Further to the north the New Zealanders and Australians prepared for their dawn landing. The men were roused from their sleep, and given a hot drink. Then from the bigger ships they clambered into small row boats manned by sailors, several of which were attached to picquets, small steamboats, which took them in tow. 'This was it,' Facey reminisced. 'We were scared stiff - I know I was - but keyed up and eager to be on our way. We thought we would tear right through the Turks and keep going to Constantinople.'[8] Several hundred metres from the shore the row boats were cast adrift and the sailors took to the oars. As the boats struck the sand banks Queenslanders from the 3rd Australian Brigade leapt into the often neck high water and struggled toward the shoreline.

The Turks had not been anticipating any landing at this point, and were better prepared several hundred metres to the south, at Brighton Beach. Yet there were about 200 Turkish soldiers at this landing, Ari Burnu, and they quickly positioned themselves against the landing force. The Australians kept moving up the hills, which they were surprised to find, having expected an open landing place. Birdwood later wrote: 'The boats did not go in the right direction. They didn't go due east but inclined left and landed a good mile further north than intended ... We hit difficult country at once in which I feared that the troops would be sure to lose their symmetry in the dark and this is exactly what happened.'[9]

'We got in without any loss in our boat.' Gardner recalls of his landing. 'We had picks and shovels ... and each of us had to take one and wade ashore. The bottom was stony and I slipped, nearly went under, but recovered myself and got ashore all right.'[10] Meanwhile the vanguard had scaled the immediate cliffs and were heading towards their objective, the Sari Bair Ridge.

Suddenly they were stopped by a number of Turkish soldiers who, while in the process of retreating, had been commanded to hold their ground by their officer, Mustapha Kemal. Kemal immediately had more reinforcements brought in, and the

---

8   Facey, A.B. *A Fortunate Life*, p. 254.
9   Letter dated 29 April, 1915, Birdwood Papers, 3 DRL 3376, Australian War Memorial (AWM). Quoted in *The Anzac Landing - the Great Gamble* by D. Winter, *Journal of the Australian War Memorial*, April 1984, p. 13.
10   Morice, Janet., *Six Bob A Day Tourist*, p. 34

advancing Anzacs were stopped. And that was as close at they got to their objective that day, and indeed for another three and a half months.

The remainder of the Anzac force landed during the course of the day. The New Zealanders observed the initial landings from their boats, before they too headed for shore. 'Ours was the first New Zealand boat ashore,' recalls Tony Fagan 'about eight thirty or nine in the morning.' One of the first scenes he saw were two boats full of dead Australian soldiers which drifted past their boat. 'It stunned us all,' he continued, 'those two boats of dead Australians. It was the first time I had seen death.'[11]

But there was no time for contemplation. The New Zealanders too had to scale the imposing hills, seek out the enemy, and establish a position. Another New Zealander who came ashore that day was Colonel Edward Chaytor, the Assistant Adjutant General, who assumed command of General Godley's headquarters while Godley remained aboard the ship *Lutzow*.

Baptism of Fire - *Zion Mule Corps*

While the beach and hills of Gallipoli on 25 April 1915 had been a baptism of fire for New Zealand and Australia, it also marked a baptism of fire for the Jewish Zionists from Eretz Israel. Although Patterson's troops were transport and not infantry, they too had to endure the terrible conditions of landing. The *Zion Mule Corps* men landed the following day, enduring shelling from the Turks on the Asiatic side in the process. 'I watched my men very carefully' recalled Patterson, 'to see how they would stand their baptism of fire, and I am happy to be able to say that, with one solitary exception, all appeared quite unconcerned and took not the slightest heed of the dangerous position they were in.'[12]

Once landed the *Zion Mule Corps* was called up to W Beach where stockpiles of ammunition and supplies were located. These they loaded onto their mules, and with the help of a guide, headed towards the front line. Shortly afterwards it began pouring with rain, hampering them severely throughout that first day of work on 26 April.

The Cost

By 26 April there was a general stalemate along the entire line of landings. As Turkish reinforcements kept pouring in, Birdwood in the Anzac sector recommended withdrawal. He foresaw a massive stalemate Western Front style. Hamilton however decided to dig in - so dig in they did. The cost for the first day of fighting for the two new nations of New Zealand and Australia was high. Of the 16,000 Anzacs landed on 25 April, some 2,000 lay dead. The beaches, hillsides, gullies and ravines of that

---

11 Shadbolt, Maurice. *Voices of Gallipoli*, p. 20.
12 Patterson. J. *With the Zionists in Gallipoli*, p. 98.

rugged landscape became one large graveyard for New Zealander and Australian. This rugged landscape soon received names such as Anzac Cove, Shrapnel Gully, Plugge's Plateau, Russell's Top', Monash Valley, Wire Valley, the Nek, Lone Pine, Chunuk Bair, Steele's Post, Walker's Ridge, the Farm, 7th Field Ambulance, Embarkation Pier, Baby 700, Quinn's Post, Courtney's Post, Johnson's Jolly, Hill 60, Shell Green, and entered into Australian and New Zealand folklore.

Added to these were the hundreds of mostly British dead at Cape Helles. The numbers of wounded too, astounded the authorities. They were unprepared for such a catastrophe. One of the wounded, Tony Fagan, was placed upon a barge and taken out to a troopship. But they were all crammed full with wounded. 'Eventually we arrived at a ship which had some space' he recalled, '... There were 600 wounded aboard that boat, two doctors, no nurses, no medical orderlies, no anesthetics, and there we lay. I wasn't touched all the way to Alexandria.'[13]

Reinforcements from Egypt

Following pleas from both Churchill and Fisher, Kitchener finally agreed to the release of more troops to Gallipoli, including the 42nd Territorial Division and an Indian Brigade stationed in Egypt. Then on 2 May Godley, commander of the Anzac Division, attempted, against advice, a breakout at Anzac Cove. The attack failed and the casualties were again, horrific. So much so that 1,000 volunteers were requested from the Anzac mounted forces still in Egypt to fill the gaps now in the Anzac infantry lines.

Chauvel and Major-General H.A. Russell, commander of the New Zealand Mounted Rifles Brigade, both volunteered their entire brigades rather than have them broken up. 'Thus began a memorable partnership in arms between Australian and New Zealand horsemen,' wrote A.J. Hill, Chauvel's biographer, 'which was to continue until the last blows were struck and the last battles won in 1918.'[14]

The first mounted men, minus their horses, arrived in early May, and were soon followed by the remaining Light Horse Brigades. '... jolly glad to step on shore among huge stacks of ammunition and stores,' recalled Ion Idriess of the 2nd Light Horse Brigade, after his landing had to encounter the standard dose of Turkish artillery. 'Men were toiling among the heavy stacks of stores, men trudged all over that tiny beach in ragged, clay-stained uniforms,' he wrote, 'their familiar Australian faces cheerful and grimy under sprouting beards.'[15].

The dismounted horsemen discovered a weary and exhausted infantry desperately holding onto their position - only several hundred metres from the beach front. When Chauvel's Brigade replaced the 4th Australian Infantry Brigade commanded by John

13   Shadbolt, Maurice., *Voices from Gallipoli*, pp. 20-21.
14   Hill, A.J. *Chauvel of the Light Horse*, p. 51.
15   Idriess, Ion. *The Desert Column*. Angus & Robertson, (Australia., 1973), p. 5

Monash only 1,800 men remained from the original 4,000. In no time at all the Anzac horsemen were at the front enduring the same ordeal as the infantry. And that ordeal included not just Turkish fire, but the standard heavy load of digging.

Other Fruitless Battles

The failure of the 2 May breakout convinced Hamilton of the fruitlessness to attempt more breakouts from Anzac Cove. He decided to stage one from Cape Helles. The attempt began on 6 May with the 29th British Division and French forces being reinforced by the New Zealand Brigade and 2nd Australian Brigade.

The objective, the village of Krithia and high point of Achi Baba beyond, called for an attack over open country and towards heavily entrenched Turkish positions. Most of the 50,000 Allied soldiers were very quickly pinned down and sustained heavy casualties. The Turkish resolve to protect their homeland was too great. The Turks themselves then attempted a massive assault on the Anzac positions on 19 May in a desperate attempt to drive them into the sea. They failed - again at great cost in human life, especially Turkish. This assault caused the Turks to realize that it was futile to attempt any further breakthroughs at Anzac Cove - and the stalemate continued.

Both sides had by now dug in, sometimes the trenches of the opposing sides being only metres apart. A war of attrition followed - minor skirmishes, lobbying of grenades into each other's trenches, sniping and bombing. Another futile Allied breakout was attempted in the Cape Helles sector in June. Again the objective was Krithia and Achi Baba. This time two British Divisions, the 29th and 42nd, plus two French Divisions threw all they could into the offensive. And again neither side gained a significant breakthrough, with each side suffering over 10,000 casualties. The Anzacs attacked the Turkish trenches as a feint - which succeeded in drawing off some Turks from the British sector. Further assaults were attempted in July, but all they achieved was to gain a few extra metres of land, and increase the casualty list.

Exploits of the *Zion Mule Corps*

Throughout this period the *Zion Mule Corps* continued to distinguish itself. One day volunteers were called to take several ammunition-laden donkeys through to the front line under Turkish fire. None were forthcoming until Wertheimer the man from the Old City of Jerusalem ushered forth and took the donkeys in lead. 'When Wertheimer appeared with his mules on the stretch of open ground,' Trumpeldor recalled, 'the enemy's fire redoubled. Shells fell thick and fast, exploding with frightful detonations.... The mules stiffened their backs and did not want to move. But the quiet, reassuring hand of Wertheimer held them and pulled them forward. He walked calmly, as if nothing were happening around him, and he paid no attention to the exploding shells. On either side of the open space the soldiers watched him with bated breath, saying in a whisper, 'Brave fellow, brave fellow'.'

Several metres from the trenches Wertheimer was hit. His wounded body was retrieved and he was sent on a hospital ship to Alexandria. He died soon afterwards. Later, Trumpeldor relates 'A letter arrived from his father asking to be sent his late son's *tefillin* (phylacteries). There was no suggestion of complaint or unrestrained grief. The man of *Chaluka* from Jerusalem had bravely shown his love for Eretz Yisrael.'[16]

The involvement of the Zionists at Gallipoli did elicit considerable interest, both amongst the other Allied soldiers, and from overseas. 'It may interest you to know that I have here, fighting under my orders', wrote Hamilton in response to a query from the New York Paper *The Day,* 'a purely Jewish unit. As far as I know,' he continued, 'this is the first time in the Christian era that such a thing has happened. These troops were officially described as the 'Zion Mule Corps,' and the officers and rank and file have shown great courage in taking water, supplies and ammunition up to the fighting line under heavy fire.'[17]

There were numerous interesting incidents associated with this unusual unit. Their lack of English caused many a problem in communication, and on occasion some embarrassment. Ultimately the Zionist soldier who knew no English, needed to be accompanied by one who did. And this was only natural, as the first language for most was either Yiddish (similar to German) and Arabic - and both Germans and Arabs were attached to the Turkish forces!

Sergeant S.I. Luck of the 1st Australian Base Hospital had the interesting task of censoring the letters of the wounded Zion men. '... it becomes rather ludicrous' he wrote to his father concerning the problems he was having in deciphering the language, 'when it turns out that German is the only language the patient can understand. Such was the case with one of our latest wounded from the Zion Mule Corps. He spoke Arabic, which was useless to us ... Thank goodness there was no intelligence Officer nearby.' [18]

Patterson and Trumpeldor left Gallipoli for Egypt in July to recruit reinforcements for the *Zion Mule Corps.* In Cairo Maxwell summoned the city's leading Jewish notables together, and Patterson and Trumpeldor were able to propagate the Zionist cause in the synagogues. Some 150 young Jewish men were recruited and after some brief training they embarked for Gallipoli.

Political Crisis

While the young men of Australia, England, Scotland, New Zealand, France, Wales,

---

16   Yaari, Avraham. *The Goodly Heritage*, pp. 431-432.
17   Patterson, J. *With the Zionists in Gallipoli*, pp. 213-214.
18   *Jewish Chronicle*, 6 August 1915, p. 11.

India, Ireland and the Land of Israel laboured to gain that strategic breakthrough in the Dardanelles, the politicians also faced serious problems. A severe munitions shortage, coupled with the losses on the Western Front and stalemate at Gallipoli, caused consternation amongst the opposition parties, who had until then supported the Liberal party's war effort. A major crisis was then precipitated when on 15 May Lord Fisher, the First Sea Lord, tended his resignation. Churchill was shocked. Many politicians, especially from the opposition, were deeply concerned. It seemed to confirm what many had suspected - that coupled with problems in the handling of the war effort in France and on the home front, the Dardanelles campaign had been poorly planned and executed.

To meet the emergency, Asquith, with Lloyd George's active support, called for the formation of a national unity government, which was formed on 19 May. Kitchener was retained, for he was far too esteemed by the public, while Churchill, the scapegoat, was removed from the Admiralty and replaced by Arthur Balfour. Soon afterwards Lloyd George was offered the new and imminently important position of Minister of Munitions, a task into which he immediately launched himself in an effort to quickly increase Britain's munitions production. In the process he became acquainted with an eminent Russian Jewish scientist and Zionist, Chaim Weizmann, who assisted greatly in the manufacture of acetone, a necessary ingredient for ammunition.

The War Council was thereafter renamed the *Dardanelles Committee*, and at its first meeting on 7 June Kitchener agreed to send three new divisions to Gallipoli.

The Land of Israel becomes a Political Issue

Despite the lack of immediate success at Gallipoli, the campaign itself had stimulated Britain to formulate her long term goals within the region of the Ottoman Empire. It was with this reason in mind that the *De Bunsen Committee* had been set up. The *Committee* finally submitted its report on 30 June 1915. They wrote:

> For over 100 years there has been one constant phenomenon in the political history of Europe. Dynasties have come and gone, States have expanded or been absorbed, boundaries have shifted backwards and forwards, but steadily, inevitably, whether as a result of war or of a peace congress, Turkey has lost territory in Europe ...
>
> ... The Committee have therefore sought for a solution which, while securing the vital interests of Great Britain, will give to Turkey in Asia some prospect of a permanent existence. They feel that the best chance of this lies in the adoption of the scheme of decentralization.[19]

This scheme of decentralization called for the creation of five largely autonomous provinces within a future decentralized Ottoman Empire. These provinces roughly

---

19 'Recommendation on Palestine by the Inter-Departmental Committee to consider the nature of British desiderata in Turkey-in-Asia in the event of a successful conclusion of World War I. (The de Bunsen Committee) 30 June, 1915.' PRO: CAB 27/1 No 220 B.

would be: (1) The region of Turkish *Palestine*. (2) The region of Syria. (3) The region of Armenia. (4) The region of Anatolia (the Turkish heartland). (5) A large part of Mesopotamia - modern day Iraq.

The *De Bunsen Committee* also proposed that the northern part of Turkish *Palestine* become part of a British zone of interest, and that Britain control a section of land from the Mediterranean coast around the Bay of Acre and the port of Haifa, through to the area of Mesopotamia. North of this zone, they proposed, would be a French zone, which would therefore separate the British zone from the Russians.

Concerning the Land of Israel the *Committee* expressed that they, 'desire to repeat that they see no reason why the sacred places of Palestine should not be dealt with as a separate question.' And as for the French claim for the Land of Israel, the *Committee* stated further, 'They have felt free to deliberate on the assumption that the French claim will be rejected, since they are convinced that the forces opposed are too great for France ever to make that claim good.' Concerning Turkish *Palestine* they stated 'for the same reason they consider that it will be idle for His Majesty's Government to claim the retention of Palestine in their sphere.' This land they surmised 'must be recognized as a country whose destiny must be the subject of special negotiations, in which both belligerents and neutrals are alike interested.'[20]

This recommendation of the *De Bunsen Committee* was a decisive point in the redirection of British policy within the region of the Ottoman Empire. They made it very clear that no solution for a dismembered Turkish Empire could allow France a leading or prominent role in the Land of Israel. If and when Russia took control of the Dardanelles (for a victory was still anticipated), Britain could not allow her other long term protagonist, France, proximity to the Suez Canal.

The *De Bunsen Committee* however was somewhat at a loss as to exactly how Britain was going to diddle France out of any leading role in Turkish *Palestine*, while achieving her own goals there. This would indeed be a difficult issue to tackle for the *De Bunsen Report* was just a recommendation, while Grey's 'commitment' of 1912 at this point was still binding - at least as far as the French were concerned. If and when the battle for the Dardanelles was successfully completed, and the Turkish Empire dismembered, then France no doubt would stand firmly upon that 1912 'agreement'.

While the Dardanelles campaign dragged on however, Britain could formulate a clearer position and then begin fresh deliberations with France with the aim of cutting her out of a definite position in Turkish *Palestine* come the final dismantling of the Turkish Empire. As part of this agenda Mark Sykes left Britain in June 1915 for a six months fact-finding tour of the Eastern Mediterranean. The French too, realizing that serious deliberations with Britain would soon be forced upon her, dispatched Francoise George Picot to the Middle East with the same aim. The diplomatic battle

---

20   Cmd 5974 (1939), Annex J, p. 51. Quoted in Stein, L., *The Balfour Declaration*, pp. 246-247.

was warming up, as too was the military battle.

A Last Attempt

Conditions at both Cape Helles and Anzac Cove worsened daily, especially with the onset of warmer weather. The continual bombing, mining, sniping, and grenade throwing meant that the troops rarely had any form of relaxation - the front line was only several kilometres from the sea. But it was the smell, the crampness, the lice and the flies which concerned the soldiers as much as the Turks. The flies bred by the millions, and moved with ease between the rotting corpses and open latrines and the soldiers cramped quarters. Once a can of bully beef was opened, it was liable to be instantly invaded by these green pests. Eating became a major task - and it often necessitated covering the body with some clothing and eating privately. In such conditions dysentery and disease were inevitable.

By mid summer, with the patience and endurance of the troops decreasing, the high command knew that something drastic needed to happen. Following the decision of the *Dardanelles Committee* on 7 June to send three new divisions to Gallipoli, there was another series of ludicrous delays and confusion. The original plan called for these fresh troops to land in the early part of July when there was no moonlight. Certain delays however caused this landing to be delayed till August, again when there was no moonlight. Unfortunately during that interim period, some nine fresh Turkish divisions arrived in the Dardanelles.

The Allies planned to land these divisions at Suvla Bay, north of Anzac Cove, on 6 August, while simultaneous diversionary offensives were to be launched from both the Cape Helles and Anzac Cove zones. These diversions proved to be the costliest assaults of the entire campaign.

The soldiers knew that the offensive would be a big one. 'My loving Mother, father, brothers and sisters and friends,' wrote Private T. Oliver of the 7th Australian Battalion on 3 August, 'Don't have any fear for me, I am ready for whatever comes and quite prepared to die for my king and country ...' [21] 'I expect to go thro alright,' wrote New Zealander William Malone to his wife, 'but ... if anything happens to me you must not grieve too much - there are our dear children to be brought up - ... I am prepared for death and I hope that God will have forgiven me all my sins.'[22]

On the afternoon of 6 August, the great offensive began as the Lancashire and Lowland Territorial Division advanced against the Turkish lines at Cape Helles. Unbeknown to them, the Turks had just brought two fresh divisions up to this line. The result was some fiercely contested skirmishes lasting up to one week.

The objective at the Anzac Cove zone was the capture of the Sari Bair Ridge.

---

21 McCleod, G. *Anzacs.* (North Ryde, 1985), p. 58.
22 Letter dated 5 August 1915, Queen Elizabeth II Army Museum, Waiouru. quoted in Pugsley, Christopher, *Gallipoli: The New Zealand Story*, p. 263.

British, Indian and Gurkha troops were attached to the Anzacs. The main thrust, by the Anzac Division and attached troops, was the actual capture of the high points of the ridge - Chunuk Bair, Hill Q and Koja Chemen Tepe or Hill 971. The Australian Division was to make a feint further to the south as if heading towards Gabe Tepe.

The events of the following days were disastrous for all parties involved. Thousands of young men were killed, maimed or seriously wounded near Lone Pine, the Nek, and Chunuk Bair. The Australian objective was to draw the Turkish troops away from the higher ridge. This they mostly achieved, but the casualty list was exceedingly high. At one point, at the Nek, hundreds of young Light Horsemen were mercilessly mowed down in a senseless operation. There had been an interval between the completion of the artillery and naval bombardment and the assault, and this interval enabled the Turks to move back to their trenches and systematically mow down the young Light Horsemen.

And when the New Zealanders climbed onto the Sari Bair Ridge near Chunuk Bair they too faced a massacre similar to the Nek. Colonel Malone of the Wellington's wisely refused to send his troops forward in another suicidal assault. And while through the remainder of 7 August these troops endeavoured to dig in and await reinforcements, they could observe Suvla Bay below them, and the British New Army divisions landing virtually unopposed. These British divisions achieved most of their initial objectives quite quickly. A number then moved inland while others remained on the beach - mostly oblivious to the bloody assaults only several miles away at Lone Pine, Chunuk Bair and the Nek.

Early in the morning of 8 August elements of the New Zealand Brigade and New Army Division made a desperate assault upon Chunuk Bair - and finally took it. Chunuk Bair, which had been reached on that first day of the campaign, but then lost, the key to the success of the Gallipoli campaign - was now in Allied hands. Although desperate hand to hand fighting thereafter ensued, the position was retained. 'The New Zealand Infantry Brigade ...' wrote Major Arthur Temperley, 'was for 48 hours ... at the throat of the Turkish Empire and had support been forth coming at the right time and place and had certain events turned out differently, the Turkish Army would have been beaten, Constantinople would have fallen and the war might have been shortened by two years.'[23]

But Turkish scouts had discovered the landings at Suvla Bay and soon afterwards Turkish reinforcements were rushing to the zone. Mustapha Kemal, the scourge of 25 April, was now made commander of the Suvla Bay zone as well as the Anzac Cove zone. And he knew full well the seriousness of losing any part of the Sari Bair Ridge to the Allies. It was a race against time. Reinforcements from the 13th Division, young men from Lancashire and Wiltshire meanwhile came up to Chunuk Bair and

---

23   A Personal Narrative of the Battle of Chunuk Bair, 6-10 August, 1915 (Ms 0017) by Colonel A.C. Temperley. Quoted in Pugsley, Christopher, *Gallipoli: The New Zealand Story*, p. 287.

relieved the exhausted New Zealanders, British and Gurkha troops on the evening of 9 August.

Finally on 10 August Mustapha Kemal's highly motivated forces overwhelmed these basically inexperienced young British soldiers - and Chunuk Bair returned to Turkish hands. And with that Turkish assault went the last real chance of victory in the Dardanelles campaign.

A last ditch Allied offensive was attempted in the Suvla Bay region on 21 August. For this offensive elements of the 29th Division were brought up from Cape Helles, the dismounted Yeomanry Division from Egypt, and the Anzac Division from Anzac Cove. But this offensive too ended in failure.

One of the casualties of the August fighting was Albert Facey, who had already lost one brother at Gallipoli, and who on 19 August found himself alongside hundreds of other wounded aboard the ship *Ulysses* heading for Lemnos island. 'We couldn't help thinking of our mates that we had left behind ...' he recalled. Shortly afterwards, while at No.1 Australian General Hospital in Heliopolis, Egypt, he received word that his other brother had been killed. [24] Ion Idriess was wounded in September and also moved to a hospital in Egypt.

Political Repercussions of Failure

The failure of the August offensive had serious consequences throughout the region, especially amongst the Balkan states, all of whom except Serbia, were as yet uncommitted to the War. The most unpredictable - and most strategically located, was Bulgaria. A neutral Bulgaria ensured there was no direct route between the Central Powers and Turkey. Once it became apparent that the Allies had failed at Gallipoli, Bulgaria moved to join the Central Powers. And once they did this the Central Powers felt at liberty to send forces against Serbia.

Greece could support Serbia in the event of an invasion, but firstly she required ample proof of Allied support if the Central Powers suddenly turned against her. The Allies then released two divisions from Gallipoli to prop up the Greeks at Saloniki. The question now confronting the Allies was how and to what extent, were they to support Serbia. And if so, was this to be at the expense of Gallipoli? Sentiment in Britain seemed to favour remaining at Gallipoli, while the French seemed more interested in Saloniki. The French won out and more troops were sent to Saloniki - but they had to sit on the sidelines and watch as the Central Powers and Bulgarian armies crushed tiny Serbia.

Meanwhile conditions at Gallipoli continued to stagnate on a daily basis. The enthusiasm and energy of the troops slowly deteriorated, while disease, especially dysentery increased to alarming proportions. It seemed that only a miracle could now redeem the Allied situation.

---

24 Facey, A. B., *A Fortunate Life*, p. 274-277.

Seeds of the Arab Revolt

By September rumours began filtering through of a possible Arab uprising in the Arab hinterland of the Turkish Empire. This was exactly what the Allied generals desired. Not only would such an uprising draw Turkish troops away from the Dardanelles, it could also cause enemy desertions, for many of the soldiers serving in the Turkish army were Arabs.

The concept of an Arab uprising had its origins at the beginning of the War. Germany and Turkey had endeavoured to persuade the Muslim leaders to proclaim a *Jihad* or Holy War against the Allies. To counter this Kitchener had approached the Emir Hussein, leader of the Hejaz tribe in Arabia and custodian of Islam's holy city of Mecca, imploring him not to use his spiritual prestige against Britain and the Allies.[25]

In January 1915 Hussein received news that the Turkish authorities intended to depose him at the end of the War. He sent his son Feisal to Constantinople to determine from the Turkish rulers if this indeed was true. En-route to Constantinople, Feisal stopped at Damascus, in March 1915, and while there met with leaders of the various secret Arab nationalist societies. These societies were dedicated to the overthrow of Turkish rule in Arab lands, and the establishment of independent Arab rule in its place. Apparently they were willing to barter with the British and the Turks, to determine who would offer them the best hopes of attaining their goals, and then pledge their allegiance to that particular side during the course of the War.

Feisal was obviously encouraged by what he saw and heard. But upon his return to Damascus from Constantinople en-route to Arabia, he discovered that the nationalist societies had been crushed by the ruthless Djemal Pasha. Many of the leaders had been banished to the Gallipoli front. It appeared that any hope of an Arab uprising from within Syria had gone.

Some of the remaining leaders proposed that Feisal initiate an uprising against Turkey from Arabia, and then they would join it. These leaders then presented Feisal with a document, the *Damascus Protocol* which defined the region of the proposed independent Arabian kingdom. Following Feisal's return to Mecca, Hussein seized the opportunity, and submitted a proposal to the British authorities in Cairo, requesting in effect that Britain agree to the establishment of an Arab Kingdom in the Middle East.

Hamilton, alerted to the possibility of an Arab uprising through revelations from a captured Arab soldier,[26] now pressured McMahon to take action. Kitchener too and other diplomats in Britain were anxious to see action taken. For all parties involved, and especially for Hamilton, an Arab uprising was highly desirable.

25   Fromkin, D., *A Peace To End All Peace*, p. 174
26   Fromkin, D., *A Peace To End All Peace*, pp. 176-8

McMahon however was being drawn into a situation he never particularly wanted, stating some years later:

> It was the most unfortunate date in my life when I was left in charge of the Arab movement and I think a few words are necessary to explain that it is nothing to do with me: it is purely military business. It began at the urgent request of Sir Ian Hamilton at Gallipoli. I was begged by the Foreign Office to take immediate action and draw the Arabs out of the war. At that moment a large portion of the forces at Gallipoli and nearly the whole of the force in Mesopotamia were Arabs...[27]

The Hussein proposal called for the ceding of the Syrian hinterland to the Arabs, which included the strategic cities of Aleppo, Hama, Homs and Damascus. This area was however highly desired by the French in the event of the eventual dismantling of the Ottoman Empire. It was a vital strategic region, lying between the desert to the east and the coast to the west. Moreover, the French constructed railway ran from Aleppo in the north, to Damascus in the south, where it joined the railway which proceeded onto Mecca and Arabia.

Kitchener instructed McMahon to respond to Hussein, and to specify which areas would be "promised" to the Arabs, in return for their support in revolting against Turkey. McMahon, in his letter to Hussein on 24 October 1915, stated that the Arabs would have to surrender their claims to the west of the districts of Damascus, Aleppo. Hama and Homs, that is, according to McMahon, the area of coastal Syria (including present day Lebanon) and the Land of Israel.[28]

Hussein did not fully accept McMahon's proposal for the Damascus-Aleppo line - yet he decided to join the British cause anyway. Meanwhile, a number of British politicians and officials were skeptical of any Arab uprising against Turkey. And this apprehension was well founded. By November it was clear that the Arabs would not rise in revolt unless and until British forces had first been landed on the Syrian coast. And if the Allies were divided amongst themselves over whether to reinforce Gallipoli or build up Saloniki, it was hardly likely that they would take on a new undertaking and land somewhere else in the Eastern Mediterranean.

Goodbye Gallipoli

Hamilton's last military option had now been expended. He had failed in every attempt to gain a breakthrough at the Dardanelles, and the War Cabinet had no choice now but to replace him. His replacement was General Sir Charles Monro, who arrived in the Dardanelles on 28 October. Soon after arrival Monro concluded that the only feasible option was withdrawal.

---

27 Kedourie, Elie. *The Chatham House Version and Other Middle East Studies,* Weidenfeld & Nicolson, (London,1970), p. 14. Quoted in Fromkin, D. *A Peace To End All Peace*, p. 178.

28 Fromkin, D., *A Peace To End All Peace*, p. 183.

Kitchener initially opposed any thought of evacuation. The *Dardanelles Committee*, now named the *War Committee*, and which was comprised of Asquith, Lloyd George, Balfour, Grey, Kitchener and later Bonar Law, met on 3 November to discuss the issue. It was agreed that Kitchener should proceed to the Dardanelles and determine for himself the position there. During his visit Kitchener heard protagonists advocating withdrawal, and others advocating remaining. He visited all the major battle zones.

His visit to Anzac Cove must have been a remarkable affair. Anzac soldiers, primarily privates, surrounded Kitchener, as one New Zealand soldier recalled, and with hands in pockets and in a leisurely fashion, they spoke about the esteemed one as many would discuss a prize bull in an agricultural show back home.[29]

Kitchener survived his tour of Anzac Cove and the Dardanelles, returned home and on 22 November recommended withdrawal, initially only from Suvla Bay and Anzac Cove. Apart from the military disadvantages, the onset of winter also became a major factor behind the decision to withdraw. Patterson was withdrawn sick in November, and recalled:

> A night or two before I left Gallipoli we had a sudden downpour of rain which made the trenches raging torrents, and turned the dug-outs into diving baths ... The men of L Battery, R.H.A., like all others, were flooded out in the twinkling of an eye, and I watched them, standing in their shirts on the edge of their dug-outs, endeavouring with a hooked stick to fish up their equipment and the remainder of their attire from a murky flood of water four feet deep - all the time singing gaily: "It's a long way to Tipperary".[30]

Towards the end of November a severe blizzard hit the Peninsula, covering it with several centimetres of snow and causing the temperature to plummet to the zero mark. The ground, roughed up by constant bombing and trekking, began turning into slush and mud. Hundreds of soldiers began reporting with frostbite, especially those who had not as yet received any winter clothing. At Suvla Bay alone many men died from exposure and frostbite - and 6,500 men were withdrawn due to the same effects. Prospects for the winter looked daunting indeed.

With Serbia's defeat and Bulgaria's entrance into the War on the side of the Central Powers, a direct route now connected Germany with Turkey. This in turn permitted the introduction of new and more powerful German artillery. The Australians felt the brunt of this when their positions at Lone Pine were shelled on 29 November, killing fifty-eight men and wounding 204.

The War Cabinet finally agreed to a withdrawal on 8 December - from all locations. The Allies then pulled off one of the great feats of modern warfare history - the

---

29   Burton, O.E. *A Rich Old Man,* unpublished manuscript, p. 117. Quoted in Pugsley, Christopher, *Gallipoli: The New Zealand Story,* p. 339.

30   Patterson, J. *With the Zionists in Gallipoli,* p. 290.

evacuation of an entire army without alerting the enemy and without the loss of one soldier. The soldiers from Anzac Cove and Suvla Bay completed their evacuation on the early morning of 20 December. The rest of the Allied forces were withdrawn from Cape Helles on 8 and 9 January 1916.

The Sentiments of Departure

Many Anzacs were indignant and disappointed to leave. Their mates lay dead and buried there. A "Special Order of the Day" was issued by Major-General A.L. Ball on 25 December, and stated:

> No soldier relishes a withdrawal before the enemy. It is hard to leave behind the graves of 9000 comrades and to relinquish positions so hardly won and so gallantly maintained as those we have left, but all ranks in the Dardanelles army will realize that they were carrying out the orders of H.M. Government so that in due course they could more usefully be employed elsewhere for their King, their Country and the Empire. There is only one consideration: what is best for the common cause. In that spirit was the withdrawal carried out and in that spirit the Australians and New Zealanders of the 9th Army Corps have proved and will continue to prove themselves second to none as soldiers of the empire.[31]

Altogether Britain lost 21,255 soldiers at Gallipoli, France 9,874, Australia 8,907, India 7,594, and New Zealand 2,701. The degree of suffering and loss incurred by New Zealand and Australia far surpassed anything in their brief national histories, and had a far reaching impact upon their national consciousness. This was their first campaign as sovereign nations - and they had to withdraw in defeat. Hence their reluctance to leave. For those whose mates lay dead and buried on the slopes and in the gullies of Anzac Cove, there was a debt to repay and a memory to erase. Next time they came up against Johnny Turk, Australia and New Zealand would not be found wanting - nor sneaking away in the middle of the night and betraying those dead mates. And this legacy was entrusted to a loyal band of surviving Anzacs, the Australian Light Horse and the New Zealand Mounted Rifles.

The *Zion Mule Corps* lost only eight men dead and fifty-five wounded. Nevertheless a Jewish unit from Eretz Israel, serving at Gallipoli under the Star of David, was a major psychological and political turning point for the Zionists. Trumpeldor had proved that Jews could fight. And his assumption that all fronts ultimately lead to Zion, passed the first test at Gallipoli.

And in the context of the restoration of Israel, Gallipoli was even more important for the British Government. Britain had been humiliated by a second rate Oriental army. This humiliation could only be compensated for by a future victory over the same foe, to be followed by substantial strategic and political gains.

---

31   Adam-Smith, Patsy. *Anzacs*, pp. 181-182.

Chapter 11

Defending the Suez Canal

Return to Egypt

The Gallipoli evacuees returned first to Lemnos Island, then to Egypt. 'The original 10th Light horse has arrived in camp from Gallipoli (or rather what is left of them),' wrote Reg Walters a 10th Light Horse reinforcement. 'They look pretty weary on it.' He concluded, especially after spotting an old mate from home who was 'looking a bit thin and tired but otherwise well.'[1]

Some of the wounded were now re-acquainted with their old units. 'With the old regiment at Ma'adi again,' wrote Trooper Idriess in January 1916 following recovery from his wounds. 'It was real lonely,' he reflected, 'wandering down the old familiar lines looking for familiar faces, and saddening to find only an odd one here and there.'[2]

The *Zion Mule Corps* also returned to Egypt. Their future however looked bleak. Although Trumpeldor repeatedly pleaded for their preservation as a unit, it was finally disbanded. About 120 members managed to re-enlist into other British units and slowly made their way to Britain.

Move to the Suez Canal

Prior to the return of the Gallipoli veterans, Senussi tribesmen from the desert area were threatening the Delta and Nile region, causing anxiety to the authorities. 'Arabs are attacking in the vicinity of Suez Canal,' wrote Walters on 16 December 1915, 'we are expecting a general upheaval any minute in Egypt.'[3] Such a threat reinforced the British concern for the defence of the Suez Canal region, now that the Turkish-German troops were also released from Gallipoli.

---

1   Diary of Trooper Reg Walters, 10th Australian Light Horse Regiment. Copy in author's possession. Hereafter *Diary of Reg Walters.*

2   Idriess, I. *The Desert Column*, p.50

3   *Diary of Reg Walters.*

The British then established a new three lined form of defence on the Sinai side of the Suez, one line at 11,000 metres east of the Canal, the next line at 6,500 metres east of the Canal and the third line on the Canal itself.[4] This system was soon to be radically improved by the arrival in January 1916 of General Sir Archibald Murray. Initially Murray shared command with Maxwell, but in March he took over completely.

Murray's task in Egypt was two-fold. Firstly, to retrain and prepare the Gallipoli evacuees for service in France.[5] Secondly, to guard the Suez Canal from Turkish attacks - and this with only the minimum of troops. From these few troops he formed a new force - the Egyptian Expeditionary Force (EEF), of which the vanguard, in defence of the Suez Canal was known as the *Desert Column*. The Suez Canal was divided into sector one with the Head Quarters (HQ) at Suez; sector two with the HQ at Ismailia, and sector three with the HQ at Port Said. Most of the Anzac Division was in sector three, which was under the command of Major-General H.A. Lawrence.

Following recuperation the Gallipoli returnees and reinforcements began moving eastwards, in January 1916, to take up new defensive positions on the Egyptian side of the Suez Canal. Describing the move of the New Zealand Mounted Rifles Brigade from Zeitoun camp, Lieut.-Colonel Guy Powles wrote   '... We looked across the green fields to the minarets of Cairo and the mighty Pyramids shimmering there in the sun; even as no doubt Moses beheld them when he, too, turned his face to the East and took his leave of Egypt.'[6] Walters unit moved some time later, and on 1 March he wrote: 'We are right on the banks of the Suez Canal. Had a swim in the Canal tonight going from Africa to Asia.'[7] Powles, Walters and the other Anzac and British members of the EEF were now entering part two of the Turkish campaign - to them was entrusted the Gallipoli legacy. Many had in fact been at Gallipoli.

Yet as shiploads of British 'Tommy' and Anzac infantry were being shipped off 'to the excitement' of France, some of the remaining horsemen became discontent with the mundane programme of drills, sand and heat. Many cleared out and stowed away in the troop ships. Anything, they thought, would be better than remaining in Egypt.

Formation of the Anzac Mounted Division.

Although the forward Turkish position lay well east of the Suez Canal, Murray

---

4   These new fortifications were supplied with fresh water piped from Cairo to Ismailia, where it was processed in a filtration system of plants, and then piped to the defences east of the Canal. The railroad to Ismailia was improved to hasten supplies, and in order to accomplish these logistical wonders, the Egyptian Labour Corps (ELC) was formed. Consisting of only 500 men at its inception, the Corps had, by June 1917, some 185,782 Egyptians in its employ. Bullock, David. L. *Allenby's War*, Blandford Press, (London, 1988), p. 23.

5   By June 1916 he had transferred nine infantry divisions to France and one to Mesopotamia.

6   Powles, Lieut.-Col. C.Guy, *With the New Zealanders in Sinai and Palestine*, Whitcombe and Tombs, (New Zealand, 1922), p. 7.

7   *Diary of Reg Walters*.

informed the Commander-Imperial-General-Staff (CIGS) General William Robertson in February 1916, that in his view El Arish, some eighty kilometres further east, would be a better position from which to defend the Canal. Control of El Arish, and El Kossaima inland, would seal the two main routes across the Sinai to the Suez Canal. The main route, the coastal road, the *Via Maris* of antiquity, was the more important, for although sandy, it had the better water supplies. Murray was permitted, initially, to take possession of a series of oases around Romani and Katia, some forty kilometres east of the Canal.

Meanwhile the deployment of the troops at the new defensive positions continued. On 6 March Walters' unit crossed the Suez Canal. 'Have now shifted camp across the Canal - 8 miles into Turkey-in-Asia on to the first line of defence.' He wrote rather excitedly. At this point the British began to re-organize their new defence system. Murray realized that the most effective way to achieve his goals was by the formation of a strong mounted force. On 18 March an exceptional unit, the Anzac Mounted Division was formed, 'the flower of Commonwealth chivalry,' claims Bullock.[8]

The Anzac Mounted Division (or Anzac Division), commanded by Major-General Harry Chauvel was comprised of the 1st Light Horse Brigade under Lieut.-General L.C Cox, the 2nd Light Horse Brigade under Lieut.-General Granville Ryrie, the 3rd Light Horse Brigade under Lieut.-General J.M. Antill, and the New Zealand Mounted Rifles Brigade, commanded by Lieut.-General Edward Chaytor. There were also auxiliary forces, including Royal Horse Artillery (R.H.A.-British artillery units), Machine-Gun squadrons, Signals Troop, Mounted Field Ambulance, Field Troop (Engineers) and a Mobile Veterinary Section.

The Anzac Division HQ was initially based at Salhia, west of Kantara from where Napoleon had organized his army for the advance to Syria in 1799. Lieut.-Col. Guy Powles came onto Chauvel's General Staff.

Another significant formation at this time was the beginnings of the Imperial Camel Corps (ICC), comprised initially of three Australian battalions and one British Yeomanry battalion. This force later grew and would prove of tremendous benefit during the Sinai campaign.

To consolidate the area of oases near the Mediterranean coast Murray commenced, in mid-April 1916, building a railway from Kantara on the Canal to Romani. A British reconnaissance force, men from the British 5th Mounted Brigade, proceeded ahead of the railway to protect it from Turkish attacks. To assist in the detection of possible Turkish attack, the Royal Flying Corps (RFC) began playing what turned out to be a vital role in the campaign.

The mounted men also aided by making large reconnaissance patrols into the desert wastes. 'During this period we made several very long patrols across the

---

8   Bullock, David. L. *Allenby's War*, p. 24.

desert,' wrote Henry Bostock of the Light Horse. 'Our first' he continued, 'was to locate a lost plane and airman ... We rode all one day, camped and skirmished the desert next morning and then were ordered back to camp.'[9]

First Skirmish

Observing all the EEF movements from further east while awaiting the arrival of his Gallipoli reinforcements and for the opportune time to attack was the German commander Kress von Kressenstein. On 23 April he struck the first blow of the campaign which would end several years later at Damascus and Aleppo. Crawling through dense fog, Turkish troops and Bedouins surprised and pounced upon the British forces. At Oghratina Oasis the British force, reduced to half by casualties, surrendered. Better luck at Katia (Qatiya) Oasis where some of the forces, although surrounded, managed to break out and escape. Substantial casualties however were received at Dudeidar Oasis.

News of the Turkish assault travelled quickly to the EEF camps. Idriess recalls receiving the order to move into the desert, and then galloping along the metalled road out of Kantara. The new reinforcements were quite excited, as indeed was Idriess and the other Gallipoli veterans.[10] Although excited by the prospect of seeing action, both the Gallipoli veterans and the reinforcements were appalled when they approached the first British position, Hill 70. Hundreds of Bedouins and soldiers, both Turkish and British died in this brief but fierce encounter. Although most of the enemy escaped, they managed to damage the prestige of the British Army.

Consolidation at Romani

The attack prompted Chauvel to bring the Anzac Division, which now included the 5th Mounted (Yeomanry) Brigade, to Romani, where he established his forward base. The railway thereafter encountered no further hindrances until its arrival at Romani in May. Soon afterwards the 52nd Lowland (Scottish) Division moved up and dug in from the coast through to Romani.

The presence of the Scottish infantry enabled Chauvel to send daily patrols eastwards into the vast Sinai desert region. One year after the Gallipoli landing Reg Walters wrote: 'Anzac Day 25th April. We are preparing to move out and meet our enemy the Turk in a day or 2, but perhaps as usual it will blow over.' These patrols often came across British soldiers, some still alive, in the region of the Oases. The Anzacs were disgusted to discover that many of them had been tortured to death by the Bedouins.

The move of the Anzacs to Romani caused the EEF strategy to be modified.

---

9   Bostock, H. *The Great Ride*, Artlook Books, (Perth, 1982), p. 33.
10 Idriess, I. *The Desert Column*, p. 55.

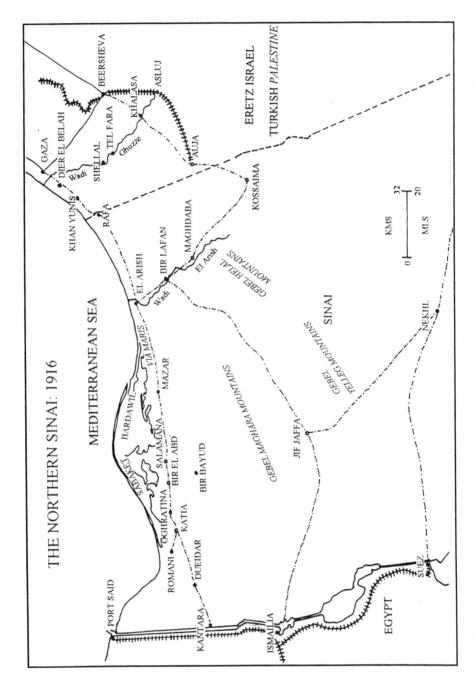

THE NORTHERN SINAI: 1916

Trenches were dug from the coast inland to the region of the Oases. When the inevitable major Turkish assault came, the EEF could then be covered by the Royal Navy on its left flank. Also, to ensure that the Turks would not use the inland route, daily patrols rode deep into the Sinai and destroyed all water facilities - wells and cisterns. One of the prime locations destroyed was at Jif-Jaffa, a former police station and strategic position on the central or Beersheva-Ismailia route.

'We are out here at the well' wrote Walters from Jif-Jaffa on 10 June 'and have just about pumped her dry preparatory to destroying it ... It was rather peculiar,' he continues, 'after travelling so many miles over a desert to strike this beautiful well.'[11] The following day the wells were completely destroyed - and any hopes of a Turkish thrust by the central route were destroyed with them. But the Turks weren't passive during this period. They too sent out patrols, while German planes, *Taubes*, were constantly bombing and photographing the EEF positions.

British Interest and the Arab Bureau

While the lines were being drawn in the desert, the politicians were busily attempting to determine future British interests in the region. Sykes at the completion of his six month fact finding tour returned to Britain with the suggestion that the discontented Arabs living under Turkish rule be encouraged to rise up and rebel.

He also perceived that British attitudes were divided concerning the future of the Middle East. One group maintained that Britain should control Syria (including the Land of Israel). This party seemed to favour a single Arab speaking entity, under the spiritual leadership of an Arab Caliph (Muslim spiritual leader), while temporal rule over this Arabic empire would be exercised by the king of Egypt - acting in conjunction of course with the British High Commissioner.

The other viewpoint seemed to favour joint British-French rule in the Middle East, based upon the 'agreement' reached between the two countries in 1912. Sykes also saw that there were many separate Middle East departments operating both in Britain and in Cairo, each with its own agenda. He proposed the establishment of a centralized department - to be known as the *Arab Bureau* - which would deal with all matters related to the Middle East. Asquith agreed and the Arab Bureau was set up in January 1916.

The task of this *Bureau* was to determine the best approach to consolidate British imperial interests within the Arab world, and how best to induce the passive, neutral Arabs into rising in revolt against their Turkish overlords. The first and most favoured candidate was Sherif Hussein of Mecca, to whom some assistance was sent. A young Thomas Edward Lawrence was soon involved in the *Bureau's* activities, impressing many with his knowledge of the Arab language, and the history, culture and mind-set of the Arab people.

---

11 *Diary of Reg Walters.*

New Arrangements with France

Sykes and others pressed the Government to act quickly upon the Arab interest to revolt. But Britain could make no further overtures to the Arabs until clearer arrangements had firstly been made with the French. Negotiations with the French over the British reassessment, as outlined in the *De Bunsen Report*, had already began in November 1915.

The French negotiator was Francois George Picot, a representative of that section of French society which believed in France's historic right to the area of Syria, which to them included the Land of Israel. There was even a French *Syria movement* in the Parliament. These, often prominent advocates, believed it would be a strategic mistake to allow Syria and Damascus to fall into the hands of any other power following the disintegration of the Turkish Empire.

Picot advocated direct French control over the coast from northern Syria to the Sinai, and even the Suez region, and indirect control over the hinterland of Syria. Britain was willing to concede part of this proposal, providing France with a section of the territory of Mosul (Upper Mesopotamia), thereby giving France a zone which stretched from the Syrian/Levantine coast to Mosul, which would act as a buffer zone between Britain's zone of interest and Russia.

The negotiations with France acquired new urgency when on 25 December 1915, the Russians received information that the Turkish commander in Syria, Djemal Pasha, might be willing to revolt against Constantinople. In return, Djemal Pasha demanded an assurance from the Russians that he become Sultan over the areas of Syria, Arabia and Mesopotamia. He proposed that Russia would have Constantinople and the Straits. Although the proposal fell through, it nevertheless put a sense of urgency into the negotiations.[12]

Sykes joined the negotiating team in early January 1916, at which point they were stalemated. He soon thrashed out an agreement with Picot, proposing that there be a British zone in the area of Haifa and the Bay of Acre with a railroad connecting this British zone with Mesopotamia. The rest of Turkish *Palestine* (which according to the 1912 'agreement' was ceded to France) was to be *internationalized.*

It was surprising that the French relented on the 1912 'agreement' which gave them control over the Land of Israel, but in fact she had no choice. France was too dependent upon the forces of the British Empire on the Western Front, and it was the forces of the British Empire, not the French, that were on the spot in the Eastern Mediterranean. France needed to gain what she could while she could. Russian consent however was now required before this Anglo-French agreement could be implemented.

---

12   Stein, L. *The Balfour Declaration,* p. 256.

The Zionist Factor

The British diplomats now had to ensure that France would not gain any advantage within the *internationalization* scheme. It was with this thought in mind, that the Jewish people and Zionist organization entered the picture. The Allied powers, especially France and Britain, as well as the *Conjoint Foreign Committee*, comprised of the Anglo-Jewish Association and the Board of Deputies of British Jews, were endeavouring to influence the neutral nations, especially the United States, to enter the war on their side.

A sizable Jewish minority lived in the USA, mostly around the important political area of New York, where they wielded a proportionally high influence in the media. It was imperative that this media-force be swayed positively toward the Allied cause. The Zionist movement in the United States, like the majority of the Jewish population, were of Russian-Jewish origin. Many were refugees or children of refugees who had fled from the Russian pogroms, and thereby hated Russia because of her anti-Semitism. Consequently, at the beginning of the War, the majority of the USA's Jewish population were opposed to the Triple Entente, due to Russia's involvement. Britain had to determine how best to induce this influential minority of Americans to espouse the Allied cause.

The British Foreign Office commissioned a prominent English Jewish diplomat, Lucien Wolf, to prepare a memorandum on this very subject and also on United States Jewry as a whole. Wolf submitted his Memo on 16 December 1915. Although not a Zionist, Wolf stated that if Britain wanted to gain the support of the United States Jewish community, she needed to state clearly her present position on the Land of Israel.

It was well known that by 1914 France held the stakes for Turkish *Palestine*. The question in 1916 was: 'Had the British position changed?' [13] American Jews also wanted to know if the Allies were willing to challenge Russia about her anti-Semitic policies.

Another prominent English-Jewish politician, Herbert Samuel, also wrote a Memo at this time concerning Zionist aspirations in the Land of Israel. Mark Sykes read this Memo prior to his departure for Russia in early March 1916, where he was to discuss the Anglo-French agreement with the Russians. On 3 March 1916, Wolf submitted a proposal which was soon adopted by the *Conjoint Foreign Committee*, calling for Jewish aspirations in Turkish *Palestine* to be taken seriously by the Allies, if and when they took control of the land during the War.[14] Foreign Minister Grey considered the proposal, liked it, and then instructed his ambassadors round the world on 11 March 1916:

---

13   Stein, L. *The Balfour Declaration.*, pp. 220-1.
14   Stein, L. ibid, p. 222.

... it has been suggested to us that if we could offer to the Jews an arrangement in regard to Palestine completely satisfactory to Jewish aspirations, such an offer might appeal strongly to a large and powerful section of the Jewish community throughout the world. [15]

Grey further stated that the Zionist idea could be very useful in persuading Jewish people in the USA, the East and elsewhere to join the Allied cause. He even alluded to the idea of future Jewish independence in *Palestine* (excluding the Holy Places) once they had grown stronger than the indigenous Arab population.[16] Shades of the Palmerston-Shaftesbury era were evident.

In Sykes' initial meeting with the Russian Foreign Minister Sazanov and the French delegate the Zionist cause was briefly discussed. Sazanov did not commit himself one way or the other, his main concern being to preserve Russian interests in *Palestine*. The French, however, never pursued the idea. They still had not given up hope of attaining the controlling interest in the Land of Israel and would not condone another party's involvement. [17]

'Sykes-Picot-Sazanov' Agreement

The Russians had certain reservations about the Anglo-French agreement. They had just recently imposed a crushing defeat upon the Turks in Armenia, an area which according to the Anglo-French agreement would be ceded to France. Russia objected to the proposal and claimed this area for herself.

France needed to be compensated for the loss of these areas and therefore proposed that part of the Land of Israel be included in her mandated territory. Negotiations then took place between the Russians and the French. The Russians were cautious. Sazanov stated that the areas of *Palestine* which incorporated Greek Orthodox interests should be under an international administration, with the guarantee of free access to the Mediterranean coast. Better an international administration, in Russia's view, than a French one!

Had the Russians not objected to the French proposal for administering at least a part, if not the whole of the Land of Israel, then the British proposal of *internationalization* would have failed. Hence the age-old animosity and rivalry between the Greek Orthodox and Roman Catholic Churches, and their protecting nations Russia and France, had again been influential in determining the future shape of the *land between.*

Russia and France had ensured that the Land of Israel would not be grasped exclusively by one of the Great Powers. Its future was still open for negotiation. The

---

15   Stein, L. ibid., p. 223.

16   Stein, L. ibid., pp. 223-4.

17   Stein, L. ibid., p. 232.

Russians were satisfied but the French were not. When the 'Sykes-Picot-Sazanov' (Anglo-French-Russian) agreement was signed in May 1916, it fell far short of the hopes cherished by Frenchmen who dreamed of a veiled annexation of a Greater Syria, stretching to the Egyptian frontier.[18]

The British politicians got what they wanted - an assurance that if and when Turkey collapsed, they would not find France occupying the east bank of the Suez Canal. Exactly who would occupy that strategic region was now a matter for the politicians to determine. But all such negotiations were still as yet premature. The Land of Israel remained in Turkish hands, and it was they and not the British and French who were on the offensive.

Summer in the Sinai

While the EEF awaited the expected Turko-German assault, the mounted troops patrolled intensively into the Sinai hinterland. All the while the increasing heat was beginning to tell. Idriess tells of a journey out into the desert where each man had only one water bottle. Some of the men went 'raving.' Others managed to return to camp only barely conscious, upon horses whose eyes were bulging out.[19]

Occasionally these patrols met their Turkish counterparts. George Harper of Christchurch wrote how during one skirmish the heat descended upon them like a wave. Then their water finished and soon men were collapsing. And to top it off, the Turks attacked. Thankfully they too were suffering from the heat, and withdrew. Then Harper himself collapsed and fell from his horse and had to be revived. [20] Following a reconnaissance trip during a *khamsin*[21] in mid-May, when temperatures were over 120 degrees Fahrenheit, Murray signalled Chauvel:

> The Commander-in-Chief wishes to convey to General Chauvel and troops of the Anzac Mounted Division his appreciation of the excellent work done in the arduous reconnaissance yesterday. The Commander-in-Chief does not think that any other troops could have undertaken this operation successfully in the present weather.[22]

It soon became apparent that the soldiers had two enemies to conquer. One was the desert. It never gave respite from the scorching heat and when combined with rocky and sandy ground, could easily envelope the troops and horses, struggling through it. The other enemy the Turk, they seldom encountered apart from long patrols into the desert. And the German *Taubes* were a constant menace. They could strike at any time, and any where, and often left behind a mess. Following a return from a patrol

---

18 Stein, L. *The Balfour Declaration*, p. 263.
19 Idriess, Ion., *The Desert Column*, p. 69.
20 King, M. *New Zealanders at War*, Heinemann, (Auckland,1981), p. 144
21 *Khamsin* - hot dry wind coming from the desert.
22 Hill, A.J. *Chauvel of the Light Horse*, p. 71.

Idriess recalled an aerial attack which left numerous soldiers dead, and many more wounded. Scores of horses were also killed, and countless more stampeded into the desert, although they were mostly rounded up.[23]

The Battle of Romani.

These battles with the heat and desert, minor skirmishes and aerial attacks continued during the summer months, trying the stamina and heart of man and horse. It did not seem to be the season for any full scale assault. Yet the EEF was being prepared. The Anzacs reconnoitered deep into the desert, the Scottish infantry were coming forth, and reinforcements of the mauled 5th Mounted Brigade arrived.

'After an eventful journey,' Lieutenant Robert Wilson of the Royal Gloucestershire Hussars Yeomanry wrote home on 18 June, 'I reached the Regiment and found them in rather a state of depression. Only a few weeks before my arrival they had lost a complete squadron except for a few survivors.'[24] Wilson and his fellow reinforcements helped re-invigorate the Yeomanry.

On 19 July General Chaytor, while on a reconnaissance flight over the eastern section of the oases, noticed the movement of large Turkish forces westward. On his return he dropped a message from the airplane to the forces below, informing them of the Turkish movements. During the following two weeks the number of skirmishes increased. Idriess wrote on 21 July of clashes involving brigades and of numerous casualties. The Turks, he said, were now preparing themselves for the big clash.[25]

Day by day the Turks edged forward. Chauvel had counted upon the Turks attacking Romani on the inland side, and positioned his forces accordingly. Von Kressenstein intended overpowering the forward positions, taking the railroad station at Romani and from there driving onto the Suez Canal, which he had been ordered to capture at all costs. He was only waiting the arrival of heavy artillery. Once they arrived, he attacked.

Just after midnight on 4 August 1916, some 8,000 bayonet-wielding Turkish infantry leapt out of the shadows of the night and raced towards the forward positions yelling 'Allah! Allah! Finish Australia.' Numerically outnumbered, the Australians were forced to withdraw from Mount Meredith, raked by German machine-gun fire as they went. They retired to the nearby Wellington Ridge where although constantly shelled by the Turks, managed to hold on until Chauvel personally brought up the 2nd Light Horse Brigade to support them in the morning.

Chauvel, realizing the Turks were heading for the railroad, headed to stop this movement. The Turks spread out and their left flank came up against the New

---

23   Idriess, Ion., *The Desert Column*, p. 72.
24   Wilson, Robert. *Palestine 1917*. Edited by Helen D. Millgate, D.J. Costello, (Tunbridge Wells, 1987), p. 42.
25   Idriess, I., *The Desert Column*, p. 82.

Zealanders at Hill 70. Due to force of numbers they steadily progressed, and despite the heat, had gained Wellington Ridge by the morning. Beyond, only 700 metres away, lay the Anzac camp at Etmaler, and beyond that the Suez Canal

From atop Wellington Ridge they poured fire down into the Anzac camp. Shortly afterwards Chaytor and the Canterbury and Auckland regiments, arrived and bolstered the Australian position. With the arrival of the New Zealanders and Yeomanry, the Australians gained a second wind and held off any further Turkish advance. Together, they pressed on and by early morning on the 5 August had regained Wellington Ridge.

This action was Walter's baptism of fire. 'The artillery is booming forth again.' He wrote. 'Temperature is anything over 100 ... poor old Jim Frost was shot dead. We rode up to a slope, dismounted and all but the horse holders had orders to advance in small rushes ... the bullets were pinging around us like hailstones from 2 machine guns the Turks had. We had to crawl on our stomachs for 50 yds pushing little ridges of sand up in front of us as we went 1/2 way up. I was next to Jim Frost and ... he was shot through the arm and heart.' [26]

As Walters and his mates, Will and Morey, found shelter in a nearby trench, the artillery opened up on the Turks. Soon the white flag went up and Walters wrote of the capture of '500 prisoners, 5 machine guns, several camels and other miscellaneous goods.' In all, some 1,000 prisoners were taken by 0500 on the morning of the 5 August, and thousands more were streaming eastwards.[27]

Generals Murray and Chauvel planned to surround the retreating Turks with the mounted troops - but a combination of heavy sand and hasty movement by the Turks defeated them. Of the battle and pursuit Wilson of the Gloucester Yeomanry wrote: '... It was impossible for Infantry to cross the plain so they said we had to go - that was our Brigade and three Anzac Brigades - what a sight! We all extended over about three and a half miles and started quietly off for the low ridge, the only cover to be seen, and only just high enough to hide the horses.' At that point Wilson wrote, the Turkish artillery opened up on them, and shrapnel was falling everywhere, forcing them to halt and retire. The next morning he relates, they went out again in pursuit of 'Johnny Turk', but he was not to be found.[28]

The Turks and German advisers withdrew to Salmana and Bir-el-Abd and then further back to El Arish. They mounted a spirited and desperate defense at Bir-el-Abd, causing Chauvel to break off the advance. By that time however, after several days of desperate fighting in the Sinai sun, the troops were exhausted. Just how exhausted is revealed by Wilson who lay down, only 'to be awakened almost immediately by a horse putting his foot plumb in the middle of my chest. I sat up just

26 *Diary of Reg Walters.*
27 Laffin, J. *Anzacs at War.* Abelard-Schumen, (London, New York, Toronto, 1965), p. 59.
28 Wilson, R. *Palestine 1917*, pp. 48-49.

in time to be knocked flat again by his hind foot hitting me a hefty blow on the forehead. I looked up to see an Australian, fast asleep in the saddle, his horse aimlessly drifting about among sleeping soldiers.' Wilson was so tired he didn't bother doing anything about it, and continued with his sleep.[29]

Results of the Battle.

The battle and associated skirmishes cost the Turks some 1,250 men, while the EEF lost 202 killed, 882 wounded and 46 missing. Most of the casualties were from the Anzac Mounted Division.[30] 'It was considered a great win for us,' Walters wrote, 'but after being in action for the first time and seeing a mate of mine killed alongside of me, it makes me wonder how such a mad and horrid state of affairs can exist. But one must not get sentimental here. The other man is out to kill you, so it is best to get in first.' Several days after the battle he wrote again 'Yesterday Sunday 6th. Jim with 2 others was buried beneath the palms of an oasis. A cross marks the spot where this fine chap lies.'[31]

The battle of Romani marked a turning-point, not just in the Sinai campaign, but indeed, in world history. Until 4 August the basic British policy was defensive - protecting the Suez Canal from a combined Turkish-German attack. Even Murray's suggestion of taking El Arish was with this view in mind. However after that decisive victory at Romani, and subsequent pursuit of the Turkish forces, the British policy makers quickly adapted their strategies. And those revised strategies were no more than the suggestions, advice, proposals and hopes of countless Jewish people, British strategists and Evangelicals during the previous one hundred and twenty years - the conquest of the Land of Israel. The stage was now set for one of the most colourful campaigns in modern history.

---

29   Wilson, R. ibid., page 50.
30   Laffin, J. *Anzacs at War.* page 60.
31   *Diary of Reg Walters.*

*C*hapter 12

To the Gates of the 'Promised Land'

Enter the Arabs

Following the Anzac-British entry into the Sinai, and victory at Romani, the Arabs decided it was an opportune time to initiate a revolt against the Turkish garrisons in Arabia. The most significant Turkish garrisons were at Mecca, Medina, At Taif, Jiddah, Rabegh and Yenbo. Hussein's sons Feisal and Ali began attacking some of these in June. In late September they captured At Taif outside Mecca. Now the entire southern Arabian Peninsula except Medina was under their control. But from Medina, where the railway terminated, northwards, considerable numbers of Turkish troops remained.

By October 1916 however it seemed that the *Arab Revolt* was losing momentum. Ronald Storrs, a senior British official, then travelled from Cairo to Jedda to meet Hussein and discuss the future of this secondary, yet albeit important campaign against Turkey. Thomas Edward Lawrence accompanied him. Lawrence quickly sized up the situation. The so-called *Arab Revolt* was likely to fizzle out if substantial British support was not forthcoming, and if there was no charismatic leader to carry it on. Lawrence believed that of all Hussein's sons, only Feisal had that potential. His superiors in Cairo accepted Lawrence's views on the subject, and then dispatched him back to the Arabian desert to act as a liaison with the Arab 'guerrilla' force.

Other British support was forthcoming in the form of weaponry, naval assistance and military advisors, including Lieut.-Colonel S.F. Newcombe, who was the head of the British Military Mission in Arabia. By mid December everything seemed in order for the *Arab Revolt* to begin in earnest.

Crossing the Sinai

As the Turkish-German force retreated eastwards, Murray persisted in obtaining War Office permission to move to El Arish, closer to the Land of Israel, the *Promised Land.* From there, he maintained, he could both defend the Suez Canal, and press forward offensively. While he awaited confirmation, Murray brought the pipeline forward to Romani and pressed on with the railroad.

Between Bir-el-Abd and El Arish lay the strategic Turkish post of Mazar, which according to Walters was 'on Napoleon's road to El Arish.' The *Desert Column* rode out to Mazar on 16 and 17 September during which men and horses had to travel over large distances with little sleep or water. Being basically a reconnaissance trip there was little actual fighting. Several days later, fearing a return by the *Desert Column*, the Turks withdrew to El Arish.

While preparing for the move towards El Arish, Chauvel sent his troops in rotation back to Egypt for rest and recreation. Meanwhile Romani was now being inundated with British *Tommy* and Scottish *Jock* infantry in large new camps. These new arrivals then began moving forward towards the front line.

To aid the advance of the infantry over the fine Sinai sand a wire meshed road was laid down, an innovation of bush-men from Queensland who used such a method in the outback to cross sandy river beds. The significance of the road on which these men were now traversing was not lost on many of the men. 'Two thousand years ago, the child Christ passed along this road when Herod drove His parents into Egypt.' Idriess wrote on 6 October. He then confessed that it was quite queer to think that Australian soldiers were now walking where Christ had been.[1] And as Christ Jesus and his parents crossed the Sinai to the gates of the Land of Israel, so now also did men from the uttermost ends of the earth.

But the Turks were still anxious to stop them. Powles recorded that the EEF intelligence had confirmed that the Turks were busy constructing a railroad from Beersheva through Magdhaba, some forty-eight kilometres south-east of El Arish aimed at the Suez Canal through the central route.[2] As there was danger of a Turkish attack along this route, reconnaissance patrols increased, primarily by the Imperial Camel Corps.

The further the *Desert Column* moved eastwards the further it moved away from Murray's control. With wide ranging responsibilities, including authority over the British forces at Saloniki (The Levant Base) and all of Egypt, Murray had to move his headquarters from Ismailia back to Cairo. In October he placed all forces east of the Suez Canal, henceforth known as *Eastern Force*, under the command of General Sir Charles Dobell. The vanguard of this force, the *Desert Column*, became a Corps in December, under the command of General Sir Philip Chetwode. The Corps comprised the Anzac Mounted Division, the 42nd and 52nd British Infantry Divisions and the Imperial Camel Corps Brigade (ICC), which was now comprised of ten Australian, six British and two New Zealand battalions. The ICC had been formed and was commanded by Lieut.-Col. C.L. Smith V.C.

Other significant changes in command at this time included 'Galloping' Jack Royston, who replaced Antill. Royston, a South African, was a huge man, and very

---

1   Idriess, I., *The Desert Column*, pp. 158-9.
2   Powles, Lieut.-Col. C. Guy, *The New Zealanders in Sinai and Palestine.*, p. 46.

popular with the Anzacs. Chetwode too was popular with the Anzacs, although he and his officers were not always happy with the Anzacs, especially their lack of decorum. Once Chetwode protested to Chauvel 'Not only do your men fail to salute me when I ride through your camps, but they laugh aloud at my orderlies.'[3] This comment was indicative of the internal dynamics of the EEF force. Anzac respect for the common British soldier did not extend to most of the officers whom they considered pompous, while these officers considered the Anzacs uncouth.

Breakthroughs for Jabotinsky

While the EEF moved towards the gates of the *Promised Land*, Jabotinsky continued his efforts for the formation of a *Jewish Legion* to fight with them. It was a difficult task, with as many opponents as supporters. Yet there was progress. On one occasion he met Lord Newton, Minister of Propaganda and proposed to him the *Jewish Legion* idea as a means of negating the American Jewish opposition to the *Entente Cordial.*[4]

Jabotinsky also met with Patterson who had just been discharged from hospital in London. Patterson in turn introduced him to various British officials who showed an interest in the proposal of a *Jewish Legion*. A number of these officials had heard of the exploits of the *Zion Mule Corps* at Gallipoli, causing Jabotinsky to confess to Trumpeldor, (also now in Britain), that he had been right in pursuing the formation of the unit.

A major frustration for Jabotinsky was the apathy of the young foreign Jewish men in Britain, especially those in London, who exhibited little desire to join the British forces. In late autumn 1916, prospects drastically improved. The 120 members of the *Zion Mule Corps* who had re-enlisted and were now attached to the 20th Battalion London Regiment, arrived in England. Through Trumpeldor they invited Jabotinsky to visit them in their barracks. One British official, Colonel Leopold Amery, commented to Jabotinsky that this would become the nucleus of his *Jewish Legion.*[5] Jabotinsky's dream was now nearer fulfillment.

Capture of El Arish

At base camp at Mazar preparations were in progress for the advance upon El Arish. On 20 December many horsemen were preparing for a pre-Christmas meal. 'We were going to have our Christmas Dinner today.' Walters recorded. 'In fact I had an invite over to the Engineers ... where a great dinner of <u>Turkeys</u> etc was being prepared. We have just been issued with tin fruits galore, plum puddings ... and then we all got the order to move at 11 a.m.' So they picked up their meal and took it with them on

---

3   Gullet, H. S. *The AIF in Sinai and Palestine,* p. 207.
4   Jabotinsky, V., *The Story of the Jewish Legion,* pp. 65-66.
5   Jabotinsky, V., ibid., p. 78.

their horses. He wrote the following day: 'We have been travelling since yesterday dinner time and are now 4 miles from "El Arish" and I think we will attack this morning. Maybe it has been evacuated' [6]

The *Desert Column* surrounded El Arish in the early morning of 21 December. 'As soon as it got light we peeped over a hill and there were these Turkish trenches' wrote Wilson of the Gloucesters, 'but no sign of Johnny Turk ... they had all cleared out in the night.' [7] The Turkish garrison had withdrawn. Not a shot had been fired and as the *Desert Column* entered the oasis they were greeted as victors. 'The praise for this bloodless victory,' wrote Powles, 'was in a great measure due to the horses, for the Turk was beginning to feel a wholesome dread of the speed and wide striking range of our mounted arm.' [8]

The first priority for many of the soldiers was to strip off and head for the beach, which according to Walters 'was absolutely the best beach I have ever seen.' But such enjoyment ended disastrously for two Light Horsemen - Gallipoli veterans. After emerging from the water they noticed and examined a sea mine on the shore. It exploded killing them both.

Battle of Magdhaba

The respite from riding and fighting for some was brief. The Turkish garrison from El Arish had withdrawn to Rafa on the border with Turkish *Palestine*, and to Magdhaba, inland south-east along wadi El Arish. Chetwode decided to strike immediately, and the Anzac Mounted Division concentrated after dark south of El Arish on the wadi and then resumed its march, each hour divided into forty minutes riding, ten minutes leading to warm the men, and ten minutes rest. [9]

The well illuminated Turkish camp at Maghdaba was sighted at 3.50 am. They were not anticipating an EEF attack. British planes bombed the Turkish positions in the early morning, drawing Turkish fire which in turn exposed their positions to the mounted men. Soon after the order came to attack. The New Zealanders and 3rd Light Horse Brigade advanced in order to cut off the Turkish retreat. The Camel Brigade was released directly upon the position, while the 1st Light Horse Brigade was held in reserve.

The battle was long and thirsty. The longer it continued the better for the Turks - they possessed the water while the *Desert Column* had limited supplies. The *Desert Column* had begun boring at nearby Bir Lahfan, but when at 1 pm it was announced that the boring was unsuccessful, their position became desperate. The nearest water was at El Arish.

6   *Diary of Reg Walters.*
7   Wilson, R., *Palestine 1917.*, p. 59.
8   Powles, Lieut. Col. C. Guy., *The New Zealanders in Sinai and Palestine*, p. 50.
9   Powles, Lieut. Col. C. Guy., ibid., p. 50.

A swift victory was required or otherwise retreat would be inevitable. Chauvel signalled Chetwode in mid-afternoon advising that the attack be called off. But when General Cox of the 1st Light Horse Brigade received orders to withdraw, he instructed his orderly to take the message away and return with it later. Cox subsequently unleashed his horsemen against the Turkish stronghold - and the first scent of victory was in the air. The other regiments followed suit.

'At 2 pm' wrote Walters, 'the order came for all to advance and then the fun began. We practically surrounded the Turks who were strongly resisting. All fixed bayonets and it was a grand and exciting sight to see all our horsemen galloping ... Small bodies of Turks were holding up their hands and of course we quickly made them prisoners.'[10] 'By 3.30 pm' Powles recalls, 'the New Zealanders with fixed bayonets were swarming over the trenches ... and the Turks were surrendering in all directions.'[11] Shortly afterwards the *Desert Column* completed the job and rounded up between 1,300-1,500 Turkish prisoners.

By 4.30 pm the village of Maghdaba was in Anzac hands. The assault had cost the *Desert Column* some twenty-two men killed and 124 wounded. It was an important victory. Addressing his troops later Chetwode said: '... the mounted men at Maghdaba had done what he had never known cavalry to do in the history of war: they had not only located and surrounded the enemy's position, but had got down to it as infantry and carried fortified positions at the point of the bayonet.'[12]

Agonizing Return to El Arish

The captured water supply was insufficient for all the troops and their horses - as well as for the Turkish prisoners. So while some troops remained behind, the remainder trudged back to El-Arish - another forty-five kilometres on a ration of one water bottle. 'They had been marching and fighting for 30 hours without pause' wrote Powles, 'and for most of them it meant the third night without sleep. To pass one night without sleep is trying; two nights is absolutely painful; but the third night without sleep after heavy fighting with all the added strain and excitement that it means - is almost an impossibility.' [13]

Throughout that night ride both men and horses collapsed. Hundreds of soldiers had hallucinating dreams. Some saw large buildings well lit up; two, including Chauvel, thought they saw a fox and presuming to be in a fox hunt, galloped off into the desert after it; others saw weird looking soldiers riding next to them; while others saw flower covered fields. 'Many discussions have followed these happenings' wrote Powles, 'and our wise ones laid it down that the brain had temporarily lost certain of

---

10 *Diary of Reg Walters.*

11 Powles, Lieut.-Col. C. Guy., *The New Zealanders in Sinai and Palestine*, p. 53.

12 Quoted in: Idriess, I., *The Desert Column*, p. 165.

13 Powles, Lieut.-Col. C. Guy, *The New Zealanders in Sinai and Palestine*, p. 54.

its powers of endurance, which sleep alone could restore.'[14]

Walters wrote from El Arish the following day: 'We arrived back here 9 a.m. this morning. It was a particularly rough job on the horses ... The men are all dead beat & are at this moment sleeping just as they laid down in the lines. We have had 3 night rides during the last 4 nights. So can say we all feel a bit weary.' Always the optimist, Walters concluded: 'But the Ocean is as at our feet & hope to have a dip & change of clothes this afternoon and all will be well.'[15]

The return journey was even more difficult and agonizing for the wounded. Some 150 camels were fitted up with stretchers, named *cajolets,* and carried the men back to camp. Due however to administrative mishandling it was another five days before many of the wounded received proper medical care.

Nearing the *Promised Land*

At this point the winter rains descended, drenching the weary troops. Their tents were still far behind the front line, and firewood was in demand, although some supplies were now arriving from Cyprus. The lack of firewood was a problem. With Christmas only several days away, the main concern was, 'How were the Christmas dinners to be cooked?' Yet soldiers have that uncanny ability to discover solutions to the most pressing of problems.

A telegraph line stretched along the Sinai coastline from Kantara into the *Promised Land*, the poles of which were constructed of iron and wood. This line was essential for future communication purposes, and orders had been issued that these poles were not to be touched. Yet with Christmas dinners beckoning and no wood supply, orders were bound to be forgotten. Disguised as Signallers, some members of the Camel Brigade, dismantled a few of these poles, and brought the wood back to El Arish. The ploy worked well - until mid-afternoon on 25 December, when it was discovered. By this time however the Christmas dinners had not only been cooked, but well and truly digested. His Majesty's Signallers were, unfortunately, now minus eight kilometres of essential telegraph line![16]

Several days after the Christmas banquet, a violent storm hit El Arish, causing considerable damage. Rain and sand were now the curse of the trooper. 'Wet blankets,' wrote Charles Malone, a reinforcement from Auckland to join the Camel Corps, 'are not the most comfortable things in the world to turn into especially if the sand is driving in on top.' [17]

An added problem for the troops, indeed one which had plagued them from the

---

14   Powles, Lieut.-Col. C. Guy, *The New Zealanders in Sinai and Palestine,* p. 55.
15   *Diary of Reg Walters.*
16   Powles, Lieut.-Col. C. Guy, *The New Zealanders in Sinai and Palestine,* p. 58-9.
17   Diary of 16419 Trooper Charles Lockton Malone, 16th Coy Camel Corps. Queen Elizabeth II Army Memorial, Waiouru. Diary 9001620.

outset of the campaign, concerned the rapacious attitudes and actions of the Bedouin. When the British authorities offered the Bedouin material inducements, in their efforts to woo them away from the Turks, many of the troops were upset. They resented these desert Arabs as they dug up the dead EEF soldiers from the battlefields and stole their boots and clothes, slit the throats of the wounded EEF soldiers, and alerted the Turks to any EEF movements.[18]

By the beginning of 1917 the troops, who had spent nearly a whole year in the Sinai, were looking forward to leaving the harsh and dry desert and its inhabitants behind. It still was not clear however if there would actually be a move into the *Promised Land.* The clue would be the railway. '... many and anxious were the eyes directed upon the railway line as it crept up to El Arish.' Wrote Powles. 'The great question of the day - a question which caused as much speculation as the Melbourne Cup - was "would it cross the wadi?"... Then one joyful day,' he continued, 'a patrol was ordered as escort to the surveying engineer ... who went away across the wadi; and we said, looking into each others eyes, "It seems too good to be true, we *are* for the Promised Land after all!'[19]

Lloyd George's Vision Prevails

Lloyd George replaced Asquith as Prime Minister on 7 December 1916. Arthur Balfour became the Foreign Secretary. Lloyd George, an advocate of the eastern campaign, wrote: 'When I formed my Government, the instructions under which Sir Archibald Murray was operating charged him to confine himself to the defence of Egypt and the Canal, in maintaining which he was recommended if possible to advance as far as El Arish on the eastern side of the Sinai Peninsular - still within the Egyptian frontier - and maintain his front there.' He describes how he then '... at once raised with the War Office the question of allowing him (Murray) to embark on a further campaign into Palestine when El Arish had been secured.'[20]

CIGS Sir William Robertson then telegrammed Murray on 9 December 1916 to ascertain what was required to further the advance. Although Lloyd George was keen to pursue the offensive, 'having for its objective the capture of Jerusalem',[21] Robertson wanted to stop any unnecessary withdrawal of troops from France.

The French too were concerned for the loss of British troops. But they had other, more long-term concerns with this likelihood of an offensive into Turkish *Palestine.* They also wanted to be involved. At the Anglo-French Conference held in London on 28 December 1916, the French requested that such military co-operation be possible, and that a French Political mission be attached to such a force. Lloyd

---

18 Idriess, I., *The Desert Column,* p. 172.
19 Powles, Lieut. Col. C. Guy, *The New Zealanders in Sinai and Palestine,* p. 64.
20 Lloyd George, D. *War Memoirs.* p. 1081.
21 Lloyd George, D., ibid., p. 1083.

George was able to temporarily postpone both.

At the War Cabinet meeting held on 29 December 1916 Robertson submitted a proposal stating that 'In the opinion of the General Staff, an offensive in Syria should not be undertaken until next autumn, and in the meantime our commitments in the minor theatres should be reduced to a minimum in order that our maximum effort may be made in France ... ' Robertson's proposal also stated that 'If the War Cabinet approves this policy, Sir A. Murray will be directed to establish himself in such a position as can be held defensively during the summer with the minimum force and is at the same time suitable as a starting-point for an offensive campaign in the autumn.'[22]

The War Cabinet meeting held on 2 January 1917 agreed to accept this proposal, and Murray was instructed to obtain the most satisfactory defensive position. And at the same time that Murray was active on the border of Turkish *Palestine*, Jabotinsky and Trumpeldor increased their exertions to form a *Jewish Legion* to join in the subsequent conquest. On 21 January 1917 they 'sent a formal petition to Mr. Lloyd George, proposing to the War Cabinet the formation of a Jewish Legion for Palestine.'[23]

Rafa on the Border

Murray's next move was the conquest of Rafa thereby clearing the Sinai of Turkish forces. A force comprising Anzac and British mounted troops, the *Camel Corps* and artillery, set out on the forty-eight kilometre journey to Rafa on 8 January. The movement of this force from the four corners of the earth, a truly representative force of the British Empire, towards the Land of Israel, caused Guy Powles to write:

> There are Australians among them and Yeoman from the British Isles and our own New Zealanders, and following them a band of tall, silent, swarthy Sikhs on huge Indian camels. There are the Hong Kong and Singapore Mountain Battery, who so ably serve the Camel Brigade.[24]

During that night march, horses munched upon the first green grass many of them had seen since leaving the Nile Delta many months before. The advance went smoothly, until near the border, when they were spotted by the Bedouin, who in their customary fashion, sent up the regular Arab cry and flares, thus alerting the Turks. Yet at six o'clock the following morning the Auckland Regiment in advance reached the boundary line separating Egypt from Turkish *Palestine*. The commander then 'rode forward alone,' records Powles, 'past the Boundary Pillar, and taking off his hat, there thanked Almighty God that he had at last been permitted to enter the Holy

---

22   Lloyd George, D. ibid., p. 1083.
23   Jabotinsky, V. , *The Story of the Jewish Legion*, p. 79.
24   Powles, Lieut. Col. C. Guy., *The New Zealanders in Sinai and Palestine*, p. 68.

Land (and was the first New Zealander to do so!).[25]

The Battle for Rafa

Shortly afterwards the battle for Rafa began in earnest. The main line of defence around Rafa was a defensive hill named El Magruntein to the west of the town, which was assaulted by the British and Anzac troops. The Turks stubbornly held their ground, despite concerted efforts by the EEF troops. 'The New Zealanders,' wrote Bostock, 'had the toughest job. They were attacking the toughest position.' The New Zealanders had by mid afternoon captured the Police Station, and the other EEF forces had made some headway. Aerial reconnaissance however had located the movement of large Turkish reinforcements coming from Shellal, some sixteen kilometres away, and from nearby Khan Yunis.

By 4.30 p.m. with ammunition running short, and the horses in desperate need of water, Chetwode gave orders for withdrawal. But, Wavell wrote, 'Before the order to withdraw could reach them, the New Zealand Mounted Brigade cleared the central keep by a fine bayonet charge. A little later the Camel Corps carried one group of works by assault. After this', he continues, 'the remainder of the defences soon fell, and as darkness came, the victory was complete.'[26]

This New Zealand assault caused considerable grief to one family that day. One section was comprised of four brothers, three in the firing line and one horse holder for the day. 'In the final attack on the trenches the Turks surrendered and white flags went up.' Henry Bostock wrote. 'However, just as the New Zealanders were a few yards from the trenches, a German machine-gunner opened fire, killing all three brothers. The New Zealanders then took no prisoners' [27] The total Anzac and British losses that day were seventy-one killed and 415 wounded.

One of those casualties was Lieutenant Wilson of the Gloucestershire Yeomanry. Not being seriously wounded himself, he escorted the other wounded back to camp. On the way, he wrote, 'I was grieved to see an officer of the Warwicks, a man named Jack Ware with whom I had soldiered at Tidworth, among the dead. He had been hit exactly between the eyebrows.'[28]

Wilson arrived at base camp at 3 o'clock in the morning, and was greeted rather abruptly by a big bearded Australian, 'What in Hell's the matter?' The Australian asked. Wilson explained that he had some wounded soldiers. Then some other Anzacs appeared and the wounded were taken care of. 'My bearded friend took me to a tent with one bed in it,' Wilson recalls, and then 'handed me some pyjamas. He never asked me what was the matter but gave me a bottle of port and said, "Get that

---

25 Powles, Lieut.-Col. C. Guy, ibid. p. 69.
26 Wavell, Colonel A. P. *The Palestine Campaigns,* Constable, (London, 1931), p. 66.
27 Bostock, H. *The Great Rid,* p. 55.
28 Wilson. R. *Palestine 1917,* p. 61.

inside you Digger, and you'll be all right in the morning", which, Wilson admitted, 'was quite true.'[29]

The battle of Rafa marked the end of part one of the campaign, the clearing of the Sinai, and the beginning of part two, the conquest of the Land of Israel. The clearing of the Sinai had been completed primarily by the Anzac mounted men, ably supported by British troops. It was they who had provided Murray with the necessary launching pad for the conquest of the *Promised Land.* Murray said as much in a dispatch he sent to CIGS Robertson in London stating: 'These Anzac troops are the keystone of the defense of Egypt.'[30]

It was primarily due to the ordinary Anzac and British soldier like Jack Frost, the three New Zealand brothers and Jack Ware, that the British Government had a platform for its future deliberations concerning the future status of the Land of Israel once the conquest was complete.

The Race to Damascus Begins

The capture of Rafa and the entrance into the *Promised Land,* the Land of Israel proper, was essentially the beginning of the race to Damascus. Almost simultaneously offensive operations began in earnest in Arabia. Feisal and Lawrence had conceived of a daring plan to take the port of Wejh in northern Arabia. The plan was carried out in late January 1917.

It was imperative for the cause of the Arab nationalist movement that the Arab 'army' put up a good show and be recognized by the British authorities as an essential adjutant to the main operations in the Sinai and Turkish *Palestine.* It was becoming clearer to Lawrence, the liaison officer-cum-Arab nationalist spokesman, that Arab aspirations and the conquest of Damascus were virtually synonymous. The Arab nationalist quest for taking Damascus was now set in motion.

---

29   Wilson, R. , ibid., p. 62.
30   Hill, A.J. , *Chauvel of the Light Horse,* p. 95.

*C*hapter 13

Gaza - The Gates are Closed

Towards Gaza

While Lloyd George was battling with his 'westerner' generals and the French concerning his goal of advancing into Turkish *Palestine*, Murray decided to move onto Gaza. This would be the ideal springboard for the proposed autumn offensive. After Chaytor captured the small village of Khan Yunis, lying between Rafa and Gaza, on 23 February, Von Kressenstein withdrew his remaining forces north to the Gaza - Beersheva line, vacating many strategic positions along the Wadi Ghuzze (Wadi Gaza or the ancient Nahal Besor), stretching from the coast through to the springs at Shellal. The remaining Turkish positions in the central Sinai were also captured, thereby minimizing any Turkish penetration on the EEF right flank.

By the beginning of March the *Eastern Force* was comprised of the Anzac Mounted Division; the newly formed Imperial Mounted Division, (commanded by a Briton, Major-General H.W. Hodgson), comprised of the 3rd and 4th Australian Light Horse Brigades and 5th and 6th British Mounted Brigades; the Imperial Camel Corps Brigade; and the 52nd, 53rd and 54th British Infantry Divisions, and other minor forces. The force was now more British in character than Anzac.

To brace themselves adequately for the coming attack upon Gaza the soldiers endeavoured to increase their diet. Wilson, of the Gloucestershire Yeomanry, now recovered from his wounds, recalls how he and his mates went to a nearby farm to buy some eggs. They were told to return the following day. So, on the morrow they returned, only to find that 'the poor old chap was in an awful way because some Australians had come with a bayonet and topped all the fowls' heads off, and left them laying in rows under their perches.'[1]   While the Tommies went without eggs this day, the Aussies feasted on chicken!

First Battle of Gaza

All realized that the battle for Gaza would be tough. Gaza, the gateway to the Land of Israel, was protected on its south eastern approach by a large mound named Ali

---

1   Wilson. R., *Palestine 1917*, p. 74.

Muntar. While Murray and his staff planned their attack, Kress von Kressenstein awaited signs of the EEF assault. He consolidated Gaza and Beersheva, as well as the centre of the line at Tel esh Sheria, and Tel Hareira, and behind this line at Jemmameh and Huj.

Murray had come forward to El Arish to oversee the battle, alongside Dobell and Chetwode who were near the front line. Such an overload of commanders would later seriously affect the outcome of the battle. As surprise was necessary, the assault was to be launched while railhead, and supplies, were still some distance from the front line. To assist this element of surprise, and to provide entertainment for the troops prior to the impending big assault, a large race meeting was held on the Rafa battleground on 21 March, entitled the *Desert Column First Spring Meeting.* 'The course was excellent going', commented Powles, 'and with natural grassy slopes for lawn and grandstand, the spectators were happily provided for. The "fields" were good and races keenly contested among the Yeomanry, Australians and New Zealanders.' The *Promised Land Stakes,* Powles was able to proudly declare, was won by the New Zealand horse, 'Maori King.'[2]

Over the next couple of days three infantry and two mounted divisions began moving forward into position along the banks of the Wadi Ghuzze. During the night of 25 March and early morning of 26 March 1917, the troops of the British Empire moved to their positions, throwing a cordon around Gaza. The Anzac Division moved to the north of Gaza and cut the route to Jaffa, (capturing a Turkish divisional commander in the process) the Imperial Mounted Division moved to the south of them. The Camel Corps and the 54th East Anglia Division covered the route from Beersheva. The 52nd Scottish Lowland Division remained in reserve in the south, while the main direct thrust was to be made by the 53rd Welsh Division.

By mid morning, the cordon was complete. A dense fog which had drifted in from the sea had assisted the mounted men reach their co-ordinates almost undetected. Yet it was the fog, as well as human error, which delayed the launching of the infantry assault. Finally around noon the Welsh Division, seeing its first action since Gallipoli, began the assault towards Ali Muntar under heavy artillery, rifle and machine-gun fire. 'The poor Welshmen, coming up the open slopes towards the redoubts were utterly exposed to machine-gun and rifle-fire,' wrote Idriess who observed the assault. '... Some thousands of the poor chaps bled on Ali Muntar that day.'[3]

Anxious for a speedy victory, Chetwode also commanded the Anzacs to move into Gaza from their positions in the north. After heavy hand-to-hand fighting the British infantry and the dismounted Anzacs had linked hands by six o'clock in the evening. Tala Bey, the Turkish commander was by then preparing to blow up the water wells and wireless station, while the civic commander of Gaza was actually

2   Powles, Lieut. Col C. Guy., *The New Zealanders...*, p. 84.
3   Idriess, I., *The Desert Column.*, p.192.

preparing a feast to welcome the British and Anzac victors.

Unfortunately, the British commanders weren't completely aware of the success of the forces in the town. Also, according to a preconceived plan, if the town had not been captured by nightfall, the EEF forces would withdraw so as to water the horses, and for fear of the arrival of strong Turkish reinforcements. While the capture of Ali Muntar and the town itself was unknown to him, Dobell announced a withdrawal. Chauvel protested vigorously 'But we have Gaza!' Dobell replied: 'Yes; but the Turkish reinforcements are all over you.'[4] So withdraw they did.

Some of the Anzacs had to withdraw six kilometres through narrow streets and cactus hedges, to retrieve their horses before making the circuitous journey back to Wadi Ghuzze. When news of the capture finally reached Dobell, he ordered an immediate re-seizure of the position. But to no avail. The Turkish, German and Austrian forces, surprised at their reprieve, had quickly re-established themselves. Tala Bey was exultant.

The British and Anzac losses that disastrous day amounted to 523 killed, 2,932 wounded and 512 missing (mostly captured).[5] Most were from the gallant Welsh infantry who had toiled hard to take Ali Muntar - then to see it lost due to the incompetence of their commanders. Murray, after failing in his attempts to recapture the vacated positions, was in a very embarrassing position, and exaggerated his report of the battle to the War Cabinet.

War Cabinet Decisions

The War Cabinet wanted good reports from the 'minor' theatres as there was nothing but a bloody quagmire on the Western Front. The British led forces under General Maude had just captured Baghdad, while the overthrow of the Czar in Russia was seen as a positive development. News of a *near* victory from Gaza was insufficient. The Cabinet met on 2 April to discuss the situation at Gaza, and, wrote Lloyd George 'devoted the afternoon to an examination of the prospects in Palestine.' Lloyd George wrote: 'We realized the moral and political advantages to be expected from an advance on this front, and particularly from the occupation of Jerusalem.' The War Cabinet then passed a resolution authorizing Robertson to inform Murray '... that we were very anxious to exploit the successes already achieved to the utmost possible extent, and to capture Jerusalem; ...'[6]

On the afternoon of 3 April, Lloyd George and Lord Curzon met with and instructed Sykes prior to his departure to Egypt where he was to join the EEF as political advisor. Sykes was instructed to: (1) Make every effort to ensure that Turkish *Palestine* fell

4   Gullett, H. S., *The AIF in Sinai and Palestine.*, p. 294.
5   Wavell, A. P., *Palestine Campaigns.*, p. 80.
6   Lloyd George, D., *War Memoirs.*, Vol. 2, p. 1086.

within the British and not the French area after occupation. (2) To ensure that no pledges concerning Turkish *Palestine* be given to the Arabs. (3) Not to prejudice the Zionists and their possible future involvement alongside Britain in the political future of Turkish *Palestine*.[7]

Encouragement for Murray's efforts at this point was due to a realization, especially by Lloyd George, that with some extra effort Turkey could be defeated. General Maude was moving northward in Mesopotamia, while, it was planned, the Grand Duke Nicholas would move down through Armenia into northern Mesopotamia. An aggressive offensive in the Land of Israel, could very well force Turkey to sue for peace.

Lloyd George also had more forward-seeking motives for defeating the Turks. 'For the British Empire,' he wrote, 'the fight with Turkey had a special importance of its own ... The Turkish Empire lay right across the track by land or water to our great possessions in the East - India, Burma, Malaya, Borneo, Hong Kong, and the Dominions of Australia and New Zealand.'[8]

Progress with the *Jewish Legion*

On the morning of 3 April, Lloyd George informed Chaim Weizmann, now actively involved in Zionist affairs, and C.P. Scott, the editor of the *Manchester Guardian,* of his desire for the conquest of Eretz Israel. At that same meeting Lloyd George was reminded of the suggestion for the formation of a Jewish unit to serve in the Land of Israel, and of the presence of the 120 former *Zion Mule Corps* men now training at Winchester. He commented that these men should be sent to the front where their knowledge of the terrain would be invaluable for the campaign.

Several days later Jabotinsky, now serving as a mere private with the 20th Battalion, was summoned to a meeting in London with Lord Derby, the War Secretary. Jabotinsky was besides himself. What, he thought, would be the War Secretary's reaction when realizing he was only 'a full private in a British infantry battalion.' 'When they see me in my uniform,' he debated with Trumpeldor, 'won't they faint, both the minister and the general, before so unheard-of a prospect as a political consultant between such unequal partners?' They agreed to go to this critical meeting together.[9]

Indeed General Woodward, the 'Director of Organization' and Lord Derby were a little astonished. Yet the historic meeting proceeded. They were asked for details about the 'Jewish unit scheme.' 'I rolled off the "details" automatically: by that time,

7   Fromkin, David., *A Peace To End All Peace*, p. 287.
8   *War Memoirs of Lloyd George*, Vol. 4: 1917 (Boston, 1934), pp. 66-7. Quoted in Fromkin, D., *A Peace To End All Peace*, p. 282.
9   Jabotinsky, V., *The Story of the Jewish Legion.*, pp. 82-83.

I could have done it half awake,' recalled Jabotinsky. Then when queried if they expected large numbers to join up, Trumpeldor took the stand and answered: 'If it is to be just a regiment of Jews - perhaps. If it will be a regiment for the Palestine front - certainly. If, together with its formation, there will appear a government pronouncement in favour of Zionism - overwhelmingly.'[10] The conversation then turned to other matters - including the service of the *Zion Mule Corps* at Gallipoli, and Trumpeldor's role in it, which was positively acknowledged.

The following day, back at camp, Jabotinsky told his commanding officer Colonel Pownall of the episode from the previous day. 'He assured me,' wrote Jabotinsky, 'it was a breach of all the traditions of the British War Office and the first time in history that such an adventure had happened to a private soldier.'[11] Despite British traditions the vision of a Jewish unit to serve in the liberation of the Land of Israel was now almost a reality.

Later Jabotinsky met with General Geddes, the Director of the Recruiting Department. Together they determined the name of the prospective Jewish unit - the Jewish Regiment. It was to have as its insignia a menorah[12] together with the Hebrew word *Kadimah* - forward. When asked who should command this Jewish Regiment, Jabotinsky recalls having mentally recited all the Jewish candidates - Lionel Rothschild, Major Schonfield, James Rothschild, Fred Samuel, Eliezer Margolin, who Jabotinsky wrote 'had been in my thoughts ever since our first days in the Gabbari camp in Alexandria,' and 'was somewhere on the Flanders front with his Australians.'

'But with all my feelings of respect to every one of these men,' he continued, 'I considered then, and consider still today, that this historic privilege had been faithfully won by another: by the man who had not been ashamed to undertake the leadership of the Mule Drivers and who had converted them into a corps for which the War Minister had profound respect; the man who in hospital and convalescent home had us ever in his thoughts ... writing his book, *With the Zionists in Gallipoli*; the man who believed in us when we were laughed at and ridiculed ...
'There is only one nominee,' I said. 'Even though he is not a Jew, he must be our Colonel and I hope that one day he will be our General: Patterson.'[13]

French Apprehensions and Turkish Reassessment.

While Britain was moving towards modifying the 'Sykes-Picot' Agreement, France, aware of Britain's intentions, was looking at how best to counteract these British moves. Simultaneously with Sykes' departure for Egypt, Picot was sent by France

---

10 Jabotinsky, V., ibid., p. 83.
11 Jabotinsky, V., ibid., p. 84.
12 Menorah - the seven stick candle holder which used to light the Temple, and was the religious symbol of the Jewish people.
13 Jabotinsky, V. *The Story of the Jewish Legion.*, pp. 88-9.

also to Egypt, to act as *French High Commissioner for Occupied Territories in Palestine and Syria.* Picot was instructed to ensure the retention of French interests in the Land of Israel, and to be considerate towards the Jewish colonies in the region. This was in accordance with a new tactic now being adopted by the French. Realizing that the Zionist appeal was gaining in popularity, the French were endeavouring to support it - and by so doing hoping to divorce it from being a purely British idea.

While the War Cabinet had encouraged and tangibly bolstered Murray's efforts, the Turks too had strengthened their position in and near Gaza. The Turkish position, rather than being weakened by the overthrow of the Tsar, was actually bolstered by it. The Russians, tired of the war, withdrew their forces from the Caucasus. Some 25,000 Turkish troops were now released for service elsewhere, some of whom came south.

The fortifications around Gaza were substantially improved, full use being made of the high ground and the abundance of cactus plants in the area. This time there was to be no opportunity for the mounted troops to encircle Gaza as at the first battle. There was a solid defensive line stretching from Gaza through to Tel esh Sheria, half way to Beersheva.

The threatened British and Anzac breakthrough at Gaza increased Turkish sensitivity towards any potential fifth-column operating within the country. Many, especially non-Muslims, were expelled from their homes. 'Refugees arrived from Gaza and Jaffa in a destitute condition,' wrote Marie James from Safed in April, 'as they were not allowed to bring any food and scarcely any clothing. After their houses had been plundered by the Turkish soldiers, many died on the way.'[14]

The general situation in the land became progressively desperate. 'Processions of Moslems and Jews kept going to the tombs to pray for rain; paper-money daily decreased in value', wrote Miss James. 'An eyewitness who returned from Salt,' she continued, 'said she saw twenty five carriages from the train filled with women and children and with little clothing, and men were carrying old women on their backs'.[15]

Both Arab nationalists and Zionists incurred the Turkish wrath. Yet a small pro-Allied group, known as the *Nili* was active during this period collecting vital information about Turkish military operations. Most of this information was transferred to British intelligence in Cairo by the group's leader, Aaron Aaronsohn, who lived at Zichron Yaacov near Atlit on the Mediterranean coast.

The activities of the *Nili* seriously endangered the welfare of the remaining Jewish community in the Land of Israel. Only intervention by the German Foreign Ministry hindered Djemal Pasha from expelling the Jewish population of Jerusalem as well. But had the *Nili* been uncovered, then Djemal would probably not have been restrained.

---

14 Diary of Marie James, quoted in *Jewish Missionary Intelligence [JMI],* 1919, p. 69.
15 Diary of Marie James, ibid., pp. 69-70.

Second Battle for Gaza

The second battle for Gaza began on 17 April 1917 with the 52nd Scottish Lowland and 54th East Anglia Divisions, including five newly arrived tanks, moving out from the shelter of Wadi Ghuzze towards their forward positions. The main assault began on 19 April, preceded by a massive artillery bombardment, and from British and French warships off shore. The 52nd, 53rd Welsh, and 54th Divisions then began their assault in front of Gaza, while the Imperial Mounted Division made a dismounted assault further east, and the Anzac Division protected the eastern flank.

The fighting along the entire front was intense. Walters wrote 'Wednesday ... we moved out in darkness to take up a position. We dismounted and then marched a considerable distance. About daylight we were down in a hollow when the Turks at short range opened up on us. Fortunately for us we were in a crop about 15 [inches] high, so we dropped like rocks and for 2 hrs lay there with bullets whistling among us. Meanwhile our artillery and Navy got going and I will never forget that bombardment. One could hardly hear himself speak at times.'[16]

Shortly afterwards, with the completion of the bombardment, Walters, like the remainder of the troops, was on the move. 'We were ordered to fix bayonets,' he continued, 'and charged. But the Turks rushed back onto the next ridge. After popping it into them about 50 surrendered, so on again we went in small rushes about another 1/2 mile. Turks seemed to be everywhere - I could see we had a nasty job on.' He continued, 'Turkish shrapnel began to come onto us. I was about twenty yards from Will with shrapnel falling all round us.'

'It was about 1 P.M. that we got it hot and horrible. The Turks were down in a waddy [sic] about 1/2 mile away and to get to it we had to advance over open country with no cover. I had been through a fair bit of fire one way and another but the Lord save us from going through such a hell again. The shrapnel shells just formed one continual screach [sic] and the shrapnel just fell around us like hail. How many of us got to the Waddy [sic] I don't know. But the order was to advance so we just had to face it ... Men were falling all around me ... It will always remain a nightmare to those of us who got through.'[17]

Walters and his unit managed to hold off the Turks for several hours. But then he noticed Turkish reinforcements moving to try and outflank his small group, and was able to gratefully record that 'The Yeomanry relieved us shortly after and we were told to retire.' That was the good news. The bad news was that they had to retire the same way that they came. 'We were all dead beat when we got over the ridge' he recalled, but then 'the General came galloping up and told us to advance again in another direction. Many of the chaps were hit in this advance with machine gun fire,

---

16 *Diary of Reg Walters.*
17 Ibid.

rifle fire and shrapnel. A huge explosive shell burst a few yards from me and a great junk [sic] of iron flew past my body about ½ a yd away.'[18]

That night Walters' badly cut up unit withdrew from their hard fought for positions. They weren't alone. Nearly every EEF unit suffered a similar ordeal. Such was the type of battle that day - positions were only won after much effort and loss. The Yeomanry too had it tough, and Lieutenant Wilson saw another of his mates killed.[19]

Another Failure

The Turks held their ground - and not even the new deadly *tank* could dislodge them. They were not going to easily give up the gateway into the *Promised Land* having once already been let off the hook. The EEF were commanded to withdraw to the Wadi Ghuzze, dig in and prepare for the expected Turkish counter-attack. Yet the counter-attack never developed, and the two sides ended up facing each other, the British-Anzac force (EEF) on a line running along the Wadi Ghuzze, and the Turkish forces just to the north of them.

The battle that was supposed to mark the beginning of the end for the Turks, and climax with the capture of Jerusalem had failed, and at great cost. The EEF suffered some 6,444 casualties,[20] the majority being inflicted upon the 54th East Anglia Division, and to a lesser extent the 52nd Lowland Division.

Despite the successes of the *Desert Column* in clearing the Sinai, the costly defeats at Gallipoli, and first and second Gaza, made it clear that the spoils of victory would definitely not be shared with any other European power, ally or not. It was now time for the British generals and politicians to formulate clear military and political options for their future operations vis-à-vis the Land of Israel.

---

18   *Diary of Reg Walters.*
19   Wilson R., *Palestine 1917*, p. 77.
20   Bullock, D., *Allenby's War*, p. 47.

Chapter 14

Allenby, Beersheva and Balfour

Encouragement's for the Zionists

The failures at Gaza and the Allied spring offensive in France seriously affected the public confidence. A decisive Allied victory, somewhere, was essential. With this view in mind the War Cabinet decided at their 23 April meeting to press on vigorously with the campaign in Turkish *Palestine*. They also decided to introduce new leadership. Murray's achievements were significant, but after two failures fresh blood was required. The position was offered to the South African General Smuts. After serious contemplation he declined.

From this point, as the British Government sought ways of gaining a pre-eminent role in the future affairs of the Land of Israel, they took a more serious interest in Zionism. On 25 April 1917, two years after the landings at Gallipoli, Chaim Weizmann, an unofficial Zionist spokesman, met with Lord Robert Cecil at the Foreign Office. Weizmann explained his discomfort with any joint British-French (or condominium) venture, preferring a 'British protectorate.' When asked by Lord Cecil why he objected to a purely French control over the Land of Israel, Weizmann explained that the French would interfere with the population and impose an *espirit francaise*. Weizmann seemed to infer, however, that under British control there was potential for partnership, whereby the aspirations of both the British Empire and Jewish people could both be attained. A Jewish *Palestine*, especially its proximity to the Suez Canal, would, he said, be very beneficial for Britain.[1]

Lord Cecil in turn hinted that the British Government would be interested in receiving worldwide Jewish support for a British takeover in the Land of Israel. Weizmann then transferred this information to his Zionist colleagues in the USA. Balfour, while on a visit there in April and May, was impressed by the depth of support amongst American Jews for Zionism.

Nahum Sokolow, another prominent Zionist, meanwhile travelled to Italy in May, meeting with both the Pope and Italian Prime Minister. Both seemed sympathetic

---

1   Weizmann, Chaim. *Trial and Error*. Volume1. The Jewish Publication Society of America, (Philadelphia, 1949), pp. 191-2.

towards Zionism, yet they had reservations about the future of the *Holy Places* and of a British sponsored protectorate in *Palestine*. From Italy Sokolow travelled to France, and met with Prime Minister Ribot. Ribot assured him of French support and sympathy, which became official when they issued a written Memo of support on 4 June. This Memo pre-dated any official British position, and was a desperate French attempt to steer the Zionist cause away from a purely British concern.

Jewish Conflicts

The intense interest now being displayed towards Zionism by both Britain and France, was due also in part to their desperation to keep Russia from signing a separate peace with Germany. All avenues which could favourably dispose the Russian people, or at least large numbers of them, towards the Allied cause, were worth pursuing. Yet left-wing agitators in Russia were propagating a withdrawal from all Czarist-made agreements, including those made with Britain and France.

Many of these agitators were Jewish, members of the *Bund*, a newly formed Jewish socialist movement. The *Bundists* agitated for a socialist society in Russia, where Jewish people and Russians could be equal. A Jewish-Zionist entity in the Land of Israel, under a British protectorate, contradicted this *Bundist* ideology.

The Russian Zionists themselves were ambivalent. Although many favoured partnership with the British, others were hesitant, fearing repercussions upon the two and a half million Jewish people living under Austro-German control. They were also aware of the policy of the Berlin Zionist Executive at the beginning of the War, which declared for neutrality, and opposed any actions aimed against Turkey. At the All-Russian Zionist Conference held in early June 1917 there was no clear Russian Zionist consensus concerning the deliberations now beginning with the British Government.

The ideological battle within Jewry over Zionism also rocked Britain. On 20 May 1917 Weizmann declared at the Zionist Conference held in London, that the British Government was prepared to support their plans. This statement drew immediate opposition, especially from the more assimilated section of the British Jewish community. A counter statement was then released by the *Conjoint Foreign Committee*, and printed in the *Times* on 24 May. It basically expressed the view that not all British Jewish people favoured the proposed British-Zionist protectorate proposal. This in turn upset the British Government, which was now endeavouring to garner worldwide support for its proposal of taking Turkish *Palestine* and providing the Jewish people there with a protectorate. A hot debate then permeated the British Jewish community, culminating in the dissolution of the *Conjoint Committee*, and a number of changes within the Jewish Board of Deputies. Delegates more sympathetic to Zionism now joined the Board.

Consolidation in the Desert

While ideological battles raged in Britain and Russia, important military changes occurred in the field. Chetwode replaced Dobell as commander of the *Eastern Force*, while Chauvel took command of the *Desert Column*, the first Australian to attain the rank of Lieutenant-General. General Chaytor now took over command of the Anzac Mounted Division. Meanwhile the Cabinet, in its efforts to secure the region, decided to bolster the EEF by sending troops from the Saloniki front.

Chetwode set about formulating a plan for the breaking of the Turkish line, and of raising the moral of the troops, which, following two losses at Gaza was now at a low point. After the second battle of Gaza the *Eastern Force* established one almost continuous trench system in close contact with the enemy from the coast near Sheik Ajlin inland for about seven kilometres to Sheik Abbas. From Sheik Abbas the line dropped south west to Tel el Jemmi. The line then followed the Wadi Ghuzze to Shellal then to Tel el Fara and onto Gamli. Between these positions there were detached posts. Due to the lack of suitable water, the area east of Gamli was covered by mounted patrols operating out of the main posts.

All the while Chetwode continued with the sound principles initiated by Murray. The railroad continued its steady progress, aiming towards Shellal. Although the pipeline carrying fresh water from Egypt drew near, strenuous efforts were made to improve the water supplies. A large reservoir was constructed to hold ½ million gallons of water at Shellal where springs came to the surface on the edge of the Wadi Ghuzze. This and other water holes served as staging posts for the mounted patrols as they patrolled the hinterland.

The patrols journeyed both north of the Wadi Ghuzze and south-east towards Beersheva. The Turks were also active, sending patrols out to monitor the EEF activities. Contact between the rival patrols was common. '... we have been doing supports and front line duty between Gaza and Beersheva.' Wrote Walters, who continued, 'Turkish cavalry in full view on the ridges.'[2] On occasions the two opposing forces merely observed each other. But occasionally they clashed.

One interesting patrol was witnessed by Trooper Malone, whose 16th ICC Company was attached to the 5th Light Horse Regiment. He wrote on 8 May:

> Pushed onto ridge W of Auja from which we observed a train lying on track with men picking up rails. With 3 others advanced to within 400 yds of track - train moved out and as it went opened fire on another patrol to our left, but was then out of range ... caught a Bedouin and 2 Turks ... This railway runs as far as Kossiami. [3]

The Turks were pulling up the railway track they had built extending south of Beersheva, by which they intended to reach the Suez Canal via the centre of the

2   *Diary of Reg Walters.*
3   *Diary of Trooper Malone.*

Sinai. It had reached El Kossaima when the EEF captured El Arish and Magdhaba, and work was stopped. But now its rails could be pulled up and used for another line they were constructing behind Gaza. Chetwode chose to destroy the railway. On 22 May one group of engineers, accompanied by the 1st Light Horse Brigade, set out from Shellal for the station of Asluj, while another group accompanied by the Camel Corps set out from Rafa for Auja. As a decoy the Imperial Mounted Division feinted towards Beersheva. Lieutenant Wilson participated in the raid.

Some twenty-four kilometres of railway were destroyed, as well as a number of arched bridges, including one of eighteen arches at Asluj. During the operation water surveying works were also carried out. Ancient wells at Asluj and Khalasa were inspected, and it was determined that they had enough water to supply two divisions of soldiers. The existence of water at these two locations was determined by General R.E.M. Russell, the Chief Engineer, who had researched the findings of the *Palestine Exploration Fund*. The PEF had written that in antiquity large communities had lived at these locations. Interviews with local Arabs confirmed the view that large water supplies were located there.

Chetwode's Plan

Familiarization with the terrain, and location of water supplies in the vast un-populated region south of Beersheva assisted Chetwode's planning. In May he wrote his *Notes on the Palestine Campaign*, in which he formulated his opinions and plan for the next stage of the campaign. Through various intelligence sources, including the *Nili*, he had determined the approximate strength of the Turkish forces, and their general areas of deployment. He deduced that another frontal assault upon Gaza was out of the question, while an assault upon the centre would be impractical, due to its proximity to the Turkish reinforcement centres. The Turks, if hard pressed could also quickly fall back to predetermined lines of defence, in touch with their water and supply lines, and in the process draw the EEF further away from their supply lines.

Only one option remained - an attack against the extreme Turkish left flank at Beersheva. Such a move was contrary to both logic and history. No force had ever before conquered the land with an assault and victory from that direction, due primarily to the lack of sufficient water to the south of Beersheva. To be successful two essentials were required - secrecy and a shortened supply line. Construction of the railway from El Arish thereafter was quickened, a branch of which deviated north east towards Shellal.

Enter Allenby

Chetwode's plan was enhanced with the arrival of fresh troops from Salonika, initially the 7th and 8th Mounted Yeomanry Brigades and later the 60th London Division.

Units from India, Aden and Egypt were also on the move, and from them the 75th Infantry Division would be formed. Small French and Italian units were also on the way, both insignificant as fighting forces, but important political expressions of the French and Italians, as they too wanted a political share of the spoils.

A new commander of the EEF was appointed: General Sir Edmund Allenby, a veteran of the Boer War and until his arrival in Egypt on 28 June, a commander in France. He carried with him a message from Prime Minister Lloyd George, who 'wanted Jerusalem as a Christmas present for the British nation.' [4] Upon arrival Allenby moved his headquarters from Cairo closer to the front line near Rafa. He also commissioned Richard Meinertzhagen as an intelligence officer. Meinertzhagen, following contact with Aaronsohn, held strong Zionist persuasions.

Allenby's presence was quickly felt on the front line, for within days he was in his advanced HQ. He made an early effort to familiarize himself with the various units of his multi-faced force, often making quick surprise visits to the camps. Other meetings were more formal, as Wilson wrote of one review:

> ... we sat on our horses for three hours without moving an eyelash with drawn swords which ultimately weighed about five ton - whilst he rode round. This was after three hours of forming up and getting into shape - a battle is a picnic compared to a show of this sort.[5]

The German and Turkish forces too were undergoing far-reaching changes. The collapse of Russia had released thousands of German and Turkish troops, many of whom went to the European theatre, while others were available for the Middle East. Their first priority was the re-conquest of Baghdad. The German commander, General von Falkenhayn was sent to Turkey and Syria, and following his suggestions a new Turkish Army was assembled at Aleppo, which was supplemented by crack German troops, known as the *Asien Korps*. This new force was to be known as '*Yilderim*' - lighting.

The movement of the *Yilderim* to Baghdad was dependent upon tranquillity in Turkish *Palestine*. This was contrary to the British strategy. Rather than fresh Turko-German forces moving towards Baghdad, they wanted to draw them into conflict in the Land of Israel. The Turkish forces were divided into three main army groups - the 4th Army in Syria and Transjordan, and the 7th and 8th Armies based in *Palestine*.

Allenby basically accepted Chetwode's plan to hit at the Turkish left. To achieve a thorough and complete victory he required more infantry and artillery - and received most of what he requested. With their arrival he abolished *Eastern Force* and formed three Corps; the Desert Mounted Corps (DMC), under Chauvel, comprised of the Anzac, Australian and Yeomanry Mounted Divisions; the 20th Army Corps, under

---

4   Wavell, A. P. *The Palestine Campaigns*, p. 96.
5   Wilson, R. *Palestine 1917*, p. 83.

Chetwode, and comprised of the 53rd (Welsh), 60th (London) and 74th (Yeomanry) Divisions, as well as the 10th (Irish) Division which arrived later; and the 21st Army Corps, under General Bulfin, and comprised of the 52nd (Lowland Scottish), 54th (East Anglia) and 75th (British-Indian) Infantry Divisions. Other troops came directly under the command of the General Headquarters, including the Camel Corps, 7th Mounted Brigade, Imperial Service Cavalry Brigade and 20th Indian Infantry Brigade.[6]

Aqaba Captured

Changes were also imperative if Feisal's Arab 'Army' was to be of major value in the forthcoming offensive. Feisal required more British supplies and the support and allegiance of the Arabs and Bedouin tribes of Syria and Transjordan. It was uncertain if these tribes would accept the authority of the Sherifians from Mecca. To determine and to encourage such allegiance Lawrence set out, under disguise, in the summer of 1917, travelling through Transjordan and Syria as far north as Baalbek. Simultaneously he engineered raids upon the Hejaz railway in Transjordan intending to mislead the Turks into thinking that the Arab 'Army' was actually operating from the east. This was to direct attention away from their next objective: the capture of Aqaba.

Aqaba, at the tip of the Red Sea, was the most strategic point for linking up with the EEF, as well as acting as the base for the northern thrust of the Arab 'Army'. The Turkish garrison, supremely outnumbered, surrendered to the Arab forces on 6 July 1917. Following the victory Lawrence set out by camel across the Sinai to Suez to inform the British authorities of Aqaba's capture, and of the need for immediate provision of supplies. Allenby immediately recognized the potential in developing the operations in this eastern sphere. Large quantities of supplies, including armoured cars, were immediately dispatched to Aqaba, where Lieut.-Colonel P.C. Joyce became base commander. At this point the *Arab Northern Army* was formally born.

Zionist and *Jewish Legion* Breakthroughs

When rumours spread that the Germans were now making approaches to the Zionists,[7] the British interest quickened. They promptly requested the Zionist leadership to quickly submit their requests. Lord Rothschild, representing the Zionist movement, submitted a letter to the British Government on 18 July 1917 outlining the Zionist proposal for a Jewish homeland in Turkish *Palestine*. By early August all the Cabinet members had seen this letter. Some were very favourably inclined towards the

6   Wavell, A. P. *The Palestine Campaigns*, pp.101-102
7   Fromkin. David. *A Peace To End All Peace.*, p. 296.

proposal, some were indifferent - and several were opposed. The most outspoken antagonist was Edwin Montague, an assimilated English Jew who in mid-July had become Secretary of State for India. Montague represented that segment of British society to whom Zionism was a threat.

More opposition followed. The Zionist proposal was closely linked to the concept of the *Jewish Legion*. Jabotinsky's efforts were finally rewarded towards the end of July, when the Government announced the formation of a Jewish infantry regiment, complete with the Star of David insignia, to be known as the *Jewish Regiment*. It was greeted with a hail of opposition, from those very same opponents of Zionism, who saw such a concept as a direct conflict with their own position as loyal British Jews. British Jews, they said, should be fighting in ordinary British units, not in a special Jewish unit.

The War Cabinet met on 3 September and the first item on the agenda concerned *The Jewish Regiment*. It was noted that a deputation of influential British Jews had met with the Secretary of State for War, and stated that some 40,000 Jews had served with distinction with the British forces, and it would therefore be unfair to them that the reputation of British Jewish soldiers be pinned to this *Jewish Regiment.*

It was agreed therefore to drop the term Jewish Regiment, and the battalions of Jewish soldiers would receive numbers like any other unit in the British Army. The minute concluded; 'It was generally agreed that there was a close connection between this subject and the question of the attitude to be taken up towards the Zionist movement as a whole.' [8]

Due to such opposition the authorities backed down from establishing a *Jewish Legion.* Instead Jabotinsky, the former members of the *Zion Mule Corps*, as well as fresh recruits, were formed into the 38th Battalion Royal Fusiliers, and would carry no distinctive Jewish insignia. The unit was officially formed on 24 August 1917. John Patterson was commissioned as commander, Jabotinsky was commissioned as an officer, while Trumpeldor, due to his disability, failed to be enlisted.

Once it became known that this unit was set for the conquest of the Land of Israel, more volunteers enlisted. One recruit was Lieutenant Eliezer Margolin who was recovering in hospital in London from wounds received in France when Jabotinsky tracked him down. Despite his reservations Margolin agreed to join, and after the Australian Army agreed to his transfer he became the commander of the second Jewish battalion - the 39th Battalion Royal Fusiliers.[9]

Other Jewish soldiers also joined up. 'It was a visiting Rabbi who conducted a Sabbath service,' wrote Private Rubinstein from Britain who was then serving in France, 'who brought to my notice that a Jewish Regiment was being formed for service in Palestine and said to me: "Who knows, this may be the beginning of a

8   PRO: CAB 23/4, 3 September 1917.
9   Jabotinsky, V. *The Story of the Jewish Legion.*, p. 102.

National Home for our Jewish People." [10]

Although there had already been a movement in the United States and Canada to enlist Jewish volunteers in the British Army, this had not received the support of the USA government, as America at this stage was still not at war against Turkey. Yet many such volunteers awaited the call, including, surprisingly, David Ben Gurion and Yitzak Ben Zvi.

Towards the *Balfour Declaration*

The War Cabinet at its 3 September meeting also discussed the correspondence between Lord Rothschild and Balfour, the Secretary of State for Foreign Affairs 'on the question of the policy to be adopted towards the Zionist movement.' At this juncture Montague produced a statement entitled *The Anti-Semitism of the present Government* which expressed his view that 'the phrase "the home of the Jewish people" would vitally prejudice the position of every Jew elsewhere.'

Suggestions to postpone the Zionist question were opposed by Balfour, who pointed out 'this was a question on which the Foreign Office had been very strongly pressed for a long time past.' It was agreed that no further overtures would be made to the Zionist organization until the views of President Wilson and the United States Government had been ascertained.[11] So while Wilson and the Americans pondered over the proposed alliance between Britain and the Zionist movement, Montague was busy arguing to change the wording of the proposed agreement, from 'Palestine being *the* Jewish homeland', to, there being *'a* Jewish homeland in Palestine'.

Weizmann and Rothschild sent a fresh Memorandum to the War Cabinet on 3 October in which they emphasized that British help towards Zionism was necessary, and that 'Imperial interests' were involved.[12] The War Cabinet which met on 4 October was now even more sympathetic towards Zionist ambitions due to fresh news of German sympathies towards Zionism. At this meeting Leopold Amery and Lord Milner had produced a redrafted text of Rothschild's original proposal. A copy of this was sent to President Wilson, from whom no clear answer had as yet been received from the previous correspondence. Copies of this redraft were also sent for comment to both pro and anti- Zionist camps in Britain.

The opponents felt it was unwise to state that Palestine was to be *the* Jewish homeland. Also it was felt that as a result of the Armenian massacres by the Turks, and by the uncovering of the *Nili* spy network in Palestine, it would be very detrimental to the lives of Jewish people living in Turkish *Palestine* if a statement was released revealing Britain's commitment towards a Jewish national home.

Yet there were several key supporters at this point, including the Chief Rabbi and

---

10   Freulich, R. *Soldiers in Judea*. Herzl Press, (New York 1964), p. 25.

11   PRO: CAB 23/4, 3 September 1917.

12   Stein, L. *The Balfour Declaration*, p. 519.

Herbert Samuel, a Jewish Member of Parliament. Samuel was firmly of the opinion that if the Turks remained in control of *Palestine* then it would ultimately fall under German influence, or another European nation. Britain's presence in Egypt would then be threatened. He had no hesitation in stating that the best safeguard would be for a strong Jewish presence in Eretz Israel, and that a policy of support by the British Government would win for her immeasurable support throughout the world. He also added, that such a declaration of support would need to be made only when the military situation in the Land of Israel was suitable.[13]

Apprehensions concerning German intentions mounted during October, as important elements of the German press were favorable towards Zionism. The Berlin Zionist Executive had actually submitted Memo's to the German Foreign Office during the previous months, suggesting that Germany and Turkey provide some encouragement towards Zionism. They were anxious lest a British-French-Zionist policy be made, which would then prejudice the Jewish people living within the Ottoman Empire. The Germans however were reluctant to provide support, fearful lest the Turks suspect her (Germany) of having ulterior motives. This German connection however influenced the British Foreign Office who were determined to pre-empt any German move.[14]

The British position was made easier when a positive response towards a British-Zionist alliance was received from President Wilson on 16 October. The final decision now awaited the next meeting of the War Cabinet scheduled for 31 October.

Turkish Pressure in the Land of Israel

While these political deliberations, and Allenby's military preparations were under way, the Turks were attempting to consolidate their hold upon the Land of Israel. The defensive line stretching from Gaza to Beersheva was strengthened, while the supply lines were improved. Strict measures were also being enforced behind the lines to root out all potential fifth-columnists and Allied sympathizers. The seriousness of the situation is highlighted by entries made by Marie James in her diary:

> June 1917 ... Deserters from the Turkish Army were caught and taken to Acre bound with ropes ... Jamal Pasha said, "If the English take our land, they will find only bones and stones."

> July 1917. - Wheat was still being sent out of the country and wood was so scarce that the Government used the bones of camels instead for the railway engines. Boys of fifteen were ordered to join the Turkish Army.

> August 1917. - ... Typhus and malaria were still raging in Safed, and cholera was very bad in Tiberius. Deserters have been shooting the soldiers sent to guard them...

---

13 Stein, L. *The Balfour Declaration*, p. 528. Italics mine.
14 Stein, L. ibid., pp 516-7.

September, 1917. - Every one in Safed suffered more or less from the want of food. The Government would not allow the inhabitants to get any wheat, although the town was full of it. The men were forced to go as soldiers, although many bought themselves off two or three times. I saw a boy of sixteen, lame and nearly blind, who was taken from his bed to serve his country ; he was in rags and had to walk to Acre like the rest of his fellow-sufferers. "Oh, when will the English come!" was the one bitter cry.

October, 1917. - ... The inhabitants of Samaria were in sore distress. A Jew and his sister ... were caught and accused of being spies. The brother escaped, but the sister was tortured and threatened to be hanged if she did not give full information about the English. She refused to do so, and finally shot herself. Her father was beaten to death.

Many Jews and Christians were imprisoned and severely beaten. In Acre and Haifa and in Nazareth, they were tortured unmercifully; a Jew from Samaria who had been cruelly beaten was on his way to Damascus to be hanged, threw himself out of the train and was killed. The Dispensary in Samaria was closed and the water supply cut off.[15]

The Jew and his sister referred to by Miss James were from the Aaronson family. While Aaron and his brother Alexander were out of the country involved in intelligence and Zionist activities in Cairo, Britain and the United States, the Turkish authorities finally uncovered the espionage ring which operated from their home in Zichron Yaacov near Atlit. Sarah, the sister and her father were arrested and interrogated. The sixty-eight year old father died, while Sarah managed to shoot herself and died four days later.

Others suspected of espionage were hanged. Had it not been for the intervention of the Germans and Talaat Bey, Djemal Pasha would have enacted revenge upon the wider Jewish community. In view of such events, it was essential that any public announcement of sympathy towards Zionism by the British Government be coupled with a military breakthrough - otherwise it would endanger the remaining Jewish population in Turkish *Palestine*. Any known or suspected Arab nationalists also received cruel treatment by the Turkish authorities. Many were hanged outside Jaffa Gate in Jerusalem. A speedy British-Anzac breakthrough was awaited by the local inhabitants of the Land of Israel.

Allenby's Final Preparations

Impressive preparations were taking place behind the Wadi Ghuzze as both supplies and fresh troops were brought forward and placed at strategic locations. All efforts had to be made to deceive the Turkish and German High Command into anticipating a diversionary attack upon Beersheva and the main British-led thrust against Gaza.

To aid in this deception Meinertzhagen 'dropped' a haversack while on patrol in

---

15 Diary of Marie James, *JMI*, 1919, p. 70.

no-man's land south of Beersheva, which was picked up by a pursuing Turkish patrol. The haversack contained amongst other things, a note-book revealing the inability of a large British led assault against Beersheva due to the water and transport problem. Although the Turkish commander at Beersheva, Ismet Bey, was skeptical about this information, Von Kressenstein swallowed the bait. He removed a division of reinforcements from Beersheva which had only just recently arrived there. He was adamant that a large force could not approach Beersheva from the waterless south and east. Ismet Bey, still not convinced, nevertheless strengthened his defences to the west, south and east of Beersheva.

While all these preparations were in progress, the troops were, as much as possible, rested. The mounted forces had a three-way rotation, one month patrolling the desert, one month resting on the beach (not really a rest when horses had to be constantly cared for) and one month of intensive training. The rest period nevertheless did offer a break from the desert and skirmishes. Occasionally leave was granted to Kantara or even Port Said. Trooper Malone wrote of his experiences:

> Sept 16. Arrived Kantara & then entrained to Port Said. There are immense stacks of war materials of every description stacked here, guns, forage, rations, tractors, light engines and mortars...
>
> Sept 21. Sailed on harbour. Ran down a boat load of Australians & got chased down the harbour - but succeeded in escaping.[16]

Malone's entries reflect the emphasis now being given to this campaign, as shown by the immense quantities of supplies, and the sporting relationship between the Anzac forces. But for him and all the other soldiers, after a few day of leave it was back to the front, and to the ordeals of life in the desert during the summer. Heat, dust and constant patrolling was the order of the day. 'For nearly three weeks now we have been on a flying stunt,' wrote William Johns to his niece in Auckland, 'have not seen a blanket & only got my boots off once or twice,' he continued. 'Though the days are so hot, the nights,' he concluded, 'are as cold as charity.'[17]

'Finished up a 24 hours stunt yesterday,' wrote Walters. '... Had a long ride out to within 6 miles of Beersheva. Met slight opposition. We left here at 6 A.M. In position at 2 P.M. Stayed there until 10 P.M. & arrived back here just after 4 A.M. Consequently we are all pretty dopy this morning.' He wrote again on 21 October: 'The past week has been a busy one doing outposts & patrols. The big push seems very near now.'[18] Just how big few of the soldiers were aware. But for many Jewish people, both in the Land of Israel and within the Zionist movement, the *big one* would dramatically affect the destiny of their nation.

---

16 Diary of Trooper Malone.
17 Johns, William Henwood 1891-1917. Letters to Iris 1915-1917. Auckland War Memorial Museum Library MS 1392.
18 Diary of Reg Walters.

Towards Beersheva

The EEF plan called for a heavy diversionary naval and artillery bombardment of Gaza during the last days of October. The infantry attack upon Gaza, the 'feint', would be carried out by the 21st Infantry Corps. The attack against Beersheva would be carried out by the 20th Infantry Corps approaching from the south and west, while the Anzac and Australian Mounted Divisions approached from the east and north east. The Yeomanry Mounted Division would cover the region between Gaza and Beersheva. A column of cameliers under the command of Lieutenant-Colonel Newcombe, coming up from Aqaba, was to make a feint north towards Hebron. This move was to give the impression there was to be a drive up the ridge road towards Jerusalem. Simultaneous to the advance towards Beersheva, the small Arab Northern Army led by Feisal and Lawrence was to attack Turkish positions further to the east in the Transjordan, moves scheduled to climax about 5 November.

The Turko-German forces too had been preparing. Although the *Yilderim* had been instructed to move south from Aleppo, they still were not in place and even Von Falkenhayn who had overall control over the forces, was only able to set up his headquarters at Jerusalem on 5 November. 7th Army headquarters were at Hebron, while 8th Army Headquarters were at Jemmameh north-east of Gaza.

Aerial superiority by the Royal and the Australian Flying Corps hindered German planes from spying behind the EEF lines. The success of the operation depended upon secrecy and concealment. The troops began moving towards their positions in late October. The Desert Mounted Corps was to move south-east along the Wadi Ghuzze to Asluj, and then by a large arc move north-east to be situated due east of Beersheva on the morning of 31 October. These movements were to be accomplished undetected. The Anzac and Australian Mounted Divisions who had the longest to travel, set off with horses fully-fed and watered, and supplies for three days. Trooper Jim Henderson of the 4th Light Horse Brigade wrote how they packed a blanket, greatcoat plus emergency rations for the horse which weighed twice as much as a man.[19]

As the column set out it spread for some sixteen kilometres. At several locations along the route they found canvas water troughs filled and waiting for them. Engineers during the previous days had been busy locating and clearing out all the ancient wells which the Turks had stopped up, and installing oil-driven pumps, enabling the troughs to be quickly filled.

During the daytime of 30 October the horsemen rested up and hid in the surrounding wadis (gullies or dry river beds), and continued their movement that night, the Anzac Division covering some forty kilometres, and the Australian Division some fifty-six kilometres. 'We only moved at night' recalls Trooper Henderson,

---

19   Diary of Jim Henderson. *Mountain Views* Healesville Local Paper, Victoria, 19/4/1993, p. 2

'and hid as best we could in cracks and crannies in the wadis or in the shadow of our brownish horses in the daytime, while we tried to sleep ...

After torturing nights over desert or mountains, or both' he continued, 'we still had no idea where we were or where we were going, or whether this was just another toughening up routine.'[20]

The Battle Which Determined Israel's Future

By 5.10 on the morning of 31 October 1917 the Australian Mounted Division was joining the Anzac Mounted Division in the hills and wadis some five kilometres east of Beersheva. About twenty minutes later British artillery opened its barrage upon the town. Several hours later infantry of the 20th Corps, after a gruelling twelve kilometre march over difficult terrain, began their assault on the Turkish positions to the south and west of the town.

From his position to the east Trooper Malone observed: 'Oct 31. Stand to. Shells bursting on ridge SW of Beersheva. Guns on all sides belching forth shells of all sizes & descriptions until whole sky was hidden under pall of smoke ... Infantry advanced on trenches in front.'[21] The British infantry was involved in desperate fighting. The prominent position was Hill 1070, which after a heavy artillery barrage, was assaulted by men of the 60th Division, and captured. From this prominent position the artillery bombed the Turkish front lines cutting the enemy barbed wire to pieces, which permitted easier access by the infantry. By about 1.30 pm the infantry had basically achieved their goals. Corporal John Collins of the Welsh Fusiliers was later awarded the Victoria Cross for his brave actions here. Altogether they sustained some 1,151 casualties in the fighting.

The Mounted Men

The task of the Anzac Division was to cut off Beersheva from the north, by capturing the heavily defended positions of Tel el Sakaty (about ten kilometres north of Beersheva,) and also Tel el Saba, the ancient Beersheva, several kilometres north east of modern Beersheva, on the banks of Wadi Saba. Walters wrote of his part: 'We came right around Beersheva before attacking. Meantime Jacko had his hands full watching the infantry who were making the frontal attack.'[22] Despite heavy enemy artillery and machine gun fire, the Australians captured Tel el Sakaty by 1 p.m.

The New Zealanders and the 1st Light Horse Brigade moved towards the more heavily defended Tel el Saba. Theirs was a very difficult task, as the Turks had very

---

20 Diary of Jim Henderson, *Mountain Views.*
21 Diary of Trooper Malone.
22 Diary of Reg Walters.

strategic positions which commanded the fields before them. But at 2.10 in the afternoon the dismounted Auckland Brigade moved in and after a series of rushes had, within half an hour, cleared the east side of the Tel. Shortly later the remainder of this strategic position had been completely gained.[23] No direct move against Beersheva from the east was possible while this position was still in Turkish hands. Chauvel could now make his final and decisive move.

Beersheva had to be captured with its water wells intact, before nightfall. If not, the men and horses would have to withdraw to the water sources, thereby losing the element of surprise. An EEF withdrawal would allow the Turks to consolidate their defences, and the situation would be a repeat of the first battle of Gaza. As evening was fast approaching, Chauvel had no time to waste. A decisive move was required. Meanwhile the horsemen from the two brigades of the Australian Mounted Division still held in reserve waited patiently. By the late afternoon, they received word to mount.

Chauvel called together his commanders, and despite protests from Brigadier-General M.W. Fitzgerald of the British Yeomanry brigade, he entrusted the responsibility of taking Beersheva to Brigadier-General William Grant, commander of the 4th Light Horse Brigade. The men were aroused from the wadis and, wrote Henderson 'With half an hour of daylight left, things began to happen! With a sudden order to mount, the regiment packed forward into a valley in the foothills at the edge of the plain.'

Henderson then recalls his squadron leader urging: 'Beersheva is two miles across the plain. All packs to the rear. We are going to ride straight into the Turkish position in extended order. It has never been done before! There is no barbed wire, we think, thank God!' [24]

At 4.30 p.m. on 31 October 1917 about 800[25] bayonet-wielding Australian horsemen set off in three columns at a canter across the five kilometre plain to Beersheva, on what would not only become an epic 'cavalry' charge, but on a venture which was to change the destiny of the former Ottoman Empire, and the course of world history. Henderson describes the following minutes:

> The moment the leading troops had crowded out on to the plain, a storm of shrapnel, high explosives and machine gun fire began and the great spread of horses increased pace to a canter ...
> The horses were shying aside from the shell bursts. A thin haze of smoke and dust began to rise, but the three lines of horses moved steadily forward.
> ... The first half mile was the worst. After that, much of the fire seemed to be going

---

23 Powles, Lieut.-Col. C. Guy. *The New Zealanders in Sinai and Palestine.* p. 138.

24 Diary of Jim Henderson, *Mountain Views.*

25 Jones, Ian. *Beersheba: The light horse and the making of myths.* From *Journal of the Australian War Memorial.* No. 3. October 1983. Australian War Memorial, Canberra., p. 30.

over our heads. As we learned later, the Turks had ranged all their weapons on us but the sight of these Australians coming from an entirely unexpected direction and bearing down on them was demoralizing, and they had forgotten to bring their sights down as we advanced! [26]

The horsemen rode about three kilometres before reaching the first Turkish trenches. The Turkish commanders, recognizing the horsemen as mounted infantry, had instructed their soldiers to wait until the Australians dismounted from their horses, and then to open fire. Lieutenant-Colonel Bouchier however commanded his men to go forward at the gallop. The horsemen rode under the range of the Turkish artillery and rifle fire.

Many of the troops dismounted and fought the entrenched Turks in fierce hand to hand fighting, marred by Turks violating their surrender, and shooting Australian soldiers. Such violators were immediately killed.

A number of horsemen continued towards the town itself, where explosives set around the water wells were about to be detonated. Fortunately the rapid Australian advance hindered their complete destruction. By a stroke of luck the German engineer responsible for the destruction of the wells was on leave in Jerusalem at the time, and his replacement was in the process of detonating the explosives at random in the switchboard of a central building, when the Light Horsemen rode in. He was hindered from accomplishing his task. Had he succeeded then he would have turned a British-Anzac victory into defeat - and changed the destiny of the campaign. Had those valuable water wells been destroyed, Allenby's strategy of a quick and decisive victory and movement northwards towards Jaffa and Jerusalem would have been thwarted.

As it was only two of the water wells were destroyed. If more had been rendered unusable, the fruits of victory would indeed have been sour. For within hours some 58,500 thirsty and weary soldiers, and up to 100,000 animals descended upon Beersheva. These men and animals required some 1,800,000 litres of water, while the reservoirs held only some 400,000 litres. Much patience and restraint on behalf of men and animal was required while the reservoirs were replenished.

In describing the outcome of the battle to the Secretary of State for War, Allenby stated:

> ... attempts to advance in small parties across the plain towards the town made slow progress. In the evening, however, a mounted attack by Australian Light Horse, who rode straight at the town from the east, proved completely successful. They galloped over two deep trenches held by the enemy just outside the town, and entered the town at about 7 p.m., capturing numerous prisoners.
>
> The Turks at Beersheva were undoubtedly taken completely by surprise, a surprise from which the dash of the London troops and Yeomanry, finally supported by their

---

26 Diary of Jim Henderson, *Mountain Views.*

artillery, never gave them time to recover. The charge of the Australian Light Horse completed their defeat. [27]

Wavell, after giving the infantry the credit they deserved, wrote: 'The moral results of the charge were even greater than the material gains. It set the pace for the whole campaign, inspiring the brigade which carried it out with immense confidence and all the other mounted troops with a spirit of rivalry and emulation. And this demonstration of the power of mounted men to ride home on their infantry undoubtedly shook the nerve of the Turks.' [28]

War Cabinet Meeting

As the British and Anzac soldiers were capturing Beersheva on 31 October a crucial meeting was being held by the War Cabinet in London. The outcome of this meeting would change the destiny of the Jewish people, the Land of Israel, and indeed of the world. Balfour stated that he 'gathered that everyone was now agreed that, from a purely diplomatic and political point of view, it was desirable that some declaration favourable to the aspirations of the Jewish nationalists should now be made.' He went on to point out that the two main objections, '(a) That Palestine was inadequate to form a home for either the Jewish or any other people, or (b) The difficulty felt with regard to the future position of Jews in Western countries,' could both be adequately dealt with. Concerning the second point, Balfour said that he understood a *national home* to mean 'some form of British, American, or other protectorate, under which full facilities would be given to the Jews to work out their own salvation and to build up, by means of education, agriculture and industry, a real centre of national culture and focus of national life. It did not,' he continued, 'necessarily involve the early establishment of an independent Jewish State, which was a matter for gradual development in accordance with the ordinary laws of political evolution.' [29]

Lord Curzon, although sympathetic to the Zionist position, nevertheless held certain reservations about the optimism concerning the future of a Jewish homeland in the Land of Israel. He also stated the necessity of retaining the Christian Holy Places in Jerusalem and Bethlehem , and remarked 'if this were to be effectively done, he did not see how the Jewish people could have a political capital in Palestine.' Yet despite these wise reservations, Curzon concluded 'that some expression of sympathy with Jewish aspirations would be a valuable adjunct to our propaganda.' Thus ended the debate, whereupon the War Cabinet authorised the Secretary of State for Foreign Affairs 'to take a suitable opportunity of making the following declaration

---

27 Dispatch of General Allenby, 16 December 1917, in *The Advance of the Egyptian Expeditionary Force*, p. 3.
28 Wavell, A. *The Palestine Campaign.*, p. 126.
29 PRO: CAB 23/4 137. War Cabinet Meeting, 31 October 1917.

of sympathy with the Zionist aspirations:-

> His Majesty's Government views with favour the establishment in Palestine of a national home for the Jewish people, and will use its best endeavours to facilitate the achievement of this object, it being clearly understood that nothing shall be done which may prejudice the civil and religious rights of existing non-Jewish communities in Palestine, or the rights and political status enjoyed by Jews in any other country. [30]

Balfour was authorized to inform Weizmann and the leading Zionists of the acceptance of their proposal, albeit one substantially altered from the original. As the initial proposal had been submitted in a letter from Lord Rothschild to Balfour in July, Balfour was to formally write to Rothschild of the Government's decision. On 2 November 1917 the very day when the British newspapers reported the victory at Beersheva, Balfour wrote the Cabinet's decision to Rothschild, beginning by stating, 'I have much pleasure in conveying to you, on behalf of His Majesty's Government, the following declaration of sympathy with Jewish Zionist aspirations which has been submitted to, and approved by, the Cabinet.' Then followed the Declaration, to be known henceforth as the *Balfour Declaration*. Balfour concluded his letter by stating, 'I should be grateful if you would bring this declaration to the knowledge of the Zionist Federation.'

Palmerston in 1840 failed to achieve a British-sponsored Jewish takeover in the Land of Israel for four main reasons: (1) Lack of sufficient troops in the Land. (2) Opposition from the other European powers. (3) An alliance with Turkey, which was unwilling to sanction a Jewish national movement within its territory. (4) Lack of readiness of the Jewish people for a return. In 1917 Balfour and Lloyd George had all of these factors weighed in their favour.

And it all climaxed at Beersheva, a town connected to Abraham, the father of Israel, to whom, the Bible states, God had promised the Land of Israel as an eternal possession.

---

30 PRO: CAB 23/4 138. War Cabinet Meeting, 31 October 1917.

Chapter 15

The Race to Jaffa

Third Battle of Gaza - Feint towards Hebron

Allenby now wanted to quickly roll back the Beersheva-Gaza line, surround the Turkish forces, move quickly up the plain of Philistia and take Jerusalem as soon as possible. But even with the wells of Beersheva he was severely handicapped by the lack of water. In addition the hot *khamsin* wind began to blow, quickly drying the throats of man and animal. Despite these setbacks preparations were made after several days for the next objective: breaking the centre of the Turkish line at Tel esh Sheria (near present day Kibbutz Mishmar Ha Negev). This objective was dependent upon consolidation of the ground to the north of Beersheva, and another, successful, strike at Gaza.

As troops began moving north of Beersheva on 1 November Newcombe and his cameliers were already engaging the Turks near Hebron. Australian patrols also reached as far as El Dhaheriye, between Beersheva and Hebron. Trooper Idriess recalls '... our mobile regiment was detached for reconnaissance up the Hebron road down which old man Abraham had travelled to Beersheba. Although without sleep' he continued, 'we rode cheerfully into the Judean hills.'[1]

Von Kressenstein and the German staff resolved to recapture Beersheva. They were diverted from this objective however, by the news of the raiding parties at Hebron and El Dhaheriya. Believing these to be major EEF thrusts towards Jerusalem, the large Turkish force headed not towards Beersheva, but towards Hebron. They confronted the EEF forces at a dominating mound, about sixteen kilometres north of Beersheva, named Tel Khuweilfeh (present day Kibbutz Lahav). Other Turkish forces also surrounded Newcombe's force, killing some and capturing the survivors, including Newcombe.

The third battle for Gaza, led by the 21st Infantry Corps, began during the night of 1 November. The defences at Gaza, subdued by a continuous bombardment since 27 October, were softened up before troops of the 54th Scottish Division began their assault. The next few days witnessed terrible hand to hand fighting in and around

---

1   Idriess, I. *The Desert Column*, p. 253.

Gaza, primarily in the vicinity of Ali Muntar.

Fighting at Tel Khuweilfeh.

Allenby suffered two set backs to his goals in early November. Lawrence was to engineer a diversionary attack in Transjordan. He and a small number of troops chose to destroy part of the railway running down the Yarmuk River between Semakh and Deraa. The attack basically failed and only part of the required goal was achieved. The other frustration was the movement of Turkish troops towards the Hebron road. No pursuit could be possible while this large force remained at Tel Khuweilfeh, which was important both strategically, and also because of its large water cisterns.

From 2-7 November, British and Anzac troops fought an intense encounter around the ancient tel, and the nearby Ras el Nagd. Trooper Malone recalled: 'Bullets falling everywhere. Lay in all day under rifle fire.'[2] Due to the lack of water the longer the engagement lasted, the worse the position became for the EEF. The Australian Mounted Division was forced to withdraw to Karm for replenishment.

An all-out offensive was planned, both at Gaza and at Tel Khuweilfeh, on 6 November. Also on that day, the first move would be made against the central positions, especially Tel Hareira and Tel esh Sheria. The fighting at all three locations was tough. Malone's entry for 6 November from Tel Khuweilfeh read: "Filluel hit in chest & died of wounds. Friend killed - hit in stomach. Gorrie hit in head - killed. Snipers.'[3] Casualties were high everywhere. In the centre the 10th (Irish), 74th (former Yeomanry) and 60th (London) Infantry Divisions contended throughout November 6th against the strategically located Kauwukah and Rushdi Turkish trench systems between the two ancient tels.[4] The Australian Mounted Division was also thrown in, and as their horsemen charged they had to evade the dead and wounded Londoners.

The fighting continued. Malone wrote on 7 November. 'Sniped all day. Turks jolly good shots & many hits ...'[5] Walters recorded on 7 November: 'Had a pretty rough time the last few days. You would not recognize us for dirt. We have just had a quick move this morning & are now at or near SHARIA. The news has just come through that GAZA has fallen. Jacko is getting a nasty knock right along the line.'[6] At dawn on 7 November, men of the 21st Infantry Corps had gained the summit of the now famous Ali Muntar. Gaza, at the third attempt, was now under EEF control.

Tel esh Sheria was also captured during the early hours of 7 November by the London Division, and soon afterwards Tel Hareira by the Irish Division. The Turko-

2   *Diary of Trooper Malone.*
3   Ibid.
4   Tel is an ancient city, which has been covered through the centuries by dust and debris. They are natural defensive positions.
5   *Diary of Trooper Malone.*

German line had at last been completely broken, apart from some menacing rearguard actions. And finally, late on 7 November Khuweilfeh was taken. Due to this and other set backs Von Falkenhayn, from his headquarters at the Augusta Victoria complex in Jerusalem, ordered Von Kressenstein to withdraw his forces from Gaza and establish a new defensive line on the northern side of Wadi el Hesi (present day Nahal Shiqma). As they headed for their next line of defence, the British-Anzac forces were to move quickly to surround and break them before they escaped.

Up the Plain of Philistia

The majority of the mounted forces were stationed ready for the race up the plain of Philistia. The emphasis now was upon the rapid movement of the mounted troops. The next Turkish defensive line ran from the mouth of the Wadi el Hesi on the coast, through to the villages and fortifications of Huj (Har Hoga near Kibbutz Dorit) and Jemmameh (Har Jemmameh near Kibbutz Ruhama),and Tel en Nejile (Tel Nagila). Yet progress during 7 November was disappointing, due primarily to the lack of water and menacing rearguard actions. With little respite, the mounted troops had been operating almost continually since 31 October and both men and horses were tired, under-watered and underfed.

Steady progress was made during 8 November. Walters recorded that this was a 'Red Letter day' for his unit, as they ran into a position of thousands of Turkish troops. 'Of course' he continued, 'we had to face a fair amount of Gun and Machine Gun fire but completely demoralised the enemy ... What a great victory we are having. Jacko is getting back for his life.'[7] As the Londoners approached Huj they came under heavy fire and called upon the mounted troops for assistance. Men of the 5th Yeomanry Brigade then pulled off an amazing cavalry charge, emulating their Australian colleagues at Beersheva. Lieutenant Wilson recalled:

> We were advancing in line, well fanned out ... Eventually we found ourselves doing a gallop and, as we crossed the ridge there was revealed a scene witnessed by few men - enemy heavy guns and machine guns surrounded by their crews dead or wounded as were many gallant yeomen and the horses that had carried them as hunters over their farms at home. I am not particularly emotional but this was the most distressing thing I had ever seen.[8]

In this brief encounter twenty-nine Yeomanry were killed and forty-six wounded, while 100 of 170 horses were killed. By late in the evening of 8 November, the 52nd Lowland Scottish Division had gained, after very heavy losses, all the Turkish positions along the Wadi el Hesi. On 9 November the Anzac Mounted Division, followed by

---

6   *Diary of Reg Walters*
7   Ibid.
8   Wilson. R. *Palestine 1917*, p. 94

the Australian and Yeomanry Divisions, was sent in pursuit of the retreating Turkish forces, who were now falling back to the next line of defence.

During the following days the British-Anzac force moved slowly northwards, capturing position after position. The British and Australian planes, in control of the skies, gave invaluable support, supplying reliable information, and often bombing the retreating Turkish transports.

The Turks were withdrawing before the mounted horsemen to a stronger defensive line, running from the coast where the Nahr Rubin-Wadi Surar (Nahal Sorek) entered the Mediterranean, along the north bank of this small river, which ran inland over the coastal plain, through the Shephelah, passing the ancient site of Bet Shemesh and village of Artuf, and on up to Jerusalem. From a place named Junction Station, where the Jaffa-Jerusalem railway joined the Jaffa-Beersheva railway, the railway ran adjacent to the stream up into the Judean hills. Part of this line was protected by the Mughar-Katrah ridge.

Battle of Junction Station and Ayun Kara

At this point Allenby determined to split the Turko-German forces into two, force a wedge between them, and by a two pronged attack, head towards Jaffa on the left flank, and towards Jerusalem on the right flank. The crucial position was Junction Station. Troops began moving towards their positions by 12 November. If the Turks lost this defensive line - their next line was beyond the Jaffa-Jerusalem railway - then that vital line of communication and supply would be lost to them. For Allenby, any hope of securing Jerusalem before the winter rains set in would be determined by the speed in which he could break this line.

This crucial thrust began in earnest on 13 November. Along the entire line there was heavy resistance and fighting. Mounted British Yeomanry dashed at the Mughar Ridge and after courageous fighting from them and the infantry, the position was captured, as was nearby Katrah. A young Evelyn Rothschild, nephew of Edmund, was killed in the clash at Mughar.

The following day, 14 November, the 75th Infantry Division captured the strategic Junction Station while the New Zealanders fought a very tough battle near the Arab village of Ayun Kara, adjacent to the Jewish colonies of Rishon le Zion and Rehovot.

The New Zealanders were heavily outnumbered by the Turks. At one point, during a Turkish counter-attack the fighting was so intense that every available soldier, including signallers, gallopers and batmen from the Regimental Headquarters were rushed forward until reinforcements arrived from the 3rd Squadron. This squadron then advanced, dismounted under the command of Major Twistleton, and came to within a few metres of the Turkish line.[9]

---

9   Powles, Lieut.-Col. C. Guy. *The New Zealanders in Sinai and Palestine.* , p. 148.

The heavily outnumbered New Zealanders at one point were rushed by the Turkish infantry. They stood and then counter attacked with the bayonet. The Turks were no match for the tough New Zealanders, and leaving hundreds of their dead and wounded behind them, they fled the scene of battle. It was the last Turkish attempt to maintain the Jaffa-Jerusalem line. The New Zealanders lost forty-four dead and 141 wounded in this fierce encounter. Some of these died later of their wounds. That evening the Jewish mayor of nearby Rehovot sent a huge flagon of rich wine to General Chaytor, with a message, 'From the Oldest Colony in the World to the Youngest.'

The Turkish Army Split

The fighting of 13 and 14 November effectively sealed the fate of the Turkish Army. Her 7th Army now retreated into the Shephelah and Judean hills, while the 8th Army retreated towards Jaffa and the line running to the north of the Jerusalem-Jaffa railway. The British-Anzac troops were in hot pursuit. Walters recorded on 14 November: 'The last few days have been very strenuous. Shell fire every day ... We have now joined up with the Inf. [infantry] & are near the junction of Jerusalem-Jaffa Line.'[10]

On 15 November, the British-Anzac force closed in on Latrun and the nearby village of Yalo, and nearby Tel Jezar, the ancient Gezer. Tel Jezar and the accompanying ridge controlled the Valley of Ajalon, and the route from Jaffa-Ramle to Jerusalem. Latrun, further to the east, marked the point where the Gaza-Jerusalem and Jaffa-Jerusalem roads converged. From Latrun the two main routes through the Judean hills to Jerusalem, via Bab el Wad and Beth Horon, diverged.

Also on 15 November the Anzac Division galloped rapidly northwards, liberating Jewish colonies, as well as the Arab towns of Ramle and Ludd (Lod) and capturing hundreds of straggling Turks. It was a great relief for the Jewish colonists to see the visible results of their prayers, and a welcome relief for the EEF soldiers to see some form of civilization. Walters wrote:

> It seemed strange to ride through decent villages with stone buildings and tiled roofs inhabited by Jews who in some cases could speak English and who were mighty glad to see the Red, White & Blue in place of the Turkish Crescent. We fared pretty well in these villages for brown bread and fruit, which was very acceptable after the weeks of tinned dog and biscuits. The Oranges particularly are a boon. We buy them here at the rate of 30 for 1/-. They come from Jaffa and Ramley. The Jews have plenty of bread to sell and we have consumed a good bit of it, but they charge an unreasonable price for sale, i.e. 1/- for a small loaf that a man can eat for one meal. In nearly every village one finds a fine engine and pumping plant and if not blown up by the retreating Turks is of immense value for drawing water for our horses.[11]

A certain degree of homesickness was felt by some of the soldiers when seeing these

---

10   *Diary of Reg Walters.*
11   Ibid.

villages, and the 'mimosa hedges in full bloom'. One interesting event occurred in the village of Nahalat Reuben (inheritance of Reuben) which Powles explains:

> The lane led out into an open space where crowds of white men, women and children welcomed us with loud cries of "Shallome, Shallome" and much talking in Yiddish. Suddenly came a clear cut question in excellent English from a woman, "Do you know a soldier of the name of _____?" An audible smile went down the little column and the Staff Officer leading suggested that there doubtless were many soldiers of that name in the Division, but that if she knew his regiment enquiries could be made. Quickly the answer came, "Yes, he is a New Zealander and is in the N.Z. Mounted Regiment, but I do not know which. I would much like to find him because he is my son." And before any further answer could be given a burly policeman, who had been riding behind the Provost Marshal and who had been chosen by that officer quite haphazard that morning from the Divisional Mounted Police as his horse holder for the day, rode forward and said he had a letter for a Mrs _____ which had been given to the Divisional Police by Trooper_____ of the Auckland Regiment about a year ago with the request that all enquiries be made for his mother in the villages of Palestine. And here we found her after riding 200 miles through an alien land: and she was the first white woman we had spoken to in all that ride.
>
> Needless to say that Trooper _____'s C.O. was at once communicated with, and the son was given leave to go to his mother.[12]

There was a very warm welcome for the Anzac liberators in all the Jewish colonies. At Rishon le Zion, the inhabitants lined the streets, in order, wrote Idriess 'to stare at these brown, sleeveless soldiers. We must have seemed queer fighting men to them,' he continued, 'for they stared as if they had expected to see supermen, not rough-clad Australians. I don't think they could realize that we actually were the men who had driven back their taskmaster of centuries. They seem also to be on the verge of something they cannot believe, cannot understand: they tremble when they whisper Jerusalem. It appears there is some prophesy, centuries old, that one day Jerusalem will fall and will be taken from the Turk or from whatever infidel holds it.'[13]

Chauvel set up his HQ at Khirbat Deiran (Rehovot) on 16 November - in the home of Lazar Slutzkin, who had been expelled by the Turks to Alexandria in 1914-15. The parents of a young horseman from the 10th Light Horse Regiment also lived in Rehovot. Under orders from Chauvel the soldier was summoned forward and warmly welcomed by his friends and family.[14]

On 16 November the New Zealanders liberated Jaffa, reputedly one of the oldest seaports in the world, and soon after occupied the southern bank of the Nahr Auja (Nahal Yarkon). The Australian Division also occupied Latrun. The area between these two positions was occupied by other horsemen and British infantry. The Turks

---

12 Powles, Lieut.-Col. C. Guy *The New Zealanders in Sinai and Palestine.*, p. 155.
13 Idriess, I. *The Desert Column.*, p. 284.
14 Hill, A.J. *Chauvel of the Light Horse.*, p. 134.

had been pushed out of the plain of Philistia. Although there were minor skirmishes during the following days, there was a respite from constant movement, allowing the troops to rest, reflect and eat. Phase two of the campaign was now over. But the victory was won at great cost. The British-Anzac force suffered some 10,000 casualties between 7-16 November.

The Cost of Deprivation.

The liberated towns and villages were placed under the jurisdiction of representatives of 'Occupied Enemy Territory', and received supplies from the various relief agencies which followed the troops. The Royal Navy arrived off Jaffa on 19 November, and thereafter landed large quantities of supplies.

Jaffa was only a shadow of its pre-war self. Only some 10,000 of its 50,000 inhabitants remained. Many residents, especially Jewish, had been expelled in 1914-15, many had been taken into the Turkish Army, many had died of starvation and deprivation, while many had been expelled by Jemal Pasha at the time of the attacks upon Gaza. Yet, wrote Powles, within days of Jaffa's liberation, many of these former inhabitants returned, coming 'on camel back and on donkeys and on foot, with all the worldly goods they still possessed packed upon camels, mules and donkeys. It was a motley crowd,' he continued, 'that arrived day after day and it showed many signs of the privations of war. Food had been exceedingly scarce and many had actually starved to death.'[15]

The fate which had befallen Jaffa was now being felt by many other towns and villages still under Turkish control. Maria James, in her last diary entry, in November 1917, wrote from Safed:

> There is great disaffection throughout the country in consequence of the Germans buying up all kinds of food, for which they pay a high price; they also bought camels, horses, mules and donkeys in great numbers. The German soldiers are well cared for, whilst the Turks are just the reverse. It is no wonder there are so many deserters from the Ottoman Army.
>
> The Government is prosecuting its search for spies with increased vigour. We have been secretly warned to destroy or hide all letters and papers, especially those written in English, as the Turks are more suspicious of what they do not understand. It is therefore necessary for me to bring "Life in Safed during the War" to an abrupt conclusion, trusting that deliverance will soon come to this unhappy country through Him Who is the "Prince of Peace."[16]

Jewish hopes now rested even more upon a speedy British-Anzac victory. In the liberated areas of the Land of Israel young Jewish men were keen to join in the conquest. And as anticipated, the announcement of the *Balfour Declaration*

---

15 Powles, Lieut.-Col. C. Guy. *The New Zealanders in Sinai and Palestine.*, p.158.
16 Diary of Maria E. James. Quoted in *Jewish Intelligence*, 1919, p. 70.

encouraged more Jewish men to seek enlistment in the *Jewish Legion*. In the United States that ground swell of interest continued to grow, especially after 9 November when news of the Balfour Declaration became public.

A Time to Rest

For the British and Anzac soldiers in the Land of Israel however it was a time to enjoy a rest, and appreciate the change of environment from the harsh Sinai and Negev Deserts. Trooper Malone was intrigued by the different agricultural styles from those he was accustomed to in New Zealand. 'One morning whilst foraging,' he reflected, 'I came across an old Arab with a donkey and a bullock harnessed together in the same team. Other combinations I have seen are:- Donkey & horse, donkey and camel, horse and camel, and bullock and camel.' Leaving animal husbandry, he then wrote of some observations about the people of the land:

> The population is very mixed and so peculiarly so that it is not right to give the whole one name. Arabs sure make up a large % of the population, but besides these there are mixed breeds of Armenians, Circassians, Kurds, Tunisians, Ethiopians and Jews. There are many Jewish colonies of Europeans, chiefly Germans, tho' nearly all nations of Europe are represented.
>
> The colonists live in houses of stone or plaster, whitewashed. These houses with their red tiles and pretty gardens form a very pleasant contrast with the Eastern villages that surround them. Most of these people are employed in the vineyards or in the wine and spirit distilleries that are to be found near them.
>
> The natives live in the usual crowded-filthy-mudwalled villages that make up the East. Most of these villages are built on hills about two miles apart. This follows the ancient scheme for protection and also keeps the dwellings on dry ground. All native & most Jewish villages are surrounded by gardens and orchards which in turn are surrounded by prickly pear hedges of enormous height and thickness ... In the native villages it is the women that do most of the heavy work - ploughing excepted. Watercarrying has been & still is the work of the Arab women and we often see them, in their characteristically Eastern dresses - harem skirts - veils- hoods, carrying huge earthenware jars of water on their heads.

Malone, in conclusion actually found one factor which reminded him of home. 'The Jewish colonists,' he concluded, 'live in scattered open villages very much like New Lynn.'[17]

Trooper Malone may not have been aware at the time, but the goal and vision of those Jewish colonists, was to now see their villages and people as secure as those of New Zealand. The first, and vitally important part of that goal was the liberation of Jerusalem and the involvement of Jewish Zionist soldiers in the conquest of their homeland. Trooper Malone and his fellow Anzac and British soldiers were soon to be a part of the fulfillment of these goals.

---

17 *Diary of Trooper Malone*, ibid. New Lynn - a settlement then on the outskirts of Auckland.

Chapter 16

Jerusalem by Christmas

Move into the Judean Hills

History has revealed the danger involved in foreign armies pressing an attack through the Judean hills to Jerusalem. Yet despite the history lessons and lack of adequate supplies Allenby chose to proceed. He wanted to take advantage of the Turkish disorganization and the psychological edge his troops, and especially the mounted forces, held over the Turks.

Allenby's strategy was to establish a firm line along the Nahr Auja over the Samarian hills north of Jerusalem and running down to the Jordan River some sixteen kilometres north of Jericho. From this platform he could cross the Jordan River, take Transjordan, cut the Hejaz railway, and move northwards towards Damascus. His initial objectives were to capture first Jerusalem, and then Jericho.

The British-Anzac force made its entry into the Judeo-Samarian range along three routes on 18 November. But as the troops began moving towards their objectives the clouds finally burst drenching the land, the men and the animals. It now became clear that this was difficult terrain for horses to operate effectively in and thereafter the operation was primarily one for the infantry. These men suffered terribly, from the heavily entrenched Turkish troops, and also from the weather. They were still in their summer wear, and lacked warm clothes.

Heavy resistance was encountered from the Turks in the region between Latrun and Bab el Wad, on the main road to Jerusalem. Walters recorded on 21 November: 'Started off last night along the road to Jerusalem, but it came on to pour rain ... The road winds in between great hills (very beautiful and inspiring). Horses & men are dead here and there along the track from the Turkish sniper who is still busy.'[1]

On 20 November the 75th Division captured the strategic ridge upon which Saris (today near junction of Jerusalem - Moshav Shoresh road) and Kuryat el Enab were located. Further to the north the Yeomanry Division was hindered from gaining its objective by fierce fighting at the Zeitoun Ridge (just north of present day Givat Zeev). This ridge controlled the Beth Horon route - and delayed any advance towards

---

1   *Diary of Reg Walters.*

the Jerusalem-Nablus road. The 75th Division moved in to offer assistance. While moving in this direction, on 21 November, they came under fire from the strategically located Nebi Samuel mosque, located atop a commanding ridge which dominated the approaches to Jerusalem. It was here that Richard the Lion Heart's quest for the capture of Jerusalem was thwarted during the Crusades. But not this time round for the British soldiers. One Brigade of the 75th Division attacked and captured the height. Seeing this position as being the key to Jerusalem the division later adopted the key as their divisional symbol. Subsequent Turkish counter-attacks failed to recapture the position. And despite repeated assaults by the 52nd and 75th Divisions, the strategically located El Jib, lying between Nebi Samuel and Zeitoun Ridge, remained in Turkish hands. By 24 November a stalemate had occurred and a new line had been established. Allenby now called for a cessation of further advances, and a consolidation of this line. Over the following days the exhausted 75th and 52nd Divisions were replaced by the rested 60th London, 10th Irish and 74th Yeomanry Divisions.

The mounted troops, men of the 10th Light Horse Regiment, were stationed at Artuf. From here they daily patrolled into the hills, venturing up to Ein Kerem (traditional birthplace of John the Baptist), Setaf and other villages on the outskirts of Jerusalem. And while these Australian horsemen probed the outskirts of Jerusalem, the politicians in London were now tackling the thorny issues associated with the future status of the Holy City.

The Politics of Jerusalem

Jerusalem now became a major issue of the War Cabinet, which had declared that upon its capture a proclamation be issued assuring the Muslim world that the British forces were the protectors of the Muslim Holy Places. At a meeting on 26 November a message was read from Allenby, inquiring what flags were to be hoisted in Jerusalem. The War Cabinet replied: 'In view of the unique character of the city and of the many difficult political and diplomatic questions that were raised in connection with it, General Allenby should be informed that no flags should be hoisted in the event of the occupation of the city by Allied troops.' [2]

Besides these meetings there were deliberations in Cairo, especially between Sykes (until his replacement as Government liaison officer by Gilbert Claydon), and Reginald Wingate, (who had replaced McMahon as High Commissioner). The Foreign Office in a letter to Reginald Wingate in Cairo on 16 November, was concerned lest friction arise 'in connection with Holy Places in the event of an occupation of Jerusalem by the British forces' and thereupon made a number of proposals for safeguarding, especially of the Christian and Muslim Holy Places. 'In general,' the memo continued, 'Jerusalem should be kept under martial law so as to avoid Franco-Italian

---

2　PRO: CAB 23/4 WC 282. 26 November 1917.

complications ... '[3] It was clear that the Government still had apprehensions about the French especially, and the Italians.

Wingate in reply on 19 November, stated that he and Allenby had decided it best to place picked Christian guards at the Christian Holy Places, and picked Muslim, probably Indian, guards at the Muslim Holy Places. A Military Governor of Jerusalem had also been selected, Colonel Borton, the Postmaster General in Egypt. 'This arrangement' wrote Wingate, 'will effectually prevent political interference on the part of interested Powers by maintaining a purely military administrative system entirely under General Allenby until the military situation becomes much clearer than it is at present.'

Wingate went on to say that Borton has been instructed, by him and Allenby, to deal with the various representatives of the Christian, Muslim and Jewish Holy Places and communities, and to assure them that little change would be presently made, 'pending the re-establishment of a purely civil Government which is not possible as long as any enemy forces are in being in Palestine.'[4]

But despite such British plans, the French were determined to be involved politically in the conquest of Jerusalem. Wingate sent an urgent telegram to the Foreign Office on 21 November, stating he had been informed by the French Ambassador, that since Picot could not 'arrive in time at Allenby's headquarters Monsieur de France has been instructed to proceed there as soon as possible in order to enter Jerusalem with the first British troops.' Wingate also wrote, 'The French Government further request that if Borton Pasha [Colonel Borton] is appointed Governor of Jerusalem he [i.e. Monsieur de France] should receive similar instructions with regard to French participation *in the administration of Jerusalem*.'[5]

On the same day, 21 November, Allenby received instructions from the CIGS Robertson at the War Office, concerning his actual entrance into Jerusalem. His every move was being dictated by the Government planners, of which Sykes was playing a key part. Allenby was informed in these instructions to enter the Holy City on foot.[6]

Meanwhile in a letter to the Foreign Office dated 24 November, Sir Reginald Wingate, (with Allenby's concurrence), was becoming concerned about the French position. The French Government was insisting that Picot, who was now on the scene, be involved in the official entry into Jerusalem. Wingate and Allenby were strongly of the opinion that a military administration should be created for the conquered areas of Palestine 'so long as military operations are in progress.'[7]

3   PRO: FO 371/3061. No 21308 383. 16 November 1917.
4   PRO: FO 371/3061 21308, p. 403-4. 221385.
5   PRO: FO 371/3061 21308, p. 410. Italics mine.
6   PRO: FO 371 3061 21308, p. 420.
7   PRO: FO 317/3061 21308., p. 430-1.

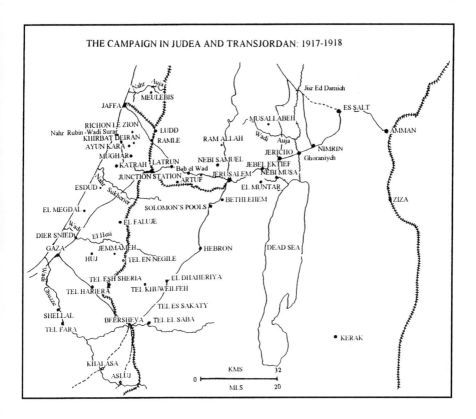

THE CAMPAIGN IN JUDEA AND TRANSJORDAN: 1917-1918

Picot however was 'sticking to his guns', and at a subsequent meeting with Wingate 'expressed his dissatisfaction with these arrangements which he considered would be strongly resented in France.' 'Picot declared' Wingate stated, that 'over a year ago it was agreed between British and French Governments that pending final settlement of peace terms, any conquered portions of Palestine should be jointly administered by us and the French, exclusive of the Italians or other nationalities.' Picot claimed that it was this understanding that warranted French officers being placed beside the British officers in the future administration of Palestine.[8]

Picot was referring to a memorandum between Grey and Monsieur Cambon on 16 May 1916 concerning the future administration of Palestine, but Wingate found this to be quite flimsy evidence to demand such an important position of authority. The Foreign Office found that their hands were tied, and instructed Wingate on 26 November that both Picot, representing the French Government and Clayton,

8   PRO: FO 317/3061 21308. 224720, p. 435.

representing the British, could enter Jerusalem with Allenby, but that both would then 'enter upon their full duties at once under General Officer Commanding.'[9] This ensured that the final word concerning the role of Picot would be entrusted to General Officer Commanding, meaning Allenby.

The *Balfour Declaration* and presence of a large British Empire force, still did not guarantee a purely British takeover of Turkish *Palestine*. The French were still in the race.

Consolidation of the Gains

To hinder the Turko-German command from disrupting his objectives in the Judean hills, Allenby attacked across the Nahr Auja on 24 November. The Turks counter-attacked the following day, and drove the British and New Zealanders back. The Turko-German forces then also attempted to thwart the EEF changeover in the hills by counter-attacking with special *Yilderim* or "storm troopers" between 27 November till 3 December along the entire EEF line from Beth Horon to the coastal plain. The fighting in many sectors was very intense. 'Fronting us,' recalled Idriess, 'the country was dotted with villages, one very pretty Jewish one, Muleubis, being all smoke from bursting shells.' Despite battle conditions, this trooper managed to discover a point in common with his native land:

> Groves of dark green gums were everywhere. The inhabitants are very jealous of each individual tree. They import the Australian "sucker" gum, the gum that our pastoralists find almost impossible to kill by ring-barking. When these people cut one tree, six young ones spring up from the old stump. When I was "suckering" in Australia I little dreamt that one day I would be in a strange land where people would treasure as more precious than gold, the very trees that we sought so hard to kill as pests. [10]

Shortly later Idriess was one of the many casualties suffered during this assault. He, like many of the wounded was then transported back to Cairo. His involvement in the War against Turkey, which took him to Gallipoli, the Sinai, Gaza, Beersheva and Judea, was now over.

This desperate Turkish attempt to wrest back the initiative, failed. It lacked the necessary penetration and their gains were small compared to their losses. They were again forced onto the defensive.

Second Attempt at Jerusalem

While the Turkish *Yilderim* counter-attack had further exhausted their 7th Army, the EEF had been invigorated, and was now fully prepared for a second assault upon Jerusalem. Plans for the assault were slightly complicated by orders not permitting

---

9   PRO: FO 371/3061 213408, p. 433.
10   Idriess, I. *The Desert Column*, p. 292.

substantial fighting within eight kilometres of the Old City. The plans were basically to surround Jerusalem and compel the Turks to withdraw. In this operation the Royal Flying Corps played a vital role by surveying Turko-German troop movements and dropping countless pamphlets calling upon the Turks to surrender.

While the main advance would come from the west, the 53rd Welsh Division, also known as *Motts Detachment,* would move from the south along the ancient Jerusalem-Hebron-Beersheva road, and would then move east and cut off the Jerusalem-Jericho road. The 60th London and 74th British-Indian Divisions would move towards Jerusalem from the west, and then circle to the north of Jerusalem and cut the Jerusalem-Nablus road near ancient Gibeah. Between these infantry bodies, were the 10th Light Horse Regiment and a regiment of the Worcestershire Yeomanry.

All the great plans for the capture of Jerusalem were much dependent upon the weather and transport. The Jerusalem-Jaffa railway was repaired as far as Ramle, enabling supplies, off-loaded at Jaffa, to come half way, and then transported onwards by the Egyptian Labour Corps (ELC) teams, which included some 2,000 donkeys, and scores of camels. The main road had been sufficiently repaired to permit these teams to make the arduous journey - although many an unfortunate camel would slip and splay its body. Nevertheless until late on 7 December preparations were going well. On that same day the Jewish people were recalling their liberation from the Greek-Syrian tyranny, and where possible, were celebrating the first day of the *Hanukah* festival.

Then during the evening, the clouds burst open again. Yet despite such ordeals, the feelings of the soldiers were attuned to higher matters. '...all ranks of the 10th Light Horse Regiment,' wrote Brigadier-General L.C Wilson, 'had been engaged in continuous duties for many days and nights, during which time wind and rain squalls prevailed. The thoughts of entering Jerusalem,' he concluded, 'counteracted all personal discomforts.'[11]

The final offensive for the capture of Jerusalem began with an artillery barrage at 2 am on 8 December. The 60th and 74th Divisions then headed towards Jerusalem along the old Jerusalem-Jaffa road. Their steady advance was slowed down as the 53rd Welsh Division moving northward from Hebron was delayed due to fog. The Australians, in their sector between the 53rd and 60th Divisions, endured various skirmishes as they attempted to reach the Jerusalem to Bethlehem road. Bethlehem was finally reached, and taken, and by the evening of 8 December the Welsh and Australian troops were ordered to halt and hold their line. Allenby's official report says the rest:

> Towards dusk the British troops were reported to have passed Lifta, and to be within sight of the city. On this news being received, a sudden panic fell on the Turks west

---

11 Wilson. Brig-Gen. L.C. *Operations of the Third Light Horse Brigade.* No publishing details., p. 19.

and south-west of the town, and at 5 o'clock civilians were surprised to see a Turkish column galloping furiously cityward along the Jaffa road. In passing they alarmed all units within sight or hearing, and the wearied infantry arose and fled, bootless and without rifles, never pausing to think or to fight.

After four centuries of conquest the Turk was ridding the land of his presence in the bitterness of defeat, and a great enthusiasm arose among the Jews. There was a running to and fro; daughters called to their fathers and brothers concealed in outhouses, cellars and attics, from the police who sought them for arrest and deportation. 'The Turks are running' they called; 'the day of deliverance is come'. The nightmare was fast passing away, but the Turk still lingered. In the evening he fired his guns continuously, perhaps heartening himself with the loud noise that comforts the soul of a barbarian; perhaps to cover the sound of his own retreat. Whatever the intention was, the roar of the gun fire persuaded most citizens to remain indoors, and there were few to witness the last act of Osmanli authority.

At 2 0'clock in the morning of Sunday, December 9th, tired Turks began to troop through the Jaffa Gate from the west and south-west, and anxious watchers, peering out through the windows to learn the meaning of the tramping were cheered by the sullen remark of an officer, 'Gitmaya mejburuz' (We've got to go), and from 2 to 7 that morning the Turks streamed through and out of the city, which echoed for the last time their shuffling tramp.[12]

The liberation of Jerusalem gave the Jewish people a double reason for celebrating *Hanukah*.

The Surrender

Early in the morning of 9 December a delegation, including the mayor and other Jerusalem notables, then made their way towards the western suburbs of Jerusalem in search of the forward British-Anzac troops, in order to surrender the city. But their efforts were more complicated than anticipated. Several hundred metres from Lifta, and behind the present Central Bus Station (a memorial marks the spot) the delegation met, as the story goes, two mess cooks (perhaps one) from the 2/20 Battalion 60th Division, who were in search of eggs. They declined the honour to accept the surrender. Then one, or perhaps two, outpost sergeants, Hurcombe and Sedgwick, of the 2/19 Battalion met the delegation. They quickly referred the matter to Lieutenant Colonel H. Bailey, 303 Brigade, RFA, who in turn contacted Brigadier-General Watson, commanding the 180th Brigade, 60th Division. Watson made haste to meet the mayor and assure him that the surrender would be accepted.

Meanwhile Chetwode was informed of the impending surrender, and he delegated Shea, commander of the 60th Division, to officially accept it. It seems that Watson,

---

12   Falls, Cyril & MacMunn, General Sir G. *Military Operations, Egypt and Palestine*. (London, 1928), p. 260-1.

in his eagerness to accept the surrender, received the keys of the city. He had wanted to reassure the people that all was well, and to apprehend any lawlessness, as looting had already begun. Bertha Spafford Vester wrote of Watson's entrance, '... suddenly there came a subdued shout, for people were still afraid to show their joy. *"Aju Aju* (They've come)"' came the shout, and Brigadier General Watson was sighted escorted by Hassain Effendi, Mr. Salameh, and a crowd of followers.' It was indeed an emotional time. 'For us the joy of that hour,' Mrs Vester continued, 'was indescribable. I rushed down and kissed the general's stirrup and rushed back. I feel quite sure that he never knew who the person was who did that impulsive act.'[13]

Mrs. Vester, her husband and brother-in-law then invited General Watson into the nearby hospital where three EEF wounded were located. 'It would be hard to find words to describe the joy of these men at seeing their brigadier general again,' wrote Mrs. Vester. 'Poor Roberts, in his weak mental state, upbraided the general for having left him to suffer so long. But the general soothed him with kind words.'[14]

Meanwhile, General Shea it seems, had decided that he wanted to accept the surrender and keys of Jerusalem. So Watson, upon hearing of this, returned the keys to the mayor. Some time later, 'Fresh cheering in the streets,' wrote witness Ernie Meyer, a British soldier 'announced the ceremonial arrival of the divisional commander in his car, accompanied by a glittering staff.'[15]

While all these deliberations were taking place, the EEF troops began filing into Jerusalem. 'My goodness, the people of Jerusalem gave us a warm reception,' recalled Private Alec Wilson of the 60th Division of that eventful morning. Yet Wilson, like many of his colleagues, was unable to savour this welcome. 'We marched up Jaffa road,' he continued, 'past Damascus Gate and took up positions near Shuafat, to protect Jerusalem from the expected counterattack by the Turks from the north.'[16]

Indeed as Shea accompanied the Vesters to the top of the Italian Hospital for a view of Jerusalem, they noticed skirmishing to the north, in the region of the Mount Scopus. Here the British infantry were encountering stiff resistance from a Turkish rear guard, who finally were defeated after a bayonet charge. The retreating Turks were being hassled along the road northwards by the aircraft of the Royal Flying Corps, especially near Shuafat where Wilson was heading. The aircraft also bombed the Jerusalem-Jericho road to the east of Jerusalem, which eased the movement of the 53rd Division as they moved from the south. This Division then cut the Jericho road, and moved to link up with the 60th and 54th Divisions on the Mount of Olives.

13 Vester, B. *Our Jerusalem,* Ariel Press (Jerusalem, 1981), p. 275.
14 Vester, B. ibid., p. 275.
15 Meyer, Ernie. 'With Allenby', *Jerusalem Post Magazine.* 15 December 1978, p. 16.
16 Meyer, Ernie. 'With Allenby', *Jerusalem Post Magazine,* p. 17.

The Anzacs Ride In

The first mounted forces, men of the 10th Light Horse Regiment, entered Jerusalem about 7 pm. These men represented the Desert Mounted Corps, which had fought every battle and skirmish from the Suez to Jerusalem. 'Their first greeting was from a nun,' wrote Gullett, 'who was busy repairing the tiles on the roof of her convent at the edge of town, and who ceased her task to wave to the light horsemen.' As the representative Anzacs then rode 'with their emu plumes stirring in the breeze ... through the streets, they were rushed by the populace,' Gullett relates, 'who marveled at the size of their big, long-tailed horses.'[17]

The villagers on the outskirts of Jerusalem 'were coming along,' recalls Henry Bostock, 'with anything to sell, but mostly it was wine.' Trooper Dinnie Connaughton was determined not to upset their hospitality, and, Bostock continues, Dinny 'made them to understand that he was there to sample the wine to see if it was fit to be sold'. Whether he found some to his liking, or overdid the sampling we are not told, but Bostock does tell us that 'when it came time to mount and ride into Jerusalem, I had to help him onto his horse.'[18]

'We passed a house,' Bostock recalls of that entrance, 'where the occupants were holding a dance in what appeared to be a large verandah with glass sides and well lit. Truly a sight to remember on such a memorable night.'[19] Yet serious and exciting as that day was, it was not without its lighter side. 'Dinnie,' Bostock recalls, 'after all his wine sampling, fell off his horse.' Some people in a nearby house, who were watching the parade of Australian horsemen, saw Dinnie's fall, whereupon they 'took him inside, gave him a nice meal and a bed for the night.' The rest of the Australians continued into Jerusalem and took over the Turkish cavalry barracks. After several weeks in the cold and wet, both men and horses enjoyed some warmth and comfort. The warmth however came at a cost to some of their neighbours - some of the wood came from the shutters from the nearby Christ Church!

Walters' wrote on 10 December of his part: 'Had a great 2 days trip. Was just on the outskirts of Jerusalem. People welcomed us offering wine, fruit etc ... Plenty to eat. Had a wet night riding home but stayed in a Jews House at ARTUF. Good bed and food. Thought I was home again. Indeed the Jewish inhabitants enjoyed the news they [the Light Horsemen] brought.'[20] On another occasion he wrote: 'We were the first to bring tidings of Jerusalem falling to this village and they were pleased. One old Jew came in and asked us if it was quite correct and when we told him it was he threw his hat down on the floor packed up his goods .... and off to Jerusalem. I suppose his relatives were there,' Walters concluded judging by the hasty departure

---

17 Gullett, H.S. *The A.I.F. in Sinai and Palestine*, p. 519.
18 Bostock, H. *The Great Ride*, p. 110.
19 Bostock, H. ibid., p. 113.
20 *Diary of Reg Walters.*

of his Jewish friend.[21]

Chauvel too enjoyed such a privilege. On 9 December he was able to announce the capture of Jerusalem to a large Jewish audience at a *Hanukah* banquet in Rehovot.[22]

The Day After

On 10 December Walters' squadron joined the rest of the 10th Light Horse Regiment in Jerusalem. 'The people,' he recalled, 'who seemed a very mixed race, with Jews in the ascendancy were mighty glad to see the British troops take control of their Holy Town. In fact at first they were jumping over themselves to give us anything and do anything for us.'[23] This enthusiasm, Walters pointed out, later became more passive.

For the majority of the troops, there was something special about being in Jerusalem. Gullet wrote that as the New Zealanders rejoiced in the comforts and civilization of Jaffa, so the troops who had been toiling in Jerusalem's hills, rejoiced now in Jerusalem's capture. Not one soldier who entered Jerusalem for the first time, he claimed, was left untouched by the touch of the Saviour Jesus. In the midst of the grossness of war, he concluded, each man came close to that 'pure and trusting' faith of his childhood.[24]

The new Military Governor of Jerusalem, Borton, arrived, and immediately began the transfer and re-organization of the civil administration. Allenby's major concerns were firstly, to establish law and order in the city, and secondly, to protect it against counter-attacks.

11 December 1917

The official entry of Allenby into Jerusalem, to officially end 400 years of Ottoman Turk rule, was scheduled for 11 December. He drove to Jerusalem that morning from his new HQ at Junction Station and met Chetwode at General Shea's headquarters, the doctor's residence of the mission hospital belonging to the London Jews Hospital on Prophets Street. In the weeks prior to the surrender of Jerusalem the Turks had used this institution for their General Staff Headquarters.

From there Allenby and his general staff proceeded on horseback along Jaffa Road towards the Old City. Most of the inhabitants of Jerusalem came out to witness this historic event. 'I saw Allenby on a beautiful horse,' recalls Rivka Amdursky-Buxbaum, a young Jewish eyewitness, 'I believe it was a greyish-white horse,' she continued, 'They told us he was a king. And everyone said : "Let's go out and see the king." ' It even seemed to Amdursky-Buxbaum that he was more than just a king,

21 Letter of Reg Walters to family. Copy in author's possession.
22 Hill, A.J. *Chauvel of the Light Horse.*, pp. 140-1.
23 Letter of Reg Walters to family.
24 Gullet. H.S. *The A.I.F. in Sinai and Palestine.*, p. 519.

perhaps, she concluded, 'it was the Messiah.'[25]

Outside Jaffa Gate, Allenby fulfilled his instructions from the Government, dismounted, and in complete contradiction to the Kaiser's ostentatious entry in 1898, entered the Holy City on foot. He walked past a guard of honour comprised of 110 soldiers from England, Scotland, Wales and Ireland on his left, and 50 soldiers from Australia and New Zealand on his right.[26]

At the gate he was officially met by Governor Borton, and then proceeded to enter the ancient walled city, not through the opening in the wall through which the Kaiser entered in all his pomp on that October day some nineteen years before, but through the ancient door of the Jaffa Gate which had been until then closed for many years. He was met on the other side by a gleeful Jerusalem populace, and by twenty French and Italian soldiers, representing the token forces sent by those two countries.

'During the ceremony,' wrote Bertha Spafford Vester, 'I was on the balcony of the Grand New Hotel ... I knew I was fortunate indeed to be witnessing one of the great events of history. I realized that the whole Christian world outside of Germany and Austria was jubilant. People in the streets were crying at their deliverance. I saw a Jew embrace a Greek priest, and his tall clerical hat went askew in the exuberance of fraternal feeling. Truly we could sing with the Psalmist, "Then were our mouths filled with laughter and our tongue with smiling ... The Lord hath done great things for us, therefore we are glad."'[27]

Allenby then headed towards the entrance into the fortress of Jerusalem, the Tower of David, followed by his staff officers, the corps commanders, Chauvel, Chetwode and Bulfin, other generals, and representatives from the other Allied countries - including Picot, and Colonel T.E. Lawrence, for whom this ceremony 'was the supreme moment of the war.'[28] The soldiers comprising the guard of honour followed, many of whom, including the Anzacs (from the uttermost ends of the earth), then formed a semi circular guard of honour between Allenby and the representatives on the landing leading into the Tower of David, immediately opposite the entrance into the London Jews Society's Christ Church.

Here a proclamation of martial law was read in his presence to the population, in Arabic, Hebrew, English, French, Italian, Greek and Russian, the same then afterwards being posted on the walls. Following the reading of the proclamations, Allenby and his entourage proceeded to the nearby Turkish barracks (today's Kishleh Police Station) where he was introduced to the community leaders of Jerusalem. The formalities over, he returned to Shea's headquarters for lunch.

Apart from the corps commanders, Shea, Picot and Lawrence too were in

25 Lossin, Yigal. *Pillar of Fire.* Shikmona Publishing Co, (Jerusalem, 1983), p. 57.

26 *New York Times Mid Week Pictorial,* New York, December 1917. No page numbers.

27 Vester, B. *Our Jerusalem.,* p. 280.

28 Lawrence, T.E. *Seven Pillars of Wisdom.,* World Books, (London, 1935) p. 453. Courtesy of the Trustees of the Seven Pillars of Wisdom Trust.

attendance. Lawrence was basically interested in Allenby's next military move and how this would affect him. Allenby explained that operations would probably have to be curtailed until February, when a push down to Jericho would be made. Lawrence meanwhile was asked to keep an eye on the traffic of food up the Dead Sea for the Turkish forces.[29]

But Picot, the French *High Commissioner for Palestine and Syria* was not concerned about what the next few months would bring, he was concerned about the here and now. 'And tomorrow, my dear General,' Lawrence relates of Picot's conversation to Allenby, 'I will take the necessary steps to set up civil government in this town.'

Everyone in attendance, according to Lawrence, was aghast at the presumptuousness of the Frenchman. 'Salad, chicken mayonnaise and foie gras sandwiches hung in our wet mouths unmunched, while we turned to Allenby and gaped. Even he seemed for the moment at a loss.' After regaining his composure, however, Allenby related the content of his instructions. 'In the military zone the only authority,' he replied, 'is that of the Commander-in-Chief - myself.'

Picot began to protest, 'But Sir Grey, Sir Edward Grey ... ' He could not finish his statement which referred to the previous 'agreements' between the former British Foreign Minister and the French Government concerning a dual administration over the conquered areas of *Palestine*. 'Sir Edward Grey referred to the civil government,' Allenby concluded, 'which will be established when I judge that the military situation permits.' [30] There was nothing more to be said. Picot may have disagreed with this off handed answer and show by Allenby. But there was nothing he could do. The British-Anzac forces were in possession of Jerusalem and Judea and not the French. It was a *fait accompli*. This was one of the remaining nails driven into the coffin of the 'Grey-Poincare' and 'Sykes-Picot' agreements. France had tried, and failed in her attempt to gain part if not all of the administration of the Land of Israel.

While all these proceedings were taking place, a young New Zealand soldier, Louis Salek, carrying a Zionist flag given to him by Jewish people in Cairo prior to his departure, ascended to the top of the Tower of David. There he daringly flew the Jewish flag to be seen by all. It was greeted with enthusiasm by the Jewish observers, with disdain and anger by the Moslem, and was quickly taken down by order of the British authorities.[32] It violated the guidelines laid down by the War Office. This was quite an amazing way to complete the day's proceedings: A New Zealander from the uttermost ends of the earth, wearing an Australian uniform, and flying the Jewish flag from the Citadel of David - the very building left standing by the Romans in 70 CE to testify to the end of Jewish national life in the Land of Israel. The irony of history.

---

29 Lawrence, T.E. *Revolt in the Desert.*, George H. Doran Company, (USA 1927), p. 192.
30 Lawrence, T.E. *Seven Pillars of Wisdom..*, p. 455.
31 'The flag waved free,' *Jerusalem Post Magazine*, 23 May 1990.

Allenby's activities over, he then proceeded to write his report to the Government as was requested. 'I ENTERED this city officially at noon to-day with a few of my staff, the commanders of the French and Italian detachments, the heads of the Picot Mission, and the Military Attaches of France, Italy, and the United States of America. The procession was all on foot. At the Jaffa Gate I was received by guards representing England, Scotland, Ireland, Wales, Australia, New Zealand, India, France and Italy.' He referred to each of the stipulations laid down in his instructions, 'The population received me well; 'Guards have been placed over the Holy Places'; and that the Latin and Greek representatives had been contacted concerning Christian Holy Places, and Indian Mohommedan soldiers and officers had been placed around the Moslem holy places.[32]

Reactions to the Capture

Allenby, his business in Jerusalem now completed, returned to his headquarters and to matters of more immediate attention - the running of the war. Meanwhile reactions to the capture of Jerusalem were now flooding in and newspapers throughout the world were highlighting this great event. It was just as Sykes and the War Cabinet expected - the propaganda scoop of the War. A simple, un-militarist entrance, in complete opposition to the Kaiser's grandiose entrance of 1898 had greatly increased British prestige throughout the world. And thereafter, whatever Britain proposed with the future of the Holy Land, the *land between*, was sure to gain acceptance.

France, at least for the time being, had been subdued over the issue. The Vatican, for the time being was supporting the capture. In reply to a telegram sent by the Foreign Office to the Vatican on 10 December announcing the capture, the Cardinal Secretary of State, Count de Valvis communicated to the Foreign Office on 12 December that the official organ, the *Observatore* stated 'that the entry of British troops into Jerusalem has been received with satisfaction by Catholics who cannot but rejoice that the Holy City should be in the possession of a Christian power', and that there 'is every hope that interests and rights of the Catholic Church will be respected.' It concluded with these startling words: *'They add that they thank Providence for not allowing Jerusalem to fall into the hands of Government of the Czar (sic).'*[33]

As for the Russians, they too had communicated with the British Government on 12 December, not so much offering congratulations, but 'suggesting that a special provisional Russian agent might be allowed to proceed to Jerusalem to assist in the administration of the various Russian institutions in that city'. The British Foreign Secretary replied that he 'has the honour to state that as Jerusalem is in military occupation the presence of foreign agents is in the opinion of the British military

---

32   PRO: CAB 23/4 WC 296., p. 247.
33   PRO: FO 371/3061 21308, p. 480. Italics mine. Sic in original

authorities undesirable'

'The General-Officer-Commanding', Balfour continued, 'has however been asked to render any protection to Russian institutions which he may render desirable.'[34] Any Russian thoughts of getting a 'toe in the door' at this juncture were firmly squashed by this emphatic message from the British Government. The British had no intention at all of allowing the Russians to gain from their hard-fought political and military victories.

It was vital for the Jewish people that no other European power be allowed any voice in the future of the Land of Israel. The British Government had made its commitment via the *Balfour Declaration*. Hopes of a future Jewish restoration lay firmly upon that promise. Neither the French nor the Russian Governments had historically given serious consideration to a Jewish restoration.

As could be expected none were more enthusiastic than the pro-restoration Evangelicals, especially those in Britain. The official LJS response to the *Balfour Declaration* and subsequent events stated:

> With one step the Jewish cause has made a great bound forward. For centuries the Jew has been downtrodden, depressed, hated and unloved by all the nations. For 2,000 years now the Jew has suffered as no other nation on the earth's surface in his restless wanderings. Wherever he has gone he has been ill-treated, but now there is at least a prospect of his settling down once again in his own country, and of becoming in the eyes of men a Nation amongst the Nations, in place of being a wanderer in every clime. He is now to have a home for himself in his God-given land. The day of his exile is to be ended.
>
> What does all this mean for us Christians? In the light of prophetic Scripture we recognise that such an action on the part of our Government and on the part of the Allied Powers, in being united in their resolve to reinstate the Jew in his own land, is full of significance. Our Lord, when asked the question, 'What shall be the signs of Thy coming and of the end of the age', gave one of the signs, in Luke 21:24, to be that 'Jerusalem shall be trodden down of the Gentiles (nations) until the times of the Gentiles (nations) be fulfilled.' Ever since A.D. 70 Jerusalem and Palestine have been under Gentile domination, and now we seem to be on the very verge of a literal fulfillment of the last prediction, and it is certainly a distinct warning to us that the Lord 'is near, even at the very doors'. (St Matt. 42:32)[35]

Indeed those events leading up to 11 December 1917 were the culmination of the dreams of many a Jewish person and Evangelical from the previous decades and centuries. Yet the significance of the *Balfour Declaration* and capture of Jerusalem would remain dormant while the Turks retained control over the remainder of Eretz Israel. There still remained the challenge of taking Jericho, Amman, Nazareth, Tiberias, and the ultimate goal - Damascus.

---

34 PRO: FO 371/3061 21308., p. 486.
35 JMI, 1917., pp. 129-30.

*C*hapter 17

Enter the 'Jewish Legion'

Consolidating the Gains

While the Turks awaited the arrival of reinforcements, primarily from the *Asien Korps*, Allenby planned to consolidate his position, primarily the areas north of Jaffa and Jerusalem. Despite heavy rainfall the 52nd Lowland Scottish Division crossed the Nahr Auja north of Jaffa at three points on the night of 20-21 December, surprising the Turks who considered a crossing impossible in such appalling conditions. During 21 December, bridges were built, and artillery moved over to the north shore. By 22 December the EEF line reached Arsuf on the coast, some twelve kilometres north of Jaffa.

Bad weather delayed the movement of EEF infantry and dismounted horsemen north of Jerusalem. The delay ensured there would be no fighting on Christmas Day. But oh, what a Christmas day it was for the soldiers. 'A word about yesterday Xmas Day,' wrote Walters. 'Will we ever forget it. Place SUFFA. It had been raining off and on for the past fortnight but yesterday was the limit. Rained hard nearly all day. My section mates (H. Conning, Mick McSwain & Sam James) were out on Post, so for Xmas dinner, I crouched up in the wet bivy and ate cold cake and milk. At night the blankets being wet we all sought different shelters.'[1]

The Jewish inhabitants of Khirbet Deiran (Rehovot) provided a hall for use as a church and wine for the communion so that Chauvel and his staff could enjoy Christmas. [2] Chauvel, desiring to identify with his men on this depressing day, also rode around to their camps in the cold and rain.

On the night of 26-27 December the Turks pre-empted the EEF offensive and counter-attacked Tel el Ful, the ancient Gibeah, several kilometres north of Jerusalem. Although the *Asien Korps* had not arrived, the Turks had to attack before the EEF did. While they battled against the British infantry around Tel el Ful, men of the 74th (Yeomanry) and 10th (Irish) Divisions moved forward from the Beth Horon ridge, aiming to cut off the Turkish force.

---

1   *Diary of Reg Walters.*
2   Hill, A.J. *Chauvel of the Light Horse*, p. 141.

The fighting was fierce, but by 29 December the Turkish offensive had lost its impetus, while the British infantry moved forward in a line on both sides of the Jerusalem-Nablus road. By 30 December the advance halted, with the EEF force running in a line from just north of Ram Allah (Ramallah). Despite heavy EEF casualties, by the end of 1917, both Jaffa and Jerusalem were safely out of reach of the Turko-German forces.

Capture of Jericho

Allenby's next major move was to capture Jericho and then Transjordan. The Arab Northern Army was instructed to strike north from Aqaba at Turkish positions to the south of Amman, thereby restricting the Turks from moving forces against the EEF moves. On 25 January they captured, in quite a brilliant fashion the strategic location of Tafila. Allenby now proposed to consolidate his position in the Jordan Valley, then launch a Spring offensive to capture the Transjordan plateau with its dearth of agricultural supplies.

His objectives were discussed with General Smuts who was sent out by the War Cabinet in early February. The overall plan in taking Transjordan was to isolate the Turkish forces in Medina and encourage Feisal's forces, and then also to move up the coast to the Plain of Esdraelon (Jezreel Valley), and from there in several movements towards Damascus, Homs and Aleppo. Smuts endorsed Allenby's plan, and then shortly afterwards proposed them to the Supreme War Council meeting at Versailles. They were mostly accepted. It was also agreed that two fresh, yet inexperienced Indian divisions would be sent from Mesopotamia.

The first objective was the capture of Jericho, to which British infantry and Anzac horsemen were committed. In mid-February most of the Anzac Division began moving into the Judean hills aiming towards the Dead Sea via Bethlehem. Riding in single file the Anzac horsemen proceeded down a goat track near Wadi Kidron, closing in on a large mount known as El Muntar, the supposed hill associated with the scapegoat of the Temple times.[3] British infantry, from the 53rd, 60th and 74th Divisions also began moving along the Jerusalem-Jericho road, aiming for the strategic Jebel Ekteif, about half way to Jericho.

By 20 February both the Anzacs and the British were attacking their objectives. The British captured, lost and then re-captured their position, and sustained many casualties. The Anzacs squared off against well-entrenched Turkish positions close to the ancient Moslem shrine of Nebi Musa, traditional Moslem burial place of Moses. On the morning of 21 February while the New Zealanders were moving onto Nebi Musa, and the British were moving towards Jericho along the road, Light Horsemen wound their way down the precipitous Wadi Qumran to the Dead Sea, and then

3   Powles, Lieut.-Col. C. Guy. *New Zealanders in Sinai and Palestine*, p. 176.

galloped into Jericho from the south.

As Jaffa, one of the oldest ports in the world was liberated by the New Zealanders, now Jericho, one of the oldest cities in the world was liberated by the Australians. But, as the New Zealanders revelled in the capture of Jaffa, the Anzacs were repulsed by their first sight of Jericho, as it was, in the words of Powles, a 'degenerate city full of loathsome disease ... Of all the cities of the east that our men had passed through,' he continued, 'Jericho led the way as the filthiest and most evil smelling of them all.'[4]

The Turks had withdrawn to the east side of the Jordan River across the Ghoraniye bridge, which they then destroyed. From there they sniped and bombed the British-Anzac forces. Chauvel and Chetwode had arrived in the town soon after its capture, and were about to eat breakfast with Chaytor when the Turks decided to lob a few artillery shells in their direction. They very quickly found a new location to enjoy their morning 'tucker!'

Jewish Legion on the Move

The *Jewish Legion* - the 38th Battalion Royal Fusiliers, (known also as the 'tailors battalion' due to its large number of tailors) marched through the streets of London on 2 February 1918 to tumultuous applause. It was the first time troops were permitted to march through central London bearing bayonets! Two days later they sailed for Egypt, from where they would proceed onto the Land of Israel.

Upon arrival at Alexandria on 1 March, Jabotinsky, Patterson and the fellow men of Zion were met by old friends from the Jewish community, who said 'The Zion Mule Corps was our son, the Jewish Legion is our grandson.'[5] They were feted by the Jewish community before leaving for their training ground at Helmieh near Cairo. Meanwhile the Jewish population of Judea had petitioned the British authorities to allow them to join the *Jewish Legion* - a petition awaiting authorization. Still they were hopeful.

Patterson's optimism was dampened several days after arrival. He met Allenby, whom he knew from the Boer War period. Yet his meeting with Allenby's Chief of Staff, Major-General Louis Bols proved a great disappointment. Bols was unsympathetic to Zionism and the *Jewish Legion*. 'I found, to my amazement,' Patterson wrote later, 'that the policy adopted by the Staff towards this Jewish Battalion, and the Jewish problem generally, ran counter to the declared policy of the Home Government.'[6] This setback was a harbinger for Patterson and the *Jewish Legion*, and later the Zionist Organization, who thereafter would receive many rebuffs from the British officers, many of whom had their own agenda for the future of the

---

4   Powles, Lieut.-Col. C. Guy. *New Zealanders in Sinai and Palestine.* p. 181-2.
5   Jabotinsky, V. *The Jewish Legion*, p. 107.
6   Patterson, J. *With the Judeans in the Palestine Campaign.*, p. 57.

Middle East.

The British Government finally agreed on 21 February 1918 to permit United States Jews to volunteer for the *Jewish Legion* 'if medically fit and well trained.' Yitzak Ben Zvi and David Ben Gurion were now about to join Jabotinsky's *Jewish Legion* and fight for Britain against Turkey.

Recruiting centres were set up in New York, Chicago, Cleveland and other major centres. The first recruits left for camp at Windsor in Canada on 28 February, and from there to England for further training.

Onto Transjordan

The EEF now had to consolidate its position in Jericho against any Turko-German counter offensive down the Jordan Valley or from Transjordan. The Turko-German command structure also changed at this time. General von Falkenhayn was replaced by the man who earned a reputation at Gallipoli, Liman von Sanders.

The four day long British-Anzac offensive was launched on 9 March. The infantry in the Samarian hills moved further north on both sides of the Nablus road, at the same time as forces moved north from Jericho past Wadi Auja, and onto the strategic positions of Abu Tellal and Musallabeh. This later move secured the water supplies of the Wadi Auja, and provided a strong position to block any movement down the Jordan Valley from Beisan (Bet Shean) or from the Nablus-Es Salt road. The offensive brought the EEF half way to Nablus.

Now the way was open for a move into Transjordan. Allenby's motives were two-fold. One was to encourage the uprising led by Feisal's forces. They were to destroy a railway tunnel and viaduct near Amman, and sever the Turkish forces in the south from those in the north and then invest the Turkish garrison at Maan. The second was to plant a seed in the minds of the Turko-German leadership that he was planning his advance to Damascus via Transjordan. In fact Allenby's main advance would be up the coastal plain, using the flat country for a quick movement by his mounted forces. The Turks would hopefully take the bait, beef up their defences east of the Jordan, and thereby deprive their defences along the coastal plain.

As the EEF forces gradually made their way towards the Jordan Valley, Trooper Malone was able to visit one of the sites of the Holy Land: Solomon's Pools near Bethlehem. He wrote: 'Watered camels at Solomon's Pools on the Hebron road. There are three large stone reservoirs supposed to have been built to give a supply of water for Jerusalem - another story is that they were made for Solomon's wives to bathe in. They must have been good swimmers,' he concluded, 'for the pools are from 70 to 100 ft deep.'[7]

As could be expected many of the troopers were intrigued by such antiquities.

---

7   *Diary of Trooper Malone.*

But this wasn't all that interested them. 'It certainly was pleasant to see some sort of civilization and a few pretty faces again,' Malone continued. 'The people around Bethlehem,' he observed, 'are very fairskinned, but all swear that they are Arabs, but make the distinction "Bethlehem Arab". The girls are especially beautiful and do not coarsen as they grow older as most Arabs do.'[8]

Unfortunately Solomon's Pools and beautiful Bethlehem women had to be left behind as the Camel Corps and the other forces continued their move onto the Jordan Valley and assembled for the attack into Transjordan, scheduled to begin on 21 March. Heavy rains however swelled the Jordan River, making the crossing very difficult. By 23 March the Anzac Bridging Train and 60th Division troops had established pontoon bridges and the bulk of the troops crossed over and a bridgehead established around Ghoraniye.

'Halted 0230 in valley of Jordan,' Malone wrote on 24 March. 'Crossed Jordan two miles from Dead Sea - which we saw - on pontoon bridge ... Moved across flat to edge of foothills ... moved on 0700 ... Met artillery, rain, steep rocky path almost impassable ... Travelled all night.' The Londoners aimed for Shunet Nimrin, where the road left the valley and wound its way up to Es Salt, and finally captured it on March 24th. The Anzacs and Camel Corps either moved up on their flank, or made their way by irregular paths, straight towards Amman.

The rain continued to fall, hampering the movement of man, beast and wagon. Much of the artillery was left behind, while the movement of supplies was badly affected. Malone wrote: 'March 25. Stopped 20 minutes for breakfast. Moved 2 miles in 6 hours and then halted at 1400. Ravines across muddy streams ... Rain all the time & mud knee deep ... moved at 1900 & travelled all night, men walking along asleep - it was impossible to ride.'[9]

After two painful and arduous days of climbing, the troops came onto the Transjordan plateau - and found it covered with water. Temperatures plummeted and the rain continued. Short of artillery and supplies, and desperately exhausted, General Chaytor ordered the advance to hold up for much of the day. That evening troops of the 1st Light Horse Brigade and 60th Division, captured Es Salt while the advance towards Amman continued by the remainder of the troops.

The attack upon the Turkish fortifications in Amman began in earnest on 28 March. It was a hopeless cause from the very beginning. The delay in crossing the Jordan had alerted the Turkish command of the impending assault, and they subsequently strengthened their defences. The British-Anzac troops were tired, cold and exhausted by the time they arrived at Amman - and faced a spirited Turkish defence. The New Zealanders, Australians and Londoners made desperate attempts to capture the Citadel, and even to reach and destroy the railway tunnel and viaduct.

8   *Diary of Trooper Malone.*
9   Ibid.

Their brave efforts gained little.

Although some Turkish troops were withdrawn from Maan and Kerak in the south, which assisted the Arab Northern Army's objectives, the expected Arab help at Amman never crystallized. By late on the evening of 28 March there was no choice but to withdraw from Amman back to the Jordan Valley. This task was as difficult as that coming up as the tracks were by now muddy bowls. The troops were totally exhausted, supplies were in very short supply and the Turks, sensing an EEF withdrawal, were hot on their heels..

Those worst affected by the withdrawal were the wounded. They not only had to be roughly carried from the field, but then had to endure an excruciating journey over the rocky hills, and down the boggy road - strapped to his horse, as the route was too slippery for the camel. Once having reached the Jordan Valley it was a long journey over the Judean Hills to the hospital train which took them onto Cairo. Only the worst cases remained in Jerusalem. [10]

Apart from some troops who maintained a bridgehead on the east side of the Ghoraniye bridge, the last troops had crossed the Jordan by 2 April. They were a tired and dispirited force. The odds had been greatly against them, they suffered 1,348 casualties, and saw little fruit for their efforts, apart from 1,000 Turkish prisoners. Yet Allenby's ploy worked - more Turkish troops were transferred to the Transjordan to withstand future British-Anzac attacks.

Despite this, the EEF plan for moving onto Damascus in the spring of 1918 was postponed. At the same time as the British-Anzac force was beginning its assault into Transjordan, the Germans broke through the Allied lines in France, and were heading for Paris. As the situation in France looked grave, Allenby was informed that he had to surrender many of his seasoned troops. Amongst those lost were the 52nd and 74th Divisions. The replacement Indian divisions coming from Mesopotamia, were basically inexperienced, and only arrived piecemeal over the following months. It was now a time for consolidation and retraining before the final expected advance.

Arrival of the Zionist Commission

While the 38th Battalion Royal Fusiliers was in training near Cairo, the 39th Battalion, under the command of Eliezer Margolin arrived towards the end of April 1918. A Zionist Commission led by Chaim Weizmann also arrived in Egypt at this time, and soon afterwards entered the Land of Israel.

The negative attitude of the British higher command towards the Zionist venture was soon after evidenced by Weizmann. He recalls breakfasting one day sandwiched between Allenby and Bols, 'who talked war across me' and recalls that there was a 'certain strain in the atmosphere.' The strain was due to the disquieting news coming

---

10 Powles, Lieut.-Col. C. Guy. *New Zealanders in Sinai and Palestine*, p. 211-12.

from France, where the Central Powers were making one last bold attempt to reach Paris and the Channel ports, and probably to the effects of Arab propaganda. They 'lost no time in proclaiming', wrote Weizmann, 'that "the British had sent for the Jews to take over the country."[11]

Weizmann felt that few of the British officers were aware of the implications of the *Balfour Declaration* and the sympathy felt for it by many prominent Britons. He also felt that many officers believed that Bolshevism was heavily influenced by Jews, and that as Zionism was very much a Russian Jewish movement, then it was somehow associated with Bolshevism. [12] It seemed on the surface that the *Balfour Declaration* and formation of the *Jewish Legion* were observed by many British officers and administrators as hindrances to their own goals for the region.

Transjordan Again

Allenby's chief concern at this time was to continue with the offensive. He again planned an attack into Transjordan. This time his plans were aided by assurances from the powerful Beni Sakr tribe, that if the British-Anzac forces moved against the Shunet Nimrin fortress before 4 May, they too would join the assault. Such an offer could not be passed over. His own plans were put forward several weeks to meet this Arab offer.

The plan called for some mounted troops to take Es Salt, while other mounted troops and infantry were to attack and capture Shunet Nimrin, which guarded the Jordan Valley at the base of the Transjordan plateau. This would widen the defensive position and ensure the troops wouldn't need to spend the summer in the simmering Jordan Valley. The Australian, Anzac and 60th London Divisions were called up for this offensive. Many of the horsemen rode to the Jordan Valley via Jerusalem, where riding two abreast they took two hours to pass through the city. They weren't the only troops on the move. Von Sanders, anticipating a major British-Anzac assault introduced some crack German troops to the force. Meanwhile Chauvel, on Anzac Day 1918 set up his new HQ at Talaat al Dunn, traditional site of the Inn of the Good Samaritan, half way along the Jerusalem-Jericho road.

The EEF troops then began assembling on the east bank of the Jordan on 29 April. The following day the Londoners and New Zealanders quickly took the forward Turkish positions at Shunet Nimrin, but progress was then held up. Some Australians galloped up the east side of the Jordan towards the Jisr ed Damieh (ed Damieh bridge). Finding the bridge too well entrenched, they maintained a position inland along the road to Es Salt.

Other Australian and British horsemen, including Walters, headed towards Es

---

11 Weizmann, Chaim. *Trial and Error*. Volume One., p. 217.
12 Weizmann, Chaim., ibid., p. 217.

Salt. He wrote: 'After an all night ride from Jericho we attacked Es Salt & by evening after a charge took the town.'[13] In fact the 8th Light Horse Regiment galloped wildly through the Turkish lines outside Es Salt, took the town, and caused the Turks to announce on the wireless 'Es Salt has been captured by the reckless and dashing gallantry of the Australian cavalry.'[14] The Anzacs then threw a cordon around the town, while the 5th Mounted Brigade began moving along the road towards Shunet Nimrin.

The following day matters turned against the British-Anzac force. The Arab force failed to materialize, leaving the roads from Amman open for the movement of Turkish reinforcements to rush west. Further Turkish forces, a 6,000 strong *Yilderim* force came down from Nablus, crossing the Jordan River undetected on a pontoon bridge. This force quickly threatened the 1,000 dismounted Australians, throwing them back southwards from the Jisr ed Damieh area. The Jisr ed Damieh - Es Salt road was now in Turkish hands. Disaster beckoned for the heavily outnumbered Australians.

The Australians withdrew into ridge country, totally unsuited for horses. It was a precarious expedition, and a number of horses tumbled down the steep ravines. Losing a few horses could be coped with, but in the withdrawal nine artillery guns were lost.

When the Turks threatened the Um esh Shert track to Es Salt, British and New Zealand regiments were quickly sent to the rescue, and retained the area. And just as well, for Turkish reinforcements from Amman now began counterattacking at Es Salt. Walters wrote on 2 May: 'And now the Turks have counter-attacked & at present we are in a pretty precarious position. Our rations have expired, so they are killing cattle and goats in the town for us. We all feel a bit washed out on it.'[15]

Over the following days the Turks pressed in from all directions. With the Arab force out of reckoning Chauvel and Allenby had no choice but to withdraw. Again a difficult task. The last troops left Es Salt on the morning of the 4 May. Throughout the rest of the day the 4th Light Horse Brigade fought hard to keep the escape route open, not only for the exhausted Anzac and British horsemen, but also for the hundreds of mostly Christian refugees who feared retaliations once the Turks had regained control of the town and region.

Most of the troops were so exhausted when they reached the dusty valley below that they collapsed in the hot sun, no energy remaining even to erect a sun shelter. The ill-fated assault cost some 1,600 casualties. Despite these heavy losses the Turks further consolidated their position on the east side of the Jordan, now more convinced than ever that this would be the direction of the main British-Anzac assault. Negatively, the campaign further increased the distrust which the EEF, and especially Anzac

---

13 *Diary of Reg Walters.*
14 Jones, I. *The Australian Light Horse*, p. 130.
15 *Diary of Reg Walters.*

forces held towards the Arabs. The losses could have been substantially lower had the Arab force shown up as promised.

The *Jewish Legion* Arrives.

On 5 June 1918, the 38th Battalion Royal Fusiliers, the *Jewish Legion*, departed Egypt for the Land of Israel. 'Our chaplain, who was a man of insight and vision,' wrote Patterson, 'arranged that our trumpets should sound, and that a short prayer should be said by the troops as they entered, for the first time, the ancient land of their fathers.'[16]

Later that same day the Zionist soldiers arrived in the land of their forefathers, where they were met with enthusiasm by Jewish colonialists. They then marched to Surafend camp. It was, Patterson recalled 'one of the hottest days I have ever experienced, and our march to Surafend, under a blazing midday midsummer sun, loaded up as we were with full kit, was a severe test of the endurance of men.'[17] Their arrival heightened the Jewish desire to fight. The British authorities finally opened an enlistment office and many sought to enlist in the 40th Battalion Royal Fusiliers. James Rothschild took command of this interesting formation.

Although many ultra-orthodox Jewish people, especially in Jerusalem, opposed the formation of the unit, the majority of the remainder of the population favoured it. Recruitment posters were stuck up through the liberated areas. One read: "Hear, O Israel! What does your heart ask you to do? Shall we not reclaim our great heritage, and establish ourselves again in the eyes of the world? ENLIST! ENLIST! BE STRONG, ENLIST!"[18]

So many sought enlistment that Weizmann was concerned lest none be left to organize the economy. One recruit, Aaron Werner had hid in an attic in Jerusalem during the duration of the war so as not to be drafted into the Turkish Army. Following the liberation of Jerusalem he left his attic, and later joined the 40th Battalion.[19] He and the other recruits initially assembled at Tel el-Kebir, and then set out by train to their training grounds in Egypt.

Captain Redcliffe Salaman, the medical officer of the 39th Battalion wrote of their arrival:

> The Palestinians have arrived. On Thursday at 1 P.M. a long train of open cattle trucks rolled into the military siding at Helmieh, and, on a given signal, seven hundred of the most bizarre looking ragamuffins jumped out, and in a trice these seven hundred oddments had grouped themselves with perfect military precision into their ranks and platoons under banners resplendent with rampant lions and crossed triangles. Never

---

16 Patterson, J. *With the Judeans in the Palestine Campaign.*, p. 69.
17 Patterson. J., ibid., p. 70.
18 Freulich, R. *Soldiers in Judea.*, Herzl Press, (New York, 1964), p. 72.
19 Freulich, R., ibid, p. 76.

in your life have you seen such a crowd - they were in rags, but what rags! Garments of every nationality and shape, from a coat and trousers to a white torn sheet wound around their lower half, and, for headgear, fezes, caps, sombreros, towels and women's straw bonnets ... They carried their belongings in every conceivable type of package, from a handkerchief to a biscuit box.

Salaman concluded: 'Here, indeed, one finds Jews with spirit, who are ready to do and die for their ideals ... the children of slaves but of the blood of princes. Difficulties are there, and will be, but the spirit is there and it is recognized by everyone who has come into any contact with them ...'[20]

Zionists to the Front

While the spirited ragamuffins of the 40th Battalion were heading towards Egypt, the 38th Battalion was heading towards the front line. They were initially placed under the 10th Irish Division, and stationed on the front line between Nablus and Jerusalem, near the Arab villages of Abouein and Jiljiliah. 'On the 13th June,' Patterson wrote, 'the Battalion was placed in Divisional Reserve. On Saturday 15th it first came under shell fire while we were holding Divine Service. Shells exploded quite close to the men, but no damage was done, and the battalion took its baptism of fire quite cheerfully.'[21]

One recalls similar words expressed by Patterson when the *Zion Mule Corps* came under enemy fire on the beaches of Gallipoli. On that occasion Trumpeldor was present, and Jabotinsky not. Now the tables were turned. Trumpeldor was busy attempting to raise a Jewish fighting force in Russia, while Jabotinsky was beside Patterson.

Jabotinsky described that their task was to observe the activities of the Turks on the opposite hill during the day time, while during the night a patrol would descend into the valley and stay there throughout the night, in order to warn them in case of attack.[22] Each platoon was sent to occupy the nearby deserted village of Abouein for a week at a time - a task not always eagerly anticipated, as they were rather isolated from the main position. Apart from isolated skirmishes and times of excitement, the battalion endured the summer well. In a letter to Dr. Salaman, Patterson wrote: 'The battalion has done an enormous amount in the way of wiring, trenches, hangers, strongpoints and roadways. I am agreeably surprised to find my tailors taking kindly to the pick and shovel. What a great thing all this will prove for the young generation of Israel.'[23] He concluded his letter by stating 'I go to Jerusalem tomorrow for the laying of the foundation stone of the Jewish University.'

20 Freulich, R., ibid., pp. 74-5.
21 Patterson, J. *With the Judeans in the Palestine Campaign*, p. 72.
22 Jabotinsky, V. *The Story of the Jewish Legion.*, pp. 123-4.
23 Freulich. R. *Soldiers in Judea.* ,p. 78.

Zionist Struggles and Triumphs

For the Zionist movement, the laying of the foundation stone for the Hebrew University on Mount Scopus overlooking Jerusalem, represented the first major tangible expression of the promises held out in the *Balfour Declaration*. Patterson, Margolin and other representatives from the *Jewish Legion*, were to lay one of the thirteen foundation stones. Yet Allenby, afraid lest such a move stimulate a local Arab revolt, forbade them from doing so. He was making every effort to distance himself and his forces from any move linked to the Zionist Organization.

The negative attitude towards the Zionist venture continued to grow. On one occasion Weizmann was handed a copy of a small booklet brought back from Russia by some British officers, entitled *The Protocols of the Elders of Zion*. This fabrication claimed that there was a world-wide sinister plan of Jews and Communists to conquer the world. A sympathetic officer, Wyndham Deedes assured him 'You will find it in the haversack of a great many British officers here - and they believe it.'[24]

Weizmann's relationship with Allenby was of great importance. After the initial cool response, Weizmann confessed that this relationship improved. At a dinner in late May he discussed with Allenby the problems faced by the Jewish settlers from the British authorities. 'The Jews are anxious to help the British;' he said, 'they had received the troops with open arms ; they were on the best of terms with the Anzacs. But,' he continued, 'it seemed as though the local administration was bent on ignoring the Home Government's attitude toward our aspirations in Palestine, or, what was worse, was going out of its way to show definite hostility to the policy initiated in London.'[25] Despite this frank analysis, Allenby still seemed determined to minimize Zionist initiatives.

Changes and Challenges

By May most of the troop changes had been executed; experienced British infantry going to France, and inexperienced Indian infantry and cavalry arriving. The number of infantry who would see the campaign through from the beginning to its dying stages was now very small indeed. The Desert Mounted Corps too went through structural changes. The Yeomanry Division and 5th Mounted Brigade were broken up and combined with the Indian units to form 4th Cavalry Division under Major-General Barrow, and the 5th Cavalry Division under Major-General MacAndrew. The Imperial Camel Corps was later broken up, the Australian battalions forming the 5th Light Horse Brigade of the Australian Division, the New Zealanders joining the Mounted Rifles.

---

24   Weizmann, Chaim. *Trial and Error*. Vol. 1., p. 218.
25   Weizmann, Chaim., ibid, p. 223.

The Australian Division opted to adopt the sword, thereby becoming cavalry, while the Anzac Division decided to remain purely as mounted rifles. The summer months were spent practicing and adapting to the new structures.

Despite daily temperatures of well over 38 degrees Centigrade Allenby wanted to maintain a strong presence in the Jordan Valley to increase the effect of his ruse. 'Probably no collection of civilized people had ever endured a full summer in this horrible valley before,' wrote Wavell.[26] While two of the mounted divisions were in the valley, the other two were either resting in the Judean mountains or near the sea or training.

Even in these trying conditions there was no time for boredom. 'Tenchdigging. Marched 4 miles & back' wrote Malone on 10 May.[27] Walters wrote on 4 June. '9 enemy planes dropped 50 bombs on us killing 70 horses besides wounded. 7 men wounded for the Brigade. A great lump of shell fell through one of the Sigs Bivies. I had been sitting there a minute previously & I shook hands with myself.'[28] Wilson, now part of the 5th Cavalry Division, wrote of life in the desert:

> Our unpleasant companions included scorpions black and yellow, huge tarantula spiders and, even more venomous, centipedes six inches long with pincers that could inflict an almost fatal injury. Once, in the middle of the night, there were cries of agony from my troop sergeant who had been bitten by one. He was in terrible pain, his arm visibly swelling. The doctor did what he could but the sergeant had to be evacuated to hospital in the morning. Deadly snakes, including the "horned viper" which actually killed two or three of the Australians, were there too. [29]

And then there was the worst danger: malaria. The number of swamps and pools of stagnant water in the region, results of winter floods, were ideal breeding grounds for malignant types of malarial mosquito. Strenuous efforts were made by both New Zealand and Australian veterinary and medical teams to eradicate this problem. Often times success was countered by a change in the direction of the wind, which blew mosquitoes into the EEF lines from the untreated Turkish areas.

'We are now camped near Ghoraniah Bridge on the Jordan.' Walters wrote on 17 June. 'We are having a very rough time, what with heat, sickness & dust. We are sending an average of 6-7 men per day away mostly from <u>Malaria</u>. I am keeping pretty right myself, had a touch of fever 1 night. We are subjected to a little shellfire daily.'[30] During that summer some 200 EEF soldiers died from malaria.

The troops were more than glad to see the last of the Valley. Malone, writing on 12 May, said 'During time we were in Jordan Valley did not have dew. Grass was

---

26   Wavell, A. P. *The Palestine Campaigns*, p. 188.
27   *Diary of Trooper Malone.*
28   *Diary of Reg Walters.*
29   Wilson, R. *Palestine 1917*, p. 108.
30   *Diary of Reg Walters.*

burnt and dry in early April - partly owing to alkaline nature of soil. Malaria & dysentery very prevalent. We are heartily sick of it and glad to see the last of it.' He wrote the following day 'Moved at 2000. Travelled all night via Bethany & Jerusalem. Change in climate very noticeable in 8 miles, cold & heavy dew.'[31]

For those remaining in the Jordan Valley furnace the ordeals continued. Many hankered after some action. It finally came on 14 July. The Turko-German forces made their last effort to break the British-Anzac line. The attack was primarily aimed against the Australians at Abu Tellal and Musallabeh, (near present day Moshav Gilgal). Three crack German battalions belonging to the *Asien Korps* and a Turkish division attacked the Anzac positions along the Abu Tellal ridge, overpowering the first line of defence. But they proceeded no further, as the Light Horsemen counterattacked, and by nine in the morning drove off the attacking force. The German battalions were decimated, and the surviving 375 were taken prisoner.

'I went down and saw the German prisoners.' Walters wrote, 'They were having a bathe at the time. The heat is very bad so they must have been tired after their fight and march when captured. A fine body of men they are ... It is a nasty knock for the enemy.'[32] It was indeed a nasty knock, and signalled Von Sanders' last offensive assault of the war.

The *Jewish Legion* in the Valley

The *Jewish Legion* was removed from its position in the Samarian Hills on 9 August, spending several days first in and near Jerusalem, and then heading eastwards towards the Jordan Valley taking up positions at Mellaleh. They now came under the command of the Australian Division.

'From a military point of view,' wrote Patterson, 'our position in the Mellaleh was a hazardous one. 'We were now on the extreme right flank and extreme north front of the British Army in Palestine,' he continued, adding, 'the post of honour and danger in the line, with the Turks practically on three sides of us in the salient we held.'[33]

Almost as bad as the peril of the Turk, were the nearby swamps, and the dreaded mosquito which they bred. They too made strenuous efforts to drain the swamps, often drawing Turkish fire in the process. Their main task was to patrol and probe near the Turkish lines, thereby maintaining Turkish attention upon its eastern defences in preference to the coastal defences. Such a strategy was often dangerous and over the weeks the casualties amongst the EEF and *Jewish Legion* grew.

On numerous occasions the Zionist soldiers exchanged fire with the Turks, causing

---

31 *Diary of Trooper Malone.*
32 *Diary of Reg Walters.*
33 Patterson, J. *With the Judeans in the Palestine Campaign.*, p. 105.

and receiving casualties. On one occasion the bodies of several Zionist soldiers were retrieved, but that of H.B. Cross was not. It was presumed that his body had been swept down the Jordan River and he was presumed dead. On other occasions the Zionist soldiers acquaintance with Arabic and even Turkish, was used to good avail. They would return from patrol with Turkish prisoners, won over with reports of the comforts of British captivity.

By late August Allenby's new plans were being polished up - a fact attested to by those remaining in the Jordan Valley. 'Our position,' wrote Jabotinsky, 'was made even more dangerous by the fact that we were left almost entirely without artillery support. As part of a secret plan, Allenby concentrated all his cannon in the Jaffa district, in order to direct the decisive blow. The results,' he concluded, 'demonstrated the excellence of the plan, but in the meantime, both we and the Anzac cavalry divisions, which were stationed just behind us in the valley, were left without cannon cover.'[34]

Jabotinsky's observations were endorsed by Walters, who wrote on 18 August, 'But now Jacko shells us daily especially at the water troughs. I was down there yesterday & was 100 yds from the trough (was going to give my horse a drink) when Jacko started shelling & put 1 shell ... fair in [the] trough blowing it to smitherins (sic)... The pumping party had just filled the trough & went off some over losing all the water.'

Those British and Anzac soldiers who had endured the campaign from its inception and now the Jordan Valley during the summer, were tired by the end of August. 'We will be out of this cursed Valley in a few days,' Walters wrote again on 18 August. He continued, 'off to Duran (Cavalry training). I won't be sorry as I feel rather down.'[35]

While the Australian Division moved out of the valley they were replaced by the Anzac Division. Of this change Patterson wrote, 'When the Australian Division was removed we were attached to Major-General Sir Edward Chaytor, who commanded the Anzac Mounted Division of immortal fame. This was a piece of rare good fortune for us, for we found in General Chaytor a man of wide sympathy and understanding, a demon for work and efficiency, but always ready to give honour where honour was due - even unto Jews.'[36]

The connection between the soldiers of Zion, Australia, New Zealand and Britain would now be continued into the last phase of the campaign for the liberation of the Land of Israel.

---

34 Jabotinsky, V. *The Story of the Jewish Legion.*, p. 133.
35 *Diary of Reg. Walters.*
36 Patterson. J. *With the Judeans in the Palestine Campaign.*, p. 108.

*C*hapter 18

The Race to Damascus and Amman

The Master Plan

As the Australian Division moved out of the Jordan Valley and into the cooler climes of the Judean hills, Walters wrote, 'Great change. There are none of us sorry to leave the malarial stricken valley.' He wrote again on 28 August, 'Camped out at LUDD. Right among the olives. First rate camp. Issued with swords, so we are now cavalry.'[1]

The Australian Division joined the 4th and 5th British-Indian Cavalry Divisions, the British/Indian Infantry Divisions, and the small *Detachment Francais de Palestine et de Syrie (DFPS)*. This detachment was a political gesture to allow France some active role in the campaign. Also attached to the 5th Light Horse Brigade was the 2nd New Zealand Machine Gun Squadron. All these troops were kept hidden among the many orange and olive groves in the region between Jaffa, Rishon le Zion, and Ludd.

Meanwhile the small force in the Jordan Valley, comprised of the Anzac Division, the *Jewish Legion*, some Indian infantry, and the British West Indies Brigade, came under Chaytor's command, and were known as *Chaytor's Force*. Thanks to Allenby's deception, to the Turk and German observers the Jordan Valley force was much larger. During the daytime, troops, especially the West Indians, travelled from Jerusalem to the valley, often dragging branches in order to kick up dust. They returned to Jerusalem by lorry the same night, and played the same ploy the following day. In the Jordan Valley large dummy camps were set up, resplendent with dummy horses with nose bags and water troughs. Allenby also set up a phony headquarters at the Fast Hotel in Jerusalem.

Allenby's plan was to break through the Turkish lines on the coastal plain north of Tel Aviv-Jaffa with infantry of the 21st Corps, and then release his mounted troops through the gap. They were to gallop up the coastal plain to the passes through the Carmel Range, at Abu Shusheh (today Yokneam) opposite Nazareth and El Lejjun or Megiddo (Har Megiddo) opposite El Afule (Afula) into the Jezreel Valley. From here they were to cut off the retreating Turks, as well as move quickly in the main

---

1   *Diary of Reg Walters.*

northward directions from the Jezreel Valley, taking El Afule (Afula), Nazareth, Jenin, Beisan (Bet Shean), Haifa and Acre.

Archibald Wavell wrote of this plan, and especially the mounted role:

> It was a daring plan even against an enemy so inferior in numbers and morale. It would involve a continuous ride of over fifty miles for the majority of the horsemen, and over sixty for some, in the course of which they would have to cross a range of hills in the enemy's possession, passable only by two difficult tracks. There is no parallel in military history to so deep an adventure by such a mass of cavalry against a yet unbroken enemy.[2]

Simultaneously, infantry of the 20th Corps in the Samarian Hills were to move towards Nablus and cut off the Turkish retreat routes towards the Jordan Valley. In the Jordan Valley *Chaytor's Force* was to move against the forces in Transjordan, while the Arab Northern Army force was to hassle Turkish troop movements on the extreme eastern flank. They began their action by cutting the rail link between Amman and Deraa on 16 September.

Facing the initial EEF thrust were three Turkish Armies, the 4th Army in Transjordan with headquarters at Amman; the 7th Army (under Mustapha Kemal) in part of the Samarian hills and Jordan Valley, with headquarters at Nablus; and the 8th Army on the coastal plain and part of the Samarian hills, with headquarters at Tul Keram (Tulkarem). The headquarters of the Commander-in-Chief, Liman von Sanders, was at Nazareth.

To maintain secrecy Allenby only convened a meeting on 17 September with his corps, divisional and brigade commanders, and informed them of his overall plan. He told them 'I have come, gentlemen, to wish you good luck, and to tell you that my impression is that you are on the eve of a great victory. Everything depends - well, perhaps not everything, but nearly everything - on the secrecy, rapidity and accuracy of the cavalry movement.'[3]

Also on 17 September the rail lines between Deraa and Damascus, and between Deraa and Semakh were cut, and the Flying Corps raided Deraa. Von Sanders took the bait and sent reinforcements from Haifa to Transjordan. The 53rd Welsh Division then made its initial move on 18 September, moving towards Nablus via the Jerusalem-Nablus road.

The Great Race Meeting Begins

While these initial operations were in progress a large race meeting was scheduled for 19 September near Jaffa. The evening before the troops and horses were being prepared for the great race. Wilson of the Gloucesters wrote 'We had spent three of

2   Wavell. A.P. *The Palestine Campaigns.*, p. 224.
3   Jones. I. *The Australian Light Horse.*, p. 148.

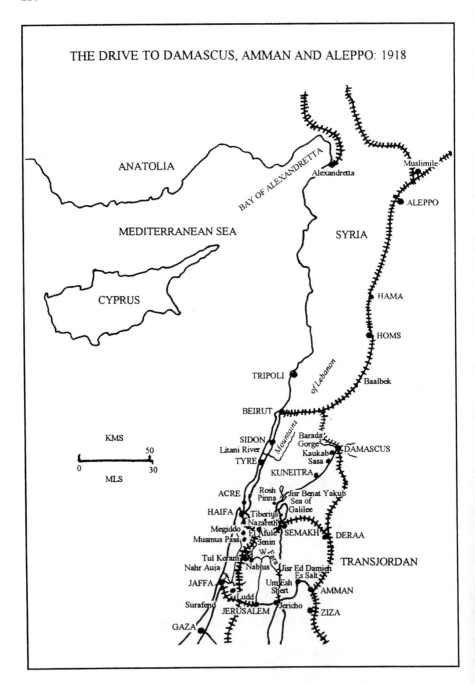

THE DRIVE TO DAMASCUS, AMMAN AND ALEPPO: 1918

the most pleasant days of the entire campaign living in the orange groves of Sarona near Jaffa so that we should not be seen by enemy aircraft. The shade of the trees and the delicious fruit, added to the anticipation of a really [good] gallop, put us on our toes.'[4]

The men and horses of the EEF received extra supplies, the soldiers an extra water bottle, the newly issued rifle pouch for some, and extra ammunition. As the soldiers slept, many next to their beloved horses, the Turks were completely oblivious to the forthcoming attack. Even the desertion of a Muslim Indian soldier made no impact. His fantastic story convinced the Turks that he was nothing more than a plant.

On the evening before the big race meeting, Reg Walters was absent. He had been sent to Port Said on regimental matters, and was not due to return until the morning of the 19 September. He wrote on 18 September 'Stunt in the wind I think.' When he arrived back at Ludd the following morning he found that his Division had moved out the previous evening. 'I could have kicked myself for missing them' he recorded, 'as it is some stunt.' Indeed it was.

At 4.30 in the morning of 19 September, the sleepy Sharon plain was rudely awakened by the roar of some 350 EEF artillery guns. After fifteen minutes of continuous barrage, men of the 21st British-Indian Infantry Corps attacked and broke through the startled Turkish lines of defence. Immediately afterwards the 4th and 5th Cavalry Divisions galloped through the gap, followed by the Australian Division.

'No one engaged in that wild ride will ever forget it' wrote Sergeant M. Fitzpatrick of the New Zealand 2nd Machine Gun Squadron. 'The pace was terrific. Our horses were very fit. They had need to be. We rode light, but still each horse carried three day's rations and bore about twenty stone in weight.'

'The blow was so sudden and swift,' he continues, 'that resistance was slight. Those who opposed were galloped down, machine guns were blanketed, there was neither halt nor check. Most of the fleeing enemy made for the hills, or the Tul Keram road, leading to Nablus. For a time the Indian Lancers and Yeomanry Cavalry, who had broken through nearer the coast, were galloping on our left. With swords and lances flashing in the sunlight, this great host thundered over the rolling ridges. It was a wonderful and inspiring spectacle.'[5]

While the British-Anzac-Indian cavalry streamed northwards, the Flying Corps bombed the central communications centre at El Afule, and the 7th and 8th Armies headquarters at Nablus and Tul Keram. The damage so confused the enemy communications that Von Sanders was oblivious to the speedy breakthrough on the coastal plain.

Chaos reigned on the coastal plain, as the Turkish forces sought every possible

4   Wilson, R. *Palestine 1917*, p. 122.
5   Powles, Lieut.-Colonel. C. Guy. *The New Zealanders in Sinai and Palestine*, p. 240.

means of escape. Many passed through Tul Karem and up the narrow Dotham Valley towards Messudieh Junction. While the Air Force bombed this disorganized group, the 5th Light Horse Brigade by-passed Tul Karem and cut them off. While the 3rd and 7th Indian Divisions continued moving through the lower sections of the Samarian Hills, the 60th Division moved into Tul Karem in the early evening. The 20th Corps troops continued their progress up the spine of the Judeo-Samarian Ridge towards Nablus, the 10th Irish Division on the left of the main road and the 53rd Welsh Division continuing northward along the right side of the road.

Chaytor's Force meanwhile was inactive in the Jordan Valley, awaiting the outcome of activities along the coastal plain. Patrols were still being sent out to probe the Turkish lines. The *Jewish Legion* even made a small frontal attack upon Turkish trenches near Mellaleh on 19 September. Margolin and the 39th Battalion Royal Fusiliers had by now joined the 38th Battalion. That same day Patterson received his instructions from Chaytor. The Jewish battalions, to be known as *Patterson's Column*, were to 'capture both sides of the ford across the Jordan known to the Arabs as Umm Esh Shert, and thereafter to advance on the town of Es Salt in the Hills of Moab, far beyond the Jordan.'[6]

As the Anzac Division and auxiliary troops prepared for the offensive, the Jewish troops were solemn. It was *Yom Kippur*, the Day of Atonement, the holiest day in the Jewish calendar. There was supposed to be total quiet on the front. Nevertheless cantor Philip Brodsky, wrote Freulich '... was wide awake. Completely forgetful of the order to be silent, he softly began to chant Kol Nidre. Emotion choked every word, making the chant more poignant. Several other soldiers joined in, and within a few minutes, all the soldiers were singing in unison, completely oblivious to the captain's command. Suddenly,' Freulich continued, 'the translucent and magical singing was shattered by distant shots.'[7]

Into the Jezreel Valley

Early in the morning of 20 September the 5th Cavalry Division passed through the Abu Shusheh track into the Jezreel Valley. One brigade headed directly for Nazareth. 'You never saw such fun in your life as we had at Nazareth,' wrote Wilson, 'only our Regiment were in the town and they didn't expect us at all and were in bed in different houses. Those we woke up,' he continued, 'of course were easy prey but street fighting of the very first order soon developed and lasted nearly all day.'[8]

Von Sanders was one of those taken completely by surprise, but managed to escape in his pyjamas. He later re-organized his troops and mounted a counterattack. Street fighting ensued for much of the day, and the outnumbered British cavalry

---

6   Patterson, J. *With the Judeans in the Palestine Campaign*, p. 135.
7   Freulich, R. *Soldiers in Judea*, p. 109.
8   Wilson, R. *Palestine 1917*, p. 138.

were forced to withdraw. Another brigade had meanwhile moved onto El Afule.

The 4th Cavalry Division moved through the Musmus Pass and emerged near Megiddo. It was immediately met by a large Turkish force - which was quickly subdued by the lancer-bearing Indians. They then proceeded onto El Afule joining men of the 5th Division, and then heading eastwards towards Beisan (Bet Shean). The Australian Division meanwhile entered the Jezreel Valley about 11 am on 20 September. Chauvel then arrived and established his HQ near Lejjun - Megiddo. He wrote to his wife that day: '... from my tent door I can see Nazareth, Mt Tabor, El Afule, Zenim (Jezreel), Mt Gilboa and Jenin ... We have been fighting what I sincerely hope will be the last "Battle of Armageddon" all day.'[9]

Capture of Jenin

While the 4th Cavalry Division was capturing Beisan, aerial intelligence had spotted large numbers of Turks converging onto Jenin. These were the remnants of the 8th Army fleeing up the Dothan Valley, and part of the 7th Army coming from Nablus. Orders were given at 4.30 for the 3rd Light Horse Brigade to capture Jenin. Galloping with swords drawn at the speed of sixteen kilometres an hour, and in formation of thirty abreast, the Light Horsemen took all before them. Prior to reaching the town they had already bagged hundreds of Turkish prisoners. Their quick and decisive movement totally confused the Turks and thousands more surrendered. [10]

Apart from some isolated sniper fire, the battle for Jenin was over. Now the Anzacs had to preserve the town from pillaging and destruction by the local Arabs. Some Light Horsemen were fortunate enough to 'rescue', after a fight with the local Arabs, a wagon loaded with some 250,000 pounds worth of bullion - as well as a number of cases of quality German champagne!

The Light Horsemen then had to block the Jenin - Nablus road south of Jenin and stop the movement of Turkish reinforcements or escapees. A machine-gun section, commanded by Lieutenant R.R.W. Patterson was sent ahead, and soon found itself well in front of the main body of Light Horsemen. Then, thanks to the moonlight, they noticed a large movement of some 2,800 Turkish and German troops coming nonchalantly towards them. Patterson put a quick burst of machine gun fire over their heads.

The Turko-German column was confronted in a narrow gorge. The Australians, hopelessly outnumbered, managed to convince the Turks, via a German nurse, that they were the vanguard of a larger force. The bluff worked and several thousand more prisoners were added to the bag. [11]

9   Hill, A.J. *Chauvel of the Light Horse*, p. 171.
10   Wilson, Brig-General. L.C. *Operations of the Third Light Horse Brigade, AIF*, p. 38.
11   Wilson, Brig-General. L.C. ibid., p. 39.

During the course of that day the Light Horsemen captured some 8,000 Turkish and German prisoners, many of whom, wrote Wilson, 'admitted being taken completely by surprise at our unexpected appearance at the northern exits of Jenin, stating that they thought we must have landed at Haifa, never believing it possible that we have made such rapid progress up the coast.'[12]

Capture of Nablus

After their exhausting time on 19 September, the 5th Light Horse Brigade rested on the other side of Tul Karem.[13] The following day they travelled along the ancient route past Samaria-Sebaste towards Nablus, the ancient Shechem. As they approached from the west, the 10th Irish Division approached from the south. Both groups of men entered Nablus almost simultaneously, on 21 September.

Light Horseman Captain Rex Hall received the surrender of the city, being handed the keys of the city at the Town Hall. The British-Anzac forces rounded up some 3,726 prisoners, the remaining Turkish soldiers having streamed out of Nablus' north-eastern exit, along the Wadi Fara (Nahal Tirza) towards the Jisr ed Damieh. This column was detected by the British and Australian aircraft (belonging to the No 1 Squadron Australian Flying Corps) on 21 September, and bombed for four hours. Despite this harassment they refused to surrender, even when the Light Horsemen appeared on both sides of the Wadi.

Even the most war hardened of the Australian soldiers were sickened by the subsequent event, as they poured fire into the hopelessly trapped Turkish column below. The survivors either scattered into the nearby hills, many of whom were captured during the following days, while some managed to flee across the Jordan.

By the end of 21 September the EEF had completed its rout of the lower Galilee, after the 5th Cavalry Division had re-captured Nazareth. On that same day the New Zealanders belonging to *Chaytor's Force*, began moving along the west bank of the Jordan River towards the Jisr ed Damieh. Until then the Turkish 4th Army had made no initial move to either extricate itself, or to come to the aid of the 7th and 8th Armies on the west side of the Jordan. By 21 September the Turkish situation was precarious. The Arab Northern Army had cut them off from Deraa, the natives were rising against them, and the large garrison at Maan was beginning to move towards Amman.

The movement northwards along the coastal plain resumed on 22 September, with part of the 5th Cavalry Division moving towards and capturing Acre with its small Turkish garrison. Haifa was better defended, by machine guns on the plain, and artillery from the slopes of Mount Carmel. On 23 September some Indian Lancers

---

12   Wilson, Brigadier-General. L.C. ibid., p. 39.

13   Powles, Lieut.-Colonel. C. Guy. *The New Zealanders in Sinai and Palestine.*, p. 241.

climbed up the Carmel and swung in behind the artillery, while other Lancers galloped down the infantry and machine gun positions with the lance. Supplies were landed at the small port and dispatched to the various EEF forces.

Es Salt - Third Time Lucky

Chaytor's New Zealanders, assisted by the West Indians, meanwhile captured the Jisr ed Damieh on 22 September. Colonel McCarroll of the Auckland Regiment was quite impressed by the West Indians, stating 'The advance of the British West Indians was particularly keen and workmanlike. They dashed down the hill in great style.'[14] The New Zealanders and auxiliary troops then intercepted numbers of Turkish stragglers coming down the Wadi Fara (Nahal Tirza).

Von Sanders planned to establish a fresh line of defence, stretching from Deraa down to Semakh, then along the western side of the Sea of Galilee up to Lake Hula to the north, and westwards towards the Mediterranean north of Acre. The Turkish 4th Army had to reach Deraa. For those stationed in the south it was imperative they first reach Amman. Chaytor had to take Amman before the Turkish garrison from Maan reached it.

In the Jordan Valley, a company of the *Jewish Legion* including Lieutenant Jabotinsky, captured the strategic Um Esh Shert position. Soon afterwards 'hoofbeats of galloping horses could be heard from a distance,' wrote Freulich. 'A group of Australian horsemen were seen crossing the river. They were followed by wagon trains and camels loaded with ammunition and supplies. A great cheer arose among the Legionnaires.'[15] These troops were en-route to Es Salt, for the third time during 1918, as too were the New Zealanders who were moving along the road from the Jisr ed Damieh.

The New Zealanders met opposition on the outskirts of Es Salt - but quickly dealt with it. By 4.30 in the afternoon the town was finally captured by the Anzacs. From here patrols were sent east and north. One consisted of four officers and 100 men from the Auckland Regiment, who completed a successful raid upon the railway line north of Amman.

On 23 September aerial reconnaissance spotted the Turkish garrison from Maan en-route to Amman. The New Zealanders made haste for Amman, joining the Light Horsemen on the way. *Patterson's Column* followed the New Zealanders, foot slogging up the rugged track. 'This march in Transjordan,' wrote Jabotinsky, 'was the most difficult I have ever experienced.'[16]

Another Legionnaire, Herman Roberts, reminisced about that march:

---

14   Gullett, H.S. *The A.I.F. in Sinai and Palestine.*, p. 717.
15   Freulich, R. *Soldiers in Judea.* , pp. 98-99.
16   Jabotinsky, V. *The Story of the Jewish Legion.*, p. 138.

The grinding climb up the hill continued. Some of the men dropped, unable to continue; others struggled valiantly to keep up. In my own case, it was as though my ribs were being pressed against a hot stove and my feet were weighed down by lead. I was in a complete daze. But it's a long lane that has [a] turning. We had reached our objective - Es Salt, a village perched atop the plateau.[17]

Half way to Es Salt some Jewish soldiers, including Jabotinsky, were told to return to the Jordan Valley and in particular to Shunet Nimrin to guard the hundreds of Turkish prisoners now being assembled there. The remainder of the Jewish unit continued onto Es Salt where Colonel Margolin was appointed military governor.

The Anzacs pressed on enthusiastically towards Amman. 'It was felt that of all old scores yet to be wiped off against the Turks,' wrote Powles, 'this was the most important. The memory of those four days of bitter fighting in the rain and cold were yet fresh in everyone's memory.'[18] Both New Zealanders and Australians, wrote Gullett, were 'animated by friendly but sharp rivalry for the capture of the town.'[19] The battle raged throughout 25 September, with the New Zealanders capturing the Citadel, scene of acrid fighting in the previous encounter. New Zealanders and Australians shared the other victories and Amman was soon captured. Altogether some 2,360 Turko-German prisoners were taken.

The Movements of Reg Walters

Trooper Reg Walters was representative of the soldiers and especially the Anzac mounted men, who fought in this campaign. He was highly inventive and adventurous. Profoundly upset at having missed the 'big stunt' or the 'great ride' he and a fellow Light Horseman 'sneaked off on foot' in search of his Regiment. After walking '½ a mile' they hitched a ride in a 'Motor Lorry' which took them about sixteen kilometres to Sarona (former German Colony and now site of Israel's Ministry of Defence).

Having stocked up on provisions, and another short walk, they managed a lift with an ammunition 'lorry train'. When the train stopped later that day, the 'Tommy' soldiers invited Walters and his mate for dinner, and then breakfast the next morning. The following day they hitched onto Tul Karem, where he noticed '1,000's and 1,000's of prisoners, the Turkish guns, the 1000000's pounds worth of Turkish Transport. It was a wonderful but awful sight. Motors by the dozens knocked over all the way along the road.'

Having restocked their supplies, it was off again, this time in a 'Ford Car' which took them some thirty kilometres, and 'dumped us at another big Railway Centre behind NABLUS.' They had not long been there when, he wrote, 'up comes 3 Flying Corps Cars … from the direction we wanted to go. They pulled up for the night and

---

17   Freulich. R. *Soldiers in Judea*, p. 113.
18   Powles, Lieut.-Colonel., C. Guy. *The New Zealanders in Sinai and Palestine*, p. 250.
19   Gullet, H. S., *The A.I.F. in Sinai and Palestine*, p. 720.

we joined them for Tea. They told us all that had happened up in the Line.' That night he slept in one of the lorries, a huge German one captured at the German airfield at El Afule.

The following morning they flagged down two big German motor lorries, and were told they could jump in the second one, driven by a captured German, and would be let off at Genene (Jenin). 'This we did' he wrote, 'so off we went keeping a sharp eye on our companion by the way.' At Jenin they heard how their Regiment had taken '7000 prisoners at this place.' 'Put in the day very nicely here.' He records quite happily. 'Had a bath, lived on tomatoes & figs & blackberries from Gardens.'

And the food wasn't all that pleased them that day, for 'at 6 o'clock the 3rd Bde [Brigade] Amb [ambulance] cars came up to a big Turkish Hospital where we were waiting & we got a lift to Afule & hopped straight out of the cars into some wagons that were going to the 10th Regt [10th Light Horse Regiment]. Arrived home safely much to the amazement of the Heads & my mates. The CO said "I wish all the Sigs [Signallers] had done the same. Although it may mean a Court Martial." (That's something', he concluded, 'I've to look forward to).'[20]

The Northern Galilee

While Walters was working his way back to his unit, Chauvel and Allenby drew up plans, on 22 September, for the capture of Semakh and Tiberias, so as to establish a line through to Acre. Early in the morning of 25 September, Australian horsemen moved cautiously towards the village and train station at Semakh, which were heavily defended by German machine gunners, and Turkish infantry. In Beersheva style, men of the 4th Light Horse Brigade galloped towards the village under heavy machine-gun fire. They dismounted and after enduring the heaviest fighting of the big ride thus far, finally took the strategic position at the cost of seventeen Australian dead and sixty-one wounded. Nearly one hundred horses were killed or wounded.[21] This encounter signalled the final breakthrough in the Land of Israel. All that now remained was the capture of Tiberias. While elements of the 4th Light Horse Brigade moved along the shores of the Sea of Galilee from the south, a regiment of the 3rd Light Horse Brigade and armoured cars were dispatched from Nazareth to move onto Tiberias via the ancient *Via Maris* past the Horns of Hattin.

Around noon on 25 September Light Horsemen approached Tiberias from the southern, and northern sides of the town. After a swift attack by mid afternoon the ancient town of Tiberias was in Anzac hands. 'The inhabitants of the town, seven-eighths of whom are Jews,' wrote Kirkpatrick, 'gave us a right royal welcome.'[22]

---

20   *Diary of Reg Walters.*
21   Wavell, A. P. *The Palestine Campaigns.*, p. 223.
22   Quoted in Powles, Lieut.-Colonel. C. Guy. *The New Zealanders in Sinai and Palestine.*, p. 242.

Walters records how having being fixed up with a new horse, his unit moved through Nazareth, 'a very large place something like Jerusalem' and 'then camped on the Sea of Galilee after leaving Tiberias.'[23]

Wilson, the commander of the 3rd Light Horse Brigade arrived in Tiberias on the morning of 26 September, and immediately dispatched Light Horsemen northwards. These patrols took possession of El Mejdel, the ancient Magdala, the birthplace of Mary Magdalene, and Tabghah further to the east on the shore front. Other patrols proceeded even to the city on the hills - Safed.[24] Such patrols confirmed that the Turkish rearguard was small in size and dispirited. Encouraged, Chauvel and Allenby decided to press on towards Damascus.

Into Gilead (the Golan Heights)

Also on 26 September Chaytor consolidated his position around Amman and sent troops north and east to capture the main water supplies and consolidate any alternative escape routes for the Turks. Then he sent another Anzac brigade to the south to make contact with the Turkish force.

Chauvel meanwhile instructed the 4th Cavalry Division to move from Beisan, across the Jordan River and up into Transjordan towards Deraa. Here Barrow was to intercept the Turkish 4th Army, and if they eluded him, to pursue them up the Hejaz railway towards Damascus. The Arab Northern Army was to continue to hassle the fleeing Turks from the desert side. The Australian Division was to head north of the Sea of Galilee, following the ancient route, the *Via Maris*, cross the Jordan River at the Jisr Benat Yakub (Bridge of the Daughters of Jacob) and continue along the ancient route through Kuneitra towards Damascus. The 5th Cavalry Division was to follow the Australian Division.

On 27 September, while the 4th Cavalry Division was engaged in fighting between Irbid and Deraa, the Australian Division began its trek towards Damascus. Passing through the Jewish village of Rosh Pina they reached the west bank of the Jisr Benat Yakub about midday. They found the old stone bridge had been destroyed by the retreating Turkish and German troops, and a strong rearguard, comprised mostly of machine-gunners was placed on the opposite bank.

After several attempts, and in spite of the machine-gun fire, a crossing was made and the Australian horsemen moved into the hills of Gilead. The enemy rearguard then quickly jumped into German lorries and made a hasty retreat towards Damascus, with the Anzac-British-Indian force in hot pursuit. One veteran who was not able to partake in this part of the action was Reg Walters. After all his efforts to rejoin his unit, he became violently sick. 'I was feeling sick when I started,' he wrote, '& after

---

23 *Diary of Reg Walters.*
24 Sarah Pearl of Safed, although only two years old at the time, vaguely recalls her parents later speaking of the Australian cavalry coming to the town. Interview with Sarah Pearl July 1996.

going 18 miles had to report to the Doctor who said I could not go on. So if that wasn't the worst bit of luck a man ever had after going through everything to fall foul just on the eve of taking Damascus.'[25]

The Farce at Ziza

The Anzac Division continued its move to tighten the knot south of Amman. They learned from a captured Turk that the Maan garrison, of some 6,000 had withdrawn and was moving along the railway towards Amman. Preparations were made to meet this strong force. The following morning, 28 September, British airmen informed Chaytor that the Turkish force had reached the village of Ziza, south of Amman. One airman dropped a note into the camp, informing them that *Chaytors' Force* controlled Amman and the nearby water supplies. He proposed that the Turkish force surrender, or be heavily bombed from the air. Shortly afterwards Lieutenant-Colonel Donald Cameron, commanding two squadrons of Queenslanders from the 5th Regiment, began surrender negotiations with the Turkish commander, Ali Bey Wahaby.

Wahaby was willing to surrender to the vastly inferior Anzac force, but he was concerned about laying down his arms while thousands of Bedouin belonging to the Beni Sakr tribe waited nearby to pounce. It was a serious situation. The Flying Corps was preparing to bomb the Turkish position during the evening, so Cameron stepped up his efforts to force a surrender. Chaytor meanwhile called upon Ryrie to proceed quickly with the remainder of the 7th Light Horse Regiment, while he himself drove at haste to the scene.

Ryrie's force arrived just before dark - to discover a most bizarre scene. 'The 5th Regiment,' wrote Richardson afterwards, 'were concentrated waiting reinforcements, while the Turks in their trenches were standing to arms holding off the Arabs with shell and machine-gun fire. The vulture appearance of the Arabs, who were willing that we should do the fighting and they the looting, will not readily be forgotten.'[26] The Arab leaders beckoned Ryrie to attack the Turks. Ryrie however knew full well the so-called fighting ability of these would-be allies, and refused.

Instead, he took the two Arab sheiks with him, galloped through the Arab lines into the Turkish centre in order to explain his decision. The Turks could retain their arms during the night until further Anzac reinforcements could come on the morrow. To press home his point to the Arabs - he kept the two sheiks hostage, explaining that if there was any violation of this decision the sheiks would be killed.

The evening of 28 September 1918 would have to be the most ironical of the War. Throughout that night the Anzac soldiers camped together with the armed

---

25 *Diary of Reg Walters.*
26 Gullett, H.S. *The A.I.F. in Sinai and Palestine*, p. 726.

Turks, and together held off any threat from the ravenous Bedouin force. Gullett summarizes the scene:

> The Turks, demoralised by the swift and complete overthrow of their fortunes, and disconcerted by the presence of the Australians, still feared massacre by the Arabs; all night they stood to arms, and engaged in bursts of machine-gun and rifle fire. The light horsemen, revelling in the strange situation, could be heard cheering on their activities. "Go on, Jacko," they would shout, "give it to the blighters" -and then indulge in shouts of laughter ... What was grim tragedy to the Turks was farce to the Australians.[27]

The following morning, 29 September, the New Zealanders arrived and the Turkish force of some 5,000 finally laid down their arms - much to the disgust of the nearby Arabs who wanted to deal with matters their way - and collect all the booty. Some Turks retained their arms so as to assist with the escort. Hereby ended all Turkish resistance in Transjordan. Chaytor's Anzac Division and attached forces had, in just over a week, enacted terrible casualties upon the Turkish 4th Army, and taken some 10,300 prisoners. The horsemen from New Zealand and Australia lost some twenty-seven killed and 105 wounded, with seven missing.[28]

Kuneitra and Sasa

After Deraa had fallen on 28 September, the 4th Cavalry Division pursued the remnants of the 4th Turkish Army northwards. Fear of the Arabs on their eastern flank compelled many Turks to keep trudging towards the refuge of Damascus rather than surrender. On 29 September Light Horsemen captured the village of Kuneitra on the main road to Damascus. Australian engineers meanwhile repaired the bridge over the Jordan, allowing supplies, as well as the remainder of the force including the 5th Cavalry Division easy passage. By the evening of 29 September most of the Australian and 5th Cavalry Divisions were resting in the vicinity of Kuneitra.

The advance guard, the 3rd Light Horse Brigade, continued northwards, and discovered the large rear guard of some 300 Germans and 1,200 Turks among the rocks near Sasa. This rearguard force was dislodged early the next morning.

Then the 4th and 12th Light Horse Regiments under Colonel Bouchier, took the lead in the advance towards Damascus. All of the Australian regiments and brigades vied for the privilege of entering Damascus first. The race to Damascus was still wide open. Also in the race were the remnants of the Turkish 4th Army, who were nearing the city by way of the ancient *Kings Highway* some kilometres to the east.

This large Turkish force decided to stop the advancing Australians and moved to a position near the village of Kaukab. While the British artillery pounded the Turkish

---

27   Gullett, H.S., ibid., p. 727.
28   Gullett, H.S., ibid., p. 727.

position Bouchier's 4th and 12th Light Horse Regiments drew the sword and charged while the small French cavalry and other Light Horse units moved around the flanks. These flank movements, as well as the frightening scene of sword wielding Australians was enough for both the German machine-gunners and the Turkish infantry. Most bolted towards Damascus.

Some 4,000 Turkish and German soldiers were forced to head towards the Barada Gorge which led out of Damascus to Beirut, the route of the railway. French and Australian soldiers from the 5th Light Horse Brigade then gained commanding positions in front and above this fleeing force, and poured fire into the advance columns. As the remainder turned back, they were confronted by more Light Horsemen, and either surrendered or made their way back into the city. The 3rd Light Horse Brigade was to proceed onwards around Damascus and cut off the exit of Turkish forces along the Damascus - Homs road. But the wreckage along the Barada Gorge and the steepness of the cliffs stopped them from progressing any further.

Withdrawal from Transjordan

Following the victory at Ziza, the prisoners and many of the Anzacs began to move back towards the Jordan Valley. A New Zealand officer, Colonel C.E.R. Mackesy from Whangarei, was appointed military governor over Amman and Es- Salt (relieving Margolin). However tragedy now struck the Anzac Division as well as the West Indian and Jewish troops. Many came down sick from malaria, pneumonic influenza and other sicknesses.

At the beginning of the assault many of these troops had been exposed to the malignant malarial mosquitoes in the Jisr ed Damieh region, an area which had not been cleaned up over the previous months due to its proximity to the forward Turkish lines. As the incubation period for these mosquitoes was between 10-14 days, the exposed soldiers were now beginning to be affected by the malaria.

Several days after the campaign ended some 900 stretcher cases were at Jericho alone. Numerous veterans from the campaign and even from Gallipoli, whose bodies were now worn out by fatigue, fell to the sickness. Meanwhile as the men of the Anzac Division rested at Jericho and then began moving into the Judean hills, the men of the Australian Division were preparing for the final move into Damascus.

Damascus Invested

By the evening of 30 September Damascus was invested. Elements of the Arab Northern Army and Barrow's 4th Cavalry Division coming from the south were linking up with the Australian Division, followed as it was by the 5th Cavalry Division. Yet although the closest, the Australians were ordered not to enter the capital city of the province of Syria. It seems that politics dictated this decision. Had the Australians entered first, the population of Damascus may have construed that the British intended handing Damascus over to the French.[29]

No 'Christian' soldiers were to enter Damascus, and all fighting and policing was to be done by Feisal's Arab irregulars. These decisions were part of the delicate political scenario now reaching its climax. Britain's promises to the French and the Arabs made during the war - and which often appeared contradictory - were to be fulfilled, or at least to appear so. According to these agreements, France was to administer the coastal region of Syria, including the Lebanon, while the inland region was to be administered by the Hashemite Arabs, that is Feisal, with some French influence.

Hence Allenby, acting upon orders from Sykes and the Foreign Office, decreed on 29 September that only Feisal's troops were to enter Damascus. Chauvel, as military chief, was to initially seek out the Turkish Vali or Governor, and entrust the civil administration to him. An Arab administration would then later be set up in the Syrian hinterland, under a French protectorate. Time would be needed before such a provisional Arab administration could be set up. And ultimately all rested upon the peace conference at the conclusion of the War. It all sounded so neat and tidy.

Yet the ordinary British-Anzac-Indian soldier of the EEF was completely unaware of these political complexities. All he wanted was for some rest right now, and then a complete victory. Most of the horsemen had ridden some 400 kilometres or more in twelve days of almost continuous riding, with intermittent fighting and minimal supplies. Now, while the politicians awaited the unfolding of their plans, these battle-weary men watched the skyline over Damascus light up as the Turks set light to ammunition dumps and supplies.

Meanwhile Lawrence, the self-acclaimed spokesman for the Arab nationalist movement, awaited in Barrow's camp to the south. He had with him various elaborate clothes, and a Rolls Royce car, all ready for a victorious entrance into Damascus the following day. But he was a worried man. So much rested upon his Arab forces being the first to enter Damascus.

'The sporting Australians,' he wrote, 'saw the campaign as a point-to-point, with Damascus the post; ... In their envelopment of Damascus the Australians might be forced,' he anxiously thought, 'despite orders, to enter the town. If any one resisted them,' he remorsefully concluded, 'it could spoil the future.'[30]

Unbeknown to Allenby, Sykes, or Chauvel, the situation in Damascus that night of 30 September, was quickly deteriorating. Over the previous couple of days there had been growing tension between the German and Turkish soldiers on one hand, and between the Turko-German troops and the local populace on the other. Anarchy

---

29   Fromkin, D. *A Peace To End All Peace.*, p. 336.
30   Lawrence, T.E. *Revolt in the Desert.*, p. 319.

was in the air. On 30 September the situation became desperate, as Djemal Pasha, much of the standing army, as well as the Turkish Governor and civil administration, fled the city.

To stem the flood of disorder a provisional council was set up by Emir Said Abd, and the Hejaz flag hoisted over the city. Some of Feisal's followers then infiltrated into the city during the evening in order to prepare for the official Arab delegation with Feisal and Lawrence at the head on the following day.

The Surrender of Damascus

Early in the morning of 1 October 1918 men of the 3rd Light Horse Brigade continued on their way to block the Damascus- Homs road. Crossing over the Barada Gorge they firstly had to clear away the debris and the dead, and move the wounded to the side, so as to make a passage through. Then, in order to quickly obtain their objective - they rode through the centre of Damascus!

Nearing the centre of the city, reputed to be the oldest continually inhabited city in the world, the Australians saw a large crowd milling around the Hall of Government. Major Olden stopped at the City Hall and was led to the office of the Governor. Here, recalled Olden, ' … a large gathering, clad in the glittering garb of eastern officialdom, stood formed up in rows. Their general demeanour,' he wrote, 'was quiet and dignified. Behind a table, in a high-backed gold and plush chair, sat a small man of distinguished appearance, wearing European clothes and a tarboosh.'[31]

The Governor in question was Emir Said, who now surrendered to the first representatives of the Egyptian Expeditionary Force to enter Damascus. This was an extraordinary incident - soldiers from one of the youngest countries in the world receiving the surrender of one of the oldest cities in the world.

Meanwhile other Light Horsemen had now entered the outskirts of Damascus. About 100 men of the 4th Light Horse Regiment charged with drawn swords into the Hamadieh Barracks which housed some 11,000 Turkish soldiers. After some brief fighting, the shocked and startled Turks raised their hands in surrender. The Australians then found, to their horror, hundreds of desperately sick Turkish soldiers suffering from influenza and other sicknesses. Unfortunately a number of the Australians became too exposed to these sick Turks, and themselves fell sick.

Olden by this time had completed his formalities, and continued on towards his initial objective, the Homs-Aleppo road. He wrote:

> The march now assumed the aspect of a triumphal procession … the dense masses of people rapidly hysterical in their manifestations of joy. They clung to the horses' necks, they kissed our men's stirrups, they showered confetti and rose water over them; they shouted, laughed, cried, sang and clapped hands. From the windows of

31   Olden, A.C.N. *Westralian Cavalry in the War.* Alexander McCubbin, (Melbourne, 1921)., p. 278.

high buildings, Moslem women, raising their dark veils, called out "Meit allo Wesahla! Meit allo Wesahla!" ('A hundred welcomes'). The cry was taken up and carried along the line of march in one continuous chant.[32]

Once through all the festivities the Australian horsemen continued their ride northwards pursuing the retreating Turkish and German soldiers. Some twenty-five kilometres or so north of Damascus however they were forced to halt. They had out-ridden their supplies, the men and horses were exhausted, and further progress without artillery support, which was by now far behind, was dangerous. They managed however to bag some 750 Turkish prisoners during the day (and added another 1,500 the following day as they rode down another Turkish column).

While the Australians were rounding up many Turkish prisoners they unknowingly liberated another prisoner. Lieutenant H.B. Cross of the *Jewish Legion*, whose body was presumed lost to the flowing Jordan River, had in fact been wounded and then taken prisoner and ended up in a murky prison-cell in Damascus. Here he was completely forgotten. Then, wrote Freulich:

> Weeks later, Cross woke up one morning to find the iron door of his cell wide open, and the guard gone. He got up, walked out of the cell, and found the other prisoners gone. No one was around. The door to an office was ajar, and he walked in. He stepped to the window, looked out and saw a mob of fleeing people.
>
> Bewildered, Cross staggered into the center of the city to discover that it was being occupied by the Australian cavalry. He managed to get some food and a clean uniform ... A few days later he was back with the battalion, and reported to Colonel Patterson.
>
> Patterson thought he was seeing a ghost. Cross had been missing and presumed dead. His wife had already been sent official word from the War Office, and Colonel Patterson had written her a personal letter. The Colonel embraced Cross, ordered some food to be brought to him and dispatched a telegram to his wife, telling her that her husband was alive and well.[33]

Chauvel and the Political Stakes

While the Australian horsemen were being festooned and then chasing down the retreating Turks, Chauvel was also chasing. His quarry was Lawrence. He arrived at Barrow's camp early on the morning of 1 October to meet Lawrence who was to act as his liaison officer. Lawrence, however, contrary to orders, had slipped away and entered Damascus. Chauvel, desperately needing the services of his Arab advisor, had only one choice - to go after him. [34]

Lawrence meanwhile was very active. He and a chief pro-Feisal loyalist, Nuri el-Sa'id, had quickly deposed Emir Said, and replaced him with their own governor,

---

32   Olden, A.C.N., ibid., p. 278.

33   Freulich, R. *Soldiers in Judea.*, p. 95.

34   Hill, A..J. *Chauvel of the Light Horse.*, p. 179.

Shukri Pasha. Shortly after this under-handed affair, a chagrined Chauvel arrived on the scene. Lawrence subsequently introduced him to the 'popularly elected' governor. Chauvel, however, had been instructed to maintain the Turkish governor at first. But when it was ascertained that indeed the Turkish governor had fled, Chauvel was left with no choice but to sanction Shukri's appointment. Shukri's presence therefore gave strong credence to the probability of Feisal's regime taking control over Damascus. Such a scheme would be opposed by the French.

Afterwards Chauvel was informed by Captain Hubert Young, a British officer attached to Feisal's force, of the devious manner in which Shukri had been appointed. Young informed Chauvel that the city was in upheaval, and that the populace basically feared the Arab troops of Feisal's army.[35]

The following morning, 2 October, the situation in Damascus deteriorated still further. Lawrence had no choice but to seek Chauvel's assistance. His Arab 'policemen' were totally inadequate for the situation. Damascus was a tinderbox. Chauvel responded by dispatching a squadron of Light Horsemen, at whose appearance, wrote W.T. Massey, a British War Correspondent, 'the trouble ceased.'

'It was marvellous,' Massey continued, 'Firing stopped - the Australians saw to that - people who had been carrying rifles stole home with them, the dead were picked up from the streets, and those who had anything to lose breathed freely.'[36] Chauvel thereupon stationed two regiments of Light Horsemen in the capital city and order was quickly restored and maintained.

To further enhance a sense of security, and to show the local populace who was really in control, Chauvel ordered a show of force - a full procession of his troops. Despite the tiredness of his troops, Chauvel, on 2 October, led a full procession through the city centre. As Australian cavalry, British Yeomanry, Indian Lancers and French Saphis rode through, followed by armoured cars and horse artillery, the local populace was left in no doubt at all of the might of the EEF, and of Chauvel's seriousness to maintain order and security.

The following day Allenby arrived in Damascus to meet with Feisal and his liaison officer Colonel Lawrence. This visit was necessary due to the appointment of the Arab governor. Allenby therefore had to outline the conditions of the 'Sykes-Picot' Agreement, especially as they related to Syria.

The meeting took place at the Victoria Hotel. Allenby told Feisal clearly that France was to be the protecting power, and that he and his father Hussein would administer Syria under French guidance and patronage, that Feisal had no claim at all to Lebanon and that Feisal would receive a French liaison officer. Both Feisal and Lawrence intimated, falsely, ignorance of the conditions of the 'Sykes-Picot' Agreement. Allenby thereupon instructed Feisal that these were the conditions, and

35 Hill, A.J., *Chauvel of the Light Horse.*, p. 180.
36 Massey, W.T. *Allenby's Final Triumph*, E. P. Dutton, (New York, 1920)., pp. 261-3.

that he, Feisal, was expected to adhere to them. Lawrence, unwilling to serve under a French liaison officer, thereupon requested, and received leave from duty.[37]

Onto Beirut and Aleppo

It was now a race against time. Britain's chances of retaining *Palestine* depended very much upon France being able to attain the other areas 'promised' to her under the 'Sykes-Picot' Agreement. That meant the whole of Syria. If for any reason only part of Syria was conquered then the entire plan was faulty. It was imperative to continue with the advance, otherwise Turkey may sue for peace before the conquest was completed. All these concerns had been discussed at length at the War Council meetings held during the first days of October.

The Australian Division, including a rejuvenated Reg Walters, remained in Damascus to retain order. After falling violently sick Walters had been moved first to a hospital in Tiberias and then to Nazareth. While there he was able to record the sicknesses and wounds of some of his mates. He was then moved to Haifa on 30 September, a 'Rotten place for treatment,' he recorded. Itching to be re-united again with his unit, Walters managed to get a discharge on 3 October. He then waited at the Haifa station one whole day before catching a ration train to Semakh. 'Cow of a train ride all night.' He wrote. From Semakh he travelled north to Tiberias, and then managed to get a lift with a rations wagon all the way back to Damascus. There he recorded 'We have been guarding P of W since I arrived. The strangest time one could wish to have ... approx 200 die daily.'[38]

After departing Damascus, the 4th and 5th Cavalry Divisions proceeded towards Rayak in the interior, where the Beirut-Homs and Damascus-Homs railways meet. The railway then travelled north to Aleppo, and then into Anatolia and onto Constantinople. The Arab Northern Army moved northward towards Aleppo along the desert route. The 7th Indian Division left Haifa on 3 October, proceeding towards Beirut along the coast. They reached Beirut on 8 October, the port facilities there now becoming available for off-loading supplies for the troops further inland.

By now many of the British Cavalry too were becoming desperately sick. Malaria and influenza hit the 4th Cavalry Division so badly that they could proceed no further, and the lead was taken by the 5th Cavalry Division. At Baalbek west of Rayak, Lieutenant Wilson too fell desperately sick. He later wrote home:

> I must now relate the saddest period of my war experiences - as it saw the end of my active service and, very nearly, the end of my life. We had chased and chivied the retreating Turk from Damascus to Baalbek with only slight resistance, which was fortunate as we were now suffering very seriously from malaria - a frequently fatal

---

37 Fromkin, D. *A Peace to End all Peace.*, pp. 338-340.
38 *Diary of Reg Walters.*

type - which we had, no doubt, contracted in the Jordan Valley. There was no quinine and no medical aid. Several of my friends died, and I, myself, was in a very bad way for about two days before reaching Baalbek but I badly wanted to keep going until the Turk threw in the sponge - an event expected at any moment. I just remember sitting on the ground, shivering and shaking and trying to appreciate the wonderful ruins by midnight, covered by two or three blankets ... the MO [Medical Officer], Dr. Foster, ... took my temperature and very sympathetically said, "You bloody fool, you've got a temperature of over 105 degrees."

Six or seven of these desperately sick soldiers were then 'bundled into an antiquated Ford truck, which,' he reminisced, 'was about uncomfortable as anything could be.' Wilson and his sick mates were then 'driven over the appalling roads to Beirut and dumped, on stretchers in an empty school.' [39]   And that was the end of Lieutenant Wilson's war.

Anzacs and Zionists Separate

While the EEF forces moved north, *Chaytors Force* continued its move westwards from Transjordan, over the Judean hills (with a few days in Jerusalem) and to camps on the coastal plain. The Anzac Division returned to their camp near Rishon le Zion, close to the Arab village of Surafend. Patterson and the *Jewish Legion* were stationed nearby at Ludd (Lod).

'When we heard that we were to be severed from the Anzacs our feeling was one of regret,' recalls Patterson, 'for every individual in the battalion had the greatest admiration for General Chaytor and his Staff, and, in fact, a feeling of great comradeship for every officer and man in the Anzac Mounted Division.'[40]

Other Zionist soldiers held similar views. 'Many incidents that I came up against are better left unwritten,' wrote M. Rubenstein of Sheffield, concerning his time of service. 'The best comrades we had among the non-Jewish troops 'he continued, 'were the Australians. They were not biased, and our boys were grateful to them for gifts of water and rations, plus the handshake and smile.'[41]

At their camps the battle-weary soldiers and horses rested while their clothes and equipment were cleaned and overhauled. It was also a time when the dreaded malaria caught up with many of them. In the *Jewish Legion* camp men became sick one by one. 'Day after day the few remaining men we had left went to hospital until,' wrote Patterson, 'in the end, I was put to such straits that I had to appeal once more to the Australians, who had a reinforcement camp near us.' Patterson then rode over and spoke to the Anzac commander, telling him 'the difficulty I had in finding men even to feed my animals, and asked him to spare me a score of troopers to help with the

39   Wilson, R. *Palestine 1917.*, pp. 145-6.
40   Patterson, J. *With the Judeans.*, p. 167.
41   Freulich, R. *Soldiers in Judea.*, p. 116.

exercising, watering, grooming, etc., of the transport animals.'

It seemed as if the Anzacs remembered what service Patterson and the *Zion Mule Corps* had bestowed upon them on that fateful 24 April evening in 1915 in Mudros Harbour. 'As usual,' Patterson continued, 'the Australians were all out to help, and readily gave me all the assistance I asked for.'[42]

Next Stop Tripoli and Aleppo

After the Beirut - Rayak line had been secured, the next objective was the line from Tripoli on the Mediterranean coast through to Homs, inland, on the ancient Aleppo - Damascus road. Sickness in the 4th and 5th Cavalry Divisions however was now rampant, with up to 50% of the troops unable to proceed. Chauvel decided to press on towards Aleppo with the 5th Cavalry Division alone. The Indian infantry and other British forces pressed on quickly along the coast, and the first troops entered Tripoli on 13 October. Two days later, on 15 October, the 5th Cavalry Division entered Homs.

Hama further to the north was occupied soon afterwards, and so now it was a race against time towards Aleppo. The 5th Cavalry Division appeared before this ancient city on 22 October. General MacAndrew the following day invited the city to surrender, but its commander was unwilling to capitulate to such a small EEF force. MacAndrew then decided to wait the arrival of the remainder of his force before making the final attack. The date for the attack, in conjunction with a local Arab force, was set for 26 October,

However during the evening of 25 October some of Feisal's Arabs entered the city, and after hand-to-hand fighting, much of the Turkish garrison left, and headed towards Alexandretta the following morning as MacAndrew was entering the city. The Jodhpur and Mysore Lancers of the 5th Cavalry Division met these retreating Turks and inflicted an initial defeat upon them. However, when noticing how few and incapacitated the Indian horsemen were, the Turks regrouped and stopped the Indian assault.

The following morning, 27 October, the Turkish troops continued their withdrawal. The 5th Cavalry Division by this time was too weak to pursue. On that day the Australian Division left Damascus en-route to Aleppo. It was imperative that all the major positions running north of Alexandretta and Aleppo be taken before the Armistice was signed, and the more seasoned troops available the better.

As the Australian Division set off on the 340 kilometre journey to Aleppo, two distinguished British prisoners of war, General Charles Townshend and Lieutenant-Colonel Stewart Newcombe, were climbing aboard the ship *Agamemnon* in Mudros Harbour, Lemnos Island, to act as intermediaries between British and Turkish officials,

---

42   Patterson. J. *With the Judeans in the Palestine Campaign*, p. 168.

concerning a satisfactory Armistice Agreement.

The War Cabinet, fearing the continuation of the war for at least another year, were anxious to have Turkey quickly out of the war, and the Bosphorus and Dardanelles open for Allied shipping as soon as possible. They decided not to waste time by conferring with their Allies, and authorized Admiral Calthorpe, commander of the British Fleet in the Aegean, to conclude an armistice agreement with Turkey.

The Australians, despite their weakened state, rode quickly towards Aleppo. Here the stalemate continued. The Turkish force, commanded by Mustapha Kemal, was determined to hold on to the very last, and not to allow any EEF force to enter Anatolia proper. When however, on 29 October the combined EEF-Arab force captured the major railway terminus of Muslimile, north of Aleppo, the writing was on the wall. All that was needed now was the arrival of more troops.

Just short of Homs however, General Hodgson was informed, at 4 p.m. on 31 October, one year after the Battle of Beersheva and formulation of the *Balfour Declaration*, that the Armistice with Turkey had been signed. Trooper Reg Walters, in his second last entry, wrote on 31 October 1918:

> HOMS & not a bad place either. Took us 4 and half days to come here from DAMASCUS. Off back tomorrow to TRIPOLI. Peace with Turkey and Austria now official. So hurrah, Home soon. Parcel from my little girl today, also letters. Am feeling Goodo.[43]

And Trooper Reg Walters, like the rest of the war-weary soldiers, be they Australian, New Zealand, British, Indian, West Indian, Zionist, Arab and even Turk, German and Austrian, had every reason to feel *Goodo.* For some, especially the Anzacs, this was the completion of a campaign which had begun at Gallipoli on the morning of 25 April 1915.

---

43 *Diary of Reg Walters.*

*C*hapter 19

Churchill's Mandate

Due to their active involvement since the inception of the campaign, Allenby released the totally exhausted Australian Division, who rode on down to Tripoli on the coast. The British and Indian troops, being newer in the field, were maintained for garrison duties. It was at Tripoli on 11 November that Reg Walters scribed his last impression of the War: 'Germany accepted Allies Armistice. We got the news 5.30 P.M. Tonight is a merry one. Rockets, Whistles etc. I'm thinking of my Dear Ones.'[1]

While at Tripoli the Australians visited the sites of Lebanon, including the mountains, now beginning to fill with snow. And they, like the Anzac Division in the Land of Israel, were also entertained with various sporting events, lectures on re-adaptation to civilian life and other topics - and were photographed by Frank Hurley the official photographer.

The New Zealanders at Surafend held a memorial service at the battlefield of Ayun Kara on 14 November near the mass grave of the New Zealanders who fell there at the battle on 14 November 1917. 'The Jewish inhabitants of the colonies of Richon le Zion and Wadi Hahnien,' recorded Powles, 'out of their gratitude to the New Zealand Brigade for their deliverance from the Turk on that day, provided the material for a Memorial Column and planted trees round the grave, undertaking to look after them in the years to come.'[2]

Return to Gallipoli

The Armistice Agreement called for the occupation of the Dardanelles and Constantinople by an Allied force. Despite their weariness, all the Anzac units fought for this honour. Due to circumstances rather than credit, the Canterbury and 7th Light Horse Regiments, were commissioned for the task. The Anzac unit embarked from Kantara on 27 November and arrived at Chanak on 5 December. The journey across the Mediterranean was rough, and many of the weary men contracted influenza.

---

1   *Diary of Reg Walters.*
2   Powles, Lieut.-Colonel. C. Guy. *The New Zealanders in Sinai and Palestine*, p. 265.

Upon arrival they were billeted in a dirty and vermin infected hospital between Maidos and Kilid Bahr.

The Anzacs were attached to the 28th British Division during their six weeks at the Dardanelles. Although they managed to improve their living conditions, the weather remained bad, and a number of men died of sickness.

Most of the Anzac officers and men were veterans of the Gallipoli campaign, and their time was as much an emotional period as it was fulfilling the conditions of the Armistice. They surveyed the former battlefields in the southern tip of the Peninsula, locating the graves of fallen mates, and collected specimens for the Australian national war museum which was later to be established in Canberra. They returned in early January 1919.

The Surafend Affair

Since the beginning of the campaign the attitude and actions of the Arab population, the Bedouins in particular were a concern. They attacked several Anzacs at Rafa leaving one dead and the other badly wounded. Later they dug up the buried Anzac soldiers and stripped them. Such an outrage occurred again after the battle of Ayun Kara. The soldiers strongly suspected the Arabs from the nearby village of Surafend. Robberies and deprivations continued after the Anzacs encamped near Surafend following their return from Transjordan. [3]

In December a New Zealander was awakened by a thief in his tent. While giving chase the thief shot the soldier dead. The footprints of the murderer led to the village of Surafend, which was soon surrounded by incensed New Zealanders. Chaytor immediately informed the General Headquarters, encouraging them to apprehend the murderer. But the GHQ ordered the immediate withdrawal of the cordon of incensed troops, and their return to camp. This further incensed the Anzacs, who could see that nothing was being done to bring the culpable Arab to account. Their anger increased the following day, when the troops saw Arabs moving freely from the village with no apparent efforts being made to address the situation.

That night New Zealanders, Australians and others returned to the village. They evacuated all the women and children from the village, and then attacked the men, killing and wounding about thirty, then set fire to the village and the adjacent Bedouin camp. Allenby was enraged, and the following day called for a parade of the Anzac Division, whereupon he strongly abused them and, according to one officer, said 'they were murderers and cowards and by killing the Bedouin had taken away the good name of Anzac - in fact a worse atrocity than any the Turks had committed, etc., etc.'[4]

3   Powles, Lieut. -Colonel C. Guy. *The New Zealanders in Sinai and Palestine*, p. 266 .
4   Hill, A.J. *Chauvel of the Light Horse*,   p. 192.

The hardened Anzac soldiers merely laughed at Allenby, causing him to ride away. The Division was then ordered to march two miles in full order, and were then banished to Rafah, where they were to be kept in isolation until their demarcation. They arrived at Rafa on 22 December 1918. Allenby also withheld recommendations and decorations from the Division - a matter which greatly displeased Chauvel.

The whole affair, sad and undistinguished as it was, may not have happened had the British authorities taken a more serious view of the marauding actions and propensities particularly of the Bedouins. This situation was aggravated by the failure of the Arab forces to keep their promises during the failed attempts in Transjordan, and now by the weary troops who wanted to return home.

Awaiting Repatriation

Shortly after the war ended on 11 November, Lloyd George, called for elections while his popularity was high. He won convincingly. One of his first moves was to appoint Churchill as Secretary of State for War and for Air. On Churchill's first day in office, 10 January 1919, he was informed by the Chief of the Imperial General Staff that there was a major crisis in the army. The soldiers were demanding demobilization, and there was a threat of large scale disorders.

Lieutenant Wilson, now recovered from his dangerous bout of malaria, wrote from Kantara on 18 January ' ... everyone is getting restless about this slowness in demobilizing and several rowdy demonstrations have taken place. The camp cinema, a huge place, was burnt down two nights ago.' [5] Lloyd George fearful of the effects of Bolshevism, and of large scale disorders amongst the troops, was keen to bring them home quickly.

Churchill realized that sufficient troops needed to be in the field until peace terms had been made with the Germans and Turks. All the hard fighting could be ruined if there were no troops to enforce the peace terms. Lloyd George however basically won the argument, and it was decided to bring home as many of the British as possible. Regular British and Indian troops took over most of the garrison work in Syria and the Land of Israel, with the Light Horse, the Mounted Rifles and *Jewish Legion* performing some other garrison duties.

The withdrawal of the remainder of the British troops was well under way by the end of January. Wilson was kept waiting in suspense at Kantara for more than a week, before setting sail in late January, via Italy to Southampton.

The Role of the *Jewish Legion*

While repatriation for the Anzacs remained a logistical difficulty another group of soldiers was not so keen to be repatriated. 'The THIRD PERIOD of our service - the

---

5	Wilson, R. *Palestine 1917*, pp. 162-163.

Armistice period -,' wrote Jabotinsky, 'I consider the most important. More,' he continued, 'the main purpose of the creation of the Legion was not so much its participation in the war, though we naturally desired this, as its remaining as the garrison of Palestine after the war.'[6]

By the beginning of 1919 there were some 5,000 Jewish soldiers in the Land of Israel, with the arrival of the 40th Battalion following its training in Egypt. Altogether some 10,500 Jewish soldiers served in the *Jewish Legion*. [7] During their time at Rafa the Jewish soldiers paraded before General Chaytor, who conferred decorations upon quite a few of them. 'It was a Red Letter Day for the battalion,' wrote a very proud Patterson afterwards.[8] They also enjoyed various types of recreation, including participation in various sporting activities in which all members of the EEF participated. They did quite well at boxing and also enjoyed playing football, cricket and racing. The American Jewish soldiers naturally won the baseball quite convincingly!

On 24 February 1919 Patterson was appointed to command the 'Rafa Area' - an area encompassing the Sinai and much of the Land of Israel itself. An important aspect of this command was the safeguarding of some 240 kilometres of strategic railway line. He quickly found his hands full - especially coping with the Bedouins.

'While the Anzac Division remained with us,' he confessed, 'I felt quite easy in my mind about being able to keep these slippery customers in check, but it was quite "another pair of shoes" when the Anzacs were hurriedly called away to suppress the disorders in Egypt.'[9]

Finally in early March 1919 the 1st and 2nd Light Horse Regiments boarded ships and returned to Australia, and it was expected that the remainder would soon follow. However, as Patterson highlighted, the Anzacs were required to suppress disorders in Egypt.

Revolt in Egypt

The rise of nationalism in Syria and subsequent triumphs of Feisal's forces affected the nationalist forces in Egypt, especially as they believed the issue of Egyptian nationalism was to be raised at the Peace Conference in Versailles. In fact leading

---

6 Jabotinsky, V. *The Story of* the *Jewish Legion,* p. 144.
7 Of these 4,000 came from Britain; 5,000 from America; 1,000 from Eretz Israel; 300 from Canada and 200 from Argentina. Amongst these, apart from such notable names as David Ben Gurion and Yitzak Ben Zvi (founders of Labour Zionism, one to be future Prime Minister, the other to be a future President of Israel) and Zev Jabotinsky (founder of Revisionist Zionism), were also Eliyahu Eitan, Moshe Gur-Gurban, Nehemiah Rabin-Raitzuv, Eliezar Sukenik and Yacov Dovotrovsky - whose sons later became Chiefs of Staff of the Israeli Defence Force . *Bet HaGiddudim Museum,* Moshav AviHayil.
8 Patterson, J., *With the Judeans,* p. 187.
9 Patterson, J., ibid., pp. 193-4.

Egyptian nationalists fully expected Britain to now grant Egypt her independence. When realizing this was not the intention of the British authorities, the nationalist leader Saad Zaghlul increased his nationalist activities. The British, annoyed by these activities, deported Zaghlul in March.

Open rebellion broke out the following day in Cairo, quickly spreading throughout the country. European, especially British subjects were threatened and even killed and public facilities, especially railroads, attacked and destroyed. The situation quickly deteriorated, causing Allenby deep concern, as most of the British troops had been repatriated home. He had only one reliable force available - the Anzacs.

The Anzac soldiers at Rafa were informed on 17 March that they were to proceed immediately to Kantara to be re-equipped. The Australian Division had moved down from Tripoli to Moascar in Egypt, and then together the New Zealanders and Australians were dispatched to the places where the most serious outbreaks of violence had erupted. They were instructed to restore law and order and arrest the ring leaders.

Chauvel had just been touring with his wife all the battle sites, from the Sinai to his HQ at Aleppo.[10] When he reached Haifa on 29 March Wavell informed him of the situation in Egypt, to where he immediately set off. Meanwhile the bulk of the garrison work in Eretz Israel was entrusted to the *Jewish Legion,* except Jerusalem where a British unit was posted. After a month the uprising was suppressed following some strong arm tactics by the Anzacs.

The Anzacs Return Home

Chauvel, recently knighted and now Sir Harry, was soon afterwards summoned to Britain. He handed command over to General Ryrie. Chauvel's contribution to the war effort was significant, enhancing both the interests of the British Empire and the Zionist hopes of the Jewish people, in ways he was probably not completely aware of at the time.

Repatriation of the Anzacs began again in May. On 30 June 1919 the New Zealand Mounted Rifles Brigade was disbanded and the first batch of New Zealand soldiers began the return journey to their homeland. One of the few men to return who had arrived initially in 1914 was Edward Chaytor, whose efforts on behalf of the British Empire and Jewish people equaled that of Chauvel's.

One very important group of Anzacs did not return home - the horses. Due to economic and quarantine factors, the horses were to remain behind. They were classified into several categories, the better ones being given to the Indian troops, the poorer ones were shot. Many a grown man shed tears as in the nearby olive groves

---

10 En-route he had called in at Rehovot and visited the Slutzkin family, whose house had been his HQ for several months. There he was touched to see the Australian flag flying over the porch. Hill, A.J. *Chauvel of the Light Horse,* p. 194.

and on the beaches those faithful horses from the mountains and plains of New Zealand and Australia were shot. Of their role, and the role of their riders, British historian David Bullock wrote:

> As for the ANZACs, they were magnificent, and after Gallipoli, nothing else would have been expected. It would be hard to imagine a finer breed of man to fight on Palestine's fields than the light horseman of the outback mounted on his country-bred waler.[11]

And so the men from the countries of the outcasts and adventurers began their return journey. Their job had been done. From Gallipoli to Jerusalem and beyond, the wild colonial men from Australia and New Zealand had fought and won, and in the process, left behind a legacy. This legacy, remembered by the locals who witnessed their exploits, was also ingrained into the folklore of both New Zealand and Australia. Within a few years war memorials sprang up throughout both countries, embellished with the names of the tens of thousands of the fallen, and such places as Gallipoli, Romani, Magdhaba, El Arish, Rafa, Gaza. Beersheva, Ayun Kara, Jericho, Es Salt, Amman, Jenin, Nablus, Semakh, Tiberias and Damascus. And on one day of the year the peoples of these countries paid homage to their dead of the war. That day was 25 April - *Anzac Day*.

Challenges for the *Jewish Legion*

Although the *Balfour Declaration* had been enacted, many of the British officials and officers in Eretz Israel refused to accept it . The *Jewish Legion* was often seen as the physical representative of the *Balfour Declaration* and Zionist movement, and consequently often received discrimination. References to the existence of the *Jewish Legion* and its role in the closing parts of the campaign were often suppressed.

Perhaps the worst form of discrimination occurred in April 1919 when the Jewish soldiers were not permitted to celebrate *Passover* in Jerusalem. 'I cannot perceive' Patterson confessed 'a greater act of provocation to Jewish soldiers than this, or a greater insult ... Think of it! Jewish soldiers for the first time in their lives in Palestine & barred from the Temple Wall of Jerusalem during Passover! Only a Jew can really understand what it meant to these men, & the great strain it put on their discipline & loyalty.' [12] To compensate for their great disappointment Patterson organized a great *Passover* feast at Rafa.

The Jewish soldiers from the United States found this discrimination very difficult to accept. A number of them requested to be discharged - and some even threatened to refuse to fulfill their duties after a certain date if their demands were not met. These men were summarily court-martialled, and finally received very severe

---

11 Bullock, D. *Allenby's War*, p. 7.
12 Patterson, J. *With the Judeans*, p. 195.

sentences and dispatched to the notorious Citadel in Cairo.

The discrimination peaked in July 1919 when a British General publicly maligned the Legion, and even struck a soldier with his cane. Patterson managed to have the General offer a public apology - but the damage had been done. Discontent increased, causing concern for both Patterson and Jabotinsky. Several officers tended their resignations, and one of them, in a letter to Patterson, wrote:

> My resignation, Sir, is my only method of protest against the grossly unfair and all too prevalent discrimination against the battalion to which I have the honour to belong. I desire to point out to you, Sir, the fact that this unfair and un-British attitude affects not only my honour as a Jew, but my prestige as a British officer ...
>
> ... I resent, and resent very strongly indeed, the abusive attitude at present prevalent towards Jewish troops. I have innumerable instances of petty spite, and not a few cases of a very serious character indeed, all of which I can readily produce should the occasion ever arise.[13]

Patterson was deeply hurt. He had dedicated himself to the Jewish units to which he was associated, and was probably the only officer in the British Army to have finished the war without receiving promotion, despite distinguishing himself from Gallipoli to Es Salt. Jabotinsky too was hurt and perturbed by these intimidating tactics and attitudes - to such an extent that he wrote to Allenby:

> I was the initiator of both the Zion Mule Corps and the actual Jewish Battalions. To-day I am forced to witness how my work is breaking into pieces under the intolerable burden of disappointment, despair, broken pledges, and anti-Semitism, permeating the whole administrative and military atmosphere, the hopelessness of all effort and of all devotion.
>
> The common opinion is that you are an enemy of Zionism in general, and of the Jewish Legion in particular. I still try to believe that this is not true, that things happen without your knowledge, that there is a misunderstanding, and that the situation can yet improve.
>
> In this hope, at the last attempt to stop a process which threatens to impair for ever the Anglo-Jewish friendship throughout the world, I beg you to grant me a personal interview and permission to speak freely. This letter is entrusted to your chivalry.'[14]

Jabotinsky was thereafter hounded by the British officials against whom his complaint was directed, refused an interview, and ordered to proceed to Kantara for immediate demobilization. Despite Patterson's protests, the order was carried out. Jabotinsky himself protested, stating: 'With the deepest reluctance and regret I must say that I consider this action shows ingratitude. I do not deserve it at the hands of the British Authorities.' [15]

---

13 Patterson. J. ibid., pp. 234-235.
14 Patterson, J. *With the Judeans,* p. 252.
15 Patterson, J., ibid., p. 257.

Jabotinsky never received a reply to his appeal, and was summarily drummed out of the British Army. He had fulfilled his usefulness for the cause of the Empire - and was no longer wanted. Yet Jabotinsky's contribution to the Allied war effort, and the Jewish cause, were significant. What was just an idea before Gallipoli, a Jewish fighting force comprised of Zionist soldiers serving under the Union Jack, was a reality by the time Jerusalem was captured.

Patterson Departs

Patterson soon afterwards relinquished his post as commander of the Battalion. The War Office finally fulfilled their promise of changing the name of the Royal Fusiliers and in December 1919 the 1st Judeans Battalion was formed. The First Judeans would remain to garrison Eretz Israel. It was at this juncture that Patterson believed his time with the Jewish fighting force had come to an end. He left and returned to UK.

Prior to his departure Patterson visited the Galilee where he met with Trumpeldor. Trumpeldor, he wrote 'had only just returned from Russia, where he had been organizing a Jewish Legion for service in Palestine. The Bolsheviks however, interfered with his plans, and he was lucky to escape from their clutches.'[16]

From Gallipoli to Jerusalem, and beyond, Patterson had struggled for that dual purpose - the cause of the British Empire and the cause of the Jewish people. His name, like those of Chauvel and Chaytor, and the forces they led, should be held high in that list of the 'righteous among the Gentiles.' That special bond between the Anzac and Zionist soldiers is portrayed in a letter which Patterson later received from Chaytor from Wellington:

> MY DEAR PATTERSON,
>
> I hope the history of the 38th Battalion is out by now. So few people have heard of the battalion's good work, or of the very remarkable fact that in the operations that we hope have finally reopened Palestine to the Jews a Jewish force was fighting on the Jordan, within a short distance of where their forefathers, under Joshua, first crossed into Palestine, and all who hear about it are anxious to hear more.
>
> I shall always be grateful to you and your battalion for your good work while with me in the Jordan Valley.
>
> The way you smashed up the Turkish rearguard when it tried to counter-attack across the Jordan made our subsequent advance up the hills of Moab an easy matter.[17]

Although now retired from active involvement in the affairs of the Jewish fighting force, Patterson continued his interest in the Jewish nationalist cause.

---

16 Patterson, J. ibid., p. 246.
17 Patterson, J. *With the Judeans*, p. 192.

The Political Struggle for Damascus

Lloyd George, Churchill and Sykes had a difficult task in the post-war period maintaining British interests in view of her various commitments made during the war. Whereas at the beginning of the War Britain had to outfox France, Russia and Germany, by the end of the War only France remained as a contender for control of the Eastern Mediterranean. And the French, outplayed by the British during the War, were now determined to re-establish their name in the region.

Lloyd George, Lord Curzon and others were unhappy with the 'Sykes-Picot' Agreement. They felt it still gave France a leading role in the region, and in the event of France being a future protagonist, it provided her an unhealthy proximity to Britain's link to India. France however was determined to abide by the terms of the 'Sykes-Picot' Agreement. To assist in the ploy to take Syria from France, the office of Lloyd George distributed a report in the winter of 1919 claiming that Feisal's force had played a significant role in capturing Syria.[18] Lloyd George was in fact using Feisal as a facade for his own imperialist ambitions.

But Lloyd George now found himself contending also with the idealism of President Woodrow Wilson and his fourteen points for self-determination. Wilson was opposed to the imperialist ambitions of the European countries. At the Peace Conference, Wilson seemed favourably disposed towards Feisal. However, as Feisal was basically a puppet for the British cause, a delegation of pro-French Syrians also appeared. Yet Clemenceau, desiring to gain fullest British support for favourable French concessions in Europe, was willing to compromise French interests in the Middle East in favour of British interests. By doing so he was placing himself in an embarrassing and dangerous position. To appease Lloyd George he was bound to fall foul of that large section of French opinion that was determined not to concede but indeed to further French interests in the Middle East.

The General Syrian Congress was summoned by Feisal on 6 June 1919, in order for him to outline his proposals to be presented at the Peace Conference. The Arab delegates however called for a completely independent Greater Syria. Matters thereafter seemed to get out of Feisal's hands, as the nationalists were determined to oust the French. Small Arab forces made raids against the French forces garrisoned on the coast near Beirut. Tensions between the French and Arabs grew. Upon his return to Paris for the Conference, Feisal and Clemenceau worked hard upon coming to a French-Arab compromise agreement.

To draw the USA into the conflict, and in order to provide a firmer buffer between Britain's zone of interest and Russia, Britain then proposed that the USA accept mandates for Constantinople, the Dardanelles, and Armenia. Wilson returned home in June 1919 to gain support for the Treaty of Versailles, and for the proposal that the

---

18   Fromkin, D. *A Peace To End All Peace*, p. 377.

USA accept Mandates in the region of the Eastern Mediterranean. Wilson's campaign was impaired when soon afterwards he suffered a stroke and was partially incapacitated. This in turn held up the peace negotiations with Turkey.

A dangerous vacuum was now created in the Eastern Mediterranean region, especially in Syria. The number of British Empire troops stationed throughout the region, from the Caucasus in the north (to help stem the Bolshevik menace) to the Sinai in the south, gradually dwindled. This helped Lloyd George to finally realize that he could no longer keep the French out of Syria. He agreed, therefore, by November 1919 for the withdrawal of British troops from that area, leaving the French and Feisal to battle it out.

Clemenceau and Feisal reached a secret compromise agreement in early January 1920, whereby Feisal would retain the title of king, but Syria would become a client state of France. There were however strong imperialist elements in France who wanted complete sovereignty over Syria. There were also strong Arab nationalist elements in Syria who wanted complete independence, with no French influence at all. This Clemenceau-Feisal 'agreement' was quickly on shaky ground, and more-so when Clemenceau lost the presidency on 17 January 1920. He was replaced by the more colonialist orientated Alexander Millerand. Any final hopes of success were dashed when Feisal returned to Syria in January 1920 and submitted the 'agreement' to the Arab Congress - which rejected it.

By January 1920 it also become apparent that the USA was not prepared to accept mandates in the Eastern Mediterranean. Final deliberations could now begin with Turkey. But turmoil was mounting in the region. A second Syrian General Congress was summoned in March 1920, at which a resolution was adopted proclaiming the independence of Greater Syria, with Feisal as hereditary monarch.

Simultaneously a group of Arabs from the Land of Israel presented the British authorities with a resolution opposing Zionism, and petitioning that *Palestine* become part of Greater Syria.

Trumpeldor's Final Battle

Meanwhile the French and the Arabs were locked in a struggle to establish facts on the ground. One of the contested areas was the region of the Upper Galilee, an area left vacant after the withdrawal of the British forces, and strategically located between the British and French zones of interest. Many pro-French Christian Arab villages were dispersed throughout this region, natural targets for Feisal's forces and his rapacious Bedouin sympathizers of the Huleh (Hula) Valley region. Several Jewish villages were also located in this region, including Metulla, Kfar Giladi and Tel Hai.

The Jewish settlements were very isolated from the rest of the Jewish *Yishuv,* and were very much dependent upon any French troops in the region. Trumpeldor from his settlement of Tel Hai, wrote on 4 January 1920 of witnessing how a French force withdrew after being attacked by an Arab force.[19]   The inability of the French battalion to stem the Arab assault concerned Trumpeldor and his fellow settlers. A meeting was held to determine whether or not they should withdraw. They resolved to remain and fight to the end. [20]

Trumpeldor and his compatriots waited for help from other Jewish settlements further south, and for French reinforcements to reach the region. Neither arrived, and the expected Arab assault came on 1 March 1920. During the assault, Trumpeldor and six of his Jewish companions lost their lives. Trumpeldor's dying words were *Tov lamut be'ad Artzenu - It is good to die for our country.*

Trumpeldor had paid the supreme sacrifice for following his ideals. Believing that all roads led to Zion, he had fought for these ideals from the shores of Gallipoli, to Jerusalem, and beyond - even to Tel Hai. His bold stand there became legendary throughout Eretz Israel - and even influenced the politicians. By not evacuating the threatened Jewish settlements in the Upper Galilee, that region was eventually included in the British zone following the negotiations with the French.

Ordeals for Jabotinsky

The attacks upon the Jewish settlements sent shock waves throughout Eretz Israel and gravely concerned the Jewish population. By March 1920 the number of Jewish soldiers attached to the *First Judeans* had been drastically reduced, while the degree of anti-Zionism within the British Administration was on the increase.

Jabotinsky, troubled by the death of his friend Trumpeldor and with the deteriorating situation, approached the Zionist leadership and secured their agreement for the formation of a Jewish self defence group, *Hagana,* to be comprised primarily of veterans from the *Jewish Legion.* The British authorities refused permission for this group to carry arms, so Jabotinsky secured them by other means.

During March and April 1920 the British, French and Turkish negotiators debated terms for a peace treaty at the Italian Riviera town of San Remo. Meanwhile rumours began filtering into Jerusalem that the Arabs were planning an action to press home their demands and opposition to the British and French presence.

On 4 April a large Arab mob proceeded into the Old City through Jaffa Gate, ostensibly as part of the Nebi Musa celebrations. Once inside the Old City, the mob, one of whose leaders was Amin al-Husseini, began to attack nearby Jewish people, and then continued their pogrom into the Jewish Quarter.

Jabotinsky's self-defense group was patrolling the streets of the Jewish section of new Jerusalem, when they heard of the pogrom. They immediately set out for the Old City. On arrival they were barred from entry by British troops. The Arab mob

---

19   Diary of Joseph Trumpeldor, quoted in Yavniely, Avraham. *The Goodly Heritage,* p. 448.

20   Yavniely, Avraham. *The Goodly Heritage,* p. 449.

meanwhile proceeded to kill six Jewish people and wound some 200, many seriously.

The *First Judeans Battalion* was confined to camp at Surafend and not permitted to help put down the revolt. This caused resentment and thereafter many filed their resignation. Ultimately Margolin remained in command of only some thirty Jewish soldiers.

The British authorities quickly convened a hearing upon the pogrom, and while searching for a suitable scapegoat, marked out Jabotinsky. Despite considerable evidence proving his innocence, he and nineteen Jewish compatriots were arrested for illegally possessing firearms, and being members of an illegal para-military organization, and charged with 'banditism, instigating the people ... to mutual hatred, pillage, rapine.' It was ludicrous - but at the closed Court Martial convened on 10 April he was convicted to fifteen years imprisonment and deportation from Eretz Israel following completion of the sentence. Jabotinsky and his compatriots were then placed in the Jerusalem prison (part of the Russian Compound) and the following Sabbath began their transferal to Kantara.

En-route to Kantara the train stopped at Ludd, whereupon Margolin and the 400 remaining members of the *First Judeans Battalion*, defied the military police guarding the station, and stood at attention while their founder and visionary passed by.

Patterson, amongst other fair-minded British officials, was ashamed and angry when acquainted with the injustice meted out to Jabotinsky, and wrote: 'The whole history of this atrocious outrage is a foul stain on our fair name ... Jabotinsky was cast into prison garb, had his hair cropped, and was marched in company with two Arabs convicted of rape, through Jerusalem and Kantara, places where he was well known as a British officer.'[21]

Following Jabotinsky's arrival at Kantara a delegation of Egyptian Jews, met with Allenby and informed him that unless Jabotinsky and his compatriots were returned to Eretz Israel, there could be Jewish rioting in Egypt. Allenby subsequently ordered Jabotinsky and his compatriots to be returned to the Land of Israel, where they were interned at Acre prison.

When the British Parliament became familiar with the injustice of the court case, and the stiffness of the sentences meted out to Jabotinsky and his compatriots, there was a general outcry. The matter was raised in the House of Commons, and Churchill, as Minister of War, was called upon to make a statement.

Due to public awareness of the matter, the sentences were later commuted, and the Government realized, finally, that the military administration was not fulfilling the Government's pro-Zionist policies. Lloyd George replaced the military administration with a civil one, and Herbert Samuel was to become the first High Commissioner. All this occurred more-or-less simultaneously with the decision of the San Remo conference to confer a Mandate upon Britain for Eretz Israel, entrusting

---

21 Patterson, J. *With the Judeans*, p. 272.

her with the responsibility of fulfilling the *Balfour Declaration*. The implementation of this *Mandate* would be the responsibility of this new British administration.

The French Take Damascus

The French were now more determined to attain their long cherished dream of possession of Syria, albeit without the southern region of *Palestine*. On 27 May the French Army based in Beirut began moving inland towards Damascus. Although only numerically small, they were able to out-manoeuvre Feisal's forces, and they occupied Damascus on 26 July 1920. They then requested Feisal to depart, which he did on 28 July. The French Government then stated in clear terms their intention of retaining Syria.[22]

Feisal's forces withdrew into the surrounding areas, causing concern for Britain, which feared that they would launch attacks against the French from the British-held territories of *Palestine* and Mesopotamia. France could then, in retaliation, launch counter-attacks, and even invade such areas as Transjordan, where no British troops were stationed. An embarrassing political situation could emerge.

Churchill's Solution

Anti-Zionist propaganda now spread throughout the Land of Israel, and the *Balfour Declaration* and *British Mandate* came under increasing pressure. One politician at this stage however who fully supported the *Balfour Declaration*, was Winston Churchill. He wrote in 1920:

> If, as may well happen, there should be created in our own lifetime by the banks of the Jordan a Jewish State under the protection of the British Crown ... an event will have occurred in the history of the world which would from every point of view be beneficial and would be especially in harmony with the truest interests of the British Empire.[23]

In February 1921 Churchill became the Colonial Secretary. But he inherited a troubled portfolio, as British interests throughout the Middle East were under considerable pressure at this point. Churchill decided to convene a meeting, in Cairo in March 1921, to determine how to maintain Britain's best interests there.

Tensions heightened during the course of the Conference, especially when Abdullah, Feisal's brother, arrived in Amman with a small army of followers, obviously en-route to deliver Damascus from French control. This situation aggravated Churchill's already heavy load, which included the future of Mesopotamia, the future of Feisal's nationalist movement now that it had been ousted from Syria, and the

---

22   Fromkin, D. *A Peace to End all Peace*, p. 439.

23   Gilbert, M. *Winston. S. Churchill: Companion Volume*. Vol. 4, Part 2, July 1919-March 1921., Houghton Mifflin, (Boston, 1978), p. 1028. n. 1

increasing anti-Zionist feelings in *Palestine*.

Churchill enacted some radical decisions as a result of all these situations and tensions. He established Feisal as hereditary monarch of Mesopotamia (which hereafter became known as Iraq); requested Abdullah to remain in Transjordan to establish order there and thereafter detached Transjordan from the rest of *Palestine* and declared that no Jewish settlement was permitted there. Shortly afterwards Abdullah decided to remain in Transjordan, and the hereditary Hashemite monarchy was established with Abdullah as king. Churchill's proposals, known as Churchill's *White Paper* were later to be endorsed by Parliament.

Margolin and the May Day Riots

Churchill's compromise solutions were not accepted by the various parties. Weizmann and the Zionist movement were disappointed that some 75% of the land promised in the *Balfour Declaration* was now made off-limits to the Jewish people. The Arab nationalists however rejected the compromise solution out of hand - they wanted all promises in the *Balfour Declaration* made null and void. The representative voice of the nationalists in *Palestine* was Amin al-Husseini who had been appointed the Mufti or Muslim spiritual leader in March 1921. He thereafter spread more anti-Zionist and anti-Jewish propaganda through the land.

On 21 May 1921 rival Jewish socialist groups paraded in Tel Aviv, creating a small degree of tension. Later on the same day a bomb exploded in Jaffa, killing eighteen young Jewish immigrants. An Arab mob immediately fell upon unsuspecting Jewish people in the vicinity of Jaffa, and another pogrom began, which quickly spread outside Jaffa.

Eliezer Margolin, now the commander of a mixed Jewish-Arab militia formed by Samuel, was stationed outside Tel Aviv. The Jewish members of his unit, mostly veterans of the *Jewish Legion*, were alarmed by the news of the riots and pogroms. Margolin prepared his men for immediate action - but no orders came to move on that first day. The following day Margolin marched, without specific orders, his fully-armed men to quell the disturbances in Jaffa.

The British authorities did not condone Margolin's action, and he was forced to resign from his post, and instructed not to return to Eretz Israel. The special force was then demobilized, and with it ended the story of the *Jewish Legion*. Margolin soon afterwards returned to Australia, 'longing' wrote Jabotinsky 'for Palestine, where once he ploughed the fields in Rehovot, fought in the Jordan Valley, ruled Es-Salt in the Land of Gilead.'[24]

---

24   Jabotinsky, V. *The Story of the Jewish Legion*, p. 153.

Churchill's Role

As reversal to Britain's interests in the Middle and Far East followed reversal, opposition within Britain to her involvement in the region of the Eastern Mediterranean increased. It culminated with a vote in the House of Lords on 21 June 1922, over a Bill declaring the *Mandate* in the Land of Israel unacceptable. The vote passed resoundingly. It seemed that the death bell was about to ring over the *Balfour Declaration*.

The issue was then presented to the House of Commons for a vote on 4 July. Much hinged on the speech of the Colonial Secretary - Churchill. He declared that Britain must honour her wartime pledges and promises, and that he, in his capacities, was determined to fulfill those responsibilities. The House of Commons voted resoundingly, 292 to 35 to accept the offer of the League of Nations to administer the *Mandate* over Eretz Israel.

▲ *Soldiers of the* Jewish Legion *at the Western or Wailing Wall in Jerusalem*

▲ *Anzac soldiers visiting the Sphinx and Pyramids, Egypt 1915. Reg Walters on left.*

▲ *The* Zion Mule Corps *at Alexandria harbour prior to departure for Gallipoli*

▲ *Joseph Trumpeldor*

▲ *Col. John Patterson*

◀ *Zev Jabotinsky*

Soldiers of the Jewish Legion - *Yitzak Ben Zvi (left) and David Ben Gurion*

Trooper Reg Walters, 10th Light Horse Regiment

▲ *Turkish infantry at Gaza, 1917*

▲ *Bedouin women outside Beersheva, c. 1917*

▲ *Australian Light Horse camp, somewhere in the Sinai, 1916*

▲ *Hospital train taking wounded back to Egypt after battle of Rafa, 1917*

▲ *New Zealand graves and memorial to battle of Ayun Kara, near Rishon le Zion*

▲ *Officers of New Zealand Mounted Rifles with Ben Zev family in Rishon le Zion following battle of Ayun Kara, 1917*

▲ *Senior EEF officers, including General Allenby, crossing Jordan River on pontoon bridge, 1918*

▲ *Horse lines at camp of New Zealand Mounted Rifles Brigade, c. 1918*

▲ *Meal time. Trooper Thomas Brocket, far right, with fellow New Zealanders. Somewhere in Eretz Israel, c. 1918*

Chapter 20

Jewish and Imperial Clashes

Zionist Consolidation

Churchill's *White Paper*, which was passed by Parliament on 1 July 1922, disturbed the Zionist Organization. Jabotinsky maintained that Britain should be kept to her promises, and that as many Jewish people as possible should be permitted to enter the Land of Israel - on both sides of the Jordan River. Jabotinsky's ideas, sometimes known as '*catastrophic Zionism*' were not endorsed by most of the Zionist Executive. He resigned and later while in Paris in 1924, set up a rival *Revisionist Zionist* movement.

Also in 1924 thousands of Polish Jews, many of whom were merchants and artisans, began moving to Eretz Israel. Then in April 1925, a gathering of dignified Zionist leaders met in Jerusalem, for the opening of the Hebrew University. Amongst those present at this dedication were Allenby, Weizmann, Samuel, and Lord Balfour. An air of optimism prevailed.

Despite the protests and opposition of the Arab leadership, conditions since the 1921 riots were basically quiet. When Samuel left in 1925 he felt that the Land of Israel was 'the most peaceful place in the Middle East'.[1] Samuel's non-Jewish successor, Field Marshall Lord Plumer was a soldier of renown. During his tenure as High Commissioner security improved, causing thereby a reduction of the garrison force. Those troops were located at isolated RAF airforce bases.

Fresh Problems

While the restoration of the Jewish homeland had been progressing, many Arabs from neighbouring lands entered British *Palestine,* enjoying the economic privileges now being evidenced. Life for the average Arab was improved considerably. Haj Amin al-Husseini, the Mufti, or Muslim spiritual leader of Jerusalem, however, was unwilling to concede this. He was an avowed enemy of Zionism and the Jewish people, and was determined to thwart the Jewish National Home. From the time of

---

1   Quoted in Lossin, Y. *Pillar of Fire, p.* 159.

his appointment he worked quietly behind the scenes building up a ground swell of opposition.

On *Yom Kippur* in 1928 a seemingly minor incident occurred at the Jewish area of the Western Wall, provoked by Muslim antagonism. In no time at all the Temple Mount region had gained worldwide renown. The Mufti then used this situation to his advantage, increasing exposure to apparent Jewish abuse of this sacred Jewish area. In 1929 a demonstration of young Jewish people went to the Wall, swearing their allegiance to the Holy Place, waving the Zionist flag and singing *HaTikva,* the Zionist song. The situation was becoming explosive.

One week later the Muslims heard a screeching anti-Zionist sermon at the Al Aksa Mosque on the Temple Mount. Afterwards they streamed out towards the Jewish Quarter. The pogroms of 1929 erupted. Jewish communities throughout the land were savagely attacked, and scores of innocent Jewish people murdered, indicating that the pogroms were premeditated. Hartuv, (Artuf) which had hosted the Light Horse in 1917, was taken by the Arabs and its Jewish inhabitants ejected. Worst affected was Hebron where some sixty-six innocent Jewish people were massacred.

The new High Commissioner John Chancellor did not have the necessary manpower to stem the attacks. A SOS was quickly sent to Egypt. While naval, army and airforce personnel converged on the Land of Israel, General William Dobbie, was sent ahead to take overall command. Dobbie quickly moved his meagre forces from one location to another, giving the impression that the British force was bigger than it really was. Dobbie, like Patterson, was a Bible-believing Christian and resorted to prayer to seek the wisdom needed to stop the attacks.[2] The intervention of Dobbie's forces obviously helped save the lives of many stricken Jewish and European people. The damage done however was irreparable.

The Shaw Commission

The pogroms of 1929 assisted the opponents of the Jewish National Home. The new Labour Government led by Ramsay MacDonald, desiring to review various commitments made by previous governments, dispatched a commission headed up by Colonial Justice Walter Shaw. The Shaw Commission's report stated that the riots of 1929 were a natural reaction of the Arab population against Zionism and the *Balfour Declaration.* Later, in 1930 the Colonial Secretary Lord Passfield introduced a *White Paper* into Parliament calling for limitations upon Jewish immigration and settlement in Eretz Israel. This *White Paper* was the first official attempt by the British Government to break the commitment she had given to the Jewish people, as endorsed by the League of Nations Mandate.

---

2   Dobbie, Lieut.-General Sir William. *A Very Present Help.* (London: Edinburgh, 1944), pp. 52-3.

Strong opposition to the *Passfield White Paper* later forced MacDonald to write to Weizmann and virtually cancel its harsh declarations. Yet the incident revealed how easily an unsympathetic British Government could break a previous commitment.

Chancellor's replacement as High Commissioner, Sir Arthur Wauchope, was more positive towards Zionism than his predecessor, and so began several very positive years for Zionist-British relations. Yet the 1930 *White Paper* had served notice to people like Jabotinsky that the British could not be trusted, and that the Zionist leadership was weak by agreeing to the British compromises. The struggle within Zionism intensified, between those, like Jabotinsky, who demanded that Britain should be held to its promises and permit as many Jewish people as possible to live in Eretz Israel, from those, like Weizmann, Ben Zvi and Ben Gurion, who worked in collaboration with the British authorities, and who espoused the tenants of general and socialist Zionism. This internal Zionist struggle however was soon to be overshadowed by a far more ominous danger to the welfare of the Jewish people.

Rise of Nazi Germany

On 14 September 1930 Adolf Hitler's avowedly anti-Jewish Nazi party received 107 seats - the second highest - in the German *Reichstag* or Parliament. Despite his anti-Jewish mandate as outlined in his book *Mein Kampf* (My Struggle), many Jewish people in Germany failed to recognize the danger. Others, including the aging Gentile William Hechler did, and attempted to warn the Jewish people of coming disaster.

When Hitler came to power in 1933 his anti-Jewish sentiments became more evident. Opposition to Jewish people mounted, especially after an anti-Jewish boycott was staged on 1 April 1933. More now saw the writing on the wall. And when many of the western democracies refused entrance to Jewish emigrants or refugees, many had no choice but to come, albeit often reluctantly, to Eretz Israel.

As the number of German Jewish refugees increased, so too did local Arab opposition. In October 1933 Arabs rioted in Jaffa, resulting in the deaths of some twenty-six Arab demonstrators. Arab pressure against the number of Jewish immigrants intensified, causing the British Government to limit the quota of Jewish entry visas in 1934. At the very time when the fate of German Jewry was in the balance, their very hope, the Land of Israel was being barred to many. Many Jewish refugees entered illegally.

The peak year of immigration was 1935 when some 69,000 Jewish people came to British *Palestine*, the majority from Germany and Poland - some were even assisted by the German authorities. Much of this immigration was a natural reaction to the abhorrent *Nuremberg Laws* passed by the Nazis in 1935 which revealed the future character of the Nazi *Thousand Year Reich*. Among the many laws were those dedicated to the 'Protection of German Blood and Honour'. Jewish people were not permitted to marry non-Jews, and sexual relations between the two were forbidden. Jewish people were also stripped of their German citizenship.

Arab Reactions and Fascism

The nationalist Arabs became further alarmed at this sudden influx of European Jewish people. On 19 April 1936 Arabs rioted in Jaffa, and in quick time the disturbances spread. Sixteen Jewish people were killed in the first two days. Thereafter the Arabs called for a general strike, protesting against the British Government's Zionist policies. There followed a 170 day strike/revolt which included sabotage and terrorism, primarily against the Jewish community.

A most dangerous position emerged in August 1936 when the notorious terrorist Fawzi al-Kaukji escaped from Syria and entered British *Palestine*. Thereafter the number of Jewish casualties increased precariously, causing considerable concern for the British authorities. They seemed incapable of protecting Jewish lives, and were forced to 'legalize' a special Jewish police force. The majority of the Jewish policemen were also members of the Jewish underground army, the *Hagana*.

While the number of Jewish refugees entering Eretz Israel continued, the Arab leaders now began to accuse the British authorities of purposely abetting the Zionist cause. They turned their anger against the British Mandatory authority. Due to their familiarity with the terrain, these Arab peasants with often antiquated rifles, soon made a virtual laughing stock of the British forces. The British Government was forced to dispatch 1,400 reinforcements to *Palestine*, with clear instructions to put down the revolt. After adopting some strong-arm tactics this objective was achieved by October 1936. Although the Arabs had failed in their attempts to force the British Government to curb, even stop Jewish immigration and settlement, they nevertheless succeeded in forcing the Government to send out another Royal Commission of Inquiry.

Fascist Expansion

Hitler's vision of a world-wide Nazi led German Empire became more tangible in 1936 when Germany, in contravention of the stipulations of the Versailles Peace Agreement, began re-arming. Then her armies marched into the demilitarized Rhineland which separated Germany from France - again in contravention of the stipulations of the Peace Agreement. France protested - but made no move to oppose this open violation.

Germany's new ally, Italy, under the control of another dictator, Benito Mussolini, had, in 1935, made its initial move for re-establishing an Italian Empire. She invaded Ethiopia, a nation strategically located on the East African coast in striking distance of the link to India. Britain's ally, Emperor Haile Selassi was forced to flee to Jerusalem.

The Arab peoples of the Middle East, and more particularly in those countries under British and French control, observed these events very closely. The Arab leaders were able to detect a change in the wind. Italy and Germany were now challenging British and French hegemony in the region and in Europe. This mood was evidenced by the number of swastikas now appearing in Jerusalem. Britain could soon find herself in a difficult position if she failed to enlist the Arab nationalists as they could easily turn to Germany and Italy for support.

The Peel Commission

In late 1936 the six members of the Royal Commission led by Lord Robert Peel arrived in the Land of Israel. They endeavoured to come to grips with the complexities within the land. On one hand there was the reality of the recent riots, and on the other the reality of the thousands of German and Polish Jewish people arriving and being absorbed into the society.

Amongst the many delegates interviewed there were those on the Jewish side who viewed things only from the Zionist perspective, believing in the complete fulfillment of the promises of the *Balfour Declaration*. Other Zionists, represented by Weizmann were more conciliatory. He spoke of 'the six million Jews "pent up in places where they are not wanted, and places where they cannot live and places which they may not enter."[3] Weizmann was very concerned about the plight of Europe's Jewish population.

On the Arab side there was basically one strong viewpoint, more-or-less epitomized by their spokesman, Haj Amin al-Husseini. Haj Amin was insistent upon receiving Arab independence, as the Arabs constituted the majority of the population. When quizzed about the future of the Jewish population, he intimated that they would be liquidated.[4] The voice of the Arab moderates was hardly heard.

The Partition Plan and Arab Revolt

The *Peel Commission* members were impressed by the passion of both Jewish and Arab perspectives. The extremism on both sides was irreconcilable. It was this situation which prompted the *Commission* to propose a solution worked out by Professor R. Coupland, of partitioning Eretz Israel into a Jewish State and an Arab State (which would be linked to Transjordan.)

The findings of the *Peel Commission* and the recommendation of the *Partition Plan* were released to the public in July 1937. Three main reactions resulted. Firstly, the British Parliament, under new Prime Minister Neville Chamberlain, was in agreement and proposed to assist the fulfillment of the plan. Secondly, the Zionist organization was split. Weizmann and Ben Gurion were willing to accept, realizing that it offered a solution to the plight of the Jewish people of Europe. Others within the Zionist organization opposed it, as did for the most part the *Revisionists*. Thirdly, despite some moderate Arab leaders who were prepared to accept the plan, the radicals

---

3   Weizmann, C. *Trial and Error.* Vol. II, p. 384.
4   Lossin, Y. *Pillar of Fire*, p. 235.

led by Haj Amin, opposed it outright. There could be no Jewish State at all.

Haj Amin subsequently ignited an intimidation campaign, firstly against the more moderate Arabs, and then later against the British authorities and the Jewish people. They began their campaign by murdering the British Governor of the Galilee District, Lewis Andrews, in Nazareth on 26 September 1937. Wauchope ordered immediate and far-reaching action. Extra forces arrived. Every effort was made to locate and root out the leaders of the Arab Higher Committee. This body was disbanded and many of its leaders exiled to the Seychelles. Haj Amin was sought, but took sanctuary on the Temple Mount and from there, under disguise, escaped to Lebanon.

Despite the loss of their leadership, the Arabs organized a revolt against the British authorities and the Jewish people. Sabotage and death followed. Passage on roads, especially near Arab areas became hazardous. When the Arab rebels blew up the oil pipeline, which carried the precious petroleum from Iraq through to Haifa port, alarm bells sounded in London. The pipeline represented the prestige of the British Empire. The eyes of the world were now being focused upon *Palestine*, to view Britain's response. More forces arrived, including Bernard Montgomery, who was entrusted with organizing the army units in the north and quelling the Arab rebellion there.

Hitler Moves Again

In March 1938 Hitler's troops marched into and took control over Austria (the *Anschluss*). The fate of the Jewish people of central Europe grew progressively worse, as thousands more now sought refuge from Nazi persecution. This situation became so desperate that the western democracies called for a conference at the French resort town of Evian in 1938 to discuss the plight of the Jewish refugees.

Although all the assembled nations expressed their sympathy to the plight of the Jewish people, they refrained from offering any tangible assistance. 'The Australians, 'wrote Golda Meir, 'even went so far as to explain why not. Australia they said, had no anti-Semitism. If Jews are brought in, anti-Semitism might develop.'[5]

But anti-Semitism was now epidemic in Germany. On the evening of 10 November 1938 people throughout Germany went on a rampage of violence and destruction against the Jewish communities, destroying synagogues, shops and brutalizing any Jewish people in their way. This event, known as *Kristallnacht* - Night of Broken Glass, was a serious harbinger of events to follow.

Germany's lust for imperial power was not satisfied. Hitler then threatened small Czechoslovakia. Prime Minister Neville Chamberlain, and Chancellor Daladier of France met with Hitler and Mussolini in Munich in late 1938. The four agreed to cede the German speaking part of Czechoslovakia, the Sudetenland, to Germany, in exchange for a guarantee from Hitler not to demand any more territory. This *Munich*

---

5   Lossin, Y. *Pillar of Fire*, p. 247.

Pact of "peace in our time" was greeted favourably by most. Many Jewish people were not fooled. Neither was Winston Churchill, who saw this compromise as the beginning and not the end of trouble.

The Jewish Police Force

By 1938 the Arab attacks in British *Palestine* became uncontrollable, especially against Jewish communities. The British authorities requested the support of the Jewish Agency to enlist Jewish men into a special Jewish Supernumerary Police force. By late 1938 some 2,863 of these *Notrim,* mostly from the *Hagana,* had enlisted. Some of these patrolled the Jewish settlements on horseback, and wore the slouch hat, revealing just how the Anzac legacy had lived on in the Jewish Yishuv. One *Noter* was Moshe Dayan.

During this difficult period the Jewish Agency executive was continually advocating self-restraint. Thus the Arabs often attacked Jewish targets and could then easily retreat to safety before mounting another assault. This situation brought sharp dispute within the Jewish community. The *Irgun,* the military arm of the Revisionist movement, did not feel compelled to be restrained. Many within the mainstream Zionist movement too saw the need to take the offensive against the Arab marauders.

The British authorities ultimately saw no choice but to encourage offensive action, and dispatched a career officer, Orde Charles Wingate, nephew of William Dobbie, to take command of this fledgling idea. Wingate was to inherit the legacy of Patterson. Wingate was also Zionist in persuasion, and carried a Bible with him at all times. His units became known as the *Special Night Squad,* and they learned all the basics of lightning warfare.

While this military arm of the Jewish nationalist movement was being formed, the settlement of Eretz Israel steadily progressed. In the period after the publication of the Partition Plan proposal some fifty-two new Jewish settlements, known as *Tower and Stockade,* were established, primarily on or near the boundaries of the proposed Jewish State.

But the Arab revolt had its effect. If the flames of this revolt spread, and encouraged other Arab nationalist movements, especially in Iraq and Egypt, then Britain's interests, including the Suez Canal could be greatly jeopardized. This was just what the pro-Arab lobby group in London wanted. They wanted the Jewish State proposal rescinded - and succeeded. Anthony Eden, the new Foreign Secretary, convinced Prime Minister Neville Chamberlain in a secret cabinet meeting to radically re-adapt the proposal.

The first move was to decrease the proposed area of the Jewish State, to some 1,000 square kilometres primarily along the coastal plain from south of Haifa to Tel Aviv. Weizmann declared the idea impractical, a sentiment which assisted the British Government in declaring that the entire partition scheme was now unworkable and needed to be revised.

Such a revision was inopportune. Hitler had just declared in the *Reichstag* in January 1939 his intentions concerning the Jewish people:

> We will have to solve the Jewish question ... If international Jewish money, whether inside or outside Europe, succeeds in drawing the nations into another world war, then the result will not be world Bolshevization - and with it victory for the Jews - but the extermination of the Jewish race in Europe![6]

Then on 15 March 1939 he invaded the remainder of Czechoslovakia. The western democracies stood by motionless. Meanwhile the Jewish people of Czechoslovakia were forced to flee - but to where? Nobody wanted them, and only a few were permitted entry into Eretz Israel. Others entered illegally, alongside many Polish and German Jewish people.

The Round Table Conference

One week after Hitler's speech in the *Reichstag*, the British Government called for leading Arab delegates from the entire Arab world and Jewish delegates from British *Palestine* to convene in London in order to discuss the future of the disputed land, and of the *Partition Plan*. These discussions became known as the *Round Table Conference*, and was convened by the Colonial Secretary Malcolm MacDonald.

The findings of the Conference, known as the *MacDonald White Paper*, were released in May 1939. They all but rescinded the promises of the *Balfour Declaration*. There would be no specific Jewish State, and instead a State of Palestine which would have an Arab majority. Jewish immigration was limited to some 75,000 people over the following five years, and Jewish purchase of land and property was virtually outlawed. To the Zionist leadership it seemed like the death knell to their national aspirations.

The British policy makers realized that in the event of war against Nazism, the Jewish people would fight alongside the Allies. However the Arabs were a more uncertain proposition and efforts needed to be made to woo them onto the Allied side.

That inevitable war against Nazism began its ugly history on 1 September 1939, as the German Army, the *Wehrmacht,* and Air Force, the *Luftwaffe,* invaded and pounded Poland. Chamberlain and Daladier challenged the Germans to withdraw. They refused, and pressed on relentlessly towards Warsaw. Britain and France declared war on Germany on 3 September. And as British and French troops began mobilizing, a reign of terror was beginning for the three million Jewish people of Poland. The German soldiers began beating, harassing and killing indiscriminately. The words of Hitler calling for the destruction of the Jewish people began its terrible road to fulfillment.

---

6   Lossin, Y. *Pillar of Fire*, p. 269.

*C*hapter 21

The ANZAC Sons are Coming

Following Germany's invasion of Poland Prime Minister Chamberlain formed a War Cabinet, which included First Lord of the Admiralty, Winston Churchill. They immediately dispatched the British Expeditionary Force (BEF) to France, the vanguard reaching there on 4 September. It seemed a repeat of 1914.

Also, as in 1914, the War was bound to affect the Eastern Mediterranean. Yet this time Britain was more assured of victory. She controlled Egypt, Cyprus, Transjordan, Iraq, Sinai and the Land of Israel, while France controlled Syria and a large portion of North Africa. Churchill well understood the strategic importance of the Mediterranean. 'Not to hold the Central Mediterranean' he wrote 'would be to expose Egypt and the Canal, as well as French possessions, to invasion by Italian troops with German leadership.'[1] He also surmised, that if and when the Italian Fleet in the Mediterranean was destroyed, the British ships could reinforce her Far East Fleet, and effectively hinder any intended Japanese invasion of Australia and New Zealand.

The Second Anzacs

As in August 1914, so too in September 1939, the two Anzac countries (as well as other British Commonwealth countries) volunteered to defend the interests of the British Empire. New Zealand's Prime Minister Michael Joseph Savage proclaimed in 1939; 'Both with gratitude for the past, and with confidence in the future, we arrange ourselves without fear beside Britain. Where she goes, we go, where she stands, we stand ... we march forward with a union of hearts and wills to a common destiny.'[2]

Enlistment in the New Zealand Expeditionary Force began on 12 September. The commander was Major-General Bernard Freyberg, who had distinguished himself at Gallipoli and had earned the Victoria Cross (VC) in France. It was announced on 24 November that the force would be sent overseas. One of the first New Zealand volunteers was Arthur Helm, who wrote:

---

1   Churchill, Winston S. *The Gathering Storm,* Houghton Mifflin Company, (Boston, 1948), p. 415.
2   Quoted in King, M. *New Zealanders at War*, p. 168.

All classes and creeds and all conditions of men were among the volunteers ... Some looked upon it as a great lark, others enlisted from a genuine sense of duty, a few others to escape their responsibilities, or to try and make a fresh start after a life of drudgery during the depression years.[3]

After enlisting, Jim Henderson spent his last day of leave with his young nephew who was full of questions about the war and his uncle's future involvement in it. The young lad asked, 'Uncle Jim? ... How long will this war go?'

'I don't know. Nobody knows.'[4] A cautious uncle Jim replied. Indeed the lesson of the First World War had been learnt. The short conflict and home for Christmas attitude of 1914 was not so apparent in 1939.

The Australian Government announced on 15 September it's decision to raise an expeditionary force of 20,000 men. This initial force, to be known as the 6th Division Second Australian Imperial Force, would be commanded by General Sir Thomas Blamey, a Gallipoli veteran who had been Monash's Chief-of-Staff in France in 1918.

This Division quickly developed a sense of pride as being the inheritors of the Anzac legend. One young recruit was 16 year old Bob "Hooker" Holt from Lakemba, in New South Wales. 'I hot footed it to enlist' wrote Holt many years later from Palmerston North in New Zealand, 'giving my age as 21. My people protested vigorously, but upstart that I was, I informed them that if they pulled me out I would leave home and enlist under a bodgie name. With that they bowed to the inevitable and gave me their blessing - more or less, anyhow.'[5]

Life in the Land of Israel

At the outbreak of War the people of Eretz Israel were still overcoming the effects of the disturbances and the *White Paper*. The Jewish people realized the necessity of supporting the Allied cause - and a basic cease fire between them and the British came into effect. Ben Gurion summarized the Jewish situation well: 'We will fight the War as if there is no White Paper, and we will fight the White Paper as if there is no War.'

The Zionist leadership immediately recognized the danger confronting the three million plus Jewish people living in Nazi occupied Poland and quite naturally wanted as many as possible to immigrate. They also began agitating for the formation of a Jewish Army from the Land of Israel that could fight against Nazi Germany. A march was held in Tel Aviv in early September calling for volunteers. Thousands responded. The British authorities however were suspicious of this move. They felt it might provoke the Arabs, that it might later be used by the Zionist Organization to

3   Quoted in King, M., ibid., p. 168.
4   Henderson, J. *Gunner Inglorious*. Harry H. Tombs. (Wellington, 1945), p. 7.
5   Bob "Hooker" Holt, *From Ingleburn to Aitape,* (Brookvale, 1981), p. 3.

agitate against the *White Paper*, and, they claimed, they didn't have the equipment for such a force.

The British Cabinet rejected the proposal. And more than that, the British Authorities in Eretz Israel intended to neutralize the *Hagana*, in its more official capacity as the Jewish Supernumerary Police. The presence of armed Jewish policemen, the authorities felt, may well antagonize the Arabs, who were still being apprehended if caught carrying arms. Fear of an Arab uprising gripped the authorities, which they felt may occur if severe restrictions were not also placed upon Jewish immigration.

On 5 October 1939 a British patrol spotted forty-three *Hagana* men, including Moshe Dayan, marching in full uniform. They were arrested and at their trial on 27 October they stated 'We were a group of young men training to prepare ourselves for the fight against our common enemy, Nazi Germany, and should receive the understanding and indulgence of the court.'[6] They were convicted of illegally carrying arms and sentenced to severe terms at the Acre prison. The authorities stated that the *Hagana* might in the future operate against British interests.

Jewish Troops to France

The British authorities did permit the formation of a mixed Jewish and Arab non-infantry unit named the *Auxiliary Military Pioneer Corps* (AMPC). However they would not permit the Jewish men to serve in combat units, for they realized that the Jewish people would use this as a bargaining chip at the war's completion. All this seemed like a rehash of early 1915 when Jabotinsky and Trumpeldor came with a similar proposal to Murray in Egypt. To eradicate hopes of such a claim, the British drafted Arabs into the formation as well. The unit departed in late February 1940 for France where they would form part of the BEF.

Their introduction to the battle zone was somewhat different from that experienced by the *Zion Mule Corps*, who although not being infantry, at least saw action at close quarters. The AMPC saw little action in those first months, as the Allied and German soldiers squared off behind their supposedly impregnable Maginot and Siegfried Lines separating the two sides. This was the so-called *phony war*.

Anti-British sentiment in the Land of Israel however increased in February, when the Government endorsed the new land laws, as proposed by the *White Paper*. Anti-Government demonstrations broke out throughout the country - while the Arabs in Jaffa rejoiced. Despite the harsh realities facing the Jewish people they had at least one supporter on the Cabinet - Winston Churchill. On 25 December 1939 he wrote and requested his Cabinet colleagues to be more lenient in their attitude towards British *Palestine*. He felt that a harsh attitude could cause the Jewish Americans to

---

6   Dayan, Moshe. *Moshe Dayan: Story of My Life*. Warner Books, (New York, 1976), p. 35.

turn against Britain.[7]

The Anzac Sons Arrive

The first 6,600 troops of the New Zealand Expeditionary Force left New Zealand on 5 January 1940 en-route to Sydney where they joined part of the 6th Australian Division. Together they journeyed to Melbourne where they were joined by the Australian commander General Blamey and his staff.

After a further stop over in Fremantle, (not Albany this time) the Anzac force headed first to Colombo in Ceylon and then towards the battlefields of France. Again a rehash of history. Fears however of an Italian entrance into the War, demanded that British forces in Egypt and the Land of Israel be strengthened. Regular British troops from India were also dispatched to Egypt, as too were Australian and New Zealand warships and aircraft and personnel.

The first contingent of the Second AIF and the New Zealand Expeditionary Force arrived at Suez on 12 February 1940, where they were greeted by Anthony Eden, the Secretary of the Dominions. The following day the convoy moved onto Kantara. The Jewish people of British *Palestine* were excited about the arrival of this new force. Under the bold title **ANZACS BACK AGAIN**, the English language newspaper the *Palestine Post* dedicated half of the cover page to the arrival of the Anzacs on 13 February and wrote of their expected role:

> To the Dominion forces will fall a vital share in the common effort ... To maintain peace in this region, to erect a barrier against a German advance into the Balkans, or a Russian threat into the Middle East, and to buttress the position of Turkey, - these are the objects which have brought to the Middle East, for the second time in a quarter of a century, the volunteer troops from Australia and New Zealand ...[8]

At Kantara the Anzac sons boarded trains and moved off to their destinations, the New Zealanders to Egypt, and the Australians to British *Palestine.* From his camp at Maadi eight miles south of Cairo, Lance Corporal J.E.J. Westbrook wrote later back home:

> We arrived here a fortnight today and I think it's been a fortnight too long. We haven't seen green grass since we left New Zealand. Here there's nothing but desert and dust ... The sun is fierce and the heat off the sand is reflected straight into your face...
> From the camp we can see the great pyramids. The Nile is between us and the pyramids. The Nile is a dirty river, sluggish and murky.[9]

As difficult as conditions may have been, all efforts were being made to ensure the comfort of the troops - even to the extent of filling the mattresses with Egyptian

---

7   Bethell, N. *The Palestine Triangle,* Andre Deutsch Limited, (London, 1979) p. 82.

8   *The Palestine Post.* 13 February 1940, p. 6.

9   Quoted in King, M. *New Zealanders at War,* p.169.

cotton instead of the usual straw! But for many, the discomforts were outweighed by the realization that they were truly following in the footsteps of their forefathers of a generation before.

The Australians found themselves also in a region well-known by their fathers' generation. In no time at all the men were encamped in sprawling camps near Gaza, which had been erected in quick time by the British troops and locals. Wherever possible these sons of the Anzacs attempted to visit the places associated with their illustrious fathers. From his base near Gaza "Hooker" Holt wrote: 'Nothing could be seen from Gaza itself, but from several miles away the imprint of the old entrenchment's could be made out quite clearly.'[10]

The *Palestine Post* correspondent spent some time talking to the newly arrived troops, one of whom commented upon Mr. Eden's visit to his ship: 'It seemed like a sort of Empire half-way house, with us coming from Australia, thousands of miles away on one side of the world, and Eden coming from England, thousands of miles the other way, and meeting here in the Middle East.'[11] This young soldier's comment summed up the real essence of why these young Anzacs were again in the Middle East - they were in the *land between* the Empires.

All the major British newspapers dedicated prime space to the arrival of the Anzacs to the Middle East. But the new Italian Empire was also eyeing these developments very keenly. Under the title **Italians Watch Anzacs Arrival. Rome's Eyes Focused on Suez,** Reuters reported, 'It is believed that the Italian Supreme Defence Council which concluded its session here yesterday evening discussed the arrival of the Anzacs in Egypt and Palestine and General Weygand's visit to Cairo.'[12]

Despite the complexities of life in the desert and near dirty Cairo, and Gaza, the boys from Down Under realized they had a tradition to uphold and encapsulated it in song:

> We are the boys from Way Down Under
> Marching to Victory
> We're not afraid of Hitler's thunder
> We'll put his where he should be
> The Poles, the Czechs and old Stalin himself
> We're out to put the bastard on the shelf!
> For we are the boys from Way Down Under
> Sons of the Anzacs are we!

Warm Welcome by Jewish Community

The local Jewish newspapers continued to dedicate much space to the arrival of the

---

10   Holt, B. *From Ingleburn to Aitape*, p. 17.
11   *The Palestine Post*. 14 February 1940, p. 1
12   *The Palestine Post*, 16 February 1940, p. 2.

sons of the Anzacs. The *Palestine Post* carried more extensive exposure on 16 February, writing in the Editorial:

> Palestine has found favour in the eyes of our latest arrivals - the Australian troops ... in his uniform and broad-brimmed, clipped-up hat he may even be mistaken for a member of the Jewish Settlement Corps. He is welcomed here, and his characteristic good-humour together with his democratic freedom from "side" will make him popular everywhere.'[13]

It was not long before the inhabitants of the Land of Israel were to experience this so-called good humour. The first day excursion was organized for 22 February, as buses took 600 soldiers on a day trip to Tel Aviv and 400 to Jerusalem. The Yemenite children of Tel Aviv fascinated some of the soldiers, one of whom 'became so attached to a young Yemenite shoelace vendor that he ... bought out his complete stock of 40 pairs of shoelaces.'

'One group of men,' wrote the *Palestine Post* correspondent, 'hired mules and started a "race" along the Jaffa Road, causing much amusement to the passersby who cheered them, especially when the animals turned out to be intractable.' By the time they left Jerusalem at 6.30 p.m. 'people were lining the pavements along the Jaffa Road to see them off, and cheers and goodbyes were exchanged.'[14]

From 25 February the troops were to go out on four day stretches, with appropriate hostels being arranged in the major places of interest. In Jerusalem the Fast Hotel near Jaffa Gate became the Australian Soldiers Club, and fifty men at a time were released to visit Jerusalem. And fifty at a time was probably all Jerusalem or any town could handle at one time! 'The Australians were all very jolly,' recalls Yitzak Toussia-Cohen, a young Jewish student, 'and they compensated for the lack of warmth experienced from the British authorities. They loved to drink, but were very popular with the children, for they used to throw coins into the air for them to catch.'[15]

Although most of the interaction was amongst the Jewish population, some Arabs also got a piece of the action. N. Ibrahim was a young Arab from the Old City of Jerusalem, who used his knowledge of the tourist sites to good effect, by guiding the soldiers. He found them very amusing and humorous, and from his exposure began learning all about the history and geography of Australia. One of his nick-names was Ned Kelly, (Australia's most notorious outlaw-cum-Robin Hood) so naturally he became very well acquainted with this aspect of Australia's history. Ibrahim's other nick-name was 'wog.' After some time he inquired what 'wog' actually meant. 'Oh it means "*W*estern *O*riental *G*entleman" a bemused soldier replied.'[16]

---

13 *The Palestine Post*, 16 February 1940, p. 8.
14 *The Palestine Post*. 23 February 1940, p. 2.
15 Conversation with Yitzak Toussia-Cohen, October 1996.
16 Conversation with N. Ibrahim, April 1997.

The New Zealanders in Egypt

The New Zealanders truly started off where their fathers began. They visited the same sights as did the Anzacs in 1914-15, although some sported new names. The Pyramids was obviously a much frequented spot, and there was the typical photograph riding a camel. Some of the more notorious spots were also visited. And there was the same *Gyppo beer* and *Gyppo belly* which their fathers also experienced. And the people and customs were just the same - very different from back at home. One soldier wrote:

> ... Cairo ... should have a fair dinkum earthquake to mop it up. It's foul and to be more blunt - it stinks ... In New Zealand I never used to count my change, here I check over them, double check, then look through for dud coins ... You'll be taken down at every opportunity ... You can trust nobody. If you haven't got a beggar whining for backsheesh following you, you have a native 'guide' who sports a Police Dept. badge (home made more than likely) wanting to show you the way to the pyramids, museum, native bazaars and boy, does he stick around ...[17]

And being New Zealanders there was as much interest in another form of culture, something which every soldier could relate to and enjoy - a game of rugby. When they weren't playing rugby, and visiting the sights and scenes, they trained and drilled. They also had breaks from the camp and confines of squalid Egypt and enjoyed the more refreshing environment of the Land of Israel. Sarah Pearl owned and operated a small hotel in Safed high up in the Galilean hills - which had been liberated by the Light Horse in 1918. Once a week she held an open house for the soldiers, where she offered tea and homemade scones. As word gets out quickly when there's a good thing going, the New Zealanders also began joining these little tea parties. She recalls that all the soldiers were 'lovely, jolly, friendly people, who often gave her little gifts in return' and 'who behaved themselves.' No hard drinks (apart from a shandy) were allowed, which may have helped matters! The New Zealanders she recalled resented being called *Australim*, (the Hebrew word for Australians) and were just as concerned about being classified as a North Islander as distinct from a South Islander, and visa-versa.

While the men of the first contingents were settling in, both in Egypt and Eretz Israel, volunteers were being called for the formation of the 7th Australian Division, and for the 5th Brigade in New Zealand.

Anzac Day - 1940

A high point for both New Zealanders and Australians was undoubtedly 25 April, 1940 - **Anzac Day**. The New Zealanders in Egypt held one of the biggest parades

---

17   King, M. *New Zealanders at War*, p. 169.

since the War. But first they were involved in early morning manoeuvres, and then after breakfast they participated in the various services. Field Marshall Lord Birdwood also sent the following message to Freyberg:

> Nothing can ever dim my recollection of the days I passed with their elder brothers of the First New Zealand Expeditionary Force in Gallipoli and France. I am absolutely confident that when you may be called on you will follow in their footsteps and equal their great deeds.[18]

Three main services were held in British *Palestine*, at Jerusalem, Tel Aviv and at Gaza. The local population was well prepared for the event, which involved the largest military parade during the Mandate period.[19] The newspapers provided much coverage to the impending events. The *Palestine Post* gave over almost the entire cover page under the title **Anzac Day in Palestine** and the entire page three to the day's events, while the Editorial was also dedicated to the Anzacs, under the title **Over Here Again.** After having summarized the exploits of the first Anzacs, and expressing gratitude for the quality these men from the Antipodes were, the editor concluded by expressing sentiments which must have brought tears to the eyes of any who read them:

> Palestine has cause to be grateful for the statesmanship which sent this glorious young army of Anzacs to instil confidence, to soften the darkness of her later days, and to help this sorely tried land back to happiness.[20]

Surely this was one of the ironies of history. Soldiers from young far away countries coming to 'instil confidence,' 'soften the darkness' and 'help' the sorely tried land of Israel back to happiness. Well the soldiers played their part on that April 1940 day. In Jerusalem a dawn service was held at the Jerusalem War Cemetery on Mount Scopus overlooking Jerusalem. Then the large contingent of Australian soldiers gathered at the Russian Compound and marched past thousands of locals the several kilometres to the same location for the 9.20 am service. There a full memorial service was held, witnessed by many. The guard of honour included thirty ex-servicemen of the *Zion Mule Corps*, and a wreath was laid on behalf of the *Zion Mule Corps.*

At Gaza, where most of the Anzacs lost their lives in the 1916-1918 campaign, a dawn service attended by some 1,500 Australian soldiers was held at the Commonwealth War Cemetery. Literally thousands of mostly Jewish spectators watched the Anzac parade in Tel Aviv. The 500 Australian soldiers marched through Dizengoff Circle to 109 HaYarkon Street where the mayor of Tel Aviv, Mr. Rokach opened the New Soldiers Club. Later at a luncheon, which provided *Passover* food, the Mayor addressed the Anzac soldiers. 'Speaking of the significance of Anzac

---

18   *The Palestine Post.* 26 April 1940, p. 1.
19   *The Palestine Post,* 26 April, 1940, p. 6.
20   *The Palestine Post.* 25 April 1940, p. 4.

Day,' the *Palestine Post* correspondent wrote, 'the Mayor said that their fathers had delivered Palestine from the yoke of the Turks ... Now, after a quarter of a century the Anzacs were back in uniform to take their part in humanity's struggle for freedom.'[21]

Fall of France and Entrance of Italy

That struggle for freedom would very shortly become a reality. Events in Europe in May and June 1940 soon changed the complexion of matters in the Middle East, and gave the Anzac soldiers something else to think about than training and playful antics in the streets of Cairo, Tel Aviv and Jerusalem. And for those Allied and Jewish soldiers in France, the 'phony war' was also over. On the morning of 10 May 1940, the German armies overran the borders of Holland, Belgium and France. In the evening of that same day Winston Churchill became the Prime Minister of Britain.

The German forces quickly overwhelmed France, forcing the evacuation of most of the British Expeditionary Force and a number of French soldiers (some 338,226 in all) from Dunkirk between 27 May and 4 June. This was a different story from 1914. When French defeat seemed inevitable, Italy entered the war allied to Germany on 10 June. Defeat was staring France in the face by mid-June. On 16 June Premier Reynaud resigned and Marshal Petain formed a new Government, revoked the March 1940 agreement with Britain which stated that neither side would make a separate peace with Germany, and immediately asked Germany for Armistice terms. An Armistice was finally signed on 22 June.

Under the Armistice, and in an attempt to stop the French setting up a government in exile, either in North Africa or Britain, Hitler permitted about half of France to be unoccupied, and self governing, while the other half remained under German control. On 1 July this self-rule Government moved to the city of Vichy, and on 5 July they broke off diplomatic relations with Britain. The official and recognized government of France was now at Vichy.

The fall of France prompted the Australian Government to approve the formation of the 8th Division. The entrance of Italy into the war prompted the formation of the 9th Division. While the 7th Division was on its way to the Middle East, the 8th Division was sent to buttress the British Far East garrison in Malaya. And the 9th Division too was designated for service in the Middle East. On 7 June 1940, Major-General R.N. O'Connor was summoned from Jerusalem to Cairo and informed that he was to take command of Western Desert Force to ward off an expected Italian attack from Libya. When the Italians declared war he sent some of his troops over the border and wreacked havoc upon the unsuspecting Italians. The battle of the Empires for control of the Eastern Mediterranean was about to begin another phase.

---

21   *The Palestine Post.* 26 April 1940, p. 2.

Anthony Eden, Secretary of the Dominions, addressing New Zealanders at Suez, 12 February 1940.

New Zealand soldiers, part of special Long Range Desert Group, 1941

▲ *Anzac Day march along Jerusalem's Jaffa Road, 25 April 1940. Large building to left of marchers is the Australian Soldiers Club, otherwise known as the Fast Hotel. This was the largest military parade held in Jerusalem during the Mandate period. The soldiers marched to the Commonwealth War Cemetery on Mount Scopus overlooking Jerusalem for a wreath laying ceremony. Several veterans of the Zion Mule Corps also participated.*

Private John Crombie, 2/7th Battalion, 6th Australian Division, 1940

Private James Crombie (far right kneeling) 2/28th Battalion, 9th Australian Division, 1941

Palmachnick Uzi Narkiss, 1944 sporting Aussie slouch hat.

▲ *Anzac soldiers and young Jewish friends, Tel Aviv, 1940*

▲ *Australian soldier and young Jewish admirer. Somewhere in Eretz Israel*

▲ *Registration of Jewish recruits into British Army, Sarafand camp, July 1941*

▲ *Jewish Australian soldiers with children at Kibbutz Kiriat Anavim*

▲ *Australian soldiers on patrol somewhere in British* Palestine

▲ *Jewish youth of Tel Yosef teaching British, South African and Anzac soldiers how to dance the* hora

▲ *Australian Army surf carnival at Tel Aviv beach. Notice Zionist (later the Israeli) and Australian flags flying together*

▲ *Australian soldiers look over Jerusalem from the Mount of Olives*

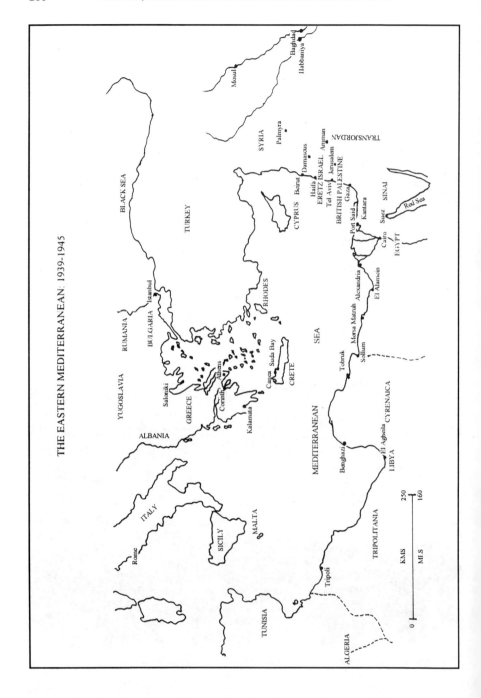

THE EASTERN MEDITERRANEAN: 1939-1945

*C*hapter 22

Italy Thrusts for Empire

New Reality in the Middle East

The fall of France and loss of the French Army in the Levant and North Africa meant that Britain now had to withstand the expected Italian invasion of Egypt alone. And the Italians could muster some 215,000 troops for such an assault. 'Mussolini might well feel,' wrote Churchill 'that his dream of dominating the Mediterranean and rebuilding the former Roman Empire would come true.'[1] Opposing him were only some 50,000 British, Indian and Anzac troops in Egypt, with more stationed and training in *Palestine.*

For many of those troops the war was now becoming a reality. 'After Italy entered the War,' Holt wrote, 'we disposed our tents and dug them into the ground ... Route marches and manoeuvres were the order of the day.'[2] When Tel Aviv and the oil refineries near Haifa were bombed, the war came into the heart of Eretz Israel. A young Alex Carmel recalls his parents sending him out of Haifa to a kibbutz for safety.[3]

Following the *Compiegne Armistice* between France and Germany, all Italian troops opposing the French in Tunisia were released to face the British across the Egyptian-Libyan border. Churchill began to panic and summoned Wavell, the Commander-in-Chief of the Middle East, to London for consultations in August.[4] Shortly afterwards many of the Anzacs were transferred to Egypt and continued their training at Helwan camp outside Cairo. Just like their fathers, they often 'painted Cairo red' with one often frequented area being the Berka. Bob "Hooker" Holt recalls the *Battle of the Berka*: 'I do not know what it was all about, but there would be a roar and a scuffling starting at one end of the crowded street and it would gradually work down to the other end of the Berka. It would die out only to start up again a hour or so later. In the main it was the Australians and New Zealanders thumping the

---

1   Churchill, Winston. S. *Their Finest Hour*, Houghton Mifflin Company, (Boston., 1950), p. 417.
2   Holt, B. *From Ingleburne to Aitape*, p. 19.
3   Conversation with Professor Alex Carmel, Haifa, April 1997.
4   Churchill, Winston. S. *Their Finest Hour*, p. 426.

tar out of anyone who happened to be near.'[5]   One immediately recalls the famous battle of the 'Wozza' in 1915.

Many a Cairene resident was probably happy when many Anzacs were then moved forward to bases, mainly near Alexandria. The British and Indian Regulars were in the forward position at Mersa Matruh. Contingency plans were also introduced in the event of the Italians breaking through at Mersa Matruh, ensuring the Italians would not have an easy passage eastwards.

With the capitulation of France, the battle for naval supremacy was to be fought between the British and Italian Fleets. Early points were won by the British and Australian ships. The British and Australian aircraft too gained pre-eminence in the region over the Italian. However it was still dangerous sending men and equipment into the Mediterranean via Gibraltar.

All the overseas territories of the French Empire were bound by the conditions of the surrender. The Vichy French authorities in Syria forbade any French troops from crossing over into *Palestine* to join the British. Few Frenchmen crossed but a Polish Brigade did. The British Government declared on 1 July 1940 that it would not permit Syria (which included Lebanon) to be either used by an enemy power or as a base for an enemy power to attack British concerns within the region.

This position was challenged when in August 1940 the Italian Armistice Commission arrived in Syria and released all German agents who had been interned at the outbreak of war. Vichy Syria now became a hive of activity for German agents, who began stirring up anti-British and anti-Zionist sentiment amongst the local Arab population.

German agents were also active in Iraq. Although Iraq broke off diplomatic relations with Germany at the outbreak of war, she did not declare war. She didn't even break off relations with Italy after they entered. Prior to the war these German agents promoted a very strong pro-Axis sentiment in Iraq. This sentiment increased as Germany won battle after battle. The Iraqi Army was becoming progressively restless by these set-backs of the British, and slowly came under the influence of four powerful pro-Axis colonels, known as the 'Golden Square'.

Such an atmosphere was only exacerbated by the presence of the Mufti, the most dangerous agitator of Arab opposition to Britain. Haj Amin, fled Syria in October 1939 for Baghdad, where he was accorded official status by the Iraqi authorities, especially by the nationalist party. From here he continued his anti-British and anti-Zionist efforts.

He sent a letter to the German ambassador in Turkey, Von Papen, congratulating Hitler upon his recent victories, and added: 'The Arab nation everywhere feels the greatest joy and deepest gratification on the occasion of these successes ... ' He further added that the end result of these successes will actually be independence and

---

5   Holt, B. *From Ingleburn to Aitape*, p. 28.

complete liberation for the Arab people. He concluded by advocating that the Arab people would 'be linked to your country by a treaty of friendship and collaboration.'[6]

It was not just a German victory over Britain that the Mufti was propagating. It was for the complete destruction of the Jewish National Home and establishment of an Arab nation. Both Berlin and Rome issued a joint statement showing sympathy towards Arab independence in October 1940.

Struggle for Jewish Division

Churchill, regarded as a pro-Zionist, disdained the *White Paper*, but had to condone it. Yet he could encourage the formation of a larger Jewish fighting force, although he realized that such a move could easily trigger off anti-British sentiment in the region. Weizmann and the Zionists persisted in their demands for a Jewish army.

As a German invasion of Britain was widely expected, Churchill's immediate concern was for home defence. He needed to raise fresh forces, and bring back home regular troops stationed in less dangerous places overseas, including British *Palestine*. He wanted the Jewish colonists armed and for reinforcements to be introduced from India. On both accounts Churchill was strongly opposed. [7]

Writing to Lord Lloyd, the Secretary of State for the Colonies, he pointed out how Britain's anti-Zionist policy had failed, as there needed to be 20,000 sorely needed soldiers stationed in Eretz Israel. 'Should the war go heavily into Egypt,' he continued, 'all these troops will have to be withdrawn, and the position of the Jewish colonists will be one of the greatest danger ... If the Jews were properly armed, ' he argued, 'our forces would become available, and there would be no danger of the Jews attacking the Arabs, because they are entirely dependent upon us and upon our command of the seas.' [8]

At the same time Jabotinsky and Patterson were agitating strongly in the United States for the formation of a Jewish Division, similar in format to the *Jewish Legion*. After being informed that Parliament had rejected the proposal, Patterson wrote to Lord Lothian on 18 June 1940:

> Can it be possible that the Cabinet is so blind that - at a moment when it eagerly wants to mobilize America on its side - it deliberately turns down the offer of an American Jewish Army. Does it not realize that such a formation born on these shores (but trained in Canada) would have brought thousands of non-Jews also to its ranks and would have aroused a flame of enthusiasm throughout this country...
>
> During the last war when our fortunes were at a low ebb, Mr. Lloyd George had the brilliant idea of bringing the Jewish people on our side by creating a Jewish Legion and solemnly promising Palestine as their national homeland ...

6   Sacher, H. *A History of Israel.* (New York, 1986), p. 228.
7   Churchill, W. *Their Finest Hour*, Houghton Mifflin Company, (Boston, 1949) p. 172.
8   Ibid., pp. 173-174.

On the 6th of March last Mr. Chamberlain did just the opposite. He forced an Act through Parliament (Mr. Churchill opposing him) devouring Israel's heritage. Chamberlain paid no heed either to England's honour or the Bible's ominous warnings - you will find it in the Second Chapter of Jeremiah and the third verse: "All that devour Israel shall offend; evil shall come upon them saith the Lord ...

Lord Lloyd and his pro-Nazi minions in the Colonial office have had their way and defeated the Jewish Army scheme, but alas they have brought England another step nearer her doom ...

Patterson ended by stating: 'Please make no mistake - one Jewish mechanized division would be worth more than all the Arabs in the Near East.'[9] More disappointment followed for Patterson as his long-standing friend and comrade, Zev Jabotinsky, died on 4 August in New York.

The War Cabinet, although refusing to endorse the formation of a Jewish Division, agreed on 15 July 1940 to the formation of six Palestinian companies of soldiers, known as the *Buffs*.[10] Churchill also encouraged a closer working relationship between the *Hagana* and the Special Operations Executive (SOE) of the British Army.

One of the first Jewish recruits to the Jewish force was Moshe Mosenson from Kibbutz Naan. 'Here I am at the training camp,' Mosenson wrote on 5 August 1940, several days after enlistment. 'There is a barbed wire fence around it and a stranger is on guard at the gate. The way home is both barred and distant ... I know that the atmosphere of uniforms and the military will be difficult for people like us to accept. But my heart remains calm.'[11] Mosenson, like many of the other Jewish recruits, was based at Sarafand (Surafend of the First World War period). Many of his fellow soldiers were recent immigrants. Meanwhile as Mosenson, his fellow Jewish soldiers, as well as the Anzacs and British prepared for battle in the training camps of British *Palestine*, the Italians prepared for their advance.

The Italians Attack

Despite his claims of unreadiness, Mussolini urged the Italian Commander-in-Chief Graziani to attack Egypt. The Italian assault began on 13 September 1940 - some 100 years after Mehmet Ali of Egypt flaunted the Europeans and provoked their involvement in the region.

The massive Italian forces quickly moved across the Egyptian border, overran Sollum and moved onto Sidi Barrani. There they re-grouped, which allowed for the arrival of much needed armour for the 7th British Armoured Division, and for the 4th Indian Division to come to full strength. Had the Italians continued their offensive, then they could have driven the Allied forces eastwards and subdued much of Egypt.

---

9   John Patterson to Lord Lothian, 18 June 1940. Jabotinsky Institute Archives, Tel Aviv. File 3-177 P.

10   Bethell, N. *The Palestine Triangle*, p. 90.

11   Mosenson, M . *Letters From the Desert*. Sharon Books, Inc. (New York ,1945), p. 3.

The Italians stalled due to their pre-occupation with other matters. Mussolini's dream of re-establishing Roman grandeur involved both the Eastern and Northern Mediterranean, especially Greece. Somewhat to Hitler's annoyance he thrust his forces into Greece on 28 October 1940. From a conquered Greece, Mussolini anticipated being in a much better position to assault the British interests in the Northern and Eastern Mediterranean.

Britain was bound to assist Greece due to an agreement between Chamberlain and the Greek government made in April 1939. While British troops then landed in Crete on 1 November 1940, Churchill impressed upon the Allied commanders in Egypt the need to assist Greece. In his opinion it would be detrimental if forces were not sent to Greece's aid, for that would show other neutral countries, in particular Turkey, that Britain does not honour her pledges.[12] A weak showing by Britain could even induce Turkey to revoke its alliance with Britain.

It was also imperative at this point to deal the Italian Fleet a telling blow, so as to keep them out of any future Allied operations vis-à-vis the Crete and Greek spheres. On 11 November 1940 aircraft flying from the carrier *Illustrious* torpedoed and disabled half the Italian Fleet at Taranto. This was just another disaster to add to Mussolini's woes. By the end of November his army was being heavily defeated by the Greeks.

In Eretz Israel meanwhile the conflict between the Jewish people and British authorities continued. In late November 1940 a large number of Jewish illegal immigrants were placed by the British authorities aboard a ship, the *Patria,* in Haifa port, intending to send them to Mauritius. In an effort to stop the sailing, members of the *Hagana* placed charges on the ship, ostensibly to damage it and prevent the sailing. The effort backfired, and instead the *Patria* sank quickly killing 267 passengers.

The Jewish community was outraged at the British High Commissioner MacMichael who had ordered the expulsion. It was a bitter pill to swallow for those who had advocated partnership with the British authorities. On 6 December 1940 Moses Mosenson wrote to his wife:

> I am writing to you this evening out of a deep need to find some refuge from myself. The story has finally reached us, in the training-camp, of what happened to the "Patria." Have you ever walked in the blazing sun without a shirt and felt the sun burn you? Do you remember the horrible pain you feel when your shirt touches your burnt skin? I have something of the same feeling today, although I haven't been out in the sun. My uniform seems to burn into my flesh ... I explain to myself that I joined the army only at the call of my conscience and political disappointments and insults cannot change this decision. All this is not new to us. But nevertheless my khaki shirt weighs heavily upon me today ...'[13]

---

12 Churchill, Winston. S. *Their Finest Hour,* p. 536.
13 Mosenson, M. *Letters from the Desert,* p. 15.

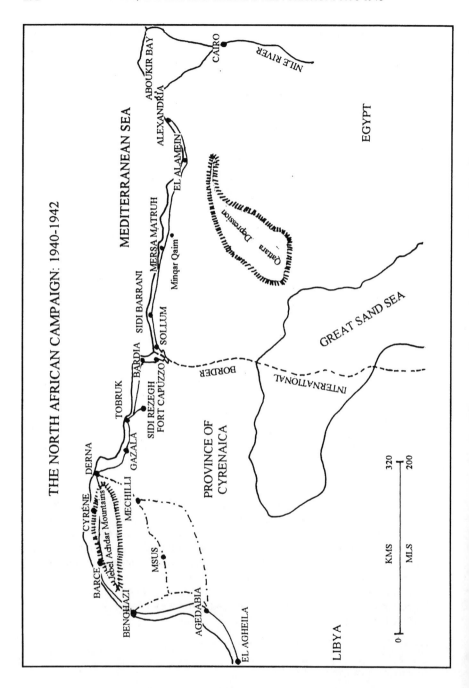

THE NORTH AFRICAN CAMPAIGN: 1940-1942

Cyrenaica Captured. First Bardia ...

Meanwhile more troops from the 9th Division left the shores of Australia in mid November and were heading towards the Eastern Mediterranean. One of those on board was Thomas Derrick from Berri, South Australia, part of the 2/48th Battalion of the 26th Brigade. He penned on 17 December: 'Disembarked at Kantara. Entrained there and went 180 miles inland to camping ground. Detrained 2400 hours.'[14] And while these troops were heading eastwards the 6th Australian Division was preparing for its first real action. On 9 December, O'Connor attacked the Italians at Sidi Barrani and quickly swept them back into Libya. After several days of intense combat the Indian Division was withdrawn and dispatched to battle the Italians in Eritrea. The Australian 6th Division was then brought forward to replace the Indians, and found themselves outside besieged Bardia.

The offensive now aimed for the strategic Italian fortifications at Bardia and Tobruk. The attacking force was comprised of the 6th Australian Division, the 7th Armoured Division, and other smaller British forces. 'We were allocated our positions outside Bardia and endeavoured to dig slit trenches,' recalls Holt, 'but it was just not possible, for six inches to a foot down we struck solid rock. We dug long trenches we could lie full length in. It was as hot as billyho through the day, but as cold as charity during the night.'[15]

On 3 January 1941 the Australians were in readiness outside Bardia. 'On our backs,' wrote Holt 'we had sewn a patch of white cloth, so that our own troops following in the dark would recognize us. I understand this device was first used by Australians at Lone Pine on Gallipoli in 1915 ... '[16] The artillery barrage then began, and the infantry broke through the perimeters at Bardia and the town was taken two days later - complete with 45,000 prisoners. In their first action of the War the Australians lost sixty-one men. Derrick at his camp in the Land of Eretz Israel, wrote on 6 January: 'Heard 6th Divy had taken Port Bardia. Hope she's right and would like to be giving a hand.'[17]

... Then Tobruk

Next after Bardia was the strategically important port of Tobruk, which was isolated by the 7th Armoured Division, with Australian support. Conditions were unpleasant as the hot dry *Khamsin* wind began blowing. Holt recalled how: '...The cutting, biting,

---

14 *Diary of Thomas Derrick.* Quoted in Farquhar, Murray. *Derrick V.C.* Rigby Publishers, (Adelaide, 1982), p. 37. Hereafter, *Diary of Thomas Derrick,* and page number from Farquhar's book.

15 Holt, B. *From Ingleburn to Aitape,* p. 35.

16 Ibid., p. 40.

17 *Diary of Thomas Derrick,* Farquhar, p. 40.

dust-laden winds blew so hard that it was virtually impossible to see and we stayed for several days in our holes covered with a blanket. It was sickening to even try to eat as everything was covered with a layer of grit the moment a can was opened. The heat was terrific and water was at a premium.'[18] The Jewish Transport Corps had also moved up to the front line.

The attack on Tobruk began on 21 January 1941 as British tanks and Australian infantry streamed through the outer fortifications. The town was taken swiftly, along with 30,000 prisoners.[19] The Reuters correspondent Desmond Tighe wrote: 'Having broken down Italian resistance in 26 hours, cheering Australians hauled down the Italian flag in the town centre and hoisted instead an Anzac hat.'[20] The port was virtually undamaged and soon supplies were being unloaded. Churchill required Tobruk's port for further advances, as it could replace Alexandria as the forward supply base. Seeking to take all of Cyrenaica before troops were needed in Greece, the thrust continued towards Benghazi. The armour moved through the inland via Mechilli, while two Australian Brigades moved along the coast road, first to Derna, and a third remained in Tobruk.

Shortly after Tobruk had fallen Mosenson found himself wandering through its ruins. 'Tobruk had a large Jewish community,' he wrote to his wife, 'and now we are living in its ruins.' His fellow Jewish soldiers found and cleaned the ruined Synagogue, writing on its walls, 'This synagogue was polluted by war and was cleansed and purified by Jewish soldiers from Palestine serving in the Jewish Transport Corps.'[21]

Mosenson's encounters with the Anzac soldiers seemed to be a repeat of the encounters between the two groups of soldiers during the First World War. Shortly later he recalled an incident in a shelter where, he wrote to his wife 'Some Australians were gathered ... as well as some enemy prisoners and English and Scottish boys. When ... the Australians noticed the Star of David that I was wearing on my helmet, they welcomed me noisily, drew out their bottles of liquor and we drank together to Palestine and to Australia.'[22]

'I am an old friend of the Australians here,' he wrote again later, 'and I am making use of the opportunity to talk about our cause with them. Some of them have been in Palestine and speak of it with fondness. Their direct personal encounter with things there conquered them completely ... Any request for help is always responded to generously ... For example, one of our boys was driving an old, broken-down machine and the Australians offered him one of theirs instead ... That's how they are.' [23]

---

18   Holt, B. *From Ingleburn to Aitape*, p. 54.
19   Churchill, Winston. S. *Their Finest Hour*, p. 616
20   *The Palestine Post*. 24 January 1941, p. 1.
21   Mosenson, M. *Letters From The Desert*, p. 26.
22   Ibid., p. 37.
23   Ibid., pp. 45-6.

Cyrenaica Captured

Wavell had been informed by the Chiefs-of-Staff that German forces were massing in Romania for a move against Greece, and that after the capture of Tobruk, the Libyan campaign was to take second place while every effort must be made to support Greece.[24] But when it became clear that Greece was unwilling to have British troops unless there could be 'sufficient numbers to act offensively', the plans were modified and it was agreed that the offensive in North Africa could continue, the next objective being Benghazi.

So the advance along the *Via Balbia* continued, and Derna fell to the Australians after some intense fighting on 30 January. The British armoured units moved through the interior while the Australians moved along the coast road towards Benghazi. O'Connor planned to trap the Italians if and when they moved around the bottom of the Gulf of Sirte towards Tripolitania.

The goal was achieved. Benghazi was entered on 6 February by the 6th Australian Division. And the 7th Armoured Division also achieved its goals to the south by reaching the coast and cutting off most of the Italian army, which finally surrendered on 7 February. Cyrenaica had been captured. In ten weeks the British-Indian-Anzac force had covered about eight hundred kilometres, destroyed ten Italian divisions and captured 130,000 prisoners. They lost 476 killed, 1,225 wounded and 43 missing.[25]

Although excited at the progress of the 6th Division the men of the 7th and 9th Divisions and the New Zealanders were beginning to wonder if they would ever see action. Thomas Derrick wrote in his diary in early February: 'Seen in the local rag the fall of Derna. Doesn't look like us getting a go at the ding. Cyrene also taken.' Following the fall of Benghazi he wrote: 'When will we get a move? Been wondering if we are going to help at all.'[26]

Hitler was about to change that situation. This Italian setback, alongside that in Greece, so concerned Hitler, that he decided to aid his beleaguered Italian ally. Hitler's Directive No 22 of 11 January 1941 was followed by the arrival on 12 February of the first German troops at Tripoli, capital of Libya. Irwin Rommel, the commander of this force, henceforth known as *Afrika Korps,* was instructed to maintain a defensive position.

The Jewish Connection

The Jewish people of Eretz Israel were keeping abreast of the events in Libya. The Hebrew and English language newspapers provided comprehensive coverage

---

24 Churchill to Wavell, 10 January 1941. In Churchill W. *The Grand Alliance,* pp. 18-19.

25 Barnett, Correlli. *The Desert Generals.* Pan Books, (London), p. 67.

26 *Diary of Thomas Derrick,* Farquhar, p. 41.

whenever news came to hand. 'Palestinian troops were among those who first entered Bardia and Tobruk, fighting with the Australians' the *Palestine Post* reported on 27 January, 'and they have been mentioned by the Commander-in-Chief.'[27] Some time later the *Vaad Leumi* (National Council) sent a message to the Chief Rabbis of the Jewish communities in Libya, stating:

> It was with unbounded joy that we heard the good news that, by the will of God, the forces of Great Britain had entered the gates of your land and entered your cities victoriously...
>
> Among the victorious British forces are many young Jews, especially in the Palestine units, who will no doubt welcome the opportunity of meeting their Jewish brethren in your towns. We would ask you to proffer them your friendship.
>
> We once more congratulate you on securing your salvation and liberation through the action of the British Army, and trust that the ties between us will never be severed.'[28]

Moses Mosenson was always on the lookout for these Jewish communities. While in Benghazi, he entered the Jewish quarter, and was immediately swamped. '... crowds of Jews' he wrote, 'saw the Star of David on the car and grew so excited that they rushed to kiss my hands.' He later met the rabbi, whom Mosenson told, 'we were a Jewish unit from Palestine stationed for some time in a certain city ... that had been abandoned by its inhabitants. I told him that we had found the synagogue there and that we had cleansed it and had worshipped there on one Sabbath Eve ... Tears of joy came to his eyes.' Mosenson was later introduced to some of the Jewish people who had fled 'that city'.

That evening he was enjoying a quiet Sabbath meal with the Ben-Dusa family, when some unwelcome Australian soldiers turned up. Mosenson attempted to get them to leave, but they remained obstinate, and refused to believe that he was a Jewish soldier from *Palestine*. 'Listen boy' one of the soldiers said, 'all of us were in Palestine and we like Jews. But a little while ago they had a big celebration here. They sang and drank and invited us too. We want to join you tonight ...' It appeared that indeed the soldiers had been present several days before, helping to celebrate the festival of *Purim*, a time of much rejoicing, and remembering the deliverance of the Jewish people from destruction while in captivity during Persian times. 'Finally', Mosenson continued, 'I persuaded them to leave and we continued singing our Sabbath hymns'.[29]

Another visitor to the region during this period was the Prime Minister of Australia, Robert Menzies, who was en-route to London for discussions with the British Government and War Cabinet. He toured the Land of Israel between 3-5 February, and was accorded a very warm welcome. Menzies gave a public interview, and said:

27 *The Palestine Post.* 27 January 1941, p. 4.
28 Quoted in *The Palestine Post.* 19 February 1941, p. 3.
29 Mosenson. M. *Letters From The Desert,* p. 42.

Australia has a very great interest in Palestine ... Wherever I have gone in the past 24 hours I have come across groups of Australian soldiers.

Palestine is in a strategic position that makes it quite important for us: it is on our line of communications. I have watched with great interest the work being done here in land reclamation and settlement ... Large tracts of country had been reclaimed from swamps. There were great fields of crops which only 20 years ago had been malarial marshes.' [30]

Menzies description of Eretz Israel as being of strategic importance due to its being on Australia's line of communication, may not have been understood by the ordinary soldier, but the politicians well understood this vital principle. This was a key element in the power struggle now engulfing the Eastern Mediterranean region.

Greece and Turkey

Wavell and his staff began planning for a quick advance into Tripolitania, and the prize of Tripoli. Yet Churchill and the Chiefs-of-Staff had other ideas. Britain was ever conscious of the needs of Greece and Turkey. Both of these countries were in danger. If they accepted British support, they could provoke a German reaction. Yet they knew what Germany intended to do. So if British support was forthcoming it had to be sufficiently large to stop a major German attack.

A quick German advance and victory in Greece would have grave consequences within the region of the Eastern Mediterranean. They could quickly subdue Crete, and with Vichy connivance, land a force in Syria, from where they could move eastwards into Iraq and Persia (and take the large oil fields) and onto India; or they could move south from Syria, into British *Palestine* and link up with the Axis forces moving across the North African coastline towards the Suez Canal. With such scenarios in mind the British Cabinet sent Foreign Secretary Anthony Eden to the Middle East to determine the best plan of operation. He was to determine how best to garrison Cyrenaica, defend Egypt and the Land of Israel, and be able to send adequate support to Greece in the first instance, and Turkey and Yugoslavia in the second. [31]

Eden and the experts in the Middle East suggested leaving one Australian division and Indian brigade in Cyrenaica, and taking one British armoured brigade, the New Zealand Division and the 6th Australian Division initially to Greece to be followed by other troops, including the 7th Australian Division. Eden, Wavell and other high officials then flew to Greece and met the King and Prime Minister of Greece on 22 February. After deliberations, the Greeks agreed to accept the offer of British help. The British Cabinet, with Menzies in attendance, agreed to accept the formula

---

30   *The Palestine Post* 4 February 1941, p. 1.

31   Instructions of Churchill to Eden, dated 12 February 1941. Churchill, W. *The Grand Alliance*, Houghton and Mifflin, (Boston, 1949), pp. 66-67.

worked out between Eden and the Greek Government on 24 February. Yet Menzies was somewhat apprehensive about the Greek enterprise.[32] So too were Blamey and Freyberg who had not even been informed of the impending campaign. Blamey wrote to Menzies on March 5th stating his objections and misgivings. 'Past experience has shown me,' he wrote, 'to look with misgiving on a situation where British leaders have control of considerable bodies of first-class Dominion troops, while Dominion commanders are excluded from all responsibility in control, planning and policy.'[33]

Command of the force nevertheless was given to the Briton, Lieut.-General Sir Henry Maitland Wilson. The Australian 6th Division was commanded by Iven Mackay, and the Australian and New Zealand forces, known as 1 Australia Corps were commanded by Blamey. Later in Greece, Blamey changed the name to *Anzac Corps*. It was intended that these forces would unite with a combined Balkan front, comprising Greece, Yugoslavia and Turkey against the impending German attack.

The task of transporting the expeditionary force across the Mediterranean fell upon the shoulders of Admiral Cunningham, who well appreciated the risks of transporting such a large amount of men and equipment across the Mediterranean. Churchill and the other leaders also realized the slight risk they were taking in removing the bulk of the Army of the Nile. He therefore at this juncture encouraged General Smuts, the South African leader, who was about to visit Egypt, to agree to the transfer to Egypt of the South African Division, which had been involved in the operations against the Italians in East Africa.[34]

It was essential during this period that the Germans have little idea of what the British and Greeks were planning, and that Yugoslavia join the Allied plan. But how to inform the Yugoslavs, while keeping Germany unaware, was a major challenge. If there was no common front, it was strongly feared that the German forces could quickly occupy Greece and Yugoslavia, subdue Turkey - and then be in a very strong position to hinder Britain's position in the Eastern Mediterranean.

The German Army moved into Bulgaria on 1 March - bringing invasion closer to the borders of Greece. In the following days it became clear to the British commanders that the Greek situation was not positive. The previous agreements had not been carried out, and an air of desperation overcame some of their leaders. Eden was forced to admit to Churchill on 5 March: 'our forces, including Dominions contingents, will be engaged in an operation more hazardous than it seemed a week ago. You will no doubt decide', he continued, 'on any communications to be made to the Dominions Governments.'[35]

The failure of Greece to live up to some of their commitments caused Churchill

32   Laffin, J. *Greece, Crete and Syria*. Time-Life Books. Australia. (Sydney, 1989), p. 17.
33   Laffin , J. ibid., p. 18.
34   Churchill to Smuts, 28 February 1941. Churchill, W. *The Grand Alliance*, p. 96.
35   Eden and C.I.G.S. to Churchill, 5 March 1941. Churchill, W. *The Grand Alliance*, p. 99.

to write to Eden: 'Grave Imperial issues are raised by committing New Zealand and Australian troops to an enterprise, which, you say, has become even more hazardous. We are bound to lay before the Dominion Governments your and Chiefs of Staff appreciation. Cannot forecast their assent to operation.'[36] Yet thoughts of abandoning the operation were quickly challenged by senior British officials, who maintained that it would be unwise for Britain to be seen reneging on her commitments. The Greek position then began to improve and it seemed obvious that she was willing to 'fight to the death', therefore any British help, limited as it may be, was essential. Despite the improvement, Churchill still wrote to Eden, now in Cairo, on 7 March, that the New Zealand and Australian Governments were to be informed that the campaign was going ahead as the senior British commanders believed there was a reasonable fighting chance of success.[37]

The Cabinet met on that same day and agreed to proceed with the planned operation, and in so doing accepting 'for itself the fullest responsibilities.' The Australian and New Zealand Governments agreed to the sending of their men. Churchill wrote to the New Zealand Prime Minister: 'We are deeply moved by your reply, which, whatever the fortunes of war may be, will shine in the history of New Zealand and be admired by future generations of free men in every quarter of the globe.'[38]

As the New Zealand Division, the 6th Australian Division and the 1st British Armoured Brigade prepared to move out, the 7th British Armoured Division moved back to Egypt for rest and the 7th and 9th Australian Divisions began moving westwards, to complete their training and act as a garrison force. '... we passed convoys carrying battalions of the Seventh and Ninth Divisions and we chiaked one another unmercifully.' Holt wrote about his journey eastwards from Libya back to Egypt. '... we exchanged the usual ribald remarks and we certainly gave them the business ... "We've won the war and you ... are just arriving"... "You're all travelling the wrong way - the war is this way."'[39] Within a short time though the war would be both this way and that as all four Anzac Divisions and the British Armoured Divisions found themselves battling against a new and more formidable foe - the armies of the German Reich.

---

36 Churchill to Eden, 6 March 1941. Churchill, W. *The Grand Alliance,* pp. 101-102.
37 Churchill to Eden, 7 March 1941. Churchill, W. *The Grand Alliance,* pp. 104-105.
38 Churchill to Savage, 12 March 1941. Churchill, W. *The Grand Alliance,* p. 108.
39 Holt, B. *From Ingleburn to Aitape,* p. 76-77.

Chapter 23

Germany's Quest: Greece and Tobruk

Move to Greece

The decision to move to Greece was based upon there being a stable situation in North Africa, which the capture of Cyrenaica had virtually ensured. The initial BEF forces began disembarking in Greece on 3 March 1941. New Zealander Westbrook wrote ' ... the people [in Athens] gave us a marvellous reception cheering and clapping throughout the short journey to the camp. Most of us went AWOL [Absent With Out Leave] that night into the city and we were literally besieged. Everyone was wanting to take us out, shout us drinks.'[1] 'New Zealand Maoris, smiling in their battle-dress and wearing tin hats, stepping jauntily', wrote Desmond Tighe(the Reuters correspondent with the BEF in Greece), 'seemed to make a special appeal to the crowds ... They caused lusty cheers - and people rushed alongside giving the "Thumbs Up" sign.'[2] The Australian 6th Division, arrived in mid-March.

Adjustments were now made to the original agreement. The majority of the Greek forces were stationed on the Albanian front. Another front, the Metaxas Line ran north of Thessaloniki (Salonika) from the coast through to the Bulgarian border to stop the German advance coming through Bulgaria. South of Thessaloniki ran a third line, manned by the New Zealand, Australian, British as well as Greek forces, from the coast, along the Aliakmon River, then northward through Veria (Berea of the Bible), Edessa, to the Yugoslav border, and then along to Florina, which lay just south of the Monastir Gap, the passageway leading from Yugoslavia into Greece.

Wilson, Blamey, and Freyberg realized the improbability of their undermanned and ill-equipped forces withstanding a numerically stronger and well equipped enemy. Other lines of defence were determined to which there could be an orderly withdrawal if needed.

The British Armoured Division reached the forward area, near the Yugoslav border on 27 March, followed by the New Zealanders, and then the Australians. Holt, describing the move northwards, wrote: 'We got off the trucks and marched into the

---

1   King, M. *New Zealanders at War*, p. 171.
2   *The Palestine Post*. 9 April 1941, p. 4.

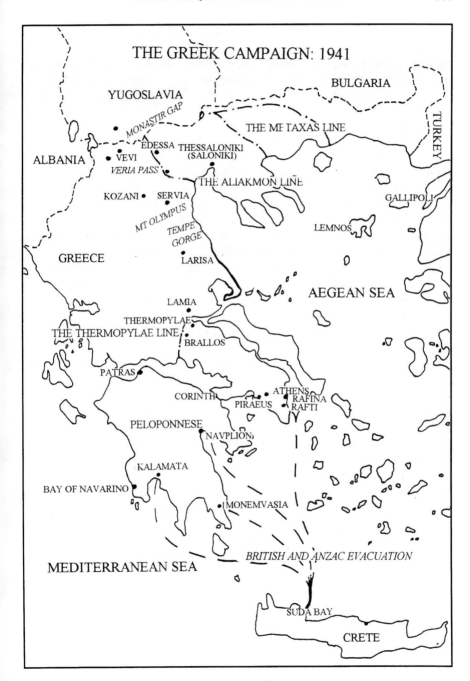

THE GREEK CAMPAIGN: 1941

BULGARIA

YUGOSLAVIA

MONASTIR GAP

THE METAXAS LINE

TURKEY

EDESSA

THESSALONIKI
(SALONIKI)

ALBANIA

VEVI

VERIA PASS

THE ALIAKMON LINE

KOZANI

SERVIA

GALLIPOLI

MT OLYMPUS

*TEMPE
GORGE*

LEMNOS

GREECE

LARISA

AEGEAN SEA

LAMIA

THERMOPYLAE

THE THERMOPYLAE LINE

BRALLOS

PATRAS

ATHENS
RAFINA
RAFTI

CORINTH

PIRAEUS

PELOPONNESE

NAVPLION

KALAMATA

BAY OF NAVARINO

MONEMVASIA

BRITISH AND ANZAC EVACUATION

MEDITERRANEAN SEA

SUDA BAY

CRETE

mountains. We eventually reached our positions and dug ourselves in at a forward defence location overlooking a small white village in Yugoslavia. It was bitterly cold,' he recalled, 'and to say the least of it, we were uncomfortable.'[3] While Holt and company were suffering the cold, matters heated up in the desert of Libya.

Enter Rommel

In North Africa Wavell and Dill inspected their positions in Cyrenaica, and realized the need to strengthen El Agheila on the border between the Libyan provinces of Tripolitania and Cyrenaica. If El Agheila was lost, there was nothing stopping the German advance to Benghazi, or via the inland route, to Tobruk - and then onto Egypt. Having committed the bulk of the army to Greece, Churchill was eager at this point to obtain additional troops, and encouraged Wavell to request Smuts to send a brigade of the South African Division.[4] The Indian Divisions meanwhile were fighting well in the Abyssinia region against the Italians.

The 9th Australian Division continued its westward journey. On 17 March they journeyed up the escarpment separating Egypt from Libya, and between the towns of Sollum and Fort Capuzzo. Derrick wrote: 'Have never seen so much destruction ... passed through Capuzzo and again we see ruins and hundreds more "ding" tanks, lorries, shells, LMG's, AkAks, heavy guns and crashed planes, some of which were destroyed on the ground.'[5]

Sensing the growing weakness of the Allied position, Rommel flew to Berlin on 19 March to obtain Hitler's permission to launch a bold thrust into Cyrenaica. He left somewhat disappointed. Hitler informed him to limit his activities to a strike against El Agheila. The reason: large numbers of German troops and equipment were earmarked for the conquest of Greece and Yugoslavia. Hitler wanted to ensure the safety of the southern flank of Europe before embarking upon his main goal - the conquest of Russia. The Germans did not want a repeat of 1915-1918 when Allied forces held down considerable Central Powers forces along the Salonika front.

Rommel finally struck out on 24 March and quickly ejected the British armoured force from El Agheila. The British were soon retiring towards Benghazi. Sensing the disorganization of the British-led force, Rommel regrouped and then on 2 April his forces struck north in pursuit. On the same day, on the other side of Cyrenaica, across the Jebel Akhdar mountains, Derrick's unit at Derna was playing cricket against an English anti-aircraft unit, quite oblivious to the events further south-west. Although top scoring with twelve runs, he confessed, 'I'm no Bradman.'[6]

The *Afrika Korps*, strongly outnumbering the British armoured forces, was soon

---

3   Holt, B. *From Ingleburn to Aitape*, p. 93.
4   Churchill to Wavell, 26 March 1941. Churchill, W. *The Grand Alliance*, p. 202.
5   *Diary of Thomas Derrick.*, Farquhar, M. p. 48.
6   *Diary of Thomas Derrick*, Farquhar, M. p. 52.

knocking at the doors of Benghazi. They also sped through the two desert roads, skirting the Jebel Akhdar range, heading for the key inland position of Mechilli, and from there to Derna and Tobruk, where one Australian Brigade was busily entrenching itself and consolidating the former Italian defences. Wavell had no choice but to order withdrawal from Benghazi on 4 April, before his British and Australian troops were cut off by the fast moving German armoured forces. He also postponed the movement of the Australian 7th Division to Greece, and ordered them to move to Mersa Matruh in readiness. Other British and Australian units east of Benghazi were commanded to dig in and await the expected German assault.

All Eyes on Tobruk

Matters grew even worse after the British commander General O'Connor was captured on 6 April. After Benghazi was evacuated it was a race against time - the German-Italian forces taking both the coastal and inland routes towards their next objective - Tobruk, the last strongly defensible position in Cyrenaica. The importance of this port is emphasized by Churchill in a memo to Wavell on 7 April:

> You should surely be able to hold Tobruk ... at least until or unless the enemy brings up strong artillery forces. It seems difficult to believe that he can do this for some weeks ... Tobruk, therefore, seems to be a place to be held to the death without thought of retirement.[7]

Tobruk was the only port of significance for 1,600 kilometres between Tripoli and Alexandria. Any army moving either west or east, needed Tobruk. Tobruk was the key position holding up a possible German thrust to Alexandria, the Suez Canal, and beyond - to the Land of Israel.

Thomas Derrick recorded on 7 April: 'Awakened 0130 hours, all the company out of Derna by 0230, taken by truck to Tobruk and lost rest of coy. Dug in and slept in a terrible dust storm. Everyone has been evacuated from Derna and valuable items blown up. Jerry attacking at Barce about 100 miles from Derna, and seems to be making the pace a cracker.'[8] It was a race against time, and against overwhelming German armour. All serviceable vehicles were put into use.

A regiment from the 7th Australian Division reached Tobruk on 8 April. Wavell went there on 8 April, and instructed Major-General John Lavarack, commander of the 7th Australian Division, 'Your main task will be to hold the enemy's advance at Tobruk, in order to give time for the assembly of reinforcements, especially of armoured troops, for the defence of Egypt.'[9] Only two undermanned infantry divisions, the 7th Australian and 6th British stood between Tobruk and the Suez

---

7   Churchill to Wavell, 7 April 1941. Churchill, W. *The Grand Alliance*, p. 207.

8   *Diary of Thomas Derrick*, Farquhar, M. p. 59.

9   Badman, Peter. *North Africa 1940-1942. The Desert War*. Time-Life Books. (Sydney, 1988.), p. 91.

Canal. By 9 April men of the other 9th Australian Division brigades made their way into Tobruk.

On that day, *Passover* eve, Mosenson managed to write a brief letter to his wife. 'It is hard for us,' he confessed, 'living in caves and hiding in rocks, with hellish noises raining down from above, to write now. I will write you at length if things get a little more comfortable.' [10] And that was how the Jewish soldiers spent *Passover* in Libya.

The fast moving Axis forces kept relentlessly moving towards the Egyptian frontier, capturing Bardia on 12 April, and also encircling Tobruk with its beleaguered force. If Tobruk could be quickly overrun, Rommel's forces would be able to hastily move into Egypt. With only a basic garrison force holding Egypt, the chances of taking Egypt were strong indeed. The Axis forces continued their eastward movement. But while Tobruk held out, Rommel's thrust would be thwarted. 'Siege operations' wrote former *Rat of Tobruk* Alec Hill, 'were the last thing that Rommel wanted as he raced to the Egyptian frontier with visions of Cairo and the Suez Canal.'[11]

The first major German assault on Tobruk began on 11 April - Good Friday, and continued for several days. It was a severely fought action, in which the first Australian Victoria Cross of the Second World War was gained by Jack Edmondson. Rommel, anticipating an easy victory, was frustrated after his famed *Panzer* tanks and German infantry made no headway against the mostly Australian defenders. The 9th Australian Division men were determined to hold on to what the 6th Australian Division had gained several months before. Following the initial battle Lavarack returned to Mersa Matruh and handed command over to Major-General Morshead.

After the initial onslaught had ended, Mosenson found some time on 13 April to write to his wife, and described how the Jewish soldiers made attempts to extricate Jewish people from the towns in Cyrenaica. That the majority remained under German-Italian control thereafter disturbed the Jewish soldiers of Eretz Israel.

The Germans invade Greece

While the battle raged in and around Tobruk, the Germans, numbering some 200,000 men, as well as heavy armour and an Air Force ten times larger than that of the Allies, began simultaneously attacking Greece and Yugoslavia on 6 April. Facing them were some 58,000 British, New Zealand and Australian soldiers, plus the ill-equipped Greek Army. The Allied position was quickly imperilled by the German *blitzkrieg* tactics, as well as by their aerial superiority. German aircraft bombed Piraeus harbour, destroying much valuable ammunition and supplies and greatly hindering the off-loading of supplies.

10   Mosenson, M. *Letters from the Desert*, p. 50.
11   Hill, A. *Tobruk*. In *Journal of the Australian War Memorial*. No 18, April 1991, p. 44.

After several days of intensive fighting along the Metaxas Line, German troops overwhelmed the Greeks and triumphantly entered Thessaloniki on 9 April. It was a dark day for the very large Jewish population of this city - several years later most were rounded up and sent to their deaths at Auschwitz concentration camp. The Allied troops on the eastern flank then began a calculated withdrawal south.

Meanwhile the main objective was to withhold the German army from moving from Yugoslavia. But following decisive victories against the Yugoslavs, the heavily armoured German columns moved into Greece on 10 April through the Monastair Gap, and followed the retreating Allied forces southwards.

On that same day it was announced that due to Rommel's decisive victories in North Africa, no reinforcements would arrive. It was at this critical period, on 12 April that Blamey sent out this message: 'As from 1800 hours 12 April, 1 Australia Corps will be designated Anzac Corps. In making this announcement the GOC Anzac Corps desires to say that the reunion of the Australian and New Zealand Divisions gives all ranks the greatest uplift. The task ahead, though difficult, is not nearly so desperate as that which our fathers faced in April 26 years ago. We go to it together with stout hearts and certainty of success.'[12]

Despite Blamey's optimism, matters grew progressively worse. Also on that same day the Greek Army in Albania began retreating, which in turn further weakened the morale of the Greek Macedonian Army. There was no choice but for General Wilson to order a general withdrawal to the next line at Thermopylae. Such a move was not so easy, considering the amount of transport heading south, the swiftness of the approaching German troops and the superiority of the *Luftwaffe* which strafed the roads. 'We travelled through the mountains' recalled Holt, 'and over the narrow winding roads. The trucks were bumper to bumper. Hold-ups were common as the truck drivers were very tired and very often went to sleep at the wheel.'[13]
New Zealander Westbrook recalled of the time:

> ... we suffered the worst machine gunning we have ever had. Twelve Messerschmitt 110s appeared very suddenly and strafed us for about half an hour and I think that that was the most scared I'd ever been. Lying face down in a outfield, the only thing that I could do to pass the time away was to try and drown the ants with the perspiration that was streaming off my nose.'[14]

Yugoslavia surrendered on 17 April, forcing further pressure upon the Greek and Allied forces defending Greece. The Chiefs-of-Staff had now to contemplate these new developments in Greece with the overall situation in the Mediterranean. Accordingly, on 18 April they released a communiqué to the Commanders-in-Chief,

---

12 Laffin, J. *Greece, Crete and Syria*, pp. 26-30.
13 Holt, B. *From Ingleburn to Aitape*, p. 96.
14 King, M. *New Zealanders at War*, p. 171.

concluding that the evacuation of Greece took second priority over victory in Libya.[15] This assessment would soon change.

The Allied troops continued their painstaking withdrawal south to the next defensible line at Thermopylae, which was reached and maintained on 20 April. Many of the troops had no choice but to foot slog it over the mountains, holding up the German advance wherever they could. Although staring a military impossibility in the face, Churchill was not willing to order withdrawal. To him, every day they could hold out at Thermopylae, and thereby hinder the German advance and defeat of Greece, the less chance Germany had of sending troops and aid to Iraq for their uprising against Britain.

The Jewish Response

The Jewish community of British *Palestine* had a vested interest in the Greek campaign. Several thousand Jewish personnel were attached to the RAF, as well as bomb-clearers, and 'diggers' with the Royal Engineers, the Service Corps and the Pioneer Corps. The Pioneers had to clear roads, and make them ready for supplies and transport. In one spate of fighting a Jewish unit was surrounded and in a desperate plight. 'A squad of Australians came to their assistance,' wrote the Reuters correspondent, 'and together the two units retreated, firing until their ammunition was exhausted. Only a few escaped.'[16]

The proximity of German forces in Libya, Greece and Yugoslavia concerned the Jewish people even more and began to create alarm in Eretz Israel. *The Palestine Post* on 8 April asked the question 'whether these dramatic developments are not bound greatly to influence our lives. This country has not only been free from attack - with the exception of air raids on our coastal towns and the inevitable toll of life - it has also escaped to a large and gratifying measure, the rigours of war time economy restrictions.' The paper's assessment concluded: '*That we should not have been obliged to modify our way of life is a tribute to the forces of the British Empire.*'[17]

Such alarm increased once news of German actions and atrocities in the newly conquered areas became public. A very sobering analysis was provided by the Editorial of *The Palestine Post* on 24 April:

> The Nazi juggernaut has driven over another corner of Europe, and in the wake of the mechanized battalions and serried divisions a mob of Gestapo jackals are already at their hideous work. As usual, it is the Jewish communities of the occupied territories which are singled out as the first victims. In all the occupied Balkan countries anti-

---

15   Chiefs of Staff to Commanders-in-Chief , 18 April 1941. Churchill, W. *The Grand Alliance*, p. 227.

16   *The Palestine Post*. 11 May 1941, p. 3.

17 *The Palestine Post*. 8 April 1941, p. 4. Italics mine.

Jewish legislation on the approved Nazi model is being introduced ... No military success, no gloating conquest can quench the Nazi hatred of the Jew.'[18]

Such sobering sentiments exacerbated the efforts of the Jewish leadership to increase enlistment in the British Army. Yitzak Ben Zvi speaking at an enlistment rally proclaimed that the front line for the Jewish people of Eretz Israel stretched from the Balkans to Benghazi. He also stated that there were over 8,000 Jewish soldiers serving on all fronts.[19] There was obvious concern for the two to three thousand Jewish personnel from Eretz Israel now serving in Greece.

Orders to Evacuate

The Greek King informed Wavell on 20 April that the Greek Army could make no sustained defence before the next German assault. The Greek Commander-in-Chief, General Papagos, realizing that disaster was facing his country, recommended to Wilson on 21 April that the BEF evacuate Greece, and save both the country and the Allied force from further destruction. Wavell had no choice but to order evacuation. The evacuation of over 50,000 New Zealand, Australian and British troops was to be a much more complicated affair than at Dunkirk. The Germans held complete dominance in the air, and the troops had to be transported a much longer distance. It was decided to get the troops as far south as possible, out of German air-range, and to embark them at night onto British and Australian warships which would then take the majority to Crete - enabling the ships to quickly turn around and move back again.

While strong rear-guards held the positions at Thermopylae and nearby Brallos, the bulk of the Allied army made its way south, to beaches near Athens, especially Rafina, but mostly to the south of the Peleponnese Peninsular, and the beaches of Kalamata, Navplion and Monemvasia. The evacuation began on 24 April - the day that Greece surrendered to Germany. On that day 26 years before, Anzac and British troops prepared to storm the beaches of Gallipoli, only several hundred kilometres away across the Aegean Sea. Now, on 24 April 1941, strong German forces attacked the Thermopylae line and were countered by the New Zealanders and Australians who were in the process of withdrawing. The Commonwealth soldiers now had to go it alone - there would be no official Greek support.

It was essential to maintain the bridge over the Corinth Canal until the last of the rear guards had crossed over to the Peleponnese. But the Germans dropped some 1,500 paratroopers near Corinth, and although the BEF soldiers managed to destroy the bridge, thus rendering it inoperable for the Germans, still some 921 exhausted Anzac soldiers were cut off and captured.

---

18   *T he Palestine Post.* 24 April 1941, p. 4.
19   *The Palestine Post.* 10 April 1941, p. 1.

On Anzac Day 1941 a combined New Zealand, Australian and British unit maintained the last rearguard, near the ancient town of Thebes, some 50 kilometres north-west of Athens. General Wilson flew out on 26 April while General Freyberg remained behind, refusing to leave while New Zealanders were still present. The evacuation was a difficult task as the German planes sank numerous ships, with much loss of life. Yet the majority of the troops managed to escape. At sea the various evacuation vessels joined up as a convoy, and headed south.

All the while it was a race against time for the rear-guards. They had the difficult task of hindering the movement of the German troops then making a hasty retreat to the next defensive position. Yet some 21,000 Allied troops managed to embark during the night of 27 April. The majority of those remaining behind, some 8,000, were at Kalamata and they would have to be embarked on 28 April. By this time however the Germans had crossed over into the Peleponnese from different directions and were quickly converging upon this southerly port. New Zealander Dennis Brickwell recalls his feelings of despondency when the Germans surrounded Kalamata and informed them of their unconditional surrender. He wrote:

> There were a few moments of stunned silence - nobody could realize the full significance of the words 'Give in' ... How we cursed the Navy, the lack of Air Force, and everything to do with the British Army. Some of us discussed the possibility of making a break for it ... and some did go into the hills, and a few found boats - the rest of us, resigned to the inevitable, dispersed along the beach ... threw ourselves down fully dressed, and slept the sleep of utter exhaustion.[20]

Several heavy skirmishes occurred against the approaching German forces, and these aided the withdrawal of more Allied troops. However on 28 April the Allied ships had to withdraw as it was feared the Italian Fleet was approaching. The remaining troops had no choice but to surrender, although many chose to flee, and eventually 1,400 managed to return to their own lines.

General Blamey's prediction proved true - it was a military failure. The casualties suffered were high. The New Zealanders lost 291 killed, 599 wounded and 1,614 captured. The Australians lost 320 killed, 494 wounded and 2,030 captured while the British suffered 256 killed, 132 wounded and an enormous 6,708 captured. Yet the presence of the BEF left an indelible mark upon the hearts and minds of most of the Greek people. Many thereafter risked their lives to assist New Zealand, Australian and British soldiers in their efforts to escape.

Sabas Stefanidis hid twelve New Zealanders in a secret place near Salonika. When he realized the Germans were closing in, he quickly sent them away into the hills. He was then arrested, and should have been executed for sheltering them. When the German judge asked why he sheltered New Zealand soldiers, he replied, 'I was hiding

---

20   King, M. *New Zealanders at War*, p. 194.

people whose lives were in danger and if your life was in danger I would hide you too, for I am a Christian.' The German judge released him. After the war one of the New Zealanders returned and married Sabas' daughter.[21]

The campaign did however slow down, albeit briefly, the *blitzkrieg* German offensive into Greece, thereby permitting time and space for squashing other Axis plans within the region. Neutral countries around the world were also impressed that Britain came to the aid of a weak defenceless country. One neutral country in particular, the USA, was impressed, and soon afterwards voted to send aid to Britain via the *Lend-Lease Bill*.

All efforts aimed at hindering the movement of German troops southward towards the Suez Canal were positive as far as the Jewish people in Eretz Israel were concerned. They knew only too well the character of the Nazi German regime. The same fate which befell the large Jewish community in Greece, and on the island of Rhodes which was closer still, death in the concentration camps, would most likely befall them if the Germans invaded. Under the title *Preparedness*, the *Palestine Post* Editorial said on 29 April: 'The progress of the struggle for the Eastern Mediterranean calls for a high degree of preparedness. The Hebrew press of this country has during the last few days been urging a sharper reaction to currents events.'[22]

Yet, despite the necessity of preparedness resulting from this latest German victory, and the resultant signs of panic, there was still one ray of sunshine: Tobruk. Speaking of the German thrust in North Africa, the *Palestine Post* wrote on 28 April:

> While Tobruk holds out - and with the Royal Navy in control it is easily reinforceable from the sea - the attacking army is in no position to concentrate its forces against the defence of Egypt proper.'[23]

Following the devastating defeat in Greece, the name of Tobruk now become synonymous with Anzac and British valour, and also with the security of the Jewish *Yishuv* in the Land of Israel.

---

21 Story related to the author by George Georgiadas, who was told it by Sabas Stefanidis.
22 *The Palestine Post*. 29 April 1941, p. 4.
23 *The Palestine Post*. 28 April 1941, p. 4.

Chapter 24

Germany Closes In: Crete and Iraq

Problems arise in Iraq

The German victories in Greece and North Africa further enhanced pro-Axis support within the Arab world. In April King Farouk of Egypt communicated with Hitler expressing his admiration for the Fuhrer and the Germans. He also stated that with the German Army poised at the gates of Egypt, the Egyptians were looking to the Germans as their liberators from the British.[1]

Matters also heated up in Iraq. Haj Amin sent another letter to Hitler in January 1941 in which he 'proposed a German-Arab alliance to achieve Arab independence, end the Jewish national home and solve "the Jewish question" on a joint basis.'[2] The following month, Haj Amin met with a number of prominent Iraqis 'to form a secret committee and break Iraq's close links with Britain.'[3] Support for Germany increased, especially within the Iraqi army. On 3 April 1941 the pro-German Rashid Ali led a *coup d'etat* and became Prime Minister. Soon afterwards the pro-British Regent, Emir Abdul Illa fled from Baghdad. 'The new Iraqi government,' wrote Bethell, 'took courage from the swift German conquests of Greece and Yugoslavia. Also, replying to the Mufti's letter, Germany recognized all Arab claims to independence and the common struggle against Britain and the Jews.'[4]

Churchill well understood the danger of this new situation. The introduction of German troops and equipment, once Greece was conquered, into both Iraq and perhaps Vichy Syria, would complete a cordon around the British possessions in the Middle East. It would be disastrous. Britain needed to act promptly to counteract this situation. Churchill duly informed the Secretary of State for India on 9 April 1941 to send troops from India to Basra.[5]

---

1   Sacher, H. *A History of Israel*, p. 228.
2   *Documents on German Foreign Policy*, Vol. XI, No 680. Quoted in Bethell, N. *The Palestine Triangle*, p. 105.
3   Hirszowicz, Lukasz. *The Third Reich and the Arab East*. Routledge and Kegan Paul, (London, 1966), p. 135. Quoted in Bethell, N. *The Palestine Triangle*, p. 105.
4   Bethell, N. *The Palestine Triangle*, p. 105.
5   Churchill to Secretary of State for India, 8 April 1941. Churchill, W. *The Grand Alliance*, p. 254.

The first British troops arrived on 18 April with more due to follow. Rashid Ali however refused permission for the entry of any new troops. He was being forced to take action against these British initiatives, playing for time while awaiting the arrival of German aircraft and airborne troops to come to his assistance. Anti-British sentiment increased, and all British civilians were evacuated from Baghdad to the nearby air base of Habbaniya. Iraqi troops, ultimately numbering some 9,000, began surrounding the air base on 13 April.

Britain was especially concerned to preserve both the oil pipeline which went from Iraq through to the Mediterranean, and the port base at Basra. To the British Government the maintenance of Iraq was vitally essential. Wavell however was not so sure. He was hard pressed on every side. Set backs in Cyrenaica, and Greece, coupled with unpromising situations in Crete and Syria had severely tested him. To add another campaign now was more than he could handle, and he expressed so in a letter to Churchill.[6]

General Claude Auchinleck, Commander-in-Chief in India, was forthcoming in sending troops from India. Wavell on the other hand was quite indignant, and felt that 'the prolongation of fighting in Iraq will seriously endanger the defence of Palestine and Egypt,' where he concluded there will be 'serious internal trouble.'[7]

London nevertheless ordered Wavell to inform Habbaniya that reinforcements were coming, and that the base had to be held at all costs. The Iraqi initiative had to be defeated before any German forces arrived. In fact Rashid Ali had only been awaiting their arrival before he began to attack British interests. The arrival of Indian troops at Basra however forced his hand before the German troops could arrive. The expected arrival of German troops had been delayed due to the rearguard action of the New Zealand, Australian and British forces in Greece.

Formation of the Palmach

The movement of the German Army into the region of the Eastern Mediterranean seriously disturbed the Jewish leadership in Eretz Israel, and in particular the *Hagana* High Command. They were concerned that with so many Jewish men now serving within the British Army away from the Land of Israel, there were none left behind who were adequately trained to withstand a German invasion. The Jewish population would be completely at the mercy of the German soldiers and Arab population.

The *Hagana* decided in May 1941 to form a special armed, mobile force to be commanded by Yitzhak Sadeh. The code name *Palmach* was adopted, an acronym for '*Shock Companies*'. According to Uzi Narkiss (later one of Israel's most famous

6 Wavell to Churchill. Churchill, W. *The Grand Alliance*, p. 256.
7 Churchill, W. *The Grand Alliance*, p. 256.

generals, and commander of the Jerusalem Brigade which captured Jerusalem in 1967), the purpose of the *Palmach* was '... to fight a guerrilla fight against the Germans.' Of such a concept, Narkiss continued, 'Everybody was naïve [including] the President, Mr. Ben Zvi our leader, who thought that a Jewish guerrilla army would be able to stop and fight the famous German Army, during the peak of its victories ... '

Referring to the odds facing them, Narkiss recalls how Sadeh 'talking with us said, "Hevreh - folks ... no problems. How many tanks do the Germans have - 500. How many Palmach people do we have - 1000. Every two Palmachnik people ... destroy one German tank with a Molotov cocktail and that's the end of the German Army." Either he was naïve,' Narkiss continues, 'or he had a fantastic sense of humour. But we related to this phenomena in the same way. Either we were very naïve or we had a sense of humour.'[8]

Renewed Attack on Tobruk

The Jewish soldiers serving on the front line in the British Army were now already facing this German threat. They well understood their role. Writing to his small daughter on Kibbutz Naan, Mosenson said, 'We are fighting the Germans; if we did not fight them here, far from home, we would have to fight them at home.'[9]

Rommel meanwhile would not be stopped, and soon afterwards was again on the offensive. Egypt awaited his forces - if only he could silence Tobruk. He renewed his attack on Tobruk on 29 April, which continued continuously until 5 May. It was a concentrated assault with Stuka dive bombers, and artillery. 'The Fritz Air Force seems to have things their own way;' Derrick wrote in his diary on 29 April, 'fear the worst and cannot hold much chance for our return home.'[10] The defenders could do little against the barrage, except where possible the British artillery retaliated. Although making ground, Rommel nevertheless lost scores of valuable tanks, and hundreds of men killed, captured or wounded. But the British and Australian defenders too sustained heavy casualties. 'Will never forget the bloody blue of May the first. My cobber Bill Grates (Hia) shot in the head with M.G. fire, died in a few minutes saying goodbye to his inseparable pal (Watha) who is in a pretty bad way about it.' The following day two more of Derrick's section died of wounds.[11]

Writing later of this battle Rommel confessed: 'The Australians fought with remarkable tenacity. Even their wounded went on defending themselves with small-arms fire, and stayed in the fight to their last breath. They were immensely big and

---

8   Conversation with General Narkiss, April 1997.
9   Mosenson, M. *Letters from the Desert*, p. 52.
10 *Diary of Thomas Derrick*, Farquhar, M., p. 68.
11 Ibid, Farquhar, M., p. 70.

powerful men, who without question represented an elite formation of the British Empire.'[12]

His second failure earned Rommel a reprimand from the German Supreme Command Mediterranean, while Morshead received congratulations from both Wavell and Churchill. The latter wrote: 'To General Morshead from Prime Minister England. The whole empire is watching your steadfast and spirited defence of this important outpost of Egypt with gratitude and admiration.'[13]

Rommel's situation was similar to that of Napoleon in 1799. Although Syria lay before him, (as Egypt did for Rommel), Napoleon could not proceed until Acre had been captured. Acre was a thorn in the flesh (as was Tobruk for Rommel), and for the sake of his pride, Acre, (like Tobruk), needed to be captured. 'It seems clear from the frequency with which Rommel mentioned Tobruk in his letters home,' wrote Foley, 'that the capture of the port became almost an obsession with him.'[14]

At this time the Mediterranean Fleet and the Royal Air Force took a leading role. Together they harassed and severely hampered the German supply line from Italy to Libya, as well as maintaining the supply line through to besieged Tobruk. The garrison at Malta also played a significant role, undergoing tremendous bombardments from the *Luftwaffe* - yet they did not yield. The garrison was admirably led by its governor, General Sir William Dobbie, the man who greatly assisted the Jewish people during the riots of 1929.

Destination - Crete

Most of the soldiers evacuated from Greece were taken to Crete. Crete was the last remaining strategic position in the central Mediterranean which could offer naval assistance to Malta, offer refuge to the Greek King and Government that had left Greece, and offer a staging post for a future re-conquest of Greece and the European mainland.

Crete had to be held at all costs. If lost, then not only would the Axis have a perfect launching pad to Egypt and North Africa, but also to British *Palestine* and Syria, and even beyond to Iraq. In these areas anti-British sentiment was being fostered by pro-German agitators. An anti-Allied uprising, coupled with a German attack in that region (simultaneous to a renewed German advance from Libya into Egypt) would have been disastrous. Wavell in a message to Churchill on 29 April actually stated that German plans for an invasion of Crete were a cover for an attack upon either Cyprus or Syria.[15]

Command for the defence of Crete was entrusted to General Freyberg. He soon realized the inadequacy of the troops at his disposal to withstand the type of attack

---

12   Quoted in Foley, J. *Tobruk Survives.* Purnell's History of the Second World War, Volume 2, Purnell & Sons Ltd, (Paulton, 1967), p. 624.

13   Badman, Peter. *North Africa 1940-1942. The Desert War,* p.100.

expected. Allied intelligence had determined that the Germans would assault Crete with a combined parachute and sea-borne force, the likes of which had never been known before. Complete German dominance in the air would greatly assist the anticipated German airborne assault. The German parachutists were regarded as the elite corps of the German army.

Freyberg duly informed both of his superiors, Wavell and the New Zealand Government, of his concerns for holding the island with the limited resources at his disposal. Freyberg's task was to prepare to defend the island from invasion at three main locations, Heraklion, Retimo and Canea. Of the three, Canea, the capital was the most strategically important, as the main airport Maleme, and the main port, Suda Bay, were close by. Preparations progressed through the early weeks of May. [16]

Concerns in Iraq and Syria

The Iraqi attack upon Habbaniya began on 2 May and fluctuated over the following ten days. The relief column from British *Palestine* meanwhile set out. It was a battle for time, and an 'audacious action now against the Iraqis,' Churchill wrote to Wavell, 'may crush the revolt before the Germans arrive.'[17] The small force at Habbaniya held out against the besieging force, and on numerous occasions actually went onto the offensive, either through infantry or the air force.

Also on 2 May Rashid Ali requested urgent armed assistance from Hitler. The German Embassy in Paris requested French permission on 3 May for German supply planes to land in Syria en-route to Iraq. By 6 May an agreement was reached between the Germans and Admiral Darlan, a Vichy French leader, whereby three-quarters of the war materials assembled in Syria by the *Italian Armistice Commission*, could be transported to Iraq. Landing rights were also given to the *Luftwaffe*. These instructions were relayed to General Dentz, the Vichy High Commissioner and Commander-in-Chief in Syria. German planes began landing in Syria on 9 May, and about 100 German and twenty Italian aircraft landed until the end of May.

The use of Syria for trans-shipment of German materials and men vexed Churchill and the Cabinet. They debated how best to counter this imminent danger, considering the few forces at Wavell's disposal. With the approval of the Defence Committee Churchill telegraphed Wavell on 9 May; 'You will no doubt realize the grievous danger of Syria being captured by a few thousand Germans transported by air.' He continued by stating that 'Admiral Darlan has probably made some bargain to help

14   Foley, J. *Tobruk Survives*, p. 624.
15   Wavell to Churchill, 29 April 1941. Churchill, W. *The Grand Alliance*, p. 272.
16   While the New Zealand Division prepared itself for battle, their Prime Minister, Peter Fraser arrived in Egypt on 17 May. He visited wounded New Zealand troops from the Greek campaign in Alexandria. While returning to Cairo shortly afterwards his car overturned and he was slightly injured.
17   Churchill to Wavell, 7 May 1941. Churchill, W. *The Grand Alliance*, p. 260.

the Germans get in there', and that if need be, the Free French may have to get involved.[18]

Wavell felt the Free French troops would be too inefficient and saw no choice but to take troops from Egypt. On 21 May he ordered the 7th Australian Division, less one brigade which was besieged at Tobruk, to return to British *Palestine* and regroup for a possible invasion of Syria. General Maitland Wilson was instructed to formulate plans for such an invasion.

The first German aircraft began arriving at the Mosul airfields in northern Iraq on 13 May. It was vital that Habbaniya be secured and Baghdad taken before the Germans came south. The advance guard coming from British *Palestine*, *Habforce* arrived on 18 May, and the following day they and elements of the Habbaniya force broke out and began pursuing the Iraqi forces towards Baghdad. Part of the force coming from Eretz Israel included a detachment of *Irgun* demolition experts, including Yaacov Meridor and David Raziel - the *Irgun* commander. While on an intelligence gathering mission, Raziel's car was hit by a bomb from a German Messerschmidt, and he was killed.

Meanwhile the RAF attacked and destroyed many of the German planes in Mosul. The German commander General Felmy carried with him instructions from Hitler outlining the German expectations in Iraq :

HITLER'S DIRECTIVE No 30. MIDDLE EAST.
Field Headquarters: May 23, 1941.
The Arab Freedom Movement is, in the Middle East, our natural ally against England. In this connection the raising of rebellion in Iraq is of special importance. Such rebellion will extend across the Iraq frontiers to strengthen the forces which are hostile to England in the Middle East, interrupt the British lines of communication, and tie down both English troops and English shipping space at the expense of other theatres of war. For these reasons I have decided to push the development of operations in the Middle East through the medium of going to the support of Iraq. Whether and in what way it may later be possible to wreck finally the English position between the Mediterranean and the Persian Gulf, in conjunction with an offensive against the Suez Canal, is still in the lap of the gods...[19]

The Battle for Crete

Almost simultaneously to the action in Iraq the battle for Crete began on 26 May. The German airborne assault, the biggest in history, took many of the defenders by complete surprise. Australian Sergeant Ian Walker wrote: 'When the invasion started we only had an onlooker position and saw thousands of paratroops dropping. It was a great sight. There seemed to be a stairway of white clouds from the ground to the

18   Churchill to Wavell, 9 May 1941. Churchill, W. *The Grand Alliance*, p. 323.
19   Quoted in Churchill, W. *The Grand Alliance*, p. 264.

planes.'[20] New Zealander, Lieutenant-Colonel H. Kippenberger added: 'The whole valley was covered with discarded parachutes, like huge mushrooms, mostly white, with different colours for those which had been dropped with supplies. Men were running about among them but though there was fire none appeared to be falling.'[21]

The main German goals were the airfield at Maleme and port at Suda Bay. The airborne assaults at Retimo and Heraklion began later in the day. In both these locations, despite heavy fighting the German paratroopers obtained few of their objectives. At Retimo the Australian soldiers under Colonel Ian Campbell held their positions and despite some set backs surrendered little ground to the paratroopers. The Germans however managed to land at Heraklion town, and some managed to find good defensive positions within the walls of the city. The following day they brought in more reinforcements. To the east of the town close to the airfield there was fierce fighting between the German and Allied troops and German raiding parties often killed civilians, accusing them of having attacked German soldiers. Many innocent Cretans lost their lives in the early part of the campaign - a harbinger of the forthcoming German occupation.

The New Zealanders bore the brunt of the initial onslaught, as they were stationed near the main German objective - the Maleme airfield. Due to weight of numbers and aerial superiority, the Germans finally captured the airfield at Maleme late on 21 May, allowing thousands more troops to land. Yet early the following morning the New Zealanders led a fierce counterattack, aiming at the airfield and nearby village of Tavronitis. Of this counterattack Captain Charles Upham wrote:

> Went on meeting resistance in depth - in ditches, behind hedges, in the top and bottom stories of village buildings, fields and gardens beside drome...
>
> We had heavy casualties but the Germans had much heavier ... With another hour we could have reached the far side of the drome...'[22]

The counterattack failed. With large numbers of German reinforcements now arriving Freyberg ordered the defenders to fall back to the next line of defense, running from the village of Galatas through to Alikianos, which was defended by the Greeks. But the New Zealanders, who had fought resolutely, were disappointed to begin the retreat on 24 May.

While the battle raged on land, an equally heavy battle raged at sea. The Royal Navy intercepted and destroyed much of the German sea borne force. Yet the *Luftwaffe* took a heavy toll upon the British Fleet and many ships were sunk or hit. It was a trial of strength between the Mediterranean Fleet and the *Luftwaffe*, which in many regards had the advantage due to its superiority in the air. But with the capture of the Maleme

---

20   Laffin, J. *Greece, Crete and Syria*, p. 63.

21   King. M. *New Zealanders at War*, p. 195.

22   Davin, D.M. *The Battle for Crete*, in *History of the Second World War*. Vol. 5, Purnell & Sons Ltd, (Paulton, 1967), p. 489.

airfield, the Germans had gained a major advantage. Allied air activity was virtually eliminated. While the Allied garrison forces maintained the Retimo and Heraklion sectors, the focus of attention now turned towards Suda Bay. Any hope of an Allied success at Crete depended upon retaining this port. If lost, then the Germans would have gained an unassailable advantage over Crete.

Further east at Heraklion the Germans threatened to bomb the city if it did not surrender. The Greek civilians were hastily evacuated, the German ultimatum not accepted, and the city was accordingly heavily bombed and damaged through 24 May. The large scale German offensive to break through the Allied line of defence guarding Suda Bay, began on 25 May. The desperate German assault succeeded in taking Galatas. Then Lieutenant Farren of the 3rd Hussars arrived with two light tanks, and Kippenberger, grouping the available soldiers, opted to counterattack.

It was a very fierce encounter, and cost the lives of seventy-one Greek and 145 New Zealand soldiers. Although it held up the German advance, they merely changed direction, and the following day, 26 May, threw their forces at the Greek and Australian defences to the south-east. Vasey, commander of the 19th Australian Brigade, and Hargest, commander of the 5th New Zealand Brigade, foresaw that their tired, ill-equipped and exhausted troops could not hold out for much longer against the overwhelming German force. Puttick, commander of the New Zealand Division, concurred, and ordered withdrawal to a line closer to Suda Bay, late on 26 May. Unfortunately some British troops were unaware of these movements, and found themselves exposed the following day.

Freyberg, although oblivious to some of the movements on the field due to breakdown in communications, knew that the situation was desperate, especially in the Canea sector. At Heraklion too, German reinforcements were causing considerable difficulties, as they were also hindering the Allied reinforcements from reaching the garrison. He proposed to Wavell that the troops be withdrawn before they were completely overwhelmed - and lost.

During 27 May, as Wavell deliberated, and Freyberg drew up withdrawal plans, the Anzac brigades had safely extricated themselves, and were now laying down a new line of defence before Suda Bay. They thought they had achieved some breathing space, when suddenly the Germans opened up fire. The German fire was quickly returned, and with the 28th Maori Battalion in the lead, five New Zealand and one Australian battalions counterattacked, and virtually wiped out the German force. Despite this brief victory, the troops could see large numbers of German troops moving eastwards along the base of the mountain range in an effort to encircle them. *The Palestine Post* later carried the headline *Maori Heroes of the Cretan Hills.*[23]

Finally it became apparent to all the leaders that with the superiority of the *Luftwaffe* the island could not be held, especially as further reinforcements could not arrive.

---

23 *The Palestine Post.* 2 June 1941, p. 1.

The Allied force at Heraklion was now running very low on ammunition, and the number of German paratroopers daily increased. But the decision to withdraw, which was finally authorized on 27 May, disappointed many of the troops and commanders, who did not relish the thought of being evacuated twice within a month.

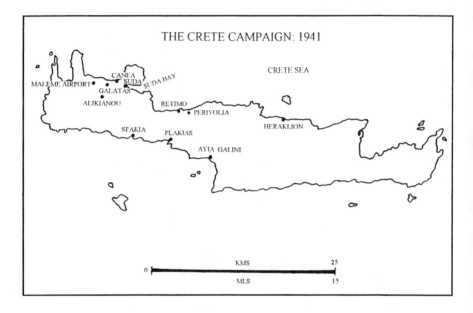

THE CRETE CAMPAIGN: 1941

While rearguards held off the attacking German force, the majority of the force began leaving the Canea sector on 28 May, heading over the rugged hill country towards the southern port of Sfakia. The British and Australian troops in the Heraklion sector were ordered to destroy all their equipment, and move towards Heraklion harbour, where, beginning on the night of 28 May, they would be embarked by British warships.

The Evacuation

And so for the second time within a month British and Anzac soldiers began a hasty retreat in order to fight another day. Unfortunately the Australian commander at Retimo was not aware of the order to evacuate, and fought on. Campbell, at the very end, ordered his men to take to the hills if they wanted, but the rest would surrender with honour. Not all went according to plan at Heraklion. The Germans bombed the harbour during the evacuation killing many of the troops awaiting to be shipped out. Yet by early morning on 29 May all but the wounded, who unfortunately had to be left behind, were aboard the British ships *Orion and Ajax* and en-route to Egypt.

Describing the march to Sfakia one New Zealand soldier told the Reuters correspondent: 'Our thirty-nine mile march to the coast was a real ordeal ... We would march a quarter of a mile and then German dive bombers would come, and we would be forced to leave the road in order to shelter on the hillsides. When they had gone we would resume the march, often with additional wounded to carry, only to be forced to scatter again almost immediately.'[24]

The embarkation of troops from Sfakia began on 28 May. A mammoth effort was again required to withdraw thousands of tired and despondent troops. And again the Mediterranean Fleet performed a tremendous job, although they lost a number of ships in the process. All the while it was necessary to maintain a strong rearguard to hinder a swift German advance which would upset the evacuation. Charles Upham performed further heroic deeds during this phase and was later awarded the Victoria Cross.

The evacuation was completed by the early morning of 1 June and some 16,500 British, Australian and New Zealand soldiers returned safely to Egypt. Yet some 5,000 remained in Crete, and although permitted by Wavell to surrender, many did not, and took to the mountains. Altogether the losses in killed, wounded and captured amounted to some 13,000, as well as nearly 2,000 naval casualties.

Consequences of the Battle

The battle of Crete had far-reaching effects. It was the beginning of a terrible ordeal for the Cretan people. Many sought to harbour the Allied soldiers who had fled into the hills. German measures against any Cretans assisting these soldiers were harsh - death and even burning of houses and villages. Andreas Braos of Sfakia recalls the execution of his uncle, who sheltered several New Zealand soldiers in a small hut high up in the While Mountains. The Germans finally located the hiding soldiers, apprehended the uncle and on a hill overlooking Sfakia harbour, shot him dead.[25]

The campaign was, to all accounts another failure. Yet the splendid German 7th Airborne Division, the elite of the German army, was virtually wiped out, as Churchill made clear later to his Parliament when grilled over the fiasco. It was this force which was intended to be the main attacking force in future campaigns in Syria and Iraq (as well as for Russia). The Germans may now be in control of Crete, within easy reach of the Levant - but their wings had been severely clipped. The cost in clipping those German wings was high, especially for the New Zealanders. From her only division, the Greek and Crete campaigns cost her 932 killed, 1,354 wounded and 4,036 captured.[26]

---

24 *The Palestine Post.* 3 June 1941, p. 3.
25 Conversation between author and Andreas Braos in October 1996.
26 Taylor, Capt. R.J. *Crete : A Tribute from New Zealand.* New Zealand Army, 1991, p. 23.

Once again the Jewish community of Eretz Israel keenly observed this campaign, due to the involvement of some of her sons in the campaign, and because of the possible consequences of a German presence even closer to her shores. '... there is the inescapable fact,' wrote Moshe Agronsky, editor of the *Palestine Post* on 22 May, 'that Crete stands between the Nazi hordes and the eastern shore of the Mediterranean. Its capture would be a great embarrassment.'[27]

Once the 'embarrassment' became apparent, a further urgency overcame the community. Moshe Shertok from the Jewish Agency, increased his calls for Jewish volunteers, stating on 24 May that 'This was the battle of the Jewish people for their very existence.'[28] Yitzak Ben Zvi, speaking after the evacuation, endorsed these views, and called for further volunteers 'now that the country is becoming a war front.' Ben Zvi also disclosed the disturbing news that 'half of the 3,000 Jewish troops sent to Greece and Crete had so far not returned.'[29] Thereafter further contingency plans were formulated for the defence of the Land of Israel.

Skirmishes in the Desert

Even while the operations in Crete, Iraq and to a lesser extent Syria were in progress, the emphasis was still upon victory in North Africa. Wavell, knowing that new German *Panzer* tanks were moving towards the front line, decided to attack with his limited forces. General Gott with a mostly British force captured Sollum and Fort Capuzzo on 15 May, although Capuzzo was later recaptured by the Axis. Not to be outfoxed Rommel counterattacked on 26 May and in the process captured the strategic Halfaya pass, separating Libya from Egypt. Wavell meanwhile prepared for a major breakout, codenamed *Battleaxe*. His intended starting date was delayed by several weeks - which allowed Rommel to bring forward more of his dreaded *Panzers*.

In the meantime the siege of Tobruk continued, the Allied soldiers being under constant harassment from the Axis forces. 'It is months now since we have taken our clothes off when going to sleep,' Mosenson informed his wife towards the end of May, 'and nobody minds in the least. We get used to everything. We get used to eating everything full of sand and dust and joke about it too.'

Yet the rare occasion of a lull in fighting and bombing did present itself, and Mosenson, the Australians, as well as British and Indian garrison troops made most of the opportunity. Describing a rare swim at the beach, Mosenson described 'how wonderful it would be if I could swim as far as the beach at Tel Aviv.'

'At the beach we met some young Australians,' he wrote on, 'who had come to rest from the front lines. We played around in the water like little boys. The atmosphere,' he described, 'was charged with joy and high spirits. We forgot about

---

27   *The Palestine Post.* 22 May 1941, p. 4.
28   *The Palestine Post.* 25 May 1941, p. 3.
29   *The Palestine Post.* 4 June 1941, p. 1.

everything. For once our bodies and heads were clean of sand. I dipped my clothes in water too, scrubbed them and laid them to dry on the rocks. But suddenly, the paradise was destroyed. Over our heads the cursed planes circled. We found shelter among the clefts of the rocks along the bay. How helpless soldiers look when they are naked, without their steel helmets and without their ammunition belts - like forlorn children.'

He continued, 'When the immediate danger was past, we jumped into the water again and dove deep down into it ... and again we enjoyed ourselves. The Australians are good playmates.' He met some old friends among them, and concluded, 'The bond of comradeship has remained undiminished.'[30]

Victory and Massacre in Iraq

Hitler's intentions in Iraq were apparent from his Directive of 23 May. He had at his disposal at this time one complete airborne force which he could have used. Had he done so he could very quickly have thrown the British out of Iraq, consolidated Syria, occupied Iran - and threatened British concerns both in India and in Eretz Israel-Egypt. He was forced to use this force in another area. Churchill later stated to the House of Commons:

> ... Rashid Ali appealed constantly to the Germans to make good their promises, but only 30-40 German aeroplanes arrived from Syria ... But meanwhile there was an explanation for this failure of the Germans. The German parachute and air-borne corps, which no doubt was to have operated in Iraq and would have been assisted on its journey across Syria by the Vichy French, had been largely exterminated in the battle of Crete ... This specialist corps was so badly mauled in the ferocious fighting that, although they forced us to evacuate Crete, they were themselves in no condition for further operations.[31]

While the remains of this elite German corps licked its wounds in Crete, the British forces approached Baghdad, reaching it on 30 May. News of the approaching British force caused Rashid Ali and others, including the Mufti, to flee to Iran. On 31 May 1941 the pro-British Regent was re-installed and a pro-British Government formed. The danger to British interests in Iraq was over.

But the danger was not over for the Jewish people. On 1-2 June pro-Axis and pro-Mufti groups ransacked the Jewish quarter of Baghdad, massacring some 180 innocent Jewish civilians. This atrocity stood as ample evidence of the brutality and intentions of the pro-Axis Arab nationalist movement and its unofficial leader Haj Amin. It highlighted the need to keep any Axis-Arab force from taking control over areas where Jewish people resided, most notably in the Land of Israel.

---

30 Mosenson, M. *Letters from the Desert,* pp. 64-65.
31 Speech of Churchill in House of Commons, 9 September 1941. Quoted in Pearlman, M. *Mufti of Jerusalem.* Victor Gollancz, (London 1947), pp. 38-39.

Chapter 25

Syria - Aussies Again in Damascus

Strategic Importance of Syria

Despite the heavy German casualties, the loss of Crete gravely concerned the Allied leaders. From Crete they realized the Germans had a natural jumping off point for Syria. On 22 May Wavell informed Churchill:

> This Syrian business is disquieting, since German Air Force established in Syria are closer to the Canal and Suez than they would be at Mersa Matruh. The [Vichy] French seem now wholly committed to the Germans. I am moving reinforcements to Palestine … because we feel we must be prepared for action in Syria, and weak action is useless.[1]

It was imperative now that Syria be occupied before the Germans could muster themselves after Crete and invade. British intelligence had ascertained that the bulk of the German army was poised to invade the Soviet Union so a small German army in control of Syria would greatly benefit the ambitions of Hitler. There would then be a greater possibility of advancing eastwards and southwards towards India.

Menzies also saw the need for quick action in Syria, as the Suez Canal could, in his opinion, be endangered. He cabled Churchill on 29 May emphasizing that possible opposition from the USA to such a campaign would not be forthcoming, and added 'I again emphasize to you that Australia and New Zealand have a large stake of four divisions in the Middle East, subject to the deductions in Greece and Crete, in addition to their vital interest in the preservation of one of the great Empire bastions. A defeat around the Suez would be a calamity of the first magnitude.'[2] It would also, wrote the *Sydney Telegraph* 'strengthen the hand of the Tokyo militarists and bring war nearer in the Pacific.'[3]

During the period of his Balkan and Crete ventures Hitler pressured the Vichy Government to forego its position of neutrality. The pressure began to take its toll and the Vichy authorities seemed headed towards an open amalgam with Nazi

---

1   Wavell to Churchill, 22 May 1941. Churchill, W. *The Grand Alliance*, pp. 325-326.
2   Quoted in Laffin, J. *Greece, Crete and Syria*, p.124.
3   Quoted in *The Palestine Post.* 5 June 1941.

Germany. When Vichy France pulled out of the League of Nations her legal basis for the Mandate over Syria was terminated. The headline of the *Palestine Post* on 23 May said it all: **Vichy Joins Axis.** Simultaneously the German ambassador to Turkey, Von Papen pressured Turkey to change her position of neutrality.[4] And indeed Turkey's position would become untenable if the Germans took control over Syria - the Germans were already controlling the remainder of the Aegean region and were poised to attack Turkey's northern neighbour, the Soviet Union.

Jewish Concerns

A German presence in Syria deeply concerned the Jewish people of Eretz Israel. Almost daily the Jewish newspapers reported the deteriorating conditions for the Jewish communities under Nazi control in Europe. The *Palestine Post* reported that only 100 out of 40,000 Jews managed to escape from Saloniki before the Germans took control of the city.[5] Reports of other atrocities also filtered through.

Such information, scant and almost unbelievable as it may have been, only confirmed to the Jewish people that it was imperative that any vestige of Nazi influence in Syria had to be eradicated. The Jewish leadership then increased their calls for volunteers to serve in the British Army. Yitzak Ben Zvi, spokesman for the *Vaad Leumi* (National Council of the Jewish people in Eretz Israel) at a meeting on 3 June which called for more volunteers, said that the Land of Israel was quickly becoming a war front, and that various contingency plans were now being formulated throughout the country against possible German action.[6] Throughout the country preparations for civil defence increased, and air raid shelters were either being readied or built. On 4 June five hundred new Jewish recruits into the British Army were addressed by Chief Rabbi Uziel at the Great Synagogue in Tel Aviv. He concluded his address: '... since the destruction of the Second Temple the Jewish people had never been engaged in a holy war as today.'[7]

The Syrian Battle Plan

The invasion of Syria, code-named *Operation Exporter,* would be commanded by General Sir Henry Maitland Wilson. It was to be carried out jointly by a Free French force (led by General Catroux, acting on behalf of General de Gaulle who had promised complete independence for Syria), the 7th Australian Division (commanded by General Lavarack), 1st British Cavalry Division, 5th Indian Infantry Brigade, with air force and naval support. The major objectives of the campaign were the large airfields at

---

4   *The Palestine Post.*, 8 June 1941.
5   *The Palestine Post.*, 29 April 1941.
6   Ibid., 4 June 1941.
7   Ibid., 5 June 1941.

Damascus, Beirut and Rayak in the Bekaa Valley lying between these two other strategic positions.

Opposing them was a large Vichy French force, commanded by General Dentz which included the *French Legion*, and French imperial troops from Africa. During the previous twenty years the French had considerably strengthened its defences from any attack from the south, and especially near the three main routes; the coastal route, the central route via Marjayoun, and the eastern route to Damascus via Kuneitra. Knowledge of the terrain and control of these strategic positions gave them a great advantage.

Moshe Sharrett head of the Political Department of the Jewish Agency, offered the services of the *Hagana,* as sappers and guides. Wilson accepted the offer. An initial operation took place on 18 May when Major Anthony Palmer accompanied by twenty-three young Jewish men, set out on a small boat, the *Sea Lion,* to destroy the oil refineries at Tripoli. The boat and men disappeared without a trace.

Yigal Allon and Moshe Dayan were chosen to lead two companies of 'guides and sappers.' They had little time to hand select the best men. The British command had been told that all those selected needed to be conversant in Arabic and would be able to pass as Arabs. Dayan's problem was that only one knew sufficient Arabic, and none knew the terrain on the other side of the border. Dayan selected an Arab, who had once been a terrorist, but who knew Syria well, to act as guide. He then broke his force into groups of two or three, and employed other Arabs to act as guides for these. While stationed at Kibbutz Hanita on the border between British *Palestine* and Lebanon, Dayan's small groups made a number of patrols across the border into Syria, between 1-7 June, providing Wilson with valuable information.

A young Yitzhak Rabin, son of a former member of the *Jewish Legion,* was visited by Dayan while on his recruiting mission, at Kibbutz Ramat Yohanan. Dayan asked Rabin if he could fire a rifle, throw a grenade, operate a machine-gun, drive a car and a motorcycle. Although answering affirmative for only half of these questions, Dayan nevertheless saw potential and signed him up.[8] And so began the military career of Yitzhak Rabin as he was co-opted into Company B.

On 6 June Dayan and his wife were driving through Moshav Nahalal, when they stopped their car next to a friend Zalman Mart, and Dayan asked, 'Do you want to see the Australians fight?' Mart answered in the affirmative, he piled into the car and joined Dayan's group of 'guides'.[9] That evening Dayan and several others made a gruelling reconnaissance patrol over the border, and although they uncovered valuable information, it was too late, for by late 7 June plans were already made. As Dayan woke up next morning trucks carrying Australian troops were already emerging upon Kibbutz Hanita.

---

8   Slater, R. *Rabin of Israel,* p. 40.
9   Teveth, S. *Moshe Dayan.* Dell Publishing, (New York. 1972), p.160.

Also on 6 June many of the Allied troops began moving northwards towards the borders of Lebanon and Syria. Lindsay Bear from Victoria recalled how the night before they left Afula, they spent the 'night under a grove of Australian gum trees and' visited 'a Kibbutz Settlement where a 2-gallon container was filled with milk from the kibbutz dairy. Lester Royle and I,' Bear wrote, 'drank the whole of the contents of the container,' adding, '(we were still eighteen year old boys.)'[10]

Desmond Tighe, the Reuters correspondent, toured the bases prior to the invasion, and wrote: 'Many Australians are fresh from their home country while others have seen service in Greece and the Western Desert. Several senior officers who served in Palestine in the last war with Allenby know every inch of the terrain. The "Diggers" are thoroughly at home in Palestine.' He also wrote how: 'The morale of Arabs and Jews throughout Palestine remains at a high level, confident that Britain will protect the country against any attempt of a German invasion.'[11]

On the evening of 7 June a group of ten Australians, including three officers, Kippen, Allen and Cowdrey, five Jewish men, including Dayan, and one Arab set out to reach their objectives, the main one of which was to secure two bridges on the coastal road near the village of Iskanderun about ten kilometres north of the border. Company A under Allon had been active on the north-eastern border in the central and eastern sectors of the impending invasion.

Rabin and two companions crossed the Lebanon border close to Rosh Haniqra on the coast and then proceeded onto the village of Binai el-Jubal some kilometres inside Lebanon. Rabin was instructed to 'watch out for the French Senegalese who were brutal, and for the advancing Australians who shoot first and ask questions later.'[12] This was sound advice as they were dressed to resemble Arab civilians. Their task was to destroy the telephone communications between Tyre and Sidon, and Rabin being the youngest and most agile of the three was instructed to climb the telephone pole and cut the wire. He later recalled, 'I must admit that my part was very simple in that invasion: a lot of walking, no fighting. Though you had to get up a telephone pole - that wasn't easy.'[13]

As these infiltrations were proceeding the Allied troops were massing at three points prior to entry into Syria, near the coastal road (aiming for Beirut), inland aimed at Marjayoun and the Bekaa Valley, and at Kuneitra aimed towards Damascus. The commanders received their briefings - as too did the Jewish scouts. One of the jump-off points was at Rosh Pina - an area familiar to the first Anzacs, as they passed there in September 1918 en-route to capture Damascus via Kuneitra. Rosh Pina in 1941 also boasted an airfield, where Allied planes assembled in readiness for the impending assault.

---

10 Letter from Lindsay Bear VX 17821 in author's possession.
11 *The Palestine Post,*. 10 June 1941, p. 1.
12 Comments by Rabin to the author in a meeting at the Ministry of Defence on 5 November 1992.
13 Slater, R. *Rabin of Israel*, p. 41.

Meanwhile the combined Australian-Jewish force of Kippen and Dayan and company located their objective, and found it abandoned. Little did they know that the French had blown the road up further to the south near the border in order to delay and obstruct any projected Allied invasion. 'It was quite clear to us,' wrote Dayan, 'that we must not abandon the bridges because they might be blown up, and we had been ordered to wait there until the invasion reached us.' So rather than waiting around, Dayan suggested that they capture the nearby French police station near Iskanderun which it was presumed was only lightly manned.[14]

So the unit comprised of eleven Australians, and the men from Eretz Israel (as well as the Arab guide) headed towards their seemingly easy objective 'talking and joking as they walked carelessly on either side of the road.'[15] Contrary to expectations however the police station was manned by a number of French soldiers, who after spotting the combined Australian and Jewish patrol, opened fire with a machine gun from the roof of the station. The Australian-Jewish force then charged the station and overcame the opposition.

The Vichy French, now alerted, sent reinforcements. The Australian and Jewish soldiers knew they could no longer wait for the invasion force, but had to fight for their survival from within the captured police station. The fighting intensified as the number of Vichy soldiers increased. At this point a bullet hit a pair of binoculars which Dayan was looking through, shattering his eye. Dayan's only hope of survival was to get to a hospital as soon as possible.

The Invasion of Syria

The invasion began in the early morning of 8 June. The Jewish people of Eretz Israel were relieved. 'There was no mistaking the dominant feeling yesterday,' *The Palestine Post* columnist reported, 'when the news came through of the Allied advance into Syria and Lebanon: it was of great relief ... Considering what is at stake - Iraq and the road to the East, on one side, Palestine and the road to Suez on the other, the British and Free French have only taken the course imposed upon them.'[16]

The main thrust of the invasion was along the coastal road - and this was held up when the Vichy forces blew up part of the road. Some of this column then proceeded to the heavily defended Litani River on foot. The crucial bridge across the Litani River was destroyed already by the Vichy. Meanwhile one Australian group captured Tibnine thirty kilometres inland. The mayor of this city then telephoned the mayor of Tyre on the coast - who said his city would gladly welcome the Australians to his city.

At about 1 pm two Australians riding a motorcycle arrived at the scene of battle

14   Teveth, S. *Moshe Dayan*, p. 165.
15   Ibid., p.165.
16   *The Palestine Post*, 9 June 1941, p. 4.

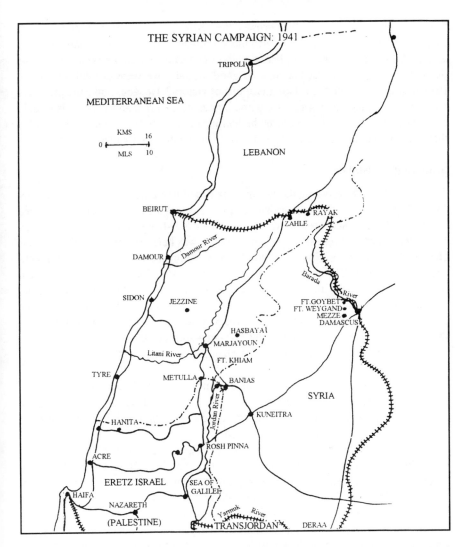

THE SYRIAN CAMPAIGN: 1941

TRIPOLI

MEDITERRANEAN SEA

KMS 16
0
MLS 10

LEBANON

BEIRUT

RAYAK
ZAHLE

DAMOUR

Damour River

Barada

FT.GOYBET
FT. WEYGAND
MEZZE
DAMASCUS

River

SIDON

JEZZINE

HASBAYA

MARJAYOUN

Litani River

FT. KHIAM

TYRE

METULLA

BANIAS

SYRIA

Jordan River

KUNEITRA

HANITA

ROSH PINNA

ACRE

ERETZ ISRAEL

SEA OF
GALILEE

HAIFA

NAZARETH

Yarmuk   River

(PALESTINE)

TRANSJORDAN

DERAA

where Dayan was seriously wounded. With permission of Kippen, Dayan and a dead Australian soldier were placed in a French truck which was driven by an Australian southward along the road which was crowded by troops moving northwards. Arriving at the demolished bridges the truck was unable to proceed, so the driver managed to procure a British ambulance, which rushed Dayan to the Hadassah Hospital in Haifa, where he was quickly operated upon.[17]

---

17   Teveth, S. *Moshe Dayan*, pp. 169-170.

The company led by Yigal Allon, crossed the border into Lebanon and returned with four Vichy French prisoners. He then met an officer of the 7th Australian Division, whom, Allon wrote 'was very pleased with us and said he would recommend us for decorations. We said that that was no good, because we were not enlisted in the British forces, but could we share the spoils of victory? He would take the prisoners and we would take their arms. He agreed, gave us the arms and invited us to help ourselves from a pile of other arms he had captured from the French. We loaded them into a van, took them away, and used them against the British years later.'[18]

Stiffening Resistance

The difficult task of crossing the fast moving Litani River was finally achieved on 9 June. That evening a pontoon bridge was placed across the river and the Allied force continued the advance northward towards Sidon - although constantly hassled by Vichy rearguards. Progress in the central sector was held up when the advance was checked by very stiff Vichy opposition from the commanding Khiam fortress southeast of Marjayoun. The next morning the artillery blasted the fort, then infantry went in and found the place abandoned. They advanced towards Marjayoun, which too was heavily defended, and after heavy fighting the town was taken on 10 June. Some Australians then began the hazardous move onto Jezzine in the central sector during the night of 13 June. The Vichy forces began a spirited counter-attack on 15 June aimed at Marjayoun. When some Australian soldiers panicked and fled, the town was lost.

The eastern sector fighting was basically entrusted to the Indian Brigade and the Free French, and they too found the going difficult. On 16 June the Vichy French attacked along the Damascus-Kuneitra road, and all but annihilated a British force of Royal Fusiliers. The survivors surrendered.

As progress was slower than expected, Wavell sent in Indian and British reinforcements from Iraq, and part of the 6th Australian Division who had been evacuated from Greece. He also changed the command structure. Major-General Lavarack was relieved of command of the 7th Australian Division and given command of 1 Australian Corps, and moved his HQ to Nazareth.

Meanwhile the 6th Australian Division men began moving out of British *Palestine* on 18 June. Holt and the 400 men of his battalion left their camp at Julis and after a series of stops, were finally stuffed like sardines into cattle trucks on a train from Haifa through to Deraa. Of this trip he wrote: 'Halfway to Deraa the worn-out engine could not take the train up a steep incline ... It took half the carriages up the mountain and was returning for us when its brakes failed and it crashed into us. This caused a number of injuries and an awful lot of swearing as we sorted ourselves out.'[19]

---

18   Bethell, N. *The Palestine Triangle*, p. 104.
19   Holt, B. *From Ingleburn to Aitape*, p. 117.

The Air War

Both the Navy and Air Force again played significant roles in this campaign. While the Navy assisted the coastal thrust by bombing some of the Vichy coastal installations, the Air Force was hammering away at key installations further inland. Australian pilots knocked out several enemy planes on 14 June while the RAF bombed Aleppo on the same day. But the enemy was hitting back - and aiming for civilian targets. Haifa endured a four hour bombing on 10 June - but there was miraculously little damage. The raid prompted the Editor of the *Palestine Post* to comment '... it does show what a deadly danger to all neighbouring countries the presence in Syria of German air planes would become if the process were not checked.'[20]

A larger-scale raid hit Tel Aviv on 12 June, scoring a direct hit on an Invalids Home and killing twelve and injuring twenty-four people. Haifa was again bombed that day, and again two days later.

Operation Battleaxe

While battles raged in Syria, Churchill was battling the politicians in London. Some were out for his blood after the Greek and Crete failures. He again declared 'Crete was only part of the Larger Battle' and reiterated that the delaying action there saved Syria and Iraq. But he did have one regret: 'One thing I regret very much is that the brunt of this fighting in the Middle East should have fallen so heavily on the splendid Australian and New Zealand troops.'[21]

Meanwhile there were plans to break out and link up with the garrison at Tobruk. Despite the hefty preparations for this operation, code-named *Battleaxe*, the Zionist soldiers from Eretz Israel managed to celebrate *Shavuot*, the Festival of the First Fruits. 'In spite of everything,' wrote Mosenson on 2 June 'we did celebrate Shevuoth. The whole company, both officers and men, gathered together in a deep gully. One of the officers made a speech about the meaning of the holiday and one of the men got up and added something to this. Rum was passed around.'[22]

Operation Battleaxe, Wavell's final attempt to effect a breakout and to throw the Axis forces out of Libya, began on 15 June 1941. There were mixed results during the first couple of days in the region of Sollum, Halfaya and Fort Capuzzo. On 17 June however events turned against the Allies, and a general withdrawal was ordered lest the force be surrounded and destroyed. Over 1,000 casualties were sustained during this intense three-day campaign. The failure of *Battleaxe* meant that the garrison at Tobruk was not relieved, but it continued to hold down considerable German and Italian forces. The failure also meant that General Wavell, like Hamilton a quarter of

---

20   *The Palestine Post.* 11 June 1941, p. 4.
21   Ibid., 11 June 1941, p. 1.
22   Mosenson, M. *Letters from the Desert,* p. 66

a decade before him at Gallipoli, had tried his last trump card, and had failed. Churchill, unwilling to concede that his venture in Greece and Crete had handcuffed Wavell, replaced him with General Claude Auchinleck. Auchinleck's place as Commander-in-Chief of India was in turn taken by Wavell.

The failure also meant that a number of troops who had endured the siege since the outset were taken out. On 23 June Moses Mosenson was evacuated on an Australian destroyer - and was soon afterwards re-united with his family on Kibbutz Naan.

Added to the recent defeats in Greece and Crete the failure also created ideal propaganda for the Germans. Enemy planes dropped pamphlets on the garrison force at Tobruk, which read:

AUSSIES

After Crete disaster Anzac troops are being ruthlessly sacrificed by England in Tobruk and Syria. Turkey has concluded a pact of friendship with Germany. England will shortly be driven out of the Mediterranean. Offensive from Egypt to relieve you totally smashed. You cannot escape. Our dive-bombers are waiting to sink your transports. Think of your future and your people at home. Come forward. Show white flags and you will be out of danger. Surrender![23]

In a manner typical of the garrison attitude to such propaganda, Derrick wrote on 25 June: 'Have thought the idea of surrendering over. Can't do it today - preserved fruit on the rations for tea.'[24]

Syria Neutralized

On 19 June the Allies began a two pronged attack upon Mezze, the last heavily defended position five kilometres west of Damascus. The Free French moved towards Damascus along the road from Deraa, the same road on which the Turks had fled northward in September 1918. They were unsuccessful. Then the assault by the Indian Brigade against Mezze was also unsuccessful and the force almost annihilated.

There was little rest for the newly arrived men from the 6th Australian Division. 'At Deraa we were told,' wrote Holt, 'we would be going into action the following day.' They then travelled throughout that night on buses towards Damascus. Arriving at the city's outskirts the following morning Holt wrote: 'It was quiet, peaceful and pleasant looking at the cool white buildings in the distance ... Our undermanned sections did not worry too much about digging in - that is until the first shell came whistling over and then we must have looked like a company of beavers.'[25]

That evening Holt's company attacked the Vichy fortress of Goybet. The going was not easy as it was surrounded by barbed wire entanglements which had to be

23 *Diary of Thomas Derrick*, Farquhar, M. pp.75-76.
24 Ibid., p. 76.
25 Holt. B. *From Ingleburn to Aitape*, pp. 117-118.

negotiated before the fortress could actually be assailed. 'The French held their fire till we were in the middle of the entanglement' he wrote 'and then they blasted shit out of us with everything they had - rifles, machine guns, mortars - the lot.' Holt was hit in the leg in this dash, and then shortly afterwards while being attended to by the stretcher bearers, 'the unsung heroes of the war' a Vichy mortar shell exploded nearby and wounded him again, this time in the chest.

While Vichy and Allied soldiers battled it out around Fort Goybet, the stretcher bearers managed to take Holt out of the fighting zone and headed into Damascus. The position in Damascus was confusing. Vichy French and Free French were battling it out - and sometimes it was difficult determining who was who.

While some men of the 2/3rd Australian Battalion attacked and captured Fort Weygand, and headed to block the Damascus-Beirut road, others were heading towards the north of Damascus, to cut the Damascus-Homs road in case Vichy forces closed in from that direction. In the process they overtook a convoy of Free French soldiers, preparing to enter Damascus to accept the impending surrender. In the convoy rode Colonel Bernard Fergusson, British liaison officer with the Free French.

Fergusson later reported that the anticipated French entrance was 'marred, unfortunately, by the sudden appearance on the road of hordes of Australian vehicles crowded with Diggers all imbued with one ambition: to be the first into Damascus. I still do not know where they came from, nor to whom, if anyone, they owed allegiance.'[26]

When it became apparent in Damascus that the road to Beirut had been blocked, the city officials surrendered to the Australian force, led by Colonel A.S. Blackburn VC. Blackburn and his staff were then given a sumptuous luncheon.[27] It almost sounds like a repeat of the entrance of the Light Horse and Major Olden's role in 1918. Several hours later the official Free French delegation entered into Damascus, led by General Le Gentilhomme. They were escorted by Circassian cavalry and were accompanied by other Allied representatives.[28]

The Vichy officers and city officials now repeated the surrender procedure, allowing the Free French to claim that they had taken possession of Damascus. However, like Lawrence and Feisal's entrance in 1918, so too with this one in 1941, the honours went to the Australians. They basked in the attention. The BBC correspondent Richard Dimbledy wrote:

> Australian hats produced more response than English uniforms, and one buxom lady who announced in a loud voice that she would kiss the first Australian soldier she saw, was nearly overwhelmed by a rush of Australian gunners from nearby.'[29]

26 Laffin, J. *Greece, Crete and Syria*, p. 151.
27 Laffin, J. *Greece, Crete and Syria*, p. 150.
28 *The Palestine Post.*, 23 June 1941, p. 3.
29 Quoted in *The Palestine Post.* 25 June 1941, p. 1.

But victory came at a cost. German planes bombed the city on 25 June, killing seventy and wounding twenty-nine people.[30] Acre was also bombed on the same day. At the same time as the battles were going on around Damascus and on the coastal plain, a striking force approached from the east, comprised of *Habforce,* and the *Arab Legion* under the command of Major John Glubb. They attacked the strategic position of Palmyra, where the *Foreign Legion* held out for some twelve days . Meanwhile progress in the central sector at Marjayoun and at Jezzine was impeded following heavy fighting.

With Damascus now secured, the British 6th Division was to aim towards Beirut across the mountain range through the Bekaa Valley and capture Rayak airfield and in the process cut off the Vichy forces in the central Marjayoun sector. The Vichy were determined to maintain Marjayoun, and all the while the Allied casualties mounted. The drive to capture Beirut via the coastal route continued. Victory at Jezzine on 27 June opened the way for a renewed advance northwards. But there was a severe obstacle on the coastal thrust, the Vichy were solidly entrenched along the Damour River and nearby hills south of Beirut.

Endeavouring to determine the enemy's strength, and to seek out alternate inland routes, Brigadier Stanley Savige, commander of the 17th Australian Brigade, sent out small groups of soldiers on reconnaissance patrols. One of them consisting of Lindsay Bear, Bruce Kingsbury (who later won the VC) and Dennis O'Connor moved inland along the Dog River (with its famous inscriptions of famous conquerors, including the Desert Mounted Corps and its mention of Australian and New Zealand as well as British and Indian troops) to the village of Ain Ksour. To ensure the *French Legion* did not attack the Australian force from the rear, they set up road blocks 'to prevent movement of motor or tracked vehicles.' Some time later while the three were sitting in a garden, they were approached by a young well-dressed Arab man. He asked, wrote Bear:

> 'Don't you know that you are in the garden of my home'? - to which we replied, "But don't you know there is a war going on." 'Yes,' he replied, 'but you are not going to harm me are you?' The occasional shell was still coming over.'
>
> 'The young man then, in turn, invited us to wash up in a bowl of hot water he had supplied - so having washed and shaved we felt better.'
>
> Following this, the young man asked us, 'Would you like some coffee?' 'Yes,' we replied. Then he carried down to us a tray of coffee - thick and treacle like - but very nice.
>
> A most enjoyable time followed with 3 Australian soldiers and a young Lebanese talking over many things.'[31]

---

30   *The Palestine Post.* 26 & 29 June 1941.
31   Letter from Lindsay Bear. Copy in author's possession. In 1971 Bear re-visited Lebanon and Ain Ksour village. The young doctor had moved to Tripoli, but Bear was able to re-establish contact with him.

But such pleasant experiences were later overshadowed by the heavy fighting which began around Damour on the coastal route during the night of 5-6 July. Again the fighting was tough, especially as the Vichy gained superior positions for their artillery. Yet Damour was finally reached on 7 July, and evacuated by the Vichy the following day. The outskirts of Beirut were sighted on 10 July. Further inland other members of the 7th Australian Division were pursuing the Vichy troops who were withdrawing from Jezzine.

The Final Capitulation

All sectors now moved steadily towards Beirut, where the HQ of the Vichy commander, Dentz was located. Dentz had meanwhile moved his HQ north to Aleppo. At this point, Lavarack increased his efforts to gain a cease-fire and end the fighting. Although Dentz procrastinated, awaiting the arrival of a German rescue, he could not hold out any longer, and the cease-fire went into operation on 11 July.

The following day Dentz met General's Lavarack and Wilson at an Australian army outpost on the Damascus - Beirut road. From there they drove down to Acre for the signing of the Armistice, which called for the occupation of Syria by the Allied forces. Again, as in 1918, Anzacs had been instrumental in subduing the region of Syria. But the cost was high, and of the 4,600 Allied casualties, some 416 Australians were killed and 1,049 wounded.

On 15 July 1941 men of the 7th Australian Division paraded through the streets of Beirut where they were given a heroes welcome by the populace. The majority of this Division now remained to garrison Syria - for although subdued, there was still the danger, following Germany's invasion of Russia on 22 June (*Operation Barbarossa*), of a German breakthrough via the Caucasus. Nevertheless Churchill stated: 'The occupation and conquest of Syria ended, as it proved forever, the German advance towards the Persian Gulf and India.'[32] The victory also placed the Suez Canal out of striking range of German aircraft operating from there. The campaign also verified the opinions of many of the statesmen of the period of 1914-1918 who saw the potential danger if France held control of the area on the east bank of the Suez, lest they one day be a belligerent power.

---

32 Churchill, W. *The Grand Alliance*, p. 332.

*C*hapter 26

Tobruk - Hope and Despair

Axis Strategy

Although the nightmare of a dual Axis movement from both Syria and North Africa had now been eradicated, there still remained the danger of an Axis victory in North Africa. The Axis, in control of Italy, Greece and Crete could easily mount attacks or send reinforcements from these areas.

Thankfully Hitler was absorbed in the invasion of the Soviet Union. Although now of secondary importance, Rommel's campaign in the Eastern Mediterranean was by no means forgotten. Conquest of the Suez Canal and the surrounding region was still very much a part of the overall Axis plan. In fact Hitler still vaguely conceived of taking this region via a two pronged assault, from Russia southwards, and from Libya eastwards. The rendezvous points would be at the Suez Canal and the oil fields of Iraq.

Much of the German strategy however was held up by the stubbornness of two locations, the garrisons at Malta and Tobruk. While Tobruk held out, Rommel could not proceed further into Egypt. And while Malta held out, it continued to thwart the Axis supply line from Italy to Libya. Both locations were mercilessly hammered by the *Luftwaffe.*

Life at Tobruk

Following the failure of *Operation Battleaxe*, Rommel consolidated his position and prepared for a major assault upon Tobruk. More German equipment and troops arrived. Auchinleck reorganized his forces into two separate armies. The Ninth Army was stationed east of the Suez Canal, in British *Palestine*, Syria and Transjordan. The Eighth Army was stationed to the west of the Suez Canal, and was commanded by Lieutenant-General Sir Alan Cunningham. Cunningham immediately set about organizing for the next thrust - the recapture of Cyrenaica and relief of Tobruk.

Life for the defenders at Tobruk, known now as the *Rats of Tobruk*, was a hazardous affair during the months of the siege. The Germans and Italians dominated the air, and together the *Stuka* dive bombers and heavy bombers blasted the Allied garrison. Numerous frontal assaults were also attempted. On 4 July Derrick recorded: 'Fritz has just scored a lucky one, and Jack Brice has been killed, Tommy Hill a nasty head wound, Jack Pascoe face injuries and head wounds. A stretcher bearer also slightly wounded.'[1]

Then on 29 July he wrote again of the trying conditions: 'Now in trenches in the salient, and did we get a reception from Fritz! Practically in the same positions as we were May 4-13. Cannot put your head up two inches during day.'[2]

The survival of the garrison was dependent upon their determination to stand, and upon the Navy. Supplies had to be brought in, and the wounded taken out, by ships secreting in from Alexandria. A dangerous undertaking The first leg of this journey, until Mersa Matruh, was safe, as the Allied Air Force, small as it was, provided air cover. But the last leg of some sixty-five kilometres was a dangerous affair. The Axis planes could be refueled from within Cyrenaica, while the closest place for the Allied planes was at Sidi Barrani, 160 kilometres from Tobruk. Many Allied ships and men were lost.

By September some of the commanders, and in particular Blamey, were concerned that the Australian soldiers, who comprised the bulk of the infantry at Tobruk, would be too fatigued to withstand a full fledged German frontal assault. Although opposed by Churchill, the Australian Government demanded that their 9th Division be relieved, after having endured the siege for five months.

From 1 September advance parties of soldiers from the British 6th Division and the Polish 1st Carpathian Brigade began moving, by boat, into Tobruk. It was imperative that the enemy remain unaware of this significant changeover Derrick wrote on 28 September: 'Have mated up with a Tommy corporal, Jim Bradley. This fellow is very interesting, and has seen a lot of action at Norway, France, Crete and Syria.'[3] Relations between the Australians and their replacements were cordial during the changeover period. Derrick himself left Tobruk aboard the HMS *Kingston* on 22 October 1941.

From Alexandria the troops were quickly moved back to the Land of Israel. At their camp at Julis, the *Rats of Tobruk* were treated to food, leave and beer - all of which had been in short supply at Tobruk. And as could be expected they were received and feted well by the Jewish people, who were well aware that the German thrust eastwards had been stopped to a large extent by these men from 'down under' and their British comrades. Throughout the period of the siege, the Jewish papers in Eretz Israel carried almost daily coverage of the battles in and around Tobruk.

---

1   *Diary of Thomas Derrick*, Farquhar, M. p. 77.
2   Ibid, Farquhar, M. p. 79.
3   Ibid, Farquhar, M. p. 80.

Thoughts of a Jewish Soldier

Following a break at home on Kibbutz Naan, Mosenson next found himself driving his truck in Transjordan. On 23 October 1941, while high up in the Transjordan hills, he wrote to his wife, echoing the thoughts of many at the time:

> When I listen to the radio I am sometimes overcome by sad and painful thoughts. The fate of the world is being decided now on the battlefields of Russia. Millions of people are dying there and thousands of villages are being turned into mounds of destruction ... the fate of the Jews looms at us out of all this. When you listen to the awful news of our ruin and the menace of the horror to come, we know that our going was not in vain, but a solemn duty to the children. For their sakes we must create a world completely different from the one we have today.[4]

Occasionally Mosenson was able to separate himself from these painful thoughts - and these often came thanks to the jovial attitude of the Anzac soldiers. On one occasion he entered the camp canteen, which was full of Australians. 'They turned up their noses a little at the sight of an English soldier' he wrote, 'but ... suddenly one of them jumped up and actually embraced me. Do you know who he was ... ?' he asked his wife in absentia. 'One of the boys who visited me at Naan after I came back from Tobruk ... He was very excited to meet me here, asked about you and even remembered your names. He turned round to his comrades in the canteen and said, "This boy is a Palestinian. He was at Tobruk with the Australians. He came home and told every one in his colony about Tobruk and the Australians there. Boys, let's drink health to the Palestinian."'[5]

Shortly afterwards he wrote of another encounter with Anzac soldiers, this time New Zealanders. 'Close by our camp is a camp of New Zealanders. They are very fine boys, as friendly as the Australians, but more restrained ... We have become friendly with many of them.' In particular Mosenson befriended a soldier named Tate, who wished to go to Naan on leave.[6]

Operation Crusader

As winter of 1941 approached, Auchinleck and Cunningham made their first major move, known as Operation *Crusader,* on 18 November 1941. It was a two pronged attack, intended to destroy the German armour and to relieve Tobruk and included British, South African, Indian and New Zealand troops. Initially all went well.

On the front line, the fighting was tough. Private Jim Henderson was at that time located to the south east of Tobruk where he endured some hostile German fire. '... somewhere out ahead,' he wrote recalling the period, 'Jerries are sprawled out in

---

4   Mosenson, M. *Letters from the Desert,* p. 80.
5   Mosenson, M   ibid., p. 81.
6   Mosenson, M.   ibid., p. 83/84

little hollows, and they've set up their guns and they're peering through their sites at us ... we're on the receiving end, and its not such fun.'[7]

Shortly afterwards Henderson was shot in the leg, while his mate Farmer next to him caught it even worse. While attempting to help his mate, Henderson copped another bullet, and that was the end of his fighting. [8] He was later picked up by a German patrol. A German doctor examined Henderson's wounded body and after commenting upon his injuries, inquired, 'Why ... did you come from New Zealand to fight us?' Attempting to outline the sequence of German aggressive acts leading up to the war, Henderson concluded 'Then we thought you would take France, then England. We knew England meant New Zealand, so we thought we'd better stop you.'

'That is not a very good argument,' the German doctor retorted. 'I know,' Henderson responded, 'but I'm not in the mood for politics right now.' [9] And who could blame him? Henderson was to spend the remainder of the war as a guest of the Axis.

When Operation *Crusader* began, Rommel himself was preparing for a further assault upon Tobruk. Although initially outmaneuvered by this Allied attack, he quickly counterattacked in certain positions, causing Cunningham to recommend withdrawal. Auchinleck disagreed and pressed on. The Allies then gained the advantage forcing the Axis forces to withdraw their positions surrounding Tobruk on 9 December 1941. Rommel withdrew westwards and established a new defensive line at Gazala.

John Blyth, who had arrived as a New Zealand reinforcement in July 1941, wrote while training at Maadi camp: 'One day we were startled to hear that the Division had become involved in heavy fighting at Capuzzo and Sidi Rezegh and that the news was grim. They had succeeded in linking up with the beleaguered troops in Tobruk but in doing so had suffered very heavy casualties.'[10]

The remaining Australian troops at Tobruk, the 2/13th Battalion, left the garrison on 16 December, thereby ending the 242 day siege - one of the epic episodes of modern military history. This battalion continued onto British *Palestine* and joined the remainder of the 9th Division who were on garrison duties.

Jewish and Anzac Friendship

The Anzacs were now celebrating their second Christmas away from home. Those in Egypt may have had conditions similar to some part of their homelands. But for

---

7   Henderson, J. *Gunner Inglorious*, p. 29.
8   Henderson, J. ibid., pp. 34-5.
9   Henderson, J. ibid., p. 39.
10 Blyth, J. *Soldiering On: A Soldiers War in North Africa and Italy*, Century Hutchinson, (Auckland, 1989), p. 25.

those stationed in Syria, Transjordan and the Land of Israel it was in the middle of winter. Mosenson happened to enter the camp canteen, and found it full of half drunk Anzacs. As usual they offered him a drink, and after several, they inquired why he didn't look too happy. He answered: 'On this very night, on this holiday, seven million of my brothers are imprisoned in Europe, without a home, crushed beneath the heel of the Nazis. Seven million of my brothers are the victims of cold, hunger and slavery.'

Despite their half drunken state, the Anzacs empathized with Mosenson's feelings for his people. 'Understanding and sympathy seemed to shine out of their eyes,' he wrote. Then one of the older soldiers present said to Mosenson: "Listen, all those millions of Jewish brothers will have a home. Palestine will be their home. Have patience; wait until victory is ours ... we'll beat those Nazis." We drank together,' he concluded, 'to victory, to the defeat of Nazism, to the rebuilding of Palestine and, finally, to a Socialist Australia. This latest was proposed by a youngster who raised his glass with great excitement and we all followed him.'[11]

Several days later Mosenson wrote again to his wife of a package and letter he had received from Eleanora Tate in far away New Zealand. She wrote to him:

> I don't know you. But I know my dear son's taste in people. If he likes you so much, you must be worthy of his love ... I and my daughter Jenny are sending you a New Year's gift. My son has written me a great deal about you. Every evening before I go to bed I pray for your safety and I pray for the safety of my dear and only son. May God grant that you will come through the war as safely as you came through the siege of Tobruk for the sake of your wife and children ... Please accept our modest gift and remember that, far from the battlefields we, the mothers and daughters of New Zealand, are praying for the triumph of justice over evil.[12]

Haj Amin and the Final Solution

For the Jewish people the triumph of justice over evil meant the defeat of both the German Army, and the anti-Zionist Arab nationalist movement. Hitler and Haj Amin together would be a deadly combination. The Jewish leadership were most concerned therefore when *Radio Rome* announced on 24 October 1941 that Haj Amin had managed to flee from Iran to Italy. He met with Mussolini on 27 October.

Mussolini, looking to expand the Italian Empire in the Mediterranean, had plans for the former Mufti. Haj Amin complied by making several broadcasts on the Arabic programme on Italian radio. The Italians were disappointed however, and the Jewish people further concerned, when a German spokesman announced in early November 1941 that the Mufti of Jerusalem was coming to Berlin and would be received there with 'full honours due to his exalted rank.'

---

11   Mosenson, M. *Letters from the Desert.*, p. 96.
12   Mosenson, M. ibid., p. 97.

The spokesman added: 'This great champion of Arab liberation and the most distinguished antagonist of England and of Jewry is expected to remain in Berlin for a long time.'[13] Haj Amin arrived in Berlin on 3 November and met with Hitler on 30 November.[14] Haj Amin reiterated his admiration for the Fuhrer and offered to raise an *Arab Legion* to fight against the Allies. He felt that raising such a force would be greatly assisted by a German proclamation of support for Arab independence. While agreeing in principle, Hitler suggested that it would be more appropriate to wait for the eventual German breakthrough at the Caucasus when they would be closer to the Arab lands.

Such a military situation, Hitler expressed, would include the liquidation of the Jewish people. Haj Amin went immediately to work, planning a massive anti-British and anti-Jewish propaganda campaign. Shortly later he declared on Berlin Radio: 'The movement for Arab independence is perfectly organized and will contribute to the fall of the British Empire.'[15] He called on the Moslems of the world to join the Axis in a *Jihad* (Holy War) against the Allies. The *New York Post* wrote that on 8 January 1942: 'Berlin announced that the Grand Mufti ... had openly announced in a telegram to the German Fuhrer before the whole world his adherence to the Tripartite Pact against Britain, Jews and Communists.'[16]

But the worst was still to come for the Jewish people. On 20 January 1942, a secret meeting was convened in the Berlin suburb of Wannsee. There Reinhard Heydrich, the head of the *Gestapo* (the German secret police), produced a document which outlined the plan for the systematic destruction of the entire Jewish population of Europe. Speaking to the fifteen senior SS officials, Heydrich said 'in the course of this Final Solution of the European Jewish problem, approximately eleven million Jews are involved.'[17] Until then the Nazis had murdered nearly a million Jewish people, primarily by shooting. But henceforth the murder would be more systematic - through mass gassings in concentration camps. The signs were ominous for the survival of the Jewish people.

Japan Enters the War

In the closing stages of *Operation Crusader* Japan struck and destroyed almost the entire United States Pacific Fleet at Pearl Harbour, and then moved quickly into South East Asia. The threat of a two pronged Axis attack, Japan from the west and Germany from the east, upon British dependencies in the region, especially India, became a real possibility.

---

13 Pearlman, M. *The Mufti of Jerusalem*, p. 41.
14 Sacher, H. *A History of Israel*, p. 229.
15 Pearlman, M. *The Mufti of Jerusalem.*, p. 42.
16 *New York Post*, 6 January 1946. Quoted in Pearlman, M. ibid., p. 53.
17 Shirer, William L. *The Rise and Fall of the Third Reich.* Simon and Schuster, (New York, 1960), p. 965.

The northern frontier separating Russia from India now took on more importance. To hinder any possible German thrust south from the Caucasus, the 9th Australian Division was moved to the Syrian-Turkish border. Derrick wrote several days later from Le Gault: 'Everything is so beautiful, quiet and peaceful that one must think again to realize the world is at war. It is hard to imagine with all this peaceful country how human beings can destroy each other.'[18] The following months were spent creating and improving the defences in the event of a thrust south by the Germans, a great deal of tough training - and some sightseeing.

Despite being away from the battle zone, the soldiers were not at ease. The war in the Far East was causing them concern. Derrick wrote on 14 February: 'Two months of the New Year with the war getting ever closer to Australia and am not in a position to do anything about it - the whole of the 9th Division are most desirous to return home and to fight for, and in, their own country.'[19] Of this new situation Churchill wrote: 'Australia and New Zealand felt suddenly plunged into the forefront of the battle. They saw themselves exposed to the possibility of direct invasion. No longer did the war mean sending aid across the oceans to the Mother Country in her distress and peril. The new foe could strike straight at Australian homes. The enormous coast-lines of their continent could never be defended. All their great cities were on the sea board. Their only four well-trained divisions of volunteers and the New Zealand Division, all their best officers, were far away across the oceans.'[20]

Despite these sentiments, tension developed between Churchill and the new Australian Prime Minister John Curtin. Curtin believed that Britain was not fulfilling its promises and obligations in the Far East, and therefore he, Curtin saw Australia's best interests laying henceforth with a closer relationship with the United States. Such an attitude however caused considerable controversy.[21]

It was finally agreed that two Australian divisions would leave the Eastern Mediterranean and return home. While the 9th Division was moving northward into Syria to strengthen the Levant-Caspian Front against a possible German breakthrough across the Caucasus, the 6th and 7th Australian Divisions, as well as Australian ships and many airmen, began the journey eastwards to defend the shores of Australia - and New Zealand.

Bob "Hooker" Holt, after recovery from his wounds, had ended up in various locations in the Land of Israel. He wrote concerning the period of early 1942: 'There have been a lot of furphies going about the camps that owing to the Japs coming into the war we would be returning to Australia. The news was too good to believe, but

---

18 *Diary of Thomas Derrick*, Farquhar, M. p. 84.
19 *Diary of Thomas Derrick*, Farquhar, M. p. 86.
20 Churchill, W. *The Hinge of Fate*, p. 4.
21 Article by Curtin in *Melbourne* Herald, 27 December 1941; and Curtin to Churchill, 11 January 1942. Quoted in Churchill, W. *The Hinge of Fate*, pp. 8 & 10.

the rumours became stronger and then became fact. We entrained, recrossed the Sinai Desert and eventually ended up at Port Tewfik.'[22]

The New Zealand Government decided not to recall its Division, a matter which caused some friction between the two Anzac Governments. Yet the entrance of Japan strengthened the Allied position by finally bringing the USA into the War. Nevertheless as far as the Eastern Mediterranean was concerned, the Allied position was considerably weakened by the withdrawal of two seasoned divisions. It was an opportune time for a quick and decisive German counter offensive.

Rommel Counterattacks

Operation Crusader continued into January 1942 and pushed the Axis forces back to the very border of Tripolitania. There at El Agheila, Rommel stopped the thrust, and regrouped. Auchinleck also regrouped, awaiting the arrival of fresh troops and equipment, and anticipated continuing the thrust by the middle of February. Rommel regrouped the quicker as German bombers operating out of Italy had severely mauled the troublesome Malta garrison. The German supply line thereafter improved.

The Axis forces launched their counter offensive on 20 January 1942. The Allied force was quickly forced back, with loss of much equipment. The Axis offensive then continued north towards Benghazi and north east towards Mechilli, the central route through Cyrenaica. The news was depressing for the Allied soldiers. Derrick wrote from Lebanon: 'Libya, the Huns have again pushed our forces back to Gazala. The East ... Japs are endeavouring to land on Singapore Island.'[23]

For the next three months the two armies faced each other at Gazala between Tobruk and Derna. It was a time of regrouping and waiting. During this period emphasis was again placed upon the strategic importance of Tobruk. Churchill and the War Cabinet emphasized to Auchinleck that Tobruk was to be held come what may and continue to be 'a thorn in the enemy's side' as it had been in 1941. It was hoped that Auchinleck and General Ritchie the commander of the Eighth Army held the same strong views.

The garrison at Tobruk was comprised primarily of the 2nd South African Division under the command of General Klopper, as well as various British and Indian units. They waited and prepared for the anticipated fresh German assault.

New Zealanders Move North

Also in January 1942 the New Zealanders returned to camp at Maadi, were rested and refitted, and then sent to Syria for garrison duties. Jack Berridge of Gisborne recalled how they 'were rushed north by motor convoys - hard travelling in 10 ton

---

22 Holt, R. *From Ingleburn to Aitape.*, p. 139.
23 *Diary of Thomas Derrick*, Farquhar, M., pp. 85-86.

trucks - to Syria ... I well remember,' he continued, 'what seemed days and nights of uncomfortable travel.' [24]

En-route they stopped in the Land of Israel. 'We moved into a transit camp at Kfar Vitkin by the sea,' Blyth recalls. 'It was a pleasant place with salmon-coloured soil, citrus trees, and Israeli girls with the longest of sun-tanned legs ... We never tired of gazing at them but as they were usually in the company of Israeli men we made no approaches.'[25]

Blyth also recalls the pleasure of watching the Jewish children 'dressed in white dresses and garlanded with flowers' perform in a festival in the nearby village. 'The Israelis' he continued, 'treated us with great courtesy. We were fighting their persecutors ... In Tel Aviv they stood aside in the bus queues, beckoning us forward. We received smiles everywhere we went and it was good to feel the return of self-esteem.'[26]

While most of the Division continued into Syria, Berridge's unit stopped in Haifa. From there they were escorted by British soldiers 'on big Harley Davidson motor cycles' eastward through a range of hills. The following morning Berridge heard 'what sounded like hundreds of Church bells echoing out from the surrounding hills.' They were in Nazareth, and it was Easter Friday. Thereafter part of Berridge's garrison duties included patrolling the hilly roads and streets of the town.

And while not on duty Berridge , like his comrades, enjoyed the hospitality of the local population, including several days on a kibbutz. 'A wonderful experience and privilege,' he recalls. 'Tremendous people. Wonderful hosts. Great meals in the big dining room.' Impressions of meals being natural for a seasoned soldier!

On another occasion he was befriended by a family in Tel Aviv and welcomed into their very humble home. 'The parents were Russian Jews,' he recalls 'the only son was in the Palestinian Army and there were two daughters.'

'I was privileged to share the Feast of the Passover in their home,' he continues 'and although Dad, a big bearded man couldn't speak English, the son ... interpreted for me as the Feast proceeded. A wonderful night - I was very privileged. What impressed me at the time,' he recalls, 'was the excitement of the family in the days preceding this special occasion. The only white linen tablecloth Mum possessed was carefully prepared, and the silver table utensils and wine glasses, polished to a real shine.'[27]

While Berridge enjoyed his *Seder*[28] in Eretz Israel, Mosenson partook of his, in Egypt, the ancient land of bondage. 'This is my second *Seder* away from home,' he wrote to his family, 'and I feel very sad about it. When I picture to myself how our

24 Letter Berridge to Marie Shaw, 22 May 1996.
25 Blyth, J. *Soldiering On*, p..29.
26 Blyth, J. ibid., p. 29.
27 Jack Berridge to Marie Shaw, 22 May 1996. Letter in author's possession.
28 *Seder* - the term for the main *Passover* meal.

dining-room looks on a holiday evening - with all the light shining in the eyes of the comrades - I am overcome by homesickness. It seems to me that this year there is a deeper meaning in this festival of freedom. For actually, we too, are at a point in history where we must fight for freedom, the freedom of our people and the freedom of man.'[29]

Some weeks later Mosenson and the Jewish soldiers of Eretz Israel celebrated their second *Shavuot* festival away from home. Despite being in the desert, they decorated their large tent with as many greens as possible, held a party, and, wrote Mosenson, even 'broke into a *Hora*[30]; just the way we do at home.'[31]

Tobruk Falls

Rommel, still fuming from his previous failure to take Tobruk, lashed out finally on 26 May 1942, and his *Operation Venezia* soon had the Eighth Army reeling backwards from Gazala. Panic buttons lit up. Blyth, with the New Zealanders in Syria, wrote of his return to camp at Baalbek from a desert manoeuvre. 'Everybody' he recalls, 'started rushing around bringing equipment up to a state of instant readiness. Word was out that the Division was returning post haste to Egypt because the 8th Army had suffered heavy defeat at the hands of Rommel, but as things had been going well in the desert we did not pay too much attention to this.' The optimists among the soldiers however, suggested that they were returning home to New Zealand.

It didn't take the men long to determine their real destination as they sped southwards through British *Palestine*, across the Sinai, and over the Suez Canal. In short time the New Zealand Division was at the front line again, alongside their fellow British, Indian, South African and Jewish soldiers. 'The dash of the New Zealand Division from Syria to the Western Desert,' wrote the *Palestine Post* correspondent, 'was made under cover of the strictest secrecy and at a "bewildering" speed.'[32]

By 20 June the Axis forces had reached the gates of Tobruk. This time Rommel was determined to capture this strategic port and threw everything into the assault. On the following day, 21 June, Tobruk fell. And with it some 35,000 Allied soldiers, mostly South Africans, were captured. The Germans, the Italians, Hitler and Mussolini were all elated. Plans for assaulting Malta were postponed, all emphasis was now placed upon a decisive drive into Egypt. Hitler wrote to Mussolini:

> Destiny has offered us a chance which will never occur twice in the same theatre of war ... The Eighth Army has been practically destroyed. In Tobruk the port installations

---

29 Mosenson, M. *Letters From The Desert*, pp. 111-112.
30 *Hora* - traditional Jewish fold dance of Eretz Israel.
31 Mosenson, M. *Letters From The Desert*., p.115.
32 *The Palestine Post*. 5 July 1942, p. 5.

are almost intact ... If, at this moment, the remains of this British Army are not pursued to the last breath of each man, the same thing will happen as when the British were deprived of success when they nearly reached Tripoli and suddenly stopped in order to send forces to Greece ...'[33]

'Bad news:' Mosenson wrote on 22 June 1942. '*Tobruk has fallen.* The heart is oppressed. There is something personal for me in this loss. It is as if I felt it on my own flesh. For this place had become a symbol of resistance to the storm. For me, too, personally, Tobruk was a testing-place. There I put myself, my nerves, and everything that is precious to me, to the test, and it left its mark on me for years to come ... There I first met with death ... In its shadow I suffered, laughed, wept and dreamed of home. There I was seized with a great fear for my home, for the country, for all of you. And now the city has fallen.'

His apprehensions for the welfare of his family were felt by most of the Jewish soldiers. 'Yesterday on the Jerusalem radio,' he continued, 'we listened to Moshe Shertok's[34] call to the Jewish community. Listening to his grave apprehensions, thoughts arose in my mind concerning what is in store for the community and how it will face what must come upon it. I am afraid to express what I have been thinking....'[35]

The remainder of the Eighth Army retreated in full flight back to Mersa Matruh, half way between Libya and Alexandria, with the Axis forces in hot pursuit. By 25 June Rommel was at the gates of Mersa Matruh itself. On that same day the 9th Australian Division received a summons to quickly rejoin the Eighth Army.

To the Gates of Alexandria

The Axis thrust continued, and on 27 June the Eighth Army was forced to retreat further east, quickly followed by Rommel's forces. General Freyberg didn't believe that Mersa Matruh could be defended against the German onslaught. So the soldiers hastily pulled down their camps and pulled out. Blyth and other New Zealanders were partly compensated for this inconvenience. 'The NAAFI canteen was thrown open,' he recalls, 'and we crammed our truck with canned apricots and beans so that every time in the next few days when we hit a bump, tins flew out. It was a pity we could not find the beer; there must have been tons of it somewhere.'[36]

The New Zealanders retreated eastwards, located a suitable position, known as Minqar Qaim, and dug in again. The following day they felt the brunt of a full frontal Axis assault. 'Heavy artillery fire numbs the mind,' Blyth wrote, 'which is just as well, but I was interested in my reaction. If this is war,' he philosophized, 'and it

---

33 Quoted in Churchill ,W. *The Hinge of Fate*, p. 419.
34 Head of the political department of the Jewish Agency in Jerusalem.
35 Mosenson, M. *Letters From The Desert*, p. 122.
36 Blyth, J. *Soldiering On*, p. 36.

undoubtedly was, it seemed to be the most stupid, scary, crazy business I had ever been involved in.'[37]

That terrible day finally ended, much to everyone's relief. The Germans had not broken through - but they held the upper hand. They had succeeded in surrounding the beleaguered Allied force comprised of the 10th Indian and 50th British divisions as well as the New Zealanders. It was a precarious situation, especially as the Allied troops were desperately low on ammunition. 'Without ammunition it is absolutely certain the Division would not have survived another day, recalls Blyth, 'and that it faced extinction, a disaster that could not be contemplated for people in a small country like New Zealand.'[38]

They had no choice but to break out during the night, crash through the surrounding Axis forces and retire further eastwards. It was a night no New Zealand soldier would forget. A hellish fire fight ensued between the two opposing forces, terrifying both Allied and Axis soldiers. Of it Rommel wrote:

> The wild flare-up which ensued involved my own battle headquarters ... The exchanges of fire between my forces and the New Zealanders reached an extraordinary pitch of intensity. Soon my headquarters were surrounded by burning vehicles, making them the target for continuous fire at close range. I had enough of this after a while, and ordered the troops with the staff to move back southeastwards. The confusion reigning on that night can scarcely be imagined.'[39]

While Rommel's staff was moving in one direction the New Zealanders were moving in another. And they miraculously broke through, although the casualties were high. The Indian and British Divisions sustained even more casualties in their breakout attempt. Yet, by the beginning of July a large proportion of the Eighth Army had managed to retreat successfully eastward and establish a new defensive line near a small railway station named El Alamein.

Renewed Jewish Concerns

On the day that the Eighth Army withdrew from Mersa Matruh, *Hagana* commanders were requested to bring the First *Palmach* Company to the Negev region and prepare for a possible German invasion. Israeli Galil, one of the Jewish soldiers, wrote 'Not all our boys were armed. There were not enough weapons for all members of the company. Some had pistols, rifles and submachine guns. Others in the company were armed with sticks.'[40]

Uzi Narkiss recalls of the time: 'I think the most naïve thing that was done at that time was that our platoon commander, a kibbutznik ... took all of us to a British

---

37 Blyth, J. ibid., p. 38.
38 Blyth, J. ibid., p. 42.
39 *Rommel*, by Desmond Young. Quoted in Churchill, W. *The Hinge of Fate*, p. 424.
40 Lossin, Yigal. *Pillar of Fire*, p. 337.

police station, [and said] "If tomorrow or the day after tomorrow the Germans will show up we will do everything to occupy the British police post before them so that we will be able to defend the Negev here." Nobody asked how are we going to do it because we did not have even one rifle. But naïve as we were ... with this sincerity and devotion for a certain cause which was defending the country now in order to establish a Jewish State, we said "OK sir" ... we didn't have any arms but we were willing to do whatever [was needed].'[41]

Indeed Jewish people throughout British *Palestine* were prepared to defend their land against the Germans with even less than sticks. On 2 July Mosensen wrote how one of the Jewish soldiers had received a paper from his kibbutz in which there was a conversation between an adult and the children of the kibbutz. The paper wrote: 'Yesterday morning, after a meeting of the *Kibutz* concerning matters of security, we had a discussion at the school. We told the children that at first we hesitated to tell them that the Germans have a great many weapons and that they have pushed the English back and conquered a part of Egypt. We did not know if they, the children, could help us.'

After explaining the story of Gideon and the Midianites, the few against the many, the correspondent continued: 'The children asked that they be allowed to drill and that they should be taught how to use guns and to shoot well.' It was then explained to the children that there were few guns. The correspondent continued: 'The discussion was tense, we ended by deciding to have them exercise in getting up quickly, aiming stones at a target, etc. We would also teach them how to overcome heat and thirst.' Mosenson and the Jewish soldiers on the front line were encouraged by the resolve of even the Jewish children of Eretz Israel to withstand the German onslaught if and when they broke through.[42]

Everyone knew the terrible consequences if the Germans invaded the Land of Israel. Jewish leaders in America, including the renowned Rabbi Stephen Wise, cabled Churchill in early July 'asking for immediate mobilization of all available Jewish manpower in Palestine, emphasizing that the German advance to Suez would threaten 550,000 Jews with annihilation.'[43] The *Statesman and Nation* journal in London emphasized the gravity of the situation even further:

> We will need every tank and gun we have got to hold Palestine and Syria ... the military case for holding Palestine has been reinforced by the duty to preserve the Jewish population from Himmler's gas chambers and firing squads.[44]

---

41   Conversation with General Narkiss, April 1997.
42   Mosenson, M. *Letters From The Desert.*, pp. 124-125.
43   *The Palestine Post.* 5 July 1942, p. 1.
44   Quoted in *The Palestine Post.* 5 July 1942, p. 1.

Chapter 27

El Alamein: Echoes of Masada

Last Stop - El Alamein

El Alamein, a small railway stop in the middle of no-where, was the last defensible position before the Suez Canal. The area was a narrow belt between the Mediterranean Sea on one side, and a huge natural barrier, the Qattara Depression some sixty-five kilometres to the south, on the other. The discouraged Eighth Army had to adequately defend this line against a revitalized German led force.

The British now faced their biggest threat since the fall of France. One eyewitness of these events, Olivier Manning, (whose husband, a civil servant was about to be transferred to Jerusalem) recalls the unease and panic which quickly spread in Egypt amongst those with Allied connections: 'When the Germans reached El Alamein, the sense of unease changed to incipient panic ... Alexandria was shaken by the sounds of guns.'[1]

The 9th Australian Division moved quickly southwards from Tripoli, ostensibly en-route to an exercise. To conceal their true destination they took the inland route through the Bekaa Valley, and on the way passed through territory familiar to both the Light Horse of 1918 and the 7th Division of 1941. A number of the men believed they were destined for Australia to fight the Japanese. Not so Derrick, who wrote: 'News from the Desert is not the best, Fritz being within 15 miles of Mersa Matruh, it now looks as though we are bound for ANOTHER ENGAGEMENT WITH MR ROMMEL.'[2] Near Gaza the long convoy turned inland towards Beersheva, a route familiar to the Anzacs and British soldiers from 1917. On 29 June the convoy progressed south of Beersheva, close to that famous staging ground of 31 October 1917, and travelling via the central route (that travelled by Enver Pasha in his ill-fated assault of February 1917), they made their way towards the Suez Canal.

While at Kantara waiting to cross the Suez Canal, Olivier Manning observed trucks heading in the opposite direction. 'These were filled with Australians' she

---

1   Manning, Olivier. *The Flap.* Quoted in *History of the Second World War*, Purnell & Sons Ltd, (Paulton, 1967), p. 1066.

2   *Diary of Thomas Derrick*, Farquhar, M., p. 92.

wrote 'thin, lanky men, darkly sunburned, who had fought their way twice up to Benghazi and had been sent for a rest to ... Syria. Now they were being rushed back to the desert. They lay about, silent, 'browned off', accepting the situation with a cynical resignation that had gone beyond disgust.'[3]

By 4 July Morshead's men, somewhat perturbed that Tobruk had been lost, were stationed near El Alamein itself, coming under the command of 30th Corps, alongside the 2nd South African Division and 10th Indian Division. Further to the south lay the 12th Corps, comprised of the 1st and 7th Armoured Divisions, the 2nd New Zealand Division and 5th Indian Division.

Renewed Concerns in Eretz Israel

'In Palestine itself,' recalls Uzi Narkiss, 'our government, the Jewish Agency, was very anxious, and everybody felt it. Anxious and pre-occupied for the future of the tiny Jewish minority living in Palestine.'[4] David Horowitz from the *Jewish Agency* affirmed Narkiss' analysis, stating that the Jewish community was almost certain 'that what awaited them was a catastrophe from Rommel's army, which had come as close as El Alamein. We knew that what stood between us and Rommel was a very thin barrier of British forces.'[5] But that thin barrier of British forces was no certainty for protection. Narkiss recalls: 'The British High Commissioner called the ... President of the Jews living in Palestine, Mr. Ben Zvi, and announced to him, "Listen Mr. President, if and when the German Army will invade and capture Palestine, we the British Army will withdraw all the way to India" ... So our President,' Narkiss continued, 'was very shocked.'

Narkiss recalled that following Ben Zvi's meeting with the British High Commissioner, Ben Zvi then, '... reported to the Jewish leaders what had happened the previous night.' After debating what the Jewish people would do in view of this new situation, they finally 'decided, number one, if the British remain or not, that's their business - we ... remain.'[6]

The Jewish leadership then increased their efforts for enlistments in the British Army. By 8 July there were over 20,000 Jewish men and women in various services - not including those involved with the *Hagana*. In an enlistment campaign in Tel Aviv on 4 July, Moshe Shertok declared '... that no nation was under a greater compulsion in facing the fateful necessity of fighting than the Jewish people, *since the remnants of its hopes were concerned with this part of the world.*'[7] Such an attitude was prevalent even before the full extent of the Nazi atrocities in Europe were apparent.

---

3   Manning, Olivier, *The Flap*, ibid., p. 1066.
4   Conversation with General Narkiss, April 1997.
5   Lossin, Yigal, *Pillar of Fire*, p. 337.
6   Conversation with General Narkiss, April 1997.
7   *The Palestine Post.* 5 July 1942, p. 5. Italics mine.

The Jewish community co-operated in every British initiative. They had no choice. If they fled, the Arab nationalist movement would greet the Germans as victors and together they would ensure that all vestiges of the Jewish National Home would be destroyed. And while the Jewish people considered their fate, nearly a third of the eight thousand Arabs in the British Army deserted with their rifles, 'mostly during Rommel's advance.'[8]

The *Carmel Plan*

'When our leaders came back from Mr. Ben Zvi,' Narkiss recalls, '[they] had several alternatives. One: that the women and children would withdraw with the British Army. The second, all the population would follow the British Army, and the last one, the entire population would remain and fight the Germans. And they chose the last one.'

'But,' Narkiss continues, 'in order to realize such an alternative you must have a fortress where you can get organized, fortified and from as a natural fortress as possible, you will be able to fight a superior power - that was the Germans. The choice was the Carmel or a certain part of it ... and to fight the German Army from there until the very end.'[9]

The British authorities were determined to establish a defensive line in the Judean mountain range and in the Carmel Range. If the Germans broke through the Allied forces in Egypt and crossed the Suez Canal, the next effective natural defence line was the Carmel Range. To proceed further northwards, the Germans would need to cross that strategically placed mountain range.

Yitzhak Sadeh and Professor Yochanan Ratner from the Technion (who was also a *Hagana* commander) devised a plan known as the *Carmel Plan*. The British authorities accepted the plan, and thereupon set about preparing the Jewish people for its implementation. In the event of a German breakthrough the entire Jewish population of British *Palestine* would be moved to the Carmel Range. There they would be governed and administered by the Jewish leaders. Supplies would be stocked up, grown locally, and dropped by the RAF and British submarines. The area would be defended by the Jewish defence forces, and become a staging post for *Palmach* guerrilla assaults upon the occupying German forces.

Many recognized a parallel and even symbolism with another famous event in Jewish history. In the first century Jewish survivors of the Revolt against Rome barricaded themselves against the occupying Roman forces on a hilltop fortress named Masada adjacent to the Dead Sea. Yigal Yadin, a senior *Hagana* commander, and Uzi Narkiss agreed that the feeling and the planning behind the *Plan* was very much

---

8   Bethell, N. *The Palestine Triangle*, p. 140.
9   Conversation with General Narkiss, April 1997.

based upon a Masada attitude.[10]   Horowitz said 'The plans were to fight down to the last drop of blood, a new version of Masada - that's how you could define it.   There was great fear.'[11]   British intelligence agents then began to train the *Palmach* how to set up an effective partisan force to operate within the Land of Israel when the Germans invaded.   Altogether 725 Palmach men were recruited for the elite units.   Added to this was a fresh recruitment drive, which was not only restricted to Jewish men.

Some 3,150 Jewish women volunteered for the Auxiliary Territorial Service (ATS), and joined the 120 non-Jewish women (Christian Arabs and Armenians).   It was significant that there were few Moslem Arabs enlisting in such a unit.   However at no time did the British authorities broadcast the fact that the majority of these enlisting were Jewish.   Britain, pushed against the wall, had no choice but to enlist greater Jewish support, while all the time attempting to maintain her position of parity with the Arabs - even though it was clear that the Arabs were now looking more and more to the Germans.

The sentiments of the Arab nationalists is expressed in a telegram which Haj Amin sent Hitler in July 1942 in which he again extended his best wishes to the Fuhrer for the latest 'Axis victory in North Africa.'   He added his opinion that the German and Italian acknowledgment of Egyptian independence was a wise policy, and one which would 'guide the German-Italian armies from victory to victory' in other Arab lands and the region, and register continual Arab support for their cause, and lead them to ultimate victory.[12]   Arab propaganda now intensified, as the Arab people living under Allied occupation were encouraged to rise up and fight the Allies, and to welcome Rommel's forces once they crossed into British *Palestine*.[13]

The Jewish people living in Egypt were filled with anxiety.   Thea Levinsohn was the head nurse of a surgical team at the Jewish hospital in Alexandria.   She wrote concerning the period when the Germans neared El Alamein, of a visit by a foreign diplomat, (whose daughter had been treated at the hospital), to see the chief surgeon, Dr. Katz.   'Katz received him,' she recalls, 'and a few minutes later called me into his room and showed me a document.   It was a copy of a command to be obeyed immediately after Rommel and his advance detachment entered Alexandria, namely, to arrest the people named in the document for deportation to Germany.   All our names and addresses, along with the German and Austrian refugees living in Alexandria, were listed.'

It was clear to those whose names appeared on the list, that they had to leave Alexandria immediately.   This opinion was confirmed shortly after by a visit from

---

10   Lossin, Yigal. *Pillar of Fire*. page 337. And conversation with General Narkiss.
11   Lossin, Yigal. ibid., p. 337.
12   Volume 13, Letters and Telegrams from Foreign Heads of State, Germany. Quoted in Pearlman, M. *The Mufti of Jerusalem*, p. 61.
13   Sacher, H. *A History of Israel*, p. 229.

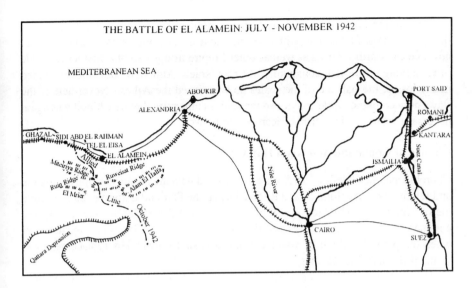

THE BATTLE OF EL ALAMEIN: JULY - NOVEMBER 1942

the British governor, who 'advised us, as Jewish refugees,' wrote Levinsohn, 'to leave the town.' [14]

First Battle of El Alamein

The battle for El Alamein recommenced on 10 July as both the Axis and the Allies made moves to break out. It was one of the fiercest assaults of the entire Desert War. While Auchinleck attempted to break out on the northern sector, near the coast, with the Australian and South African Divisions, and the central sector by the New Zealand, Indian and British Divisions, Rommel was moving to the south and attempting to come in behind the Allied lines. Small, basically insignificant places like Tel el Eisa, Ruweisat Ridge, Miteiriya Ridge, El Mrier, Ruin Ridge and others soon became household names throughout the world as many closely observed this critical action. All the nations suffered heavy casualties, with the New Zealanders suffering some 1,405 soldiers killed, wounded or captured from the Ruweisat Ridge action alone. Charles Upham won his second Victoria Cross here. At the battle of Ruin Ridge one Australian battalion, the 2/28th lost 554 men killed, wounded or captured.[15]

Unfortunately many of the casualties suffered were the result of poor planning and communications. The New Zealanders and Australians were very critical and upset with the British staff work and lack of support from the British armour.[16]

---

14 *The Jerusalem Post*, 23 October 1992.
15 See Ivor Davies, *Jim Jeans' Letters 1940-42*, (soon to be published) pp. 24-.6
16 Badman. P. *North Africa 1940-1942*, p. 153.

Despite the heavy casualties and severe problems with communication, it was this first battle of El Alamein, which stopped, at least temporarily, the German-Italian advance eastwards. Anzac as well as other Empire troops had played a leading role in preserving the Jewish community of Eretz Israel. Although both sides sustained heavy losses, the balance of the scales now favoured the Allies. Nevertheless, the flaws noticed in the battle convinced the senior authorities that new blood was again necessary if the war in North African was to be won.

Change of Command and Alam Halfa

Churchill and the Chiefs-of-Staff were dissatisfied with the progress of the campaign, and felt that both Auchinleck and Ritchie lacked the flair and initiative required for a major victory. Auchinleck was replaced by General Sir Harold Alexander, and command of the Eighth Army was entrusted to General Gott. Gott was killed however when the plane in which he was travelling was shot down. His replacement was General Bernard Montgomery.

Due to fatigue Rommel requested to be relieved, but Hitler refused permission. And not only was he tired, so too were most of his men. He was now drawing upon his last reserves, and knew that a last effort needed to be made quickly before the Allies managed to re-supply and re-equip.

The next Axis thrust, anticipated by Montgomery, was aimed at securing the Alam Halfa Ridge to the south east of El Alamein. It was to be Rommel's last throw of the dice. Montgomery planned, at the same time, striking north from the coastal sector. In fact when Rommel opened the offensive on 30 August, he made diversionary attacks against the Australian and Indian positions in the north and central sectors.

The main German offensive moved towards the Alam Halfa Ridge, where he was heavily attacked by the New Zealanders and the new 132nd British Brigade. Rommel was able to withdraw with much of his force in tact. The diversionary attack of the Australians began on 1 September and gained many positions before retiring before heavily defended Axis positions. Both sides returned to almost the same positions as before the battle. Although Allied tank losses were greater than the Axis, the Allies could more easily restock, due to the arrival of more equipment coming from the USA. The Battle of Alam Halfa proved to be advantageous to the Allies.

Preparations for the Final Thrust

During the following weeks both sides worked feverishly to prepare themselves for what all knew would be the decisive battle. For the Jewish soldiers this was the period of the *High Holidays*, which alongside *Passover,* is the most important part of the Jewish calendar. The *High Holiday* season began with *Rosh HaShanah*, the Jewish New Year. 'Three hundred guests came to our dining room this evening.'

wrote Mosenson of the *Rosh HaShanah* celebration. Besides the men from Eretz Israel, Jewish soldiers from South Africa and elsewhere, as well as a veteran of the *Jewish Legion* participated.

Rosh HaShanah is a time of celebration. 'However,' wrote Mosenson of this festival, 'there was not a great deal of gaiety in the program arranged for the evening. Uppermost at this celebration was our anguish at the suffering of European Jews and our fears for the fate of Palestine.'[17]

Although the desert still had the same everyday problems, there were definite improvements in equipment and certain conditions for the soldiers. In the weeks since the Battle of Alam Halfa both sides prepared for what all knew would be the decisive battle in the Eastern Mediterranean. Rommel, by now totally exhausted managed to return to Germany for treatment. Montgomery on the other hand, fresh and energetic, set about rectifying the many problems noticed from the previous engagements.

It seems apparent that Montgomery instilled confidence in his troops, and the sense of gloom and depression which came over them following the first battle of El Alamein, had by mid-October begun to dissipate. The soldiers by mid-October knew that the upcoming battle was to be the crucial one. The feelings of the soldiers were similar to those of the young men from Britain, Australia and New Zealand prior to the August offensive at Gallipoli in 1915 and the Battle of Beersheva in October 1917. Derrick recorded: 'This is a moment in history.'[18]

Mosenson wrote to his wife on the evening of 23 October: 'The sun has set and the world is sunk in darkness. I'll finish now. I don't know when I'll be able to write again - and perhaps not at all. This is a hallowed moment. In another three and a half hours the attack will begin and my own fate may be decided one way or another. In the shadow of death that is hovering over the very hills on the horizon that we may conquer by tomorrow the heart clings to its dear ones, to its dear and distant home....'[19]

'There was tension and excitement at Headquarters.' recalls Blyth. 'The date was 23 October 1942 and that night the 8th Army was going to make an attack along the whole front. Somebody said we had 900 guns ahead of us, almost wheel to wheel, and there was going to be the biggest gun barrage ever heard in the Middle East.'[20] Brigadier Howard Kippenberger, veteran of Greece, Crete and North Africa, addressed his men of the 23rd New Zealand Battalion on the slopes of a sand hill:

> I told them that this was the turn of the war and the greatest moment of their lives: they had the duty and the honour of breaking in, on which everything depended: our hats were in the ring and I expected them to do it no matter what the cost ...[21]

---

17 Mosenson, M., *Letters From The Desert.*, p. 129.

18 *Diary of Thomas Derrick*, Farquhar, p. 113.

19 Mosenson, M. *Letters From The Desert.*, pp. 134-135.

20 Blyth, J. *Soldiering On.*, p. 65.

21 Kippenberger, Brigadier, H. *Infantry Brigadier.* Oxford University Press, (Oxford,1961), pp. 225 & 228.

Second Battle of El Alamein

The crucial battle of the Eastern Mediterranean during the Second World War was announced by the launching of a massive Allied artillery barrage from some 800 guns. New Zealander, Sergeant Mick Kenny recalled that there were 'flashes all over the place, the air became thick with dust, smoke and burnt cordite. The sounds of the Highland Bagpipes and the Maori Battalion doing their war cries. What a scene! Something we can't ever forget.'[22] Then after this barrage had completed its initial task, the infantry and armour headed for their objectives. From the coast inland were spread the 9th Australian, 51st Highland, 2nd New Zealand and 1st South African Divisions - a Commonwealth spread if ever there was one. Behind them were the 1st and 10th British Armoured Divisions ready to break through the gaps opened for them by the infantry.

By the next morning significant gains had been made, but the Axis forces held firm in most positions. Part of the initial impetus was lost as the sappers were not able to adequately clear the minefields for the armour. The British armour took very heavy casualties in their attempts to break out.

The Germans strongly counter-attacked, concentrating upon the northern sector in and around Tel el Eisa. The fighting was intense, with Rommel, now restored, back leading the Axis forces. He later wrote: 'Attacks were launched by elements of the 15th Panzer Division, the Littorio Division and a Bersaglieri Battalion, supported by all the local artillery and anti-aircraft guns. The British resistance was desperate. Rivers of blood were poured out over miserable strips of land.'[23]

Montgomery, in the midst of the fighting, made the decision to withdraw some of his troops from the front line and have them ready for his breakout, to be known as *Operation Supercharge*. This would be led by the New Zealand Division, the 151st and 152nd British Infantry Brigades, and the 9th British Armoured Brigade.

The fighting continued almost non-stop until late on 2 November. 'Something had to break the stalemate,' Blyth wrote of the battle, 'and it was the Australians who did it. Ninth Australian Division out on the coast ... made a spectacular advance in their sector which created a serious bulge in the enemies defences which Montgomery was quick to exploit. It was the beginning of the end.'[24]

Churchill wrote of that critical breakthrough: 'The magnificent forward drive by the Australians, achieved by ceaseless bitter fighting, had swung the whole battle in our favour. At 1 A.M. on November 2 "Supercharge" began. Under a barrage of three hundred guns the British brigades attached to the New Zealand Division broke through the defended zone, and the 9th British Armoured Brigade drove on ahead.'[25]

---

22 Taylor, Capt. R.J. *Kiwis in the Desert*. New Zealand Defence Force, 1992.
23 Badman, P. *North Africa 1940-1942*, p. 157.
24 Blyth, J. *Soldiering On.*, pp. 66-67.
25 Churchill, W. *The Hinge of Fate*, p. 598.

The gap opened by the 9th Australian Division was wide enough to allow the New Zealand Division and Scottish Highland infantry as well as the British armour to penetrate into the German sector.

Rommel was directed by Hitler not to retreat. But once he realized that several Allied divisions were pouring through that gap, he had no choice but to withdraw. He was hotly pursued by the re-invigorated Allied force, led by the New Zealanders, and then the other Commonwealth units - except the Australians. Having suffered 2,694 men killed, wounded or missing since 23 October they remained at Sidi Abd el Rahman, and regrouped. Of Thomas Derrick's company of eighty men on 23 October, seventy were dead or wounded. And every company and battalion was in the same shape.

Joy and Grief for the Jewish Soldier

After two weeks of continuous activity Mosenson was able to write his next letters home. On 5 November 1942 he wrote to his precious daughter:

> We are pursuing the German armies who are fleeing before us ... We have pushed them far away from the place where they threatened our country. That danger is now over. But the job is not finished yet ...
> ... We went out to war so that our children, when they grow up, will not have to go through this horror a second time. We went out to war in order to defend our country and our work, to free our people from the dreadful fate which the cursed Nazis have forced upon them ...
> ... And after we clean Africa up we will go on and fight them in their own country, until we wipe out this Nazi-Fascist plague completely. Then, my daughter, we will go home again.[26]

Mosenson wrote to his wife the same day - and was full of sorrow. 'I have heard that my friend Tate, the New Zealander, is among the dead. I can't rid myself of this thought.'[27] Later, on 11 November he wrote how on the following day he was going out in search of Tate's grave.[28] But he searched in vain for his young friends grave. He reluctantly informed his wife several days later: 'My dear Tate, the gentle, pure-hearted lad from New Zealand has been added to the long line of unknown soldiers.'[29] Shortly later Mosenson and the other Jewish soldiers prepared to celebrate *Hanukah,* the festival of light, freedom and redemption, in the desert. Exactly twenty-five years before, the Jewish people of Eretz Israel celebrated *Hanukah* as Judea and Jerusalem were being liberated by the British-Anzac force.

But this *Hanukah* party was a sad affair. The rabbi brought the sorrowful news

---

26 Mosenson, M. *Letters From The Desert.*, pp.136-137.
27 Ibid., p. 137.
28 Ibid., p. 141.
29 Ibid., p. 142.

of the welfare of the Jewish community of Libya. The Jewish males had been taken as civilian road-builders and few survived. From the survivors he learned that most of the Jewish people of Berci, Derna and Benghazi, including the family with whom Mosenson celebrated *Purim* in 1941 had been killed or dragged away. Mosenson wrote remorsefully: 'the young daughter of the Ben-Dusa family, whose guest I was, was carried off by the Italian army; the mother was raped by drunken Italians and was then stabbed to death and the rest of the family were taken to labor battalions and no one knows how they met their death.'[30]

In his last letter of 1942, Mosenson wrote to his wife on 15 December of his feelings: 'When we appeared in Libya for the first time and went in a group to the synagogue, the Jewish quarter hummed with joy and happiness. They believed, innocently, that we had the keys to Palestine. Now they are beaten and wretched, and we have no word of hope for them. Think of the feelings of a Jewish soldier who goes to battle in order to save his people, but is completely helpless when he meets them, crushed and miserable.'[31]

The only consolation was that now the Jewish soldiers from the Land of Israel were involved in driving the Nazi menace away from the borders of their homeland. Their focus was upon eradicating that menace initially from Africa and then from Europe itself.

Australians Return Home

While the British, New Zealand, Indian and South African Divisions and Jewish soldiers from Eretz Israel continued their pursuit through Cyrenaica, into Tripolitania and then into Algeria, the 9th Australian Division made its way back to their camps in British *Palestine*, arriving by 9 December 1942. Leave programs for Jerusalem, Tel Aviv and Haifa were quickly set up.

The men of the 9th Division completed what their fathers' generation had begun in 1917, and what the men of the 6th and 7th Australian and New Zealand Divisions had achieved since 1940 - the liberation and preservation of the Jewish homeland in Eretz Israel. The words inscribed on the parchment of that Bible given to Montgomery by the Jewish leadership say it all.

On 22 December 1942, thousands of these soldiers, veterans of Tobruk and El Alamein paraded at an airfield near Gaza in one of the biggest military parades of the war.[32] They were inspected by Commander-in-Chief General Alexander, who praised them for their share in the November victory at El-Alamein.[33] Major-General Sir Edward Spears wrote of the parade:

---

30   Ibid., pp. 145-146.
31   Ibid., p. 149.
32   *The Palestine Post.* 25 December 1942, p. 1.
33   Ibid., p. 1.

...The men, I was told, had taken immense pains to be drill-perfect, for they regarded this parade as a message, a token of sorrow and respect to all those Australian soldiers whom they left behind, buried in the soil of the Levant.[34]

With their New Zealand brothers still pursuing the German-Italian army in North Africa, the 9th Australian Division was indeed signalling a message in this parade. It was not only their fellow men of the 9th Division they were honouring, but indeed the roughly 20,000 New Zealand and Australian soldiers who lay buried in the Levant-Eastern Mediterranean from Gallipoli through to Tobruk. Indeed this was a supreme contribution from two small nations from *the uttermost ends of the earth*. Shortly afterwards these tired soldiers headed to Kantara for the long sea journey back to Australia, where they would rest before fighting the Japanese threat to their own nation, homes and destiny.[35]

---

34 Quoted in Laffin, J. *Greece, Crete and Syria*, p. 162.
35 During this period a New Zealand survey unit was mapping the borders of British Palestine.

*C*hapter 28

Exit British Empire - Enter Israel

As the soldiers from the British Commonwealth and Eretz Israel continued their move westwards, they ultimately met up with the newly arrived forces of the USA. By mid 1943 the final victory over the Axis forces in North Africa was achieved, and the Allies then crossed to Sicily and thence to the Italian mainland.

Following the Allied victories at El Alamein and at Stalingrad in 1942 the Nazi policy to exterminate the Jewish people increased and millions were sadistically murdered in the gas chambers. Henceforth names like Auschwitz, Treblinka, Dachau, Buchenwald, Bergen Belsen and others became synonymous with Nazi hatred of the Jewish people and other minority and despised groups, including Evangelical Christians, Communists and Gypsies. But there were pockets of Jewish resistance to the planned extermination, especially at the Warsaw Ghetto, and also behind German lines as members of partisan groups. Jewish parachutists from Eretz Israel were also dropped behind German lines, especially in Yugoslavia. Almost simultaneously, the Haj Amin was encouraging Moslem Bosnians to join Hitler's *SS*.

Struggles in Eretz Israel

The Jewish people of British *Palestine* now concentrated upon saving their brethren in Europe, and influencing British officialdom to adopt a more pro-Zionist attitude, and managed a little success. Churchill had, in January 1944, asked the War Cabinet to seriously consider establishing a Jewish State in part of the Land of Israel. Few knew of this plan, for the emphasis first was upon the destruction of Nazi Germany.

Yet despite Churchill's sentiments, most Jewish leaders in Eretz Israel, including Ben Gurion and Weizmann, were becoming impatient. The Jewish people of Europe were being exterminated and the Land of Israel was closed to those who could flee. Others in British *Palestine* were much more frustrated than Weizmann and Ben Gurion. On 1 January 1944 the *Irgun*, under the command of Menahem Begin, (a protégé and admirer of Jabotinsky) who had fled from Nazi occupied Poland in 1943, declared an armed revolt against the British authorities - and those who collaborated with them.

The *Irgun* and another radical group, the *Stern Gang* meant business. In 1944 Lord Moyne the British Minister of State for Middle Eastern Affairs, stationed in

Egypt, (who up till 1944 had been anti-Zionist in his opinions, but had since modified his position), was murdered by the *Stern Group*. This group wanted to show the world that even the officialdom of the mighty British Empire could be touched.

The Zionist leadership and the *Irgun* condemned the murder, while Churchill roundly condemned the Zionist organization. Then the two separatist groups, the *Irgun* and *Stern Gang*, were ordered by the Zionist leadership to lay down their arms and cease from separatist acts. The *Irgun* refused to comply. The British authorities arrested hundreds of suspected activists and deported them to internment camps in East Africa.

Formation of Jewish Brigade

Despite these tensions within Eretz Israel, Churchill informed the Secretary of State for War on 12 July 1944 to implement the formation of a *Jewish Brigade* as soon as possible.[1] Later he stated that the Jewish fighting force should proceed to Italy as soon as possible. 'I like the idea,' he stated, 'of the Jews trying to get at the murderers of their fellow-countrymen in Central Europe.'[2] The British War Cabinet, agreed to the proposal on 20 September 1944 and Churchill nine days later announced the formation of the *Jewish Brigade* in the House of Commons.[3] Such an announcement had been previously withheld as the British did not want to exacerbate pro-Nazi attitudes amongst the Arabs.

The *Jewish Brigade Group* adopted the Star of David as their emblem, and flag. They were commanded by a Canadian Jew, Brigadier Ernest Benjamin. Like the formation of the *Zion Mule Corps* and the *Jewish Legion*, the *Jewish Brigade* was seen as a great political step forward

Enter the USA and the United Nations

During 1945 approaches were being made to President Roosevelt and to the United States administration by some Zionist leaders. But at the same time as the *Jewish Brigade* soldiers were participating in battles in the Senio River area in Italy, President Roosevelt was meeting with Ibn Saud, the King of Saudi Arabia. The major topic of discussion - oil. During the same meeting, Ibn Saud managed to prejudice Roosevelt against Zionism.

This meeting revealed that henceforth it would be oil and not the riches of India and the Spice Islands which would be the lure of the East. It would not be Britain's concern for her eastern Empire which would be the determining factor in the affairs

---

1   Churchill to Secretary of State for War, 10 July, 1944. Churchill, W. *Triumph and Tragedy*, Houghton & Mifflin, (Boston, 1949),p. 693.

2   Churchill to Secretary of State for War, 26 July, 1944. , ibid., p. 697.

3   Sacher, H. *A History of Israel*, p. 242.

of the Eastern Mediterranean, but the concerns of the USA and the industrialized West and its ideological battle against the Soviet Union. This period witnessed a changing of the imperial, superpower baton.

Then in April 1945, the opening session of the newly formed United Nations Organization, was held in San Francisco. The qualification for entrance - participation in the war against the Axis forces. Four Arab nations participated, including Egypt, Yemen and Saudi Arabia, who were encouraged by Britain to quickly declare war against Germany so as to qualify. Most of the leaders of the Arab countries had actually supported the German cause during the War. The Jewish people however were not formally represented. They had no nation and no flag which could represent them.

Victory in Europe was achieved on 8 May 1945. Afterwards the full extent of the *Holocaust*, the systematic murder of six million Jewish people, was revealed. The main hope and dream for the survivors was to go to the Land of Israel. But officially the *White Paper* of 1939 was still in effect, and despite Churchill's previous sentiments, there was little that could be done. In desperation the *Jewish Agency* requested permission to bring 100,000 Holocaust survivors into Eretz Israel. When the authorities procrastinated, the Zionist movement organized the illegal immigration of the 100,000 Jewish refugees - known as *Operation Briha.*

Following elections in July 1945, Churchill was ousted, and a Labour Government formed under Clement Attlee - an apparent pro-Zionist. Another apparent pro-Zionist, Ernest Bevin, became the Foreign Secretary. There was optimism for the Jewish people - and apprehension on behalf of the Arabs. Yet within a short space of time both men quickly changed their spots when faced with the weight of Arab opposition. They agreed to maintain the conditions of the 1939 *White Paper* and restrict Jewish immigration.

The USA, under new President Harry Truman, pressured Britain at this point to permit the entry of the 100,000 refugees into Eretz Israel. Would the new British government heed the pressure of the United States and the Zionist movement, or bow to Arab pressure? Bevin was apprehensive about adopting a favourable stance towards Zionism for fear that the Arabs would gravitate towards the Soviet Union, thereby providing the former Russian Empire an easy entrance into the Middle East.

The Soviet Union, sidelined during the previous decades was now again becoming an interested player in the imperial game. The West, and especially the United States, was becoming more dependent upon the oil from the Arab areas. Realizing this, the Arab states held the Russians out as a possible partner if the USA, Britain and the West did not support their position.

Bevin's compromise was to form a joint *Anglo-America Committee of Inquiry* to determine the best solution for the refugees. The *Committee* visited DP (Displaced Persons) camps in Germany and interviewed many prominent Jewish and Arab spokesmen in the Land of Israel. The *Committee* called for the immediate entry of

100,000 war refugees into British *Palestine*. Five days after the findings of the *Committee* were released, Britain granted independence to Transjordan, and signed a treaty of friendship with the new king, Abdullah. Britain also declared it would not agree to the entrance of the 100,000 refugees, and that the conditions of the *White Paper* of 1939 would remain in force.

Jewish Reactions to Britain's Policies

The pro-Allied role of the Jewish people of Eretz Israel during the war was being forgotten, as was the pro-Nazi position of many of the Arab leaders. In reaction the *Hagana, Irgun* and *Stern Group* joined together and formed a *Jewish Resistance Movement* to battle against the British policies. Many key British installations were attacked. The British authorities reacted strongly, and on *Black Sabbath*, 29 June 1946, they imposed a general curfew throughout the country, searched numerous Jewish settlements for arms, and arrested a number of key leaders.

Despite this, the struggle continued. On 22 July 1946 members of the *Irgun* blew up part of the King David Hotel in Jerusalem, seat of the Mandatory Government, killing ninety-one people. The *Hagana* was upset as they maintained that the event was not staged as planned, and the period of co-operation ceased.

A severe British clamp-down followed. The Jewish community then heeded Weizmann's plea to end armed resistance. Although many members of the *Palmach* disagreed, Weizmann's decision held the day. Henceforth the attention of the *Palmach* and *Hagana* was upon more peaceful means, such as establishing settlements and bringing in as many illegal immigrants as possible.

In late September 1946 the *Hagana* established eleven Jewish settlements in the northern Negev area in one night. Many of these settlements were established on ground over which the Anzacs rode in 1917. One of them was Kibbutz Beeri.

Meanwhile the activities of the *Irgun* and *Stern Gang* intensified, causing the British authorities to evacuate all dependents to Britain in February 1947 - *Operation Polly*. The British then hanged four Jewish freedom fighters at Acre Prison in April. This in turn precipitated a daring raid by the *Irgun* against the Acre Prison, in July 1947, in which many members of the group were freed.

Britain Turns to the United Nations

All the activities, either of the *Irgun* and *Stern Gang* as well as by the *Hagana*, and the efforts of the Zionist Organization, had a telling effect upon the British Government. They just could not find a suitable solution. Finally in 1947 Ernest Bevin, the Secretary of State, informed the Cabinet that he had exhausted all his options. Britain had no choice but to offer the future of the Land of Israel to the United Nations.

The United Nations debate on the future of British *Palestine* began on 28 April 1947. When the Soviet representatives spoke up about the 'right of the Jewish People to have a state of its own', and of the need for a partition into a Jewish and Arab state, hope permeated the Jewish community. The UN dispatched a special committee, named the *United Nations Special Committee on Palestine (UNSCOP)* to the Land of Israel in June 1947. During their period in Eretz Israel events escalated dramatically.

On one occasion a dilapidated old ship, named the *Exodus* carrying some 4,554 Jewish refugees was dragged into Haifa harbour by ships of the Royal Navy. While on the high seas there had been a running battle between the British seamen and Jewish refugees, which left three Jewish people dead and scores wounded. As the Jewish refugees were taken off at Haifa in order to be deported, two of the *UNSCOP* delegates witnessed the scene.

The refugees were returned first to France, and then unbelievably, back to Germany, a scene witnessed by the world. The British authorities were determined to hinder every effort of the Jewish people to reach their ancient homeland. It was ironical then that at the same time, in August 1947, the members of *UNSCOP* were finalizing their report in Geneva. They concluded that 'UNSCOP calls for an end to the British Mandate', and recommended the establishment of a Jewish State, an Arab State and for the *internationalization* of Jerusalem.

Partition Proposal

The Arab League and countries surrounding Eretz Israel, as well as the Arab leadership within British *Palestine,* unanimously rejected the *UNSCOP* recommendation, and began making menacing troop movements. These in turn alarmed the large Jewish population of some 700,000 living within the Arab countries. Groups of Jewish people, from Morocco and Iraq, made attempts to enter Eretz Israel. Many believed that the time of their redemption and the coming of the Messiah was drawing near.

Meanwhile attention was focused upon the United Nations which was now beginning to seriously consider the *UNSCOP* recommendation. The key players in the drama were the two major worldwide powers, the Soviet Union and the United States. While Soviet consent had already been voiced, the United States still procrastinated. Some in senior positions favoured a Jewish State - others opposed it. The critical issues revolved around the USA's need for Arab oil, and that of an Arab-Soviet alliance.

The *UNSCOP* proposal was to be finally voted upon on 29 November 1947 - 150 years after Napoleon began to prepare his fleet for the invasion of Britain. To attain statehood, the Jewish people required a two-thirds majority. The first country to vote was Afghanistan, which being Islamic, naturally voted No. Next was Argentina, which abstained. The third to vote was Australia - which voted Yes, as later did her sister Anzac country New Zealand. France also voted Yes as did, South Africa,

Canada, Netherlands, the Soviet Union, the United States and twenty-five other countries. Britain abstained and India, then with a large Muslim minority, voted against. The two-thirds majority was attained - and after some 2,000 years of national dispersion, there would again be a Jewish State in the Land of Israel.

Reactions to the Vote

The Jewish people, both in British *Palestine* and indeed throughout the world, rejoiced gleefully. The Arab leaders and much of the populace, both in the Land of Israel and throughout the Arab world reacted angrily. Shortly afterwards the Arabs of Eretz Israel began rioting and looting in the Jewish areas. Similar outbursts occurred elsewhere. The Jewish quarter in Aleppo, including the synagogue, was destroyed. A violent pogrom in Aden resulted in the deaths of some eighty-two Jewish people.

Throughout Eretz Israel Jewish communities were attacked - and often the British authorities did little in stemming the attackers. The Zionist movement decided not to abandon any settlements - but to defend them to the bitter end. It was a costly decision. The British, claiming to still be in charge of internal security, did not even patrol or secure the roads. This was left to the *Hagana* - yet if any were caught carrying weapons they were arrested.

The Mufti's forces, under the command of Abd al-Khader al-Husseini, concentrated upon cutting the roads to Jewish settlements, primarily the road from Tel Aviv to Jerusalem. The future outcome of the war, and of who would actually control Eretz Israel, depended upon who won this sector. The Arab League however, now suspicious of Haj Amin, appointed Fawzi al-Kaukji, a bitter rival of the Haj, as commander of their *Army of Liberation.*

Meanwhile a number of murderous bomb explosions occurred in Jerusalem, in which scores of Jewish people were killed. The Jewish fighters occasionally retaliated upon the Arab community. All the while the British authorities seemed reluctant to get directly involved - although they continued to expend considerable energy stopping the infiltration into the Land of Israel of illegal Jewish immigrants - while turning a mostly blind eye to the infiltration of the *Army of Liberation.*

In fact as it appeared that the Arabs were getting the upper hand, opinions at the United Nations, especially that of the United States, began to change. Truman began to have doubts, but assured Weizmann of his support. Yet in a speech at the UN Security Council session on 19 March 1948, Warren Austin, the US representative, announced a reversal of the United States position.

In Eretz Israel the Arab forces stepped up their offensive, and on 20 March they stopped a Jewish convoy getting through to Jerusalem. Jerusalem was under siege. Despite British objections, Ben Gurion saw no alternative but to go onto the offensive. The first operation, *Operation Nahshon* began on 4 April 1948. The objective being to capture Kastel, strategically located on the road between Jerusalem and Tel Aviv, and a position coveted by the EEF in its drive to Jerusalem in November and December 1917. After some heavy fighting it was finally captured. Three young *Palmach* soldiers who distinguished themselves fighting for the preservation of their homeland were Moshe Dayan, Yitzak Rabin and Uzi Narkiss

The Mufti's arch enemy Fawzi al-Kaukji meanwhile began an offensive in the Galilee, aimed at capturing Kibbutz Mishmar HaEmek, strategically located in the Jezreel Valley. From 4-11 April his forces attacked the poorly defended kibbutz, but were beaten off. This Jewish victory was soon afterwards marred by terrible events in and near Jerusalem. On 9 April the *Irgun* and *Stern Gang* captured the Arab village of Deir Yassin adjacent to the Jerusalem-Tel Aviv road. In the battle some 250 Arab civilians were tragically killed. The killings were strongly condemned by the *Vaad Leumi*. Although the *Irgun* and *Stern Gang* maintained that the casualties were killed in the course of the battle, after having been previously warned to flee, there was widespread condemnation. The Arab leadership used the killings to further their propaganda efforts. It backfired and resulted in the exodus of tens of thousands of Arabs from the land, who followed in the footsteps of the 30,000 well-to-do Arabs who had left after the passing of the *Partition* plan.

The political battle was also heating up. The USA was now determined to rescind the *Partition* proposal, and instead opted for a UN Trusteeship. The Soviet Union, sensing the opportunity to take the fledgling Jewish State under her wings, continued to support its formation. The Arabs weren't even interested. They began massing their armies - each sensing that this was an opportunity to cash in and grab a share of the coveted *land between*. Syria planned for the conquest of the north. An Iraqi army was en-route, via Transjordan. On 11 May, King Farouk of Egypt ordered his armies to begin moving eastwards, along the route familiar to Napoleon, Ibrahim Pasha, the EEF, and more recently men of the 2nd New Zealand Expeditionary Force and 2nd Australian Imperial Force. These national Arab armies awaited until after the British Mandate had formally ended - which was to be on 15 May.

The Arab army which most concerned the Jewish leadership was that of Transjordan. King Abdullah's force, the *Jordanian Legion*, was well equipped and British trained. Besides, Abdullah's kingdom was the smallest of the Arab nations surrounding the Land of Israel, and here was his opportunity to carve out for himself a larger and more viable political entity - including the hallowed city of Jerusalem. Contrary to the rules, elements of the *Jordanian Legion* entered the Land of Israel even before the end of the Mandate, and immediately set about attacking the Jewish settlements to the south of Jerusalem - the Etzion bloc.

Despite the odds, and several setbacks, the Jewish forces gained impressive victories throughout the land. Such victories however were insignificant when compared to the odds against them if they declared statehood. The Arab countries, with fully-fledged armies had vowed to invade *Falastin* - the Arabic term for *Palestine* and destroy the Jewish National Home. The question facing Ben Gurion and the

Vaad Leumi in early May 1948 was: 'Whether or not to accept the United States proposal to delay the declaration of statehood, or to proceed and face the risks without official US support? On 11 May, *the Vaad Leumi* met in Tel Aviv and voted to declare statehood when the British left in three days time.

May 14-15 1948

The British High Commissioner, Sir Alan Cunningham, left Government House in Jerusalem at 8 am on 14 May, and flew to Haifa. He then embarked upon a British warship, where he waited until midnight, when the British Mandate over the Land of Israel would officially end.

During the day Cunningham bided his time on the warship in Haifa Bay. Nearby was Acre from where Sir Sidney Smith thwarted Napoleon's attempts to conquer the region in 1799; where Sir Charles Napier ended Egyptian (and French) ambitions in 1841, and where Vichy French-Nazi German ambitions ended with the signing of the Armistice in 1941. Some kilometres to the east stood Mount Tabor, where Napoleon routed the Turkish Army and issued his famed, yet unfulfilled, proclamation calling upon the Jewish people to return and attain a place among the nations. And a few kilometres to the south, lying at the base of the Carmel Range, lay Megiddo, through which General Chauvel's *Desert Mounted Corps* streamed in pursuit of the Turkish forces in 1918. It was that final thrust by troops of the British Empire - Anzacs, Indians and British - which cleared Eretz Israel of the rule of the Turkish Empire and prepared the way for the officially recognized return of the Jewish people. And above Megiddo all the way through to the Bay of Haifa ran the Carmel Range. It was here in 1942 that the Jewish community of Eretz Israel busily constructed an enclave where they would hold out against the expected Nazi invasion. Thankfully that invasion was stopped when Anzac, British, Indian and South African troops halted the German-Italian advance at El Alamein.

As Cunningham waited, another historical event was occurring at Tel Aviv. An event in fact which was the logical conclusion to all of those previous events stretching from Acre through to El Alamein. At 4 p.m. David Ben Gurion, the former soldier of the *Jewish Legion*, rose to speak to an assembled group of Jewish dignitaries at the Tel Aviv Museum. He said:

> Eretz Israel was the birthplace of the Jewish people. Here their spiritual, religious and political identity was shaped. Here they first attained to statehood, created cultural values of national and universal significance and gave to the world the eternal Book of Books.
>
> After being forcibly expelled from their land, the people kept faith with it throughout their Dispersion and never ceased to pray and hope for their return to it and for the restoration in it of their political freedom ... which would open the gates of the homeland wide to every Jew and confer upon the Jewish people the status of a fully-privileged member of the community of nations ... This right is the natural right of the Jewish

people to be masters of their own fate, like all other nations, in their own sovereign State.

Accordingly we, members of the People's Council, representatives of the Jewish Community of Eretz Israel and of the Zionist movement, are here assembled on the day of the termination of the British Mandate over Eretz Israel and, by virtue of our natural and historic right and on the strength of the United Nations General Assembly, hereby declare the establishment of a Jewish State in Eretz Israel, to be known as the State of Israel ...

Placing our trust in the Almighty, we affix our signatures to this proclamation at this session of the Provisional Council of State, on the soil of the homeland, in the city of Tel Aviv, on this Sabbath Eve, the 5th day of Iyar, 5708, (14th May, 1948).[4]

On the same day that the new State of Israel was officially formed, the Egyptian Air Force bombed Tel Aviv, the Old City of Jerusalem was captured by the *Jordanian Legion*, and the other Arab armies invaded Israel. At midnight, the British warship carrying the official representative of the British Empire, left the waters of Eretz Israel.

* * * * * * * * * * * *

CONCLUSION

Here ends another epoch in the history of the *land between empires*. An epoch which began with Napoleon's invasion of the region in 1798 and ended with Israel's establishment one hundred and fifty years later in 1948. Who at the beginning of this period could have foreseen the unfolding of events over the following one hundred and fifty years? James Bicheno came close. How true those words of his from 1800 echoed in 1948. Concerning the restoration of Israel, he predicted that *'these events may be brought about in a more circuitous way, and by means and instruments not thought of ... For it is not from one particular event that our hope of a speedy restoration of the Jews is drawn, but from the combined direction of many, so it is not this or that particular circumstance, favourable or unfavourable, that can materially affect it.'*

That restoration, anticipated by some in 1798 and by even more in 1840, was by no means a speedy event, but it was a painstaking drawn out affair, involving the combined activities and influences of many people, nations and circumstances, many of which were unfavourable - particularly the wars and conflicts.

These wars and conflicts were invariably brought about by the lust, greed and covetousness of one or more nations, individuals or empires. The conflict of wills of

---

4   Speech of David Ben Gurion, Tel Aviv Museum, 14 May, 1948.

nations, as Oswald Chambers put it. Yet ironically, it was often as a by-product of these wars and conflicts that Israel's restoration was furthered. And in most instances, this development came from little or no pre-conceived plan or initiative.

Perhaps one of the best examples of this principle was the Gallipoli-Dardanelles campaign of 1915. What has for decades been construed as an unmitigated failure, was, in the context of Israel's restoration, a mammoth step forward. The immediate goal of that campaign, the conquest of Constantinople and freeing of the Dardanelles Straits, was definitely not achieved. But the military and political options presented by the opening up of this campaign, led all the way to Jerusalem, more-or-less as Trumpeldor had predicted.

Had Constantinople been taken and Turkey knocked out of the War, and had previous 'agreements', 'commitments' and ambitions been honoured, then Britain probably would not have gained control over the Land of Israel. France, and to some extent Russia, would have. And France and Russia, in all likelihood would not have permitted an officially recognized Jewish restoration.

With this perspective, one's attitude towards that campaign is open for re-evaluation. Something positive did emanate from it. The long-term results of that campaign provided hope for the dispersed Jewish people, who, more than any other nation in history knew the meaning of suffering. **Gallipoli** was a large step which led onto Romani, Gaza. Beersheva, the *Balfour Declaration* and **Jerusalem.**

A similar principle was apparent during the Second World War. As frightening as the prospect of a German led invasion of Eretz Israel was, it was this period which provided tens of thousands of Jewish people with military training. Without such training, how could they have withstood the Arab onslaught of 1947-48 and subsequent attacks?

This period of battles by the European empires for control and influence in the Eastern Mediterranean had, by 1948, been completed. Now a new period was about to begin. The *land between empires* was no longer sought after because of its centrality between Egypt and Mesopotamia as in antiquity, or between Europe and the spices and wealth of India and the Far East. Or between Britain and her eastern Empire. After 1948 it was to become the *land between* the industrialized West, and the oil fields of Arabia; and the land of conflict between those who adhere to the belief that Eretz Israel has been promised to the Jewish people and those who challenge this promise.

A quick look at the historical record from 1948 until the modern day reveals this fact all too plainly. No other nation in the world has had to battle such overwhelming odds in order to survive. Apart from fighting Wars in 1948, 1956, 1967 and 1973, Israel has had to battle the constant threat of local and global terrorism, the economic war, and an ideological war, as her very presence confronts and contradicts countless other belief systems.

It seems then that the Land of Israel was destined to be a clashing ground of rival and conflicting empires and kingdoms. It also seems likely that empires and kingdoms, either physical or ideological, will continue their efforts to subdue, conquer and dominate the Land of Israel. The questions now to be asked are, 'Why?' 'What is so significant about a small piece of real estate in the Eastern Mediterranean, far from the commercial centres of the USA, Western Europe and East Asia that it should provoke such profound interest? And more importantly, 'Why all the extra attention when the Jewish people return to that small piece of Land, (which is almost a forgotten Land until they reside in it), and strenuous efforts made to eradicate their presence there?'

Perhaps in fact those Jewish and Christian Bible-believing people have been right. Perhaps the return of the Jewish people to the Land of Israel, and more specifically to Jerusalem, may lead to the final conflict of the ages and be a prelude to the coming, or return of the Messiah. The Jewish prophet Zechariah actually predicts such a final conflict as the nations of the earth battle against Jerusalem. Jesus also predicted that Jerusalem would be trodden under foot by the Gentiles until the times of the Gentiles would be fulfilled.'[5]

For both the devout Jewish and Christian Bible-believer, the end of Gentile interference with the affairs of Jerusalem and Eretz Israel will be synonymous to the establishment of the Messianic Kingdom, the Messiah's seat of authority being at Jerusalem, in the midst of the Land of Israel, at the centre of the world. If this is so, then it is understandable that those ideological systems which reject the *Kitvei Ha Kodesh* - the Holy Writings of the Jewish people (the Bible), would reject Jewish sovereignty in Eretz Israel.

Perhaps those battles referred to by Churchill and the Israeli kibbutznik did indeed play a significant part in shaping the destiny of the world. Although not fully understood at the time by mortal man, are we now, with the benefit of historical hindsight, able to discern the direction in which all these events and battles have been pointing?

---

5   Zechariah 14 and Luke 21:24.

▲ *General Uzi Narkiss, Defence Minister Moshe Dayan and Chief of Staff Yitzak Rabin entering the Old City of Jerusalem, June 1967. (Courtesy the late General Narkiss.)*

Selected Bibliography

Books Used

Adam Smith, Patsy, *The Anzacs*, Penguin Books, Melbourne, 1991.

Badman, Peter, *North Africa 1940-1942 The Desert War*, Time-Life Books/John Ferguson, Sydney, 1988.

Barnett, Correlli, *The Desert Generals*, Pan Books, London.

Bethell, Nicholas, *The Palestine Triangle*, Andre Deutsch Limited, London, 1979.

Bicheno, J. *The Signs of the Times*, London, 1792.

Bicheno, J. *A Glance at the History of Christianity and of English NonConformity*, London, 1798.

Bicheno, James, *The Restoration of the Jews, And the Crisis of All Nations*, London, 1800.

Blyth, J. *Soldiering On.. A Soldiers War in North Africa and Italy*, Century Hutchinson., Auckland, 1989.

Bostock, H. *The Great Ride, Artlook Books*, Perth, 1982.

Bullock, D. *Allenby's War - The Palestine-Arabian Campaigns 1916-1918*, Blandford Press, London, 1988.

Carmel, A. *Activities of the European Powers in Palestine*, 1799-1914, in *Asia and Africa Studies*. 19, 1985.

Churchill, W. *The World Crisis*, Charles Scribner's Sons, New York, 1949.

Churchill, W. *The Gathering Storm*, Houghton Mifflin Company, Boston, 1948.

   Their Finest Hour, ibid
   The Grand Alliance, ibid.
   The Hinge of Fate, ibid.
   Triumph and Tragedy, ibid.

Davin, D.M. *Battle of Crete*, In *Purnell's History of the Second World War*. Volume 5, Purnell & Sons Ltd, Paulton, 1967.

Dayan, Moshe, *Story of My Life*, Warner Books, New York, 1977.

Dobbie, Lt-Gen. Sir William, *A Very Present Help*, Marshall, Morgan & Scott, Ltd, London: Edinburgh, 1944.

Ellern, H & B, *Herzl, Hechler, the Grand Duke of Baden and the German Emperor, 1896-1904*, Ellern's Bank Ltd, Tel Aviv, 1961.

Facey, A.B. *A Fortunate Life*, Penguin Books, Melbourne, 1981.

Falls, Cyril & MacMunn, General Sir G, *Military Operations, Egypt and Palestine*, London, 1928.

Farquhar, M. *Derrick V.C.*, Rigby Publishers, Adelaide, 1982.

Foley, J. *Tobruk Survives*. In *Purnells History of the Second World War*, Vol 2, Purnell & Sons Ltd, Paulton, 1967.

Freulich, R. *Soldiers in Judea*, Herzl Press, New York, 1964.

Friedman, I. *The Question of Palestine*, Transaction Publishers, New Jersey, 1992.

Fromkin, D. *A Peace to End all Peace*, Avon Books, New York, 1989.

Gilbert, Martin, *Winston S. Churchill, Vol 3; 1914-1916. The Challenge of War*. Houghton Mifflin, Boston, 1971.

Gilbert, Martin, *Winston S. Churchill: Companion Volume.* Vol 4, Part 2, July 1919-March 1921. Houghton Mifflen, Boston, 1978.

Gordon, Dr. H.L. *The Jewish Legions in the British Army During the World War (1914-1918).* New York, 1940.

Gullett, H.S. *The A.I.F. in Sinai and Palestine,* University of Queensland Press & Australian War Memorial, 1984.

Henderson, J. *Gunner Inglorious,* Harry H. Tombs, Wellington, 1945.

Herold, J. Christopher, *Bonaparte in Egypt,* London, 1963.

Hill, A.J. *Chauvel of the Light Horse,* Melbourne University Press, 1978.

Hodder, Edwin, *The Life and Works of the Seventh Earl of Shaftesbury,* London, 1886.

Holt, Bob, *From Ingleburn to Aitape,* Brookvale, 1981.

Hopwood, D. The *Russian Presence in Syria and Palestine, 1843-1914: Church and Politics in the Near East,* Oxford, 1969.

Hughes, R. *The Fatal Shore,* Pan Books/Collins, London, 1987.

Hyamson, Albert, *The British Consulate in Jerusalem in Relation to the Jews in Jerusalem,* London, 1934.

Idriess, Ion., *The Desert Column,* Angus & Robertson, Melbourne, 1973.

Israel Pocket Library, *Zionism,* Keter Books, Jerusalem, 1973.

Israel Pocket Librayr, *History from 1880,* Keter Books, Jerusalem, 1973.

Jabotinsky, Z. *The Story of the Jewish Legion,* Ackerman, New York, 1945.

Jones. I. *The Australian Light Horse,* Time Life/John Fergusson, Sydney, 1987.

Johnston, R.M. *The Corsican: A Diary of Napoleon's Life In His Own Words,* London, 1910.

Jurieu, P. *The Accomplishment of the Scripture Prophecies,* London, 1687.

Kett, H. *History the Interpreter of Prophecy,* London, 1799.

King, M. *New Zealanders at War,* Heinemann, Auckland, 1981.

Kinross, Lord., *Between two Seas. The Creation of the Suez Canal,* William Morrow and Company, Inc., New York, 1969.

Kippenger, Lieut-Col. *Infantry Brigadier,* 1949.

Kobler, F. *The Vision was There,* Lincolns-Prager, London, 1956.

Kobler, F. *Napoleon and the Jews,* Massada Press, Jerusalem, 1975.

Laffin, J. *Anzacs at War,* Abelard-Schumen, London, New York, Toronto, 1965.

Laffin, J. *Greece, Crete and Syria,* Time/Life & Fergusson, Sydney, 1989.

Lawrence, T.E. *Revolt in the Desert,* George H. Doran Co., New York, 1927.

Lawrence, T.E. *Seven Pillars of Wisdom; A Triumph,.* World Books, London, 1935.

Lewis, B. *The Middle East and the West,* Harper and Row, New York, 1964.

Lloyd George, D. *War Memoirs,* Odhams Press Lim., London ,1939.

Lossin, Yigal., *Pillar of Fire,* Shikmona Publishing Co., Jerusalem, 1983.

Manning, Olivier, *The Flap,* In *Purnell's History of the Second World War,* London, 1967.

Massey, W.T. *Allenby's Final Triumph,* E.P. Dutton, New York, 1920.

McClasland, David, *Oswald Chambers: Abandoned to God,* Discovery House Publishers , Nashville, 1993.

McKernan, Michael, *Padre - Australian Chaplains in Gallipoli and France,* Allen & Unwin, North Sydney, 1986.

McCleod, G. *Anzacs,* North Ryde, 1985.

Moorehead, A. *Gallipoli,* Hamish Hamilton, London, 1956.

Moorhouse, Geoffrey, *Hell's Foundations: A Town, its Myths and Gallipoli,* Sceptre/Hodder & Stoughton. UK, 1992.

Monson, James, *The Land Between - A Regional Study Guide to the Land of the Bible,* Jerusalem, 1983.

Morice, Janet, *Six Bob a Day Tourist,* Penguin Books, Australia, 1985.

Mosensen, M. *Letters from the Desert,* Sharon Books Inc., New York, 1945.

New Zealands Heritage, Number 15, Hamlyn House, Auckland, 1971.

Olden, A.C.N. *Westralian Cavalry in the War*, Alexander McCubbin, Melbourne, 1921.

Parkes, J. *Whose Land?* Penguin Books, Britain, 1970.

Patterson, J. *With the Zionists in Gallipoli*, Hutchinson & Co., London, 1916.

Patterson, J. *With the Judeans in the Palestine Campaign*, New York, 1922.

Pearlman, M. *The Mufti of Jerusalem*, London, 1947.

Pirie - Gardon, H. Editor. A Brief Record of the *Advance of the Egyptian Expeditionary Force*. London, 1919.

Powles, Lieut Col Guy., *The New Zealanders in Sinai and Palestine*, Whitcombe and Tombs, Auckland, 1922.

Pugsley, Christopher, *Gallipoli: The New Zealand Story*, Sceptre NZ, 1990.

Ridley, Jasper, *Lord Palmerston*, Constable & Co, London, 1970.

Sacher, H. *A History of Israel*, Alfred A. Knopf Inc., New York, 1976.

Sanders von, Liman, *Five Years in Turkey*, United States Naval Institute, Annapolis, 1927.

Sanders, R. *The High Walls of Jerusalem*, Holt, Rinehart and Winston, New York, 1984.

Schwarzfuchs, S. *Napoleon the Jews and the Sanhedrin*, London, 1979.

Sinclair, K. *A History of New Zealand*, Pinguin Books, Auckland, 1959.

Shadbolt, Maurice, *Voices of Gallipoli*, Hodder &Stoughton, Auckland, 1988.

Shirer, William. L. *The Rise and Fall of the Third Reich*, Simon & Schuster, New York, 1960.

Slater, R. *Rabin of Israel*, London, 1996.

Sokolow, N. *History of Zionism, 1600-1918*, 2 Vols. London, 1919.

Steel, Nigel & Hart, Peter, *Defeat at Gallipoli* ,. Macmillan/Papermac, London, 1994.

Stein, L. *The Balfour Declaration*, Vallentine, Mitchell & Co, London, 1961.

Taylor, Capt R.J. *Kiwis in the Desert*, New Zealand Defence Force, 1992.

Teveth, Shabtai, *Ben Gurion: The Burning Ground 1886-1948*, Houghton Mifflin Company. Boston, 1897.

Teveth,S. *Moshe Dayan*, Dell Publishing, New York, 1972.

Tibawi, A.L. *British Interests in Palestine 1800-1901*, Oxford, 1961.

Trevelyan, G.M. *History of England*, Longmans, Green & Co., London, 1948.

Tuchman, B. *Bible and Sword*, Minerva Press, New York, 1956.

Vader, J. *Anzac*, New English Library, Britain, 1972.

Verete, M. *The Restoration of the Jews in English Protestant Thought 1790-1840*, Middle East Studies, Frank Cass, London, January 1972.

Vester, B. *Our Jerusalem*, Jerusalem.

Wallbank, Walter, T. *A Short History of India and Pakistan*, New York, 1958.

Wavell, Colonel A.P. *The Palestine Campaigns*, Constable & Co.,London, 1931.

Weizmann, C. *Trial and Error: 2 Volumes*, The Jewish Publication Society of America, Philadelphia,1949.

Weldon, Captain L.B. *Hard Lying*, London, 1925.

Wilson, R. *Palestine 1917*, Edited by Helen D. Millgate, Costello Publishers, Turnbridge Wells, 1987.

Wilson, Brig-Gen L.C. *Operations of the Third Light Horse Brigade*. No publishing details.

Yaari, Avraham, *The Goodly Heritage*, Abridged and Translated by Israel Schen, Zionist Organization, Jerusalem. 1958.

Yavniely, S. *Sefer Ha Zionist*, Tel Aviv, 1944.

Other Sources - Journals, Newspapers, Magazines etc.

Evangelical Magazine, London, 1796

Gentleman's Magazine. London, July 1799

Jerusalem Post, Jerusalem. May 23, 1990; December 4, 1992; November 13, 1994; December 15, 1978; October 23, 1992.

Jewish Chronicle. London, September 15, 1882; January 22, 1915; January 29, 1915; March 12, 1915: April 30, 1915; August 6, 1915;

Jewish Chronicle, New Zealand, October, 1992.

Jewish Expositor, 1825.London.

Jewish Intelligence/Jewish Missionary Intelligence. 1826. London. 1826; 1833; 1839; 1840; 1841; 1915; 1919;

Jewish Repository, 1832. London.

Journal of the Australian War Memorial, April, 1984; October 1983; April 1991;

Middle East Studies. Frank Cass,London.

Mountain Views. Healesville(Victoria) Local paper, April 19, 1993.

New York Times Mid Week Pictorial. New York. December 1917.

Palestine Post, Jerusalem. Numerous papers between 1940 - 1942.

Report - London Jews Society. 1833. London.

The Annual Register, London, 1798.

The Courier, June 19, 1798.London.

The Times, London, 10 November 1914.

Archives, Libraries, War Memorials, etc.

Auckland Institute and Museum Library, The Domain, Auckland.
- Letters of William Johns.

Australian War Memorial, Canberra.

British Library, London.

Central Zionist Archives. Jerusalem.

Jabotinsky Institute, Tel Aviv.

Museum HaGidudim (Museum of the Jewish Legion,) Avihayil, Israel.

Public Records Office, Kew, London.
- CAB 21/1 No 21347
- CAB 23/4 September 3, 1917.
- CAB 23/4 137.
- CAB 93/4 WC 277
- CAB 23/4 WC 280
- CAB 23/4 WC 282. November 26, 1917
- CAB 23/4 WC 296.
- WO 1/893
- FO   78/227
- FO 371/3061 21308

Queen Elizabeth II War Memorial, Waioru, New Zealand.
- Unpublished material Diary of Trooper Malone.

Other Unpublished Materials

Diary of Trooper Reg Walters, 10th Light Horse Regiment.

Letter Private John Crombie to Jim Crombie.

Letter Lindsay Bear to author.

Letter Jack Berridge to Marie Shaw, May 22, 1996.

Various interviews, including : Prime Minister Mr. Yitzak Rabin (z.l.), Mrs. Sarah Pearl, Mr. George Georgiadas: Mr. N. Ibrahim; Mr. Yitzak Toussia-Cohen; General Uzi Narkiss (z.l.); Professor Alex Carmel; Mr. Andreas Braos; Mrs. Ruth Stark.

Index